DEMOCRACY

A USER'S GUIDE

BY JOSS SHELDON

www.joss-sheldon.com

First published in the UK in 2020.

Cover design by Marijana Ivanova.

Edited by the Saun-Jaye Brown.

Proofread by Aleksandar Bozic.

Beta read by Kajal Dhamija and Amber Ayub.

CONTENTS

INTRODUCTION

Democracy!

Whether you consider it "The worst form of government, except for all the others", "The bludgeoning of the people, by the people, for the people", or simply "The road to socialism" - one thing seems clear. Representative democracy has come to dominate the globe.

According to The Economist's "Democracy Index", 64.4% of the world's adults can vote to elect their leaders. The magazine considers twenty-two nations to be "Full Democracies". Another fifty-four are classified as "Flawed Democracies" - they do hold elections, but they have governance issues. And thirty-seven are dubbed "Hybrid Regimes" - their elections might not be free or fair. (The Economist Intelligence Unit, 2018)

Representative democracy reaches far and wide. But how deep, exactly, does it penetrate?

Is it enough to simply elect our leaders and sit back, helpless, as they rule over us like dictators? What good is selecting our politicians, if we cannot control our media, police or soldiers? If we must blindly follow our teachers' and bosses' commands, is it not a little naïve to believe that we are the masters of our own destinies? And if our resources are controlled by a tiny cabal of plutocrats, bankers and corporations; can we honestly say that our economies are being run for us?

Does representative democracy actually put power in the hands of the majority? Or could things be a little more, well, *democratic*?

***

It was not always like this. For hundreds-of-thousands of years, we humans lived in small bands, which tended to be far more democratic than modern society.

In the first section of this book, "A (Very) Brief History Of Democracy", we will see how these groups mocked, criticised, disobeyed, ostracised, expelled, deserted, and even executed would-be-chiefs, thereby ensuring that power remained with the people. We shall see how those groups combined, to form democratic confederacies - how democracy survived through the Middle Ages, on the commons, in the monasteries and guilds - and how mass movements forced the reforms that led to the rise of the representative democracies which dominate the globe today.

History, of course, is an ongoing process. In Section Two, we will see how our peers are democratising the political landscape *today*...

We shall take a peek at the types of direct democracy being practised in Rojava, Venezuela and Switzerland; before heading over to China, where "Deliberative Democracy", a modern take on sortition, is beginning to gain some traction. And we shall return to Dundee, in Scotland, to introduce "Participatory Budgeting", through which the locals are given a say in how their council's budget is spent.

In Chapter Seven, we will introduce "Liquid Democracy" - a system that allows members of political parties, such as Spain's Podemos, to propose and amend policies, vote on those proposals, and *delegate their votes* to like-minded souls. Finally, in Chapter Eight, we shall look at that last bastion of people power: The political protest.

For such tools to achieve their potential, we need a free press, to provide us with an abundance of good information, and an educated populace, with the ability to dissect fact from fiction. In Chapters Nine and Ten, we shall take a look at how this might be achieved...

We will visit Britain's Summerhill School, America's Sudbury Schools, and Brazil's Lumiar Schools - democracies, where pupils can self-educate, set the rules and hold court. We shall chart the rise and fall of the people-powered "Indymedia", its predecessor, public access television, and its democratic cousin, the member-owned paper.

Yet even with such institutions in place, democracy will remain a pipe-dream so long as policemen and soldiers serve the minority...

In Chapter Eleven, we will take a trip with George Orwell to meet the POUM - a democratic army, run by the people, for the people, without a goose-step or barked order in sight. And in Chapter Twelve, we shall look at a few ways through which we might democratise the police; considering the case for elected police chiefs, neighbourhood watches and citizen's arrests.

That just leaves Part Four. It is the largest section of the book because it covers a topic that affects us all on a daily basis: The economy.

Chapter Thirteen takes a look at workplace democracy, considering ideas such as collaborative hiring, profit-sharing, pre-approval, holacracy and worker cooperatives.

Chapter Fourteen tackles the thorny issue of corporatocracy; asking how we can make businesses produce the things *we* demand, rather than the things *they* wish to supply. We will take a look at the "Sharing Economy", epitomised by Toronto's Library of Things - consumer cooperatives, such as FC Barcelona - and advertising bans, like the one introduced in São Paulo.

In Chapter Fifteen, we will attempt to solve the "Plutocracy Problem", through which rich consumers, with their extra *spending power*, can unduly influence the distribution of resources. We shall consider the cases for fiscal policy, a return to the commons, the zero marginal-cost society, and buying clubs.

We shall finish by taking a look at some of the ways through which we might democratise the supply of money: one-hundred percent reserve banking, sovereign money, public banks, peer-to-peer lending, community currencies and crypto-currencies.

***

I hope this gives a flavour of things to come.

The book is jam-packed with many more topics than have been mentioned here. I have tried to make it as entertaining as it is informative. If you want a serious, academic tome, then this might not be the book for you! I am a novelist, after all. Although I would like to think that my degree in economics, from the London School of Economics (LSE), does qualify me to dabble in the social sciences.

These pages contain a raft of ideas and stories, but several others miss the cut. This is in part due to my own ignorance, and in part because the subject of "Democracy" is so gargantuan that even the greatest minds would struggle to do it justice.

Whilst writing "Democracy: A User's Guide", I often felt as though I had bitten off more than I could chew. Yet I still felt that it needed to be written.

My previous book, "Individutopia", tackled one of the subjects we will discuss Part Four: The corporatocracy. In Individutopia, the main character seeks to free herself from corporate control; going in search of the sort of earthy, small-scale democracies we shall meet in Chapter One.

Individutopia was well received by most readers, but a couple of one-star reviews did stand out. The first called it, "Insane leftist propaganda... (that) rang like a communist manifesto". The other suggested we should accept corporate control because, "Over one-hundred-million people were murdered by communist and socialist regimes in the Twentieth Century alone".

Such reviewers seem to believe that there are just two political systems: American-style capitalism and Russian-style communism. We should accept corporate control because the only alternative is so ghastly that its death-toll is nine digits long.

I wrote this book to lay such a belief to rest (and to add some substance to the topics covered somewhat more whimsically in my novels).

In reality, these two political ideologies *both* involve top-down control. The former gives power to corporations, banks, plutocrats, *and yes* to governments too. The latter gives all the power to the state.

I dislike both ideologies. I want to live in a world in which *no-one* rules us from the top-down. For me, this is the essence of "Democracy" - a system in which the power is held by all the people, or at least by the majority.

Perhaps this definition is different from your own. If it is, I hope you can bear with me!

***

Those two angry, I would say "Misinformed" reviewers, did have one thing correct. I suppose I do have a left-wing bias. Anyone who has read my novels or seen my tweets will confirm as much.

Born into a conservative family, and sent to private school (albeit for just four years); I never identified as a lefty until I jacked in the day job to become an author. I have always considered myself an anarchist, if the truth be told. Even before I knew the term existed, I was resisting the authority figures in my life - my parents and teachers.

This natural disdain for authority spread into my politics. I despised the authoritarian left *and* the authoritarian right - the likes of Stalin and Mao, *and* the likes of Hitler and Franco.

Still, I do have a natural inclination towards the more libertarian left; a bias I have tried to temper wherever possible...

In the bibliography, you will find seven references from The Financial Times, three from The Daily Telegraph, and even one from the International Monetary Fund! These may be outnumbered by left-wing sources, but they do hold their own.

I have also included some ideas that might sit more comfortably with those on the right than those on the left...

In the chapter on policing, we will meet the elected sheriff doing everything he can to uphold his constituents' right to bear arms. The concept of 100% reserve banking was first developed by the Chicago School economists beloved by Margaret Thatcher and Ronald Reagan. "The Zero Marginal Cost Society", which is offered as a solution to the plutocracy problem, assumes the ultimate efficiency of free markets. The chapter on workplace democracy gives credit to the likes of Google, Pret A Manger and Zappos. I may not be a fan of these large corporations myself, but I am more than willing to tip my hat to them when they empower their workers.

Even this may not be enough for some right-wingers. But that is life. As they say: "Haters gonna hate".

***

Anyway, that is enough of the preamble. Let's move on to the good stuff...

PART ONE

A (VERY) BRIEF HISTORY OF DEMOCRACY

1. PRIMITIVE DEMOCRACY

Two gorillas walk into an enclosure.

The first, Calabar, is an impressive chap. His sturdy frame and colossal thighs almost scream, "Ladies and gentlemen, I am the alpha here!"

The second, Rann, is no shrinking violet. Yet one cannot help but acknowledge his inferiority. His muscles are a fraction of the size of his companion's. His claws and teeth are far less malign.

***

These two gorillas enter the enclosure as comrades. Having spent several weeks in the same cage, at the Yerkes Primate Centre in Atlanta, they are accustomed to each other's presence.

Their alliance does not last long.

Met by the sight of four lady gorillas, each turns to the other with lust burning red in their eyes:

"This will be my kingdom. These mates will be mine!"

Calabar's iron fists pound his chest.

The walls vibrate with mirth.

Rann's leathery paws ricochet across his breasts. They create an echo. Audible, almost rhythmic, but nowhere near as loud as Calabar's pounding beat.

Slowly, these apes begin to move; sidestepping in the dust, pitter-pattering in a delicate semi-circle which belies their hulking frames.

Torso aligns with torso. Eye fixes upon eye.

A tense pause. The calm before the storm.

Rann's foot claws the earth. It seems as though he is about to make his move. Like a sprinter at the starting block, his muscles tense and his jaw juts forward.

But it is Calabar who charges first, swishing past Rann's left shoulder. His hair bristles with static, and his claws slash through the soil.

And now Rann is on the move.

Like pinballs, they crash; rebounding off one wall, then another.

A dust cloud engulfs the scene.

The lady gorillas shuffle back. They would blend into the scenery, if it were not for their hoots and hollers, flaying arms and agitated feet.

Rann and Calabar zigzag across the enclosure, bouncing off the sides, swinging from rope to rope. They almost collide. Then Rann barges Calabar, who trips, stumbles, composes himself, and resumes the charade.

The first blow, a backhanded slap, knocks Rann to the ground. He springs back up. Visibly shaken, he considers fighting, but thinks better of it.

He retreats into the shadows.

***

The alpha has dispatched the beta, and a hierarchy has been established.

Or so it might seem...

This may have been the first fight, but it is not the last.

In similar duels, over the days which follow, Calabar's superior strength continues to prove irresistible. This hulking beast dispatches his weaker rival on a regular basis.

Yet Calabar fails to land a decisive blow. The skirmishes continue...

Swipe follows swipe. Blood trickles from gashes in leathery skin. And then, during the umpteenth confrontation, Rann's knee buckles. He stumbles, tries to regain his balance, and braces himself as Calabar's shadow engulfs his entire form.

Angling his face, Rann looks into the crevices which line Calabar's palm. His enemy looms high, ready to crush his weaker foe.

Calabar's arm jolts forward, beginning its descent, but it moves no further. Held high in stunted animation, freeze-frame, it seems that time has stopped.

But time has not stopped.

Two female gorillas are clasping Calabar's shoulders. One is biting through his fur, flesh and muscle; tearing a blood-soaked clump from his spine and shaking her jowls; showering the air with fragments of hair and micro-beads of blood.

She returns to feast some more.

The second female holds tight. So tight, in fact, that her claws pierce Calabar's flesh - drawing so much blood that her fur turns from black to maroon to crimson.

A third female charges at Calabar's leg.

The fourth bounds through the air, arms outstretched, and grabs his waist.

Calabar howls:

"Aaaaagh!!!"

And now he stumbles.

Flesh is torn from his abdomen, chest and thigh.

Blood squirts fantastic.

And now he falls.

And now he whimpers:

"Ah… Ah… Aww!"

The gorillas retreat, leaving Calabar grounded, swimming in a pool of bile, saliva, mud and excrement. The fight is over in under a minute, but the result is conclusive.

Calabar must be removed from the group.

It is Rann, not his stronger adversary, who will take the throne.

And yet Rann knows, deep down, that his power will never be absolute. His position has been handed to him by an alliance of female gorillas. Those gorillas, who were strong enough to dispatch Calabar, remain more than capable of dethroning *him*. Rann's position is precarious. He knows he must rule in a way that pleases his troop, or he too will be left bruised and bloody in the dirt. (Nadler, 1976)

CHIMPANZEE CONTROL

Similar events have been observed amongst our closest relative, the chimpanzee, on Arnhem Zoo's "Ape Island" - a tree-filled enclosure, designed to replicate the chimps' natural habitat…

Yeroen, the group's alpha, was known for his puffed-up manic charges. Yelping and barking, he would dive head-first into a group of his peers, scattering them in every direction. Harried cries would fill the air, creating an atmosphere which was thick with tension.

It would take several moments for things to settle down.

When the air did finally clear, Yeroen's minions would tiptoe forward to pay homage to their leader - sitting at his feet, offering a hand and grooming his fur.

Such displays maintained the natural order. They reminded the group that Yeroen was in charge.

Yet the roles could also be reversed…

Our alpha often found himself being chased by a gang of screaming females. Outnumbered, it was clear that he was petrified by this exhibition of collective power.

Yeoren may have been in charge, but his position was never assured. The group went to great lengths to remind him that he could be ousted at any time.

***

A full coup, however, could take several months…

When Yeroen realised that he was no longer the maddest, baddest ape on the island, he attempted to shore up his supporter base - spending over 60% of his time with the female chimps, upon whose goodwill he relied.

With such backing, he would prove hard to depose.

Yeroen shared his sleeping quarters with the beta male, Luit - a younger, more playful chimpanzee who had arrived with Yeroen from a zoo in Copenhagen.

Luit had always known his place. He slunk into the shadows, and only ever ate the scraps left on his master's table.

But things had begun to change. Luit was now walking around their quarters as if he owned the place. He even took one of Yeroen's apples.

When the two apes finally came to blows, it was Luit who wounded his leader; leaving teeth-marks down Yeroen's side and indentations on his foot.

The next morning, Yeroen looked a shade of his former self. His hair, which normally stood on end, hung limply from his limbs. His eyes assumed a dusty glaze.

When he was allowed back onto Ape Island, Yeroen immediately broke down; whining and wailing, falling to his knees and imploring the heavens above.

The other chimps had never seen anything like it. In a show of awe and anguish, they lavished Yeroen with affection; restoring his confidence as best they could.

For Luit the message was clear. He may have dispatched the king, but the king had retained his kingdom.

Luit spent the day trying to make amends - nervously embracing Yeroen's subjects and tending to his master's wounds.

***

The third male, Nikkie, was a ball of nervous energy. A somewhat clownish character, known for his acrobatic displays, Nikkie was treated with disdain. His sexual advances were often rebuffed. He was sat upon and brushed aside.

But Nikkie had attached himself to Luit's rising star. As the challenger's henchman, he routinely attacked any female who was seen to side with Yeroen; discouraging them from socialising with their threatened leader.

It had the desired effect. Each day, Yeroen was granted a little less time in the company of the female chimpanzees.

As he saw his entourage dwindle, Yeroen became desperate. He threw himself to the ground, stretched forth his arms, and beseeched his mates to embrace him. He writhed like a fish on the floor of a trawler, and wailed like a newborn babe in need of his mother's milk.

So it was that he became the architect of his own demise…

Yeroen's tantrums, which had curried so much support at first, now became tiresome. Rather than provoke sympathy, they evoked pity and disgust.

Who, after all, would want to be led by an overgrown baby who cried whenever he was unable to get his way?

The females turned towards a stronger, more stable male: Luit.

For his part, the former beta male had been doing the rounds - grooming each female in turn, embracing them when he could, and playing with their offspring. He was slowly winning their support.

With more of a spark than a flame, he had risen to high office.

Yeroen finally accepted defeat. He allowed Luit to step over him, before reconciling with his erstwhile rival - greeting him with a subservient bark.

Within a month, peace had been restored. Luit was the undisputed alpha. And Nikkie, by hanging on to Luit's coattails, had become the beta. (De Waal, 1982)

FROM PRIMATES TO PRIMITIVE PEOPLES

We humans are not gorillas, nor are we chimpanzees. We do not organise ourselves into the strict, linear hierarchies that our apish cousins tend to form. Nor do we rely on intimidation or violence to gain access to food and sexual partners.

But for the vast majority of human history, we *have* lived in flexible bands, just like our hairy relatives. Like such primates, we have roamed the jungles at will; hunting animals and gathering plants.

Like the aforementioned apes, our politics have been driven by two desires. We have a selfish drive to *control others*. But we resent it when other people try to *control us*. We resist bullies, in much the same way that the female chimps resisted Calabar.

With the apes, this had two effects. The personal drive for power resulted in *hierarchical control*. At Arnhem Zoo, Luit rose to the top, Nikkie took up office as his deputy, and Yeroen was forced to accept third place. But the group's *collective resistance* ensured that no individual ape held any real power. The alpha in Arnhem has first dibs on food and sex. He can attack chimps, individually, to keep them intimidated, and may act as a mediator. But that is just about the sum total of this alpha's "Privileges".

Even in the wild, a top-ranking chimpanzee cannot compel his subordinates to go to war against other bands. A low-ranking chimp will still keep most of the food he finds. He can go wherever he likes, whenever he likes, and may even mate with a female who has gained the attention of a more senior rival.

The desire not to be controlled comes to the fore; ensuring leaders do not have *too much* power.

***

For humans, things are slightly different...

With the ability to control resources, weapons and soldiers, humans *can* win personal power over the group. When this happens, we end up with authoritarian regimes.

Occasionally, this may occur in hunter-gatherer societies. Psychopaths, shamans and the best hunters can come to rule the roost.

But in the vast majority of instances, hunter-gatherers do manage to keep power-hungry individuals in check. By *actively resisting* such people, on an ongoing basis, they maintain democratic control.

The apes showed us two methods through which this can be achieved. The female gorillas *violently dispatched* the strongest male. The female chimpanzees slowly *ostracised* their former leader.

In the wild, chimpanzees can also get up and leave; *abandoning* unpopular alphas.

Hunter-gatherers and small-scale tribes also have these weapons in their arsenal. They too can execute, ostracise and desert would-be-dictators. They also have a few other tools: criticism, ridicule, disobedience and deposition. (Boehm, 1991)

In the remainder of this chapter, we shall see how these methods have been used to maintain democratic control in primitive societies *today*.

By observing such peoples, we can infer how humans might have lived in the past. These groups offer us a sort of *living history* - a lens through which we can gaze back into the Stone Age.

They do.

But the lens may be a little blurred. Such groups have been in contact with agrarian states and empires, raiders and traders, for several millennia. Their cultures have been shaped through attempts to engage with or avoid such outsiders. Their societies may be similar to their ancestors, in some ways, but they may be different in others.

We should proceed with caution... (Graeber & Wengrow, 2018)

UTKU OSTRACISM

Deep in the Arctic Circle, life for the Utku Eskimos ambles on as it has done for millennia. The people here still live in tents and igloos; eating fish, seal and caribou. They remain as cool as the icy-breeze itself.

The Inuit *do not do anger*.

An angry person might turn violent, subdue dissenters, rise up and rule the entire group. And that, for the Utku, is inconceivable.

***

The Utku are taught not to show any sort of anger from an early age...

If an Utku child were to pick up a pebble and throw it at her mother, she might say, "Ooh, that hurts". But her voice will barely elevate above a whisper.

Rather than use harsh words or actions, to get their children to behave, parents tell them stories...

You do not want a child to wander into the icy waters? Great! Tell them about the gnarly sea monster who will drag them down into the darkest depths and gobble them up for breakfast.

You do not want a child to take food without asking? Great! Tell them that long fingers will reach out and grab them if they do.

And if a story does not do the trick? Okay. Put on a play. Let the child *see* the consequences of violent behaviour for themselves. (Doucleff & Greenhalgh, 2013)

***

The first Westerner to study the Utku was a young linguist and anthropologist named Jean Briggs.

Briggs struggled to fit in when she first arrived. Avoiding even the smallest display of anger, was no easy task.

Things came to a head when the Utku agreed to lend one of their canoes to a pair of tourists, not because they were keen on the idea, they resented such requests, but because they wished to avoid a confrontation.

When the tourists broke the canoe, Briggs informed them that her friends only had one more, which they relied upon to fish. Since it was fragile and hard to replace, Briggs asked them not to use it.

The tourists went to speak to the locals themselves.

Put on the spot, the Utku buckled. They consented to the tourists' request.

Briggs was visibly upset. She could not bear to see her beloved hosts abused in such a manner.

A tear in her eye, she stormed off and cried.

For the Utku, this emotional outburst was simply unacceptable. They left Briggs in her tent, outcast and alone, for almost ninety days.

***

Even though Briggs was trying to defend the group, and even though her anger was harmless, it was still too much for the Utku to bear. The Utku do not tolerate *any* sort of anger, no matter the circumstances. An angry person might rise up and come to rule the group.

Briggs had no desire to rule her band. But when she was angry, she confronted the tourists; speaking on behalf of the group, like a de-facto leader.

By eliminating emotional behaviour, the Utku remove the means through which individuals can come to rule their neighbours. We are left with a leaderless society, in which the people rule themselves:

"The Utku, like other Eskimo bands, have no formal leaders whose authority transcends that of the individual households. Moreover, cherishing independent thought and action as a natural prerogative, people tend to look askance at anyone who seems to aspire to tell them what to do".

***

Briggs was eventually integrated back into the group.

One of the indigenous families, however, was not...

The smallest family in Briggs' band consisted of just three members: Niqi, her husband Nilak, and an adopted seventeen-year-old daughter.

They were outcasts of their own making. Niqi never cooked, sewed less than the others, collected firewood alone, and made her own fires. She was deemed stingy - someone who did not share as much as social decorum dictated. She repeatedly failed to do her fair share of the communal work.

Nilak, meanwhile, was deemed to be bad-tempered and unhelpful.

There was a general feeling that both husband and wife were never far from displaying that emotional taboo: Anger.

Deemed an antisocial presence, Niqi and her family were pushed into a state of semi-ostracism. They did not live far from the rest of their clan, but a chasm existed between them. Perched on the other side of the rapids, a few hundred metres from the communal camp, they looked like shadow puppets; present, in motion, but not entirely real.

Her brethren never ignored Niqi completely. When she said "Hello", they replied with a similar greeting. When she smiled, the others smiled back. But they never initiated such contact.

In a tight-knit society, in which members rely upon each other to survive, Niqi's ostracism was one of the harshest punishments imaginable. (Briggs, 1970)

***

What does this tell us?

It shows that there *is* a social etiquette; an unwritten law which the Utku have to follow. They have to contribute to the economic welfare of the group, by doing their share of the fishing, cooking and sewing. And it shows that this unwritten law *is* enforced; not from the top-down, by an authoritarian chief, but by the group. Anyone who refuses to contribute is punished. They are ostracised, overlooked, and pushed to the margins of society by *every other member of the clan.*

By banning angry displays, the Utku eliminate the means through which leaders might come to power. But the absence of leaders does not mean an absence of control. It means that control is exerted by the community as a whole.

Utku society is democratic. The group is in charge.

!KUNG RIDICULE

Anger can propel an individual into a position of power. People may follow their commands, because they fear being hurt if they do not. This explains why the Utku were so keen to ostracise angry characters.

But there is another way through which an individual may come to dominate the group. Not with the stick, but with the carrot...

***

Imagine that you are the greatest hunter in your clan. It has been several days since anyone has killed an animal, when you return home with a majestic antelope.

What do you do?

You could keep that meat to yourself, and eat many meals. Or you could share it; only eating one or two meals before the group devours your bounty.

In the short term, you would be better off keeping the antelope to yourself. But, if you were to do this, your companions would die of hunger. When you encounter a bad run of luck, and are unable to find any food, there will be no-one left to help you.

In this scenario, everyone dies, including yourself, and your clan becomes extinct.

Alternatively, you could share the meat. Your loved ones would survive and, when you hit a bad run of luck, or become too old to hunt, they are likely to repay the favour; coming to *your* rescue, by sharing *their* food with *you*.

In this scenario, the whole clan survives.

***

What we have here is a simple case of "Survival of the Fittest". Only it is not the strongest *individual* who is deemed the "Fittest". It is the most egalitarian *clan*. The clan which shares survives.

This system, in which everyone shares their food, is known as "Primitive Communism". It can be found in hunter-gatherer societies all across the globe.

But here comes a dilemma…

What stops you, the best hunter, from seizing control of the group? Since you control the biggest share of the group's wealth, its meat, you could demand power, fame and glory, before sharing it amongst your peers. They would be left with just two options: Obey your commands or starve.

***

Let's take the case of the !Kung - the Kalahari Bushmen known for their ability to hunt giraffe, warthog, gemsbok, kudu, wildebeest, eland, antelope and hartebeest.

If you were to return to your !Kung clan with a freshly slain beast, your brethren would not greet you with praise, as you might expect.

Why?

"(Because) when a young man kills much meat, he comes to think of himself as a big man, and he thinks of the rest of us as his inferiors. We can't accept this. We refuse one who boasts, for someday his pride will make him kill somebody. So we always speak of his meat as worthless. In this way, we cool his heart and make him gentle".

A returning huntsman must remain modest, sit in the shade and wait to be approached by a fellow clansman, who might ask:

"What did you see today?"

"Ah, I'm no good at hunting. I saw nothing at all. Well, maybe some little thing, nothing more".

Such modesty can only mean one thing - this individual has killed a great beast. But this does not mean that he will be praised. The more wonderful the animal, the greater the ridicule he can expect to receive:

"You mean to say you have dragged us all the way out here to make us cart home your pile of bones? Oh, if I had known it was this thin, I wouldn't have come. People, to think I gave up a nice day in the shade for this. At home we may be hungry, but at least we have nice cool water". (Lee, 1979)

***

The !Kung's use of ridicule keeps would-be-leaders humble.

This is not to say that the !Kung are as fiercely anti-authoritarian as the Utku. They do have *nominal* leaders - the group's elders. These individuals get to decide where the group shall wander. They oversee the process of cutting and distributing the group's meat.

But these elders are not treated with deference. They are not given extra food, weapons or clothes. They are not given a prime position by the fire. And they do not have any *judicial* power.

If an individual threatens the group, the *group* will act as judge and jury. If an individual threatens another individual, those two individuals will be left alone to resolve their conflict. The elders cannot intervene. (Brownlee, 1943)

***

The !Kung regularly mock would-be rulers, denying them the respect they would need to rule. Power remains with the people.

Such a practice is fairly widespread...

In South India, when a group of Paliyans tried to invoke the gods, to gain power over their clan, the community mocked both them *and* their gods. In Northern Tanzania, when a Hadza man tried to form an alliance of subordinates, he was greeted with a choir of guffaws. Anthropologists have observed similar behaviour amongst Mbuti Pygmies, Ngukurr Aborigines, and the Enga of Papua New Guinea. (Boehm, 1993)

CUNA CRITIQUE AND DEPOSITION

Now let's visit the San Blas Islands, off the north-east coast of Panama - a tropical paradise, where turquoise waters lap over golden sands, palm trees rustle in the salty breeze, and the Cuna people live as they have done for centuries, albeit influenced by Panama's national government.

Unlike the Utku and the !Kung, the Cuna are not nomadic hunter-gatherers. They live in villages. And each village *does* have nominal rulers - a collection of chiefs, a spokesman and a policeman. Some also nominate leaders for individual tasks, such as house building. They might even treat these leaders with respect, showering them with flattering metaphors. Yet, like the alpha chimpanzees, these rulers have no *real* power. They are elected by the villagers themselves, can be removed from office at any time, are regularly criticised, and must always succumb to the will of the people.

Their role is educational and ceremonial. They host sacred meetings two or three times a week. They lead the villagers in song, recount folklore, perform rituals, and set out moral codes. But their decisions are only upheld if have been approved by a democratic vote.

In essence, the Cuna operate a "Direct Democracy", in which nominal leaders act as chair-people; overseeing the decision-making process, without having the power to dictate policy themselves. As moderators, they must stay calm and semi-neutral. They actually have *less* freedom to express an opinion than anyone else.

This forced-neutrality even extends to the judicial realm. If a village chief sees a conflict, they do not have the right to intervene, but they do have a responsibility to raise the incident at the next village meeting.

***

So what happens when a chief makes a decision *without* the people's consent?

The people will *criticise* that chief.

Let's consider what happened when a Panamanian official visited a Cuna village, whilst most of its inhabitants were away...

The minister, who wanted the village to produce a surplus of fish, asked a chief how many nets the village might require. The chief, speaking hypothetically, said they would probably need two.

Even though he had only made a suggestion, not a firm commitment, that chief was rebuked at the next village meeting. The villagers rounded on him, peppering the air with damning oratories. They told their chief that future discussions with government officials had to take place in the evening, when other villagers could participate, and that he could never again make such a suggestion without consulting the group.

On another occasion, when a chief tried to defend his son's indiscretions, several villagers shouted him down; rebuking him in the harshest of terms.

Such criticism is the norm in Cuna society. Lesser men regularly criticise those in office, and youngsters regularly criticise their elders.

***

This culture is inspired by the Cuna's oral histories...

Stories about poor leaders teach the villagers to be critical of their chiefs. They, after all, could turn bad at any moment.

Stories of great leaders, meanwhile, are met with a similar response: "Why aren't you, our current chief, as good as those leaders we had before?"

Through such stories, the Cuna come to distrust their leaders. This distrust encourages them to criticise their chiefs - a practice which keeps their leaders humble, and prevents them from garnering too much power.

***

So what if the chief is criticised too much, too frequently?

They will be *deposed*...

The chief will lose the respect they need to rule, be voted out of office, and a new chief will be elected in their place.

This happens so frequently, there is an official position of "Ex-Chief".

Rather than let their experience go to waste, ex-chiefs are normally welcomed onto another island, where they are made a "Repository of Tradition" - a respected storyteller and singer. After a cooling-off period, they may even be welcomed back by their original village. But they will never be chief again. (Howe, 1978)

***

The Cuna, therefore, take two measures to ensure their leaders serve the people. They criticise them whenever they stray a little, and they depose them whenever they stray a lot.

Other tribal groups also criticise and depose their leaders...

An Iban chief who acts so brazenly as to give a "Command", is sure to be rebuffed by his people. The Shavante and Mbuti Pygmies shout down over-assertive hunters. Criticising inferiors help control Navajo chiefs.

The Assiniboin, Yokuts, Yap, Nyakyusa and Somalis all boot their leaders from office, whenever they grow too big for their boots. (Boehm, 1993)

TIKOPIAN PUBLIC OPINION AND MASS DISOBEDIENCE

Tikopia is a tiny island in the furthest reaches of the Pacific Ocean. Situated atop a dormant volcano, it has very few resources, and barely a thousand inhabitants.

As with the Cuna, the Tikopians do have leaders - four "Boss Boys", who are organised in a linear hierarchy.

Unlike the Cuna, Tikopian chiefs *do* stand apart from their subjects. Islanders are not allowed to touch them or make loud noises in their vicinity. The Boss Boys are not expected to do any physical labour. They do have authority and can make political decisions without a public vote.

The Tikopians have a common expression: "This land is the land of the chiefs". It is no idle metaphor. The Boss Boys really do own the island. They can distribute its land and produce as they deem fit.

On the face of it, therefore, Tikopian society might seem authoritarian. The Boss Boys have economic control of resources and political control over island life.

So what stops them from doing as they please, and keeping all the land to themselves?

Public opinion.

Tikopian Boss Boys feel duty-bound to act with the welfare of the community in mind; to only issue decrees which the people will respect and obey. Before making a decision, the Boss Boys discuss the matter with their executive officials. They, in turn, petition the people, to get a feel for public opinion. A Boss Boy will only issue a decree when they are certain it will receive their subjects' full support.

***

Let's consider a couple of examples...

When government officials from the Solomon Islands asked the Tikopians to stop defecating on the beaches, the Boss Boys nodded sagely. They understood that public excretion was unsavoury, unsightly and unhealthy. Yet they refused the government's request.

At the same time, in 1966, Chief Pa Ngarumea forbade his people from picking turmeric leaves.

Why were the Boss Boys happy to issue one edict, but not the other?

The preservation of turmeric leaves was considered a matter of *public interest*. Turmeric leaves were used during public rituals, attended by everyone on the island. Chief Pa Ngarumea's officials had petitioned the islanders, reported back, and told him that such an edict had the support of the people. He knew it would be obeyed.

But the other issue was deemed to be a matter of *private interest*. It infringed upon individuals ability to go to the toilet wherever they chose. The chiefs did not feel they had any right to dictate such a personal matter. Their research told them that such an edict would not be obeyed. The people liked to defecate on the beach, it was a traditional custom, and they would continue to do so no matter what their chiefs decreed.

***

With this in mind, we can now answer our previous question: If the Tikopian Boss Boys control the island's land and produce, why do they not keep it all for themselves?

Whilst Boss Boys have the right to take land and produce, and may choose to take more than their fair share, the people can always reject their decrees. If the Boss Boys were to take *all* the land, without the public's support, the islanders would simply ignore their orders.

There is a word for such collective action: "Disobedience".

In fact, the very threat of disobedience keeps Tikopian chiefs from acting selfishly. It forces them to respect the will of the people.

***

This culture of collective disobedience stretches well beyond Tikopia's shores...

With permission from the Boss Boys, some Tikopian families have gone to labour on other islands, temporarily; earning money before returning home.

The national authorities encouraged such behaviour. It was good for business. But they insisted that the Tikopians pay a local income tax to support the islands on which they resided.

The Tikopian labourers refused. They said that their Boss Boys, back on Tikopia, had issued a decree, stating that all taxes should be paid to the Tikopia Development Fund. The fund had already built a rural health centre, and was planning to press ahead with a number of similar projects.

The national government summoned the Tikopian Boss Boys to court. When they did not attend, they were issued with fines. When they did not pay those fines, a boat was sent to transport them to prison.

The boat docked, and the Boss Boys boarded without any resistance. But they were not alone. Almost everyone in the vicinity also boarded that vessel!

"We've not paid that tax", they said, as if in unison. "You must arrest us as well".

"Arrest me!"

"And me!"

"Don't forget me! Take me to prison too!"

Realising that it would be dangerous to set sail with so many people aboard, the jailors released their detainees and left empty-handed.

A compromise was eventually reached - the Boss Boys agreed to pay a share of the tax on behalf of their overseas workers.

But by this point, the Tikopians had already proved their point. Through mass disobedience, not only were they able to hold their own leaders to account, they were also able to withstand a distant government. They had ensured that power remained with the people. (Firth, 1969)

***

As with the other anecdotes in this chapter, the use of public opinion and disobedience are by no means limited to a single people...

Any Iban chief who tries to command is likely to be ignored. The Chaco turn their back on leaders who try to overrule their wishes. South American Indians, Montenegrin tribesman, the Arapaho and the Bedouin have all been known to disobey unpopular chiefs.

The chiefs who govern the Cayapo, Canela, Ashanti, Navajo and Hottentots, meanwhile, are also controlled by public opinion. (Boehm, 1993)

NAMBIKUARAN DESERTION

We mentioned that a chimpanzee might abandon their community if they dislike its leader. We humans can also walk away from unruly leaders. In extreme cases, a whole clan may desert its chief...

***

Whilst they now live in villages, on the fringes of Brazil's tundra, the Nambikuara lived a semi-nomadic existence until well into the last century. Each year, when the rains subsided, they left their dwellings, formed new bands, and spent the dry season wandering from place to place.

Each Nambikuara band chose a leader, who decided where they would hunt, forage and fish. In return for his guidance, this man was awarded a special privilege -the right to take a second wife.

As with the previous examples, the leader gained his authority by consent. People only followed him when they approved of his decisions. If he were to make an unpopular decision, prove too demanding, monopolise the group's women, or fail to provide enough food; then his followers would wander off and join another group.

The Nambikuara had an easy come, easy go, sort of existence. Their groups were soon formed and soon disbanded. Their leaders rose and fell with the tides of public opinion. (Levi-Strauss, 1967)

Even today, in their more settled state, it is hard to discern who, if anyone, is the chief of a Nambikuara clan. Whilst brothers may form alliances, to maintain a degree of control, villages tend not to last for more than ten years. When they fall, their members have a great opportunity to go their separate ways. In the intervening period, the Nambikuara still spend about half their time away from their villages, and away from any leader who might reside there - a sort of temporary desertion. (Price, 1981)

***

To understand the desirability of desertion, it may be worth visiting the Batek - a nomadic group who inhabit the Malaysian rainforest.

When they were asked why they never shot the Malay slave-raiders, who had been a constant scourge upon the Batak, they responded with a look of shock and consternation:

"But... Why... Well... Because it would have killed them!"

The Batek had poisoned blowpipes. They could have used them to save themselves from the horrors of enslavement. But they abhorred violence so much that they refused to do so.

Given they are so averse to violence, the idea of fighting back against a bully, or executing a would-be-chief, have never been options for the Batek. This is why abandonment works so well. It gives them an alternative to a violent confrontation - the option to simply walk away.

Hence anyone who is considering doing something aggressive, must pause and think twice. They know that if they behave in such a way, their entire group will abandon them - a scary punishment for this ultra-social people.

And so violence becomes futile, aggressive acts are rare, and would-be-rulers are denied the tools they need to seize control. (Endicott, 1988)

***

Again, such behaviour is widespread...

The Batek and Mendrig desert headmen who are considered dishonest, belligerent or unjust. The Mizo abandon chiefs who are deemed too harsh. The Chaco walk away from leaders who are too stingy. And the Patagonians leave chiefs found guilty of misconduct. (Boehm, 1993)

EXECUTION

We began this chapter by recounting the tale of Calabar and Rann. When the gorillas turned on Calabar, the zookeepers had no choice but to transfer him. If they had not, that power-hungry ape would have been killed by the very subjects he was trying to rule.

Whilst it remains an extreme option, we humans have also been known to execute aggressive individuals who try to control our societies.

***

The Iliaura take a rather ingenious approach...

When a power-hungry miscreant is deemed a threat to their community, they do not necessarily kill that person themselves. They might hand him over to their enemies; allowing *them* to do the dirty deed on their behalf. This ingenious act kills two birds with one stone. It stops would-be-tyrants in their tracks, and it appeases a vengeful enemy intent on blood.

The !Kung also execute aggressive men who desire power, so long as there is agreement from the entire band. The Gebusi kill sorcerers. Similar executions have been witnessed amongst the Aborigines of Arnhem Land, the Hadza, Yaruro, Montenegrins and Baruya.

In such societies, however, it is often the *threat* of execution that proves more effective than the deed. Leaders feel pressured into doing their subjects' bidding - acting as their servants, not their kings - because they know they might be killed if they do not. (Boehm, 1993)

PRIMITIVE DEMOCRACY

The societies we have visited *are* democratic. Their members rule the roost. But this democracy does not appear by magic. It is actively maintained by the people, who use several different techniques to stop would-be-dictators from seizing control.

These methods are by no means obscure.

In his seminal paper, Christopher Boehm investigated forty-eight primitive peoples from across the globe. He found that every single group used at least one of the methods we have just encountered. Most used a combination of two or more.

But what about the resulting democratic systems themselves?

***

Amongst nomadic hunter-gatherers, such as the Utku and !Kung, there tend not to be any authority figures whatsoever:

"Every (Eskimo) man in his eyes has the same rights and the same privileges as every other man in the community. One may be a better hunter, or a more skilful dancer, or have greater control over the spiritual world. But this does not make him more than one member of a group in which all are free and equal". (Jenness, 1923)

These hunter-gatherer bands may not have *chiefs*. They do, however, have *leaders*. Everyone is a leader! Everyone leads themselves.

This is how the !Kung put it:

"Of course we have headmen... Each of us is headman over himself". (Lee, 1979)

And these are the words of the Ona:

"We have many chiefs. The men are all captains and all the women are sailors". (Bridges, 1948)

Some Aborigine groups take a slightly different approach...

An individual may command another person when they are fishing, but be commanded by that same person when they are building huts. A different hierarchy exists for each task. And because there are many different tasks, there are several jumbled hierarchies. Everyone is simultaneously dominant *and* subservient to everyone else, and no-one comes out on top.

The best hunter may take the lead when hunting, the best navigator may take the lead when moving from camp to camp, and the best warrior may take the lead when heading into battle. Individuals manage their own households, and the community comes together to make decisions which affect the whole group. (Sharp, 1958)

***

When tribal groups settle down and form villages, chiefs do begin to appear. We saw this with the Cuna and the Tikopians.

But such chiefs remain beholden to the people. They do not rule from the top-down, but act as mediators - enforcing the will of their subordinates. If they do not submit to public opinion, they may be disobeyed, abandoned or even killed.

These chiefs are considered "First amongst equals". They go out of their way to avoid prominence and are expected to be generous. They have been known to give away almost everything they own. For the !Kung, characteristics such as arrogance, aloofness, overbearingness and boastfulness disqualify a person from becoming a chief.

Tribal "Chiefs" are expected to act as facilitators and mediators. They can make suggestions, but tend not to make demands. Because they are respected, their suggestions are often approved, but such an outcome is never guaranteed. These people are not kings. They can be disobeyed at will. (Service, 1975)

***

In general, hunter-gatherers and settled tribes both use some sort of direct democracy. They might hold assemblies to discuss key issues, allowing everyone to have a say. They might make decisions with a group vote.

Of course, not every society is the same. We have already seen how the Tikopian Boss Boys poll the people, to understand public opinion. And we have mentioned how some groups, such as the Yokuts, delegate power to a council of elders.

The G/Wi hunters of the Kalahari take a slightly different approach. Rather than have a mass meeting, they break off into small subgroups. These give everyone the time and space they need to voice an opinion. Slowly, the clan comes together, and a consensus begins to form. Ideas which face opposition are dropped, and ideas which are acceptable to everyone come to the fore. (Silberbauer, 1982)

***

It would be wrong to get too misty-eyed. Just because such groups are democratic, does not mean they are perfectly egalitarian...

When primitive societies do have chiefs, they are almost always male. Within the home, husbands might have power over their wives. Adolescents can be used as chattels - married off by their parents for political convenience. Humans might beat or kill their animals.

Still, there are three reasons to focus on such groups...

HISTORY LESSONS

The hunter-gatherer and tribal groups we met in this chapter still exist today. We might not want to wave goodbye to our friends and family, reject the only culture we have known, live without smartphones and springy mattresses. But the option remains on the table. If we are prepared to make such a leap, we can pack our bags, travel the world, and live with the Utku or the Cuna. We can experience their democracies for ourselves.

It is a pretty extreme option, but it is an option nonetheless.

***

Why bother studying history at all?

By understanding where we have come from, we can understand where we are, the challenges we face, and the road ahead...

Fossils found at Jebel Irhoud, Morocco, prove that homo-sapiens have been around for at least three-hundred-thousand years. We may have been around for longer. Other humans, such as homo-habilis, first walked the earth many *millions* of years ago. (Hublin, Abdelouahed & Bailey, 2017)

The first civilisations, by contrast, only popped up about five-thousand years ago.

For around 98% of our time on earth, therefore, we homo-sapiens have lived in small-scale tribal groups. The societies we visited in the chapter are not niche or abstract. They are an insight into the way we have lived for the *vast majority* of our history.

Between them, they show that the urge to live in democracies is hard-wired into our nature. We have been rebelling against would-be-despots for hundreds of millennia, so it is little wonder that we continue to do so today.

***

Finally, primitive societies help to highlight several methods through which we can maintain democratic control *today* - through ostracism, ridicule, criticism, the court of public opinion, disobedience, deposition, desertion and execution...

Ostracism and exile may not be standard practice in modern society, but the likes of the Dalai Lama and Idi Amin will be sure to tell you that it does still exist. Twenty-five heads of state were exiled in the first eighteen years of the Twenty-First Century. Whether such actions had the democratic backing of the people, however, is another matter entirely.

The same could be said of executions. Four American presidents have been assassinated by their subjects. But those assassins did not secure the majority's support before completing their vicious acts. They were hardly democratic.

It is unlikely that half a nation will simply desert its leaders, but states have been known to split, and individuals do emigrate - abandoning undesirable leaders.

We may not ridicule strong hunters, like the !Kung, but a whole sub-genre of comedy, "Satire", has been developed to mock our leaders. From "Spitting Image" to "The Daily Show", funny men and women continue to use mockery to keep our politicians humble.

Columnists, bloggers and You Tubers all criticise our politicians.

Pollsters and protestors try to highlight public opinion.

Politicians who do not react to such opinions may find themselves voted out of office - a deposition of sorts.

That just leads disobedience. And yes, people can refuse to obey their leaders. Americans continued to drink alcohol, even when it was prohibited. Brits refused to pay the Poll Tax. In both cases, their governments were left with no choice but to rescind their unpopular legislation.

2. CONFEDERATE DEMOCRACY

Let's take a few steps back...

In the previous chapter, we suggested that humans react to power in two distinct ways: We try to gain a little control over *others*, and we try to prevent others from exerting control *over us*.

In hunter-gatherer societies, we saw how the second force overwhelmed the first. When would-be-dictators tried to exert control over the group, the people united and cut them down to size.

It is not hard to understand why this happened...

Those power-hungry individuals did not have any sort of advanced weaponry. The weapons that did exist were owned by the group. They did not own any land - the concept of private ownership had not yet been invented. They could have rallied a few henchmen, but they could not assemble a large army, because their entire societies only contained twenty or thirty people.

Without superior resources, weaponry or manpower, it was virtually impossible for individuals to seize power and lord it over the band.

That all changed when humans formed villages. Specialisation led to advancements in weaponry, people fenced off areas of land for themselves, and populations grew to levels which had been previously unknown. Individuals *could* now accrue land, weaponry and henchmen. They had the tools they needed to control the masses. (Olson, 1993)

And so, when farming was invented in the Middle East, about eleven-and-a-half-thousand years ago, life became steadily less democratic. Political, economic and gender inequalities began to soar. (Morris, 2015)

Depending on the time and place, this change could have been slow and imperceptible, as administrators took on more responsibilities to cope with the needs of their burgeoning societies. The people may have turned to lawmakers to resolve their differences, or they may have looked to a soldier class to protect them from outsiders. These people might have accrued more and more power, until they eventually formed a ruling class.

Elsewhere, the change could have been shockingly quick. Charismatic individuals could have risen to power after charming their peers. Strongmen could have claimed high office through acts or threats violence. Priests could have risen to power by promising their supporters a luxuriant afterlife. (Boehm, 1993)

But it would be wrong to suggest that we made some big sort of giant leap; abandoning our small democratic bands in order to live in large authoritarian states.

There was an intermediate stage…

As populations grew, contact between different groups became more common. Such encounters could be hostile, involving fights to the death. But they could also be cordial. Some bands even forged *alliances*…

Under such agreements, individual villages were still run along democratic lines, as in previous millennia. But villagers also began to attend large gatherings, along with people from *other* groups. Sometimes these gatherings were democratic. Sometimes they were not.

We shall come onto the *archaeological* evidence in a moment. This suggests that hunter-gatherers formed temporary cities, many thousands of years ago. They feasted, made merry, swapped information, and then continued on their way; returning to a nomadic existence.

But first, we shall consider the *anthropological* evidence, gathered in the last few hundred years. Here, *tribal villages* ruled themselves, democratically. But they also elected representatives to sit on *regional councils*, alongside representatives from other villages. These, in turn, sent representatives to sit on *national councils*, alongside representatives from other regions.

What we were left with was a halfway house, with direct democracies at the local level, and representative democracies at the national level…

THE IROQUOIS CONFEDERACY

The Haudenosaunee went by several names. The English called them the "Five Nations". The French called them the "Iroquois". But it is their native name which gives us an insight into the culture of these indigenous Americans.

"Haudenosaunee" means "People who live in the extended longhouse". And they really did live together, in a single, communal home. Theirs was a tight-knit society.

***

Legend has it that the people of five nations (the Senecas, Cayugas, Onondagas, Oneidas and Mohawks) were united by a single man: Dekanawida.

Born to a virgin mother, Dekanawida's grandmother sensed a scandal.

"You must drown the boy", she insisted. "It is the only way to save our family's honour".

With a heavy heart, Dekanawida's mother made her way to the lake, cut a hole in the ice, and plunged her baby into the deepest, darkest depths.

Trembling, shocked at the repulsiveness of her act, she returned home to cry.

When she awoke the next morning, she found Dekanawida at her breast.

She tried a second time. And again, miraculously, Dekanawida survived.

The third time, Dekanawida's grandmother tried herself; holding her grandson beneath those icy waters until his heart stopped beating and his lungs were still.

When she saw Dekanawida the next day, cradled in her daughter's arm, she knew this boy was special:

"We must protect him. He is sure to become an important man".

***

This survival trick was to prove crucial when Dekanawida visited the Mohawk.

"No longer shall you kill one another", he told them, rather bombastically. "Our happiness depends upon peace".

The Mohawk replied:

"What you say is surely true. We all want peace. But words are cheap. Noble stranger, you must prove yourself capable of action. Show us that you have the power to bring us the peace of which you speak".

And so Dekanawida climbed a tree, which the Mohawk cut down. They watched on as it crashed into the rapids, where Dekanawida's body was consumed by a tumult of white froth and raging waves. Then they returned home, certain that this peculiar stranger had drowned.

The next morning, they saw smoke above an empty cabin. Confused, but intrigued, they approached on tiptoes, peered through a gap in the wall, and spotted Dekanawida.

The people were convinced. This chap really was the "Great Peacemaker" they had been awaiting.

They accepted his entreaties, entered into peace negotiations with their neighbours, and formed a confederacy of nations.

The Iroquois Confederacy was born. (Greene, 1925)

***

Perhaps there really was a "Great Peacemaker". And let's not forget his trusty sidekick, the "Mother of Nations", Jigonhsasee.

Perhaps the reality was a little more prosaic than the legend.

The truth is we cannot even be sure *when* the Iroquois Confederacy was formed, let alone *who* formed it. Some say it lasted eight-hundred years, beginning in the year 1000. Others say it was not created until 1450. (Johansen, 1995) (Weatherford, 1989)

We do know that the five tribes came from a common stock. They spoke related dialects of the same language, and inhibited a continuous stretch of land. They all subsisted on fish, game, and whatever vegetables they could grow. And, of course, they all lived in those ubiquitous longhouses.

Their common roots pitched them against one another. These were squabbling cousins who had outgrown their tribes, formed their own villages, and were now competing for the same resources. It also brought them together. These were long estranged brethren who longed to be reunited. (Engels, 1902)

The confederacy was formed, and it soon began to grow - maintaining peace at home whilst waging war on other peoples - conquering land which stretched from present-day Canada, in the north, along the Great Lakes, and down into Virginia, Kentucky and the Ohio Valley.

***

Iroquois democracy, in all five nations, began at the local level, in "The Gentes". In the Seneca nation, for example, there were eight gentes - the wolf, bear, turtle, beaver, deer, sniper, heron and hawk.

The gentes were democratic assemblies in which every adult could voice an opinion. They had a judicial role; meting out justice for crimes such as murder. And they controlled membership; adopting new members into the group. (Gillin, 1919)

Each gen elected two leaders: The "Sachem", who oversaw domestic matters, and the "Chief", who led the group into war. These leaders had to be approved by the other gentes, but they could be deposed by their own community, at any time, without outside approval. They were not superior to anyone else in their gen. Every individual was "Equal in privileges and personal rights". There were no slaves or servants. And women were just as powerful as men. They controlled most of their group's possessions. (Johansen, 1982) (Engels, 1902)

***

So far, we have described a system much like those we met in the previous chapter. The one real difference was that the sachem and chief had to be approved by other local groups - a measure that helped to maintain harmony in the region.

But the Iroquois did not stop here...

The sachems and chiefs from each gen were sent to sit on councils with leaders from the *other* gentes. The Seneca sent their sachems to a "Phraty", to sit with the sachems from three other gentes, and to the "Tribal Council", where all sixteen sachems and war chiefs sat as one.

These councils dealt with international affairs - the sort of issues which were too big for the local gentes to deal with alone. They received and sent diplomatic delegations, declared war and made peace.

They should not, however, be confused with the sort of parliaments we have today. They were held in public. Any member of the tribe could attend, contribute to debates, and raise new issues for discussion. Furthermore, they were conciliatory, not confrontational. Decisions had to be made *unanimously*. This forced sachems and chiefs to compromise, to account for each other's views. There could be no "Dictatorship of the majority". (Engels, 1902)

***

With such a system in place, we can see the need for the Great Peacemaker. Nations had formed, and together they were strong. They had the power to attack, kill, raid and steal.

We can also see why such a peace-making mission could work. The infrastructure for diplomacy was in place.

And so it came to pass...

The five nations united, forming a "Grand Council". Much like the tribal councils beneath it, this international union welcomed the sachems and war chiefs from all the Haudenosaunee gentes.

By the time the Iroquois Confederacy had adopted a sixth nation, the Tuscarora, it had grown to encompass a total of fifty gentes. The Grand Council, therefore, had seats for fifty sachems and fifty chiefs.

Meetings took place in a longhouse, in the Onondaga nation, once every five years, although they could be convened during the intervening period if the need arose. As with the tribal councils, Grand Council meetings could be attended by anyone, and motions had to be approved by every single sachem and chief before they were passed.

The meetings dealt with internal conflicts between the Haudenosaunee nations, as well as matters of international diplomacy - the forming of alliances, signing of treaties, regulation of subjugated nations, acceptance of new members, and protection of weaker tribes.

There were no presidents or leaders within the Grand Council. Members had to influence their peers through acts of oratory excellence. There was no heckling or jeering - everyone was respected whilst they spoke. After they had finished, speakers were granted a brief period of silence, in case they should think of something else to say. (Weatherford, 1989)

Showing this sort of respect certainly left its mark on one of the founding fathers of the United States of America...

When Benjamin Franklin witnessed it in person, he could not help but compare it to the situation back in Europe, where politicians were regularly interrupted. Franklin wrote that many missionaries misinterpreted this practice, believing it indicated some sort of agreement. They were wrong. The Iroquois regularly listened in silence, showing the utmost respect, whilst refusing to believe a single word they had heard! (Grinde & Johansen, 1990)

***

The Iroquois Confederacy, therefore, was a system of council upon council upon council. One Jesuit witness, writing in 1647, reported that "There was nothing but the holding of councils". (Grinde & Johansen, 1990)

It all sounds rather bureaucratic, does it not?

The reality was a little different...

The Grand Council only met once every five years. There were no full-time politicians. Indeed, there were "No soldiers, no gendarmes or police, no nobles, kings, regents, prefects or judges, no prisons, no lawsuits".

The Iroquois Confederacy maintained the democratic traditions of the hunter-gatherers. Disputes were settled by the community, not by a lofty judiciary. The land belonged to the whole tribe, not an aristocratic class. There were no castles or palaces. Everyone lived together. (Engels, 1902)

But the Iroquois went one step beyond their primitive cousins. They united their gentes to form a confederacy - an informal nation that allowed them to organise on a mass scale, defend themselves, and expand their borders.

ONE OF A KIND?

Was the Iroquois Confederacy a freakish one-off?

It would be true to say that the Iroquois Confederacy was the most famous political system of its kind. It may even be fair to call it the most successful. But it would be wrong to suggest it was unique...

James Adair, a trader who lived amongst the Cherokees, noted that such confederacies were common across the southern frontier:

"The power of their chiefs is an empty sound. They can only persuade or dissuade the people... Every town is independent of the other. Their own friendly compact continues the union". (Adair, 1775)

So a "Union" did exist. A Cherokee council, with a loose and changing membership, convened on an occasional basis. But it did not have the authority to impose its will. It was beholden to the people it served, who could disobey it on a whim. (Zinn, 1980)

***

Further south, the Aztecs were divided into twenty "Calpulli" - clans, much like the Iroquois gentes, which owned everything collectively and ruled themselves from within. Each calpulli elected a speaker, the "Tlatoani", who was sent to sit on the "Supreme Council".

Unlike the Iroquois, the Supreme Council did elect a supreme speaker, the "Huey-Tlatoani" - a role which was held for life. Eventually, this position came to be reserved for members of a single family; a clear example of how democracy can descend into monarchy. (Weatherford, 1989)

***

The examples we have met so far have been *anthropological*. They are based on historical reports, written by eye-witnesses, when such confederacies were still alive and kicking.

Archaeological evidence suggests that similar confederacies could be found across the globe, long before anyone had the tools to document them. Before big cities began to form, and civilisation took root, ancient peoples came together to form *temporary* cities - to trade, socialise, find wives and form political unions. They then dismantled those cities; returning to the sort of small-scale democratic societies we met in the previous chapter...

The remains of mammoth houses, constructed from animal hides and tusks, can be found all the way from Kraków to Kyiv. These fifteen-thousand-year-old temporary structures may have been part of one of the first "Pop-up" cities to have been created and then dismantled by a group of organised hunter-gatherers.

Certainly, the eleven-thousand-year-old stone temples of Göbekli Tepe, on the Turkish-Syrian border, do feature some rather enlightening pillars - works of art, onto which images are carved, not of townsfolk, but of hunter-gatherers, who appear to be building cities, feasting in those metropolises, and then razing them to the ground.

Nomadic peoples also came together at Dolní Věstonice, in the Czech Republic. They formed a temporary city, feasted, performed rituals and completed artistic projects. They traded animal pelts, minerals and shells.

Similar sites can be found in the great rock shelters of the French Périgord and on Spain's Cantabrian coast. (Graeber & Wengrow, 2018)

Large concentrations of archaeological artefacts suggest that people also came together on the west coast of Britain, back in the Mesolithic era. Members of different bands would have socialised, exchanged vital information about their territories' river systems, and found sexual partners, before heading off alone. (Spinney, 2012)

Several millennia later, similar events took place at Stonehenge.

***

Returning to the anthropological evidence, we can see such a system at play among the Cheyenne and Lakota, back in the Nineteenth Century...

These one-time farmers, who had reverted to hunter-gathering, came together on the Great Plains, towards the end of each summer. They formed large, temporary settlements, and made preparations for the year's buffalo hunt.

In camp, they gave up a large chunk of their independence, of their own free will; appointing a police force that had the right to imprison, whip and fine anyone who threatened the success of the hunt. This was considered a price worth paying for the meat and hides that such an arrangement could produce. But once the hunt was over, and the rituals were done, the confederacy disbanded, and the people returned to their nomadic lifestyle, free from any such authority. (Graeber & Wengrow, 2018)

***

These examples should make one thing clear: Our ancestors did not suddenly abandon their hunter-gatherer lifestyles, turn to agriculture, create cities and form states. There was no incentive for them to do so. Agriculture required more work than hunting and gathering. It provided a less varied, less nutritious diet. And it created an environment, with a high concentration of animals, which enabled infectious diseases to spread. Life expectancy was far lower for the early villagers than it was for their nomadic cousins. And their societies were far less democratic. They could be despotic, patriarchal and plagued by social inequality.

Rather, there was a slow and steady transition. Nomadic peoples united to form seasonal states, for a portion of the year, before returning to wander the forests and plains. They may have practised a *little* agriculture, without being committed agriculturalists; sowing some seeds, leaving to hunt and forage, and then returning to harvest their crops.

A process of evolution ensued. Our ancestors slowly turned from hunting and gathering to agriculture. They slowly turned from a nomadic lifestyle to a settled existence. But this process was hardly linear. Agriculturalists might revert to hunting and gathering if their crops failed. Villagers might become nomads if they were expelled from their land.

Likewise, it took a few thousand years for the democratic systems, outlined in the previous chapter, to transform into centralised states. And before such a transition was complete, the early cities were fairly democratic...

In Mesopotamia and the Indus Valley, the earliest cities employed the sort of municipal councils we saw amongst the Iroquois. They had sophisticated civic infrastructures, which flourished for half a millennium, but there is no evidence of any royal burials or monuments - the telltale signs of a rich and powerful elite. There is no evidence of standing armies, nor any other means of large-scale coercion. Nor is there any hint of a centralised government, with direct bureaucratic control over citizens' daily lives.

It took a long time for centralised states to form. The first stratified, tax-collecting, walled states appear in the Tigris and Euphrates Valley around 3100BC; *more than four-thousand years after our ancestors began to domesticate crops*. That leaves a big chunk of history in which confederate democracies and seasonal states were able to flourish. (Scott, 2017) (Graeber & Wengrow, 2018)

***

In Europe, the early Romans also formed a confederacy, long before they formed an empire. The Ancient Greeks formed gentes, to deal with local issues, before uniting those gentes to form phratries, and uniting those phratries to form tribes. The very words used to describe the Iroquois' social structures were taken from the Greeks, because the anthropologists who studied them were overwhelmed by the similarities. (Morgan, 1877)

But the Greeks did not stop there. Unlike the Iroquois, they went on to form modern, centralised nations. And, after a brief period of feudal rule, they returned to their democratic roots...

THE "BIRTHPLACE OF DEMOCRACY"

And so, finally, we arrive in Athens.

"What took you so long?" I hear you cry.

Many readers might have expected a history of democracy to begin with the Greeks. The Greeks invented the word "Democracy", after all. We are often told that they invented the whole shebang.

The reality is a little different. The types of primitive democracy we met in the previous chapter predate Greek democracy by hundreds-of-thousands of years. Confederate democracy came next. Groups such as the Iroquois remained wholly democratic.

In Greece, however, only a handful of men could vote. Women, foreigners and slaves were excluded from the political arena. (Morris, 2015)

Nonetheless, it is worth a visit because, for the lucky few who *did have the vote*, Greek democracy was still fairly democratic...

***

They say, "A man's home is his castle". Once upon a time, there may have been an element of truth in this cosy expression. Before there were states and governments, individuals really could behave like small-time kings. Their homes were their "Castles". Their lands were their "Kingdoms".

This was the case in Greece. (Blackwell, 2003 (a))

Towns and villages began to form, and with them came the pre-cursor to Greek democracy: Confederations.

Village "Kings" formed councils, who ruled their regions in cooperation with an "Agora", an assembly of the people, and a "Basileus", a military commander. (Giljin, 1919)

Homer's epics tell us what happened next...

Some of these local "Kings" coveted absolute power. They expanded their domain, acquiring control of neighbouring "Kingdoms".

Then came Theseus - the sword-swinging, sandal-wearing, Minotaur-slaying, mythological hero of ancient Greece. Theseus, so the legend goes, abolished the local authorities and centralised power. The whole region of Attica came to be ruled from Athens; first by Theseus himself, and then by an aristocratic clique of three king-like "Archons". (Blackwell, 2003 (a))

The reality may not have been quite as swashbuckling as the myth, but it continued along similar lines...

Ancient Athens was built on steady foundations. Its citadel had its own water supply, and mountains protected it from invaders. But Athens' earth was thin. It was adept at growing olives, but too infertile to produce grain. Thus, in the Eighth Century BC, the Athenians pushed outwards. They colonised the Attica region and seized control of its wheat fields. In the Seventh Century BC, they began to colonise the nearby islands. (Hornblower, 2019)

During this period, six new archons were added to the mix. The region's leadership had evolved from a monarchy into an oligarchy.

After ten years of service, these archons stepped out of the limelight, but they continued to rule as members of the "Council of the Areopagus" - a sort of upper chamber, like Britain's House of Lords. (Blackwell, 2003 (a))

Yet all was not well in the corridors of power...

Trade with rich Asian civilisations had produced disparities in wealth. Conflicts brewed. In the 630s, Attica almost fell to tyranny when Cylos, the great Olympian of his time, attempted to seize power. (Hornblower, 2019)

In the fallout from this failed coup, two figures rose to power who would lay the groundwork for Athenian democracy: Draco, from whom the word "Draconian" was coined, began the process of transcribing the oral law. And a new archon, Solos, began to enfranchise the people...

Solon gave everyone the right to appeal to a jury of their peers; removing this power from the nine archons who had previously acted as judge and jury. He changed the way in which those archons were selected. He split the population into four classes, according to their wealth, allowed anyone from the richest three classes to propose a new archon, and then whittled down the nominees by taking lots. Solon also introduced the first assembly, in which any citizen could participate.

Solon made the people pledge to honour his new system, unchanged, for a full ten years. Then he waved Athens goodbye and took to the seas; living in a self-imposed exile, so that he could not be cajoled into changing a single thing!

It worked. Solon's system survived for several decades.

Then Cleisthenes took office...

Cleisthenes transformed the Greek political system by doing something which, on the face of it, might seem inconsequential: He changed people's surnames. Rather than naming citizens after their parents, "Demochares son of Demosthenes", Cleisthenes named them after their ancestral towns, "Demochares from Marathon".

This small change had a big effect. It returned power to the *regions*, or "Demes", as in the days before Theseus became king. It broke the stranglehold of the aristocratic *families*.

Each Deme was sorted into one of thirty "Thirds". Each coastal third was partnered with a city third and an inland third; creating ten pan-Attican "Tribes". These tribes each sent fifty representatives to sit on a "Council of Five Hundred".

That council governed Attica on a day-to-day basis. It also helped to administer the assembly - a direct democracy, in which any enfranchised Athenian could propose, debate and vote on motions.

Between them, these institutions ruled Attica; usurping the oligarchical archons and their Areopagus. (Blackwell, 2003 (a))

This is not to say it was plain sailing. The oligarchs tried to win back control on several occasions. Nonetheless, the council and assembly held strong for the better part of two-hundred years.

Let's take a closer look at these institutions...

THE ECCLESIA

Rising a hundred metres above Athens, this grey, rocky stage seems to erupt through the earth. Dry shrubs creep up on every side. Their uppermost leaves peer out across the modest expanse where political greats once stood.

This is the "Pnyx". A place of worship, dating from prehistoric times, it rose to fame as the so-called "Cradle of democracy". It was home to the "The Ecclesia", one of the first arenas to host *mass* democratic assemblies.

Imagine the scene, if you will...

The council of five hundred sit on wooden benches to one side. Thousands upon thousands of men jostle for position. A few officials, selected at random, attempt to maintain order.

The rituals begin. A goat emits a sharp, scratchy yelp. Blood sprays from its slashed neck. Its head falls limp.

This sacrificial beast is paraded around the arena, serenaded by the deep, sombre sounds of an ancient prayer.

The holy sanctum of Athenian democracy has been purified.

The herald stands, pauses, looks out across the gathered masses, and asks his familiar refrain:

"Who here wishes to speak?"

***

These meetings took place between ten and forty times a year.

To participate, a young man had to register with his local "Demos", when he turned eighteen, and spend two years with the military cadets. He could be disenfranchised if he prostituted himself, beat his parents, threw his shield away in battle, or squandered his inheritance.

Citizens were paid to attend. This ensured that even the poorest Athenians could take part. They would not be out of pocket should they have to forgo an afternoon's work.

Before the introduction of this payment, encouraging attendance could be a challenge. Slaves were sent to herd the people into position using a red-stained cordon. Anyone caught with red dye on their clothes was fined.

That all changed when the payment was introduced. Meetings became so popular, that same rope was sometimes used to keep people *at bay*!

***

Debates and discussions led to votes. These were conducted by a show of hands, if fewer than six-thousand people were in attendance, or by a secret ballot, at more popular meetings.

Such votes affected every aspect of Athenian life: financial, religious, legal and administrative. The people voted to launch wars, sign treaties, amend laws, host public festivals, regulate their ferries and elect some officials, including army generals. Other officials were selected at random, by taking lots.

Although most citizens never actually spoke, *everyone had the right to speak*, at any meeting, on any issue.

In practice, when it came to technical issues, only the experts were treated with respect. When Athens needed new ships for her navy, ship-builders were called to offer their opinions. The assembly asked craftsman to advise them on construction projects.

Should a citizen without such expertise enter the debate, they would be laughed at, scorned and shouted down.

But when it came to matters of general governance, anyone could have their say - be they a sea captain or a deckhand, rich or poor, beautiful or grotesque. (Blackwell, 2003 (b))

***

The assembly had another key function which deserves a section of its own: Ostracism...

Athenian democracy was under constant threat. Powerful neighbours, such as the Persians and Macedonians, could invade at any point. The aristocratic families might try to regain control, either by allying with those foreign empires, or by building alliances at home; bribing their acolytes with promises of wealth and power.

The solution was hardly original. In the previous chapter, we saw how the Utku ostracised disruptive characters - banishing them to the other side of the river. Even the chimpanzees in Arnhem Zoo practised this form of behaviour - ostracising their former alpha.

Yet it *was* efficient.

If an individual was considered a threat to Athenian democracy, the people would vote to hold an ostracism. The assembly would be convened. Every enfranchised Athenian would scratch the name of the individual they wanted to ostracise on a fragment of pottery, known as an "Ostrakan". Whoever received the most votes was required to leave Athens for ten years.

Anyone who threatened the people's sovereignty was quite literally put out of harm's way.

This system did help to exclude anyone who was deemed a menace. But it was far from perfect.

Let's consider the story of Aristides...

When his nemesis, Themistocles, began to spread rumours, the public's passions were stirred. They came to believe that Aristides had abolished the democratic courts, was judging cases in private, and had been prancing about like a de-facto king.

At the next ostracism, people began scratching Aristides name onto their ostraka.

One such chap even handed his ostrakan to Aristides himself! Unaware that he was speaking the condemned man, this illiterate Athenian asked for help:

"Please scratch the name 'Aristides' onto this fragment".

Astonished, Aristides asked the layman what wrong he had been done.

"None whatsoever. I don't even know the fellow. But I am tired of hearing him everywhere called 'The Just'."

Aristides assisted the man, writing his *own* name on the ostraka, thereby helping to seal his fate.

It was because of injustices such as this that the practice of ostracism eventually fell into disuse. Nonetheless, it served a vital role in the fledgling days of Athenian democracy, protecting the system as it matured. (Plutarch & Perrin, 1914)

THE BOULE

The council, or "Boule", contained five-hundred Athenians - fifty from each of the ten tribes. Its members had to pass a process of "Scrutiny", which ruled out anyone involved in a coup. They had to be male, enfranchised, and over thirty-years-old.

Councillors were not elected. Rather, they were chosen at *random*; a process known as "Sortition". So they included a *representative* sample of men from every district, class and profession. These were everyday folk, not career politicians. No-one could serve on the council for more than two terms.

***

Each month, the fifty councillors from one tribe would serve as "Presidents". On duty day and night, working eight-hour shifts, they helped to maintain law and order.

The presidents selected a chairman to lead them. This man was a ruler of sorts - the chief executive of Athens. But he only ruled for twenty-four hours, and could only hold the position once in his lifetime.

An Athenian, therefore, would experience about ten-thousand different chairmen every thirty years. Given that there were approximately twenty-two thousand enfranchised Athenians in 400BC, this meant each one had almost a one-in-two chance of ruling Attica himself.

***

So what, exactly, did these representatives do?

The chairmen responded to emergencies. If they heard that an army was encroaching, for example, they might take measures to defend the region. Then they would call an assembly meeting, so that the people could decide upon a full course of action.

The council also had an administrative function. It received ambassadors, maintained the cavalry, and managed the state's finances. And it had a safeguarding role. It investigated the new magistrates who had been elected by the assembly.

But it rarely showed initiative. It was a safeguard; responsible for upholding the will of the people, not for imposing a will of its own.

The council's main responsibility was to protect the assembly. It spent most of its time preparing decrees for the assembly, arranging assembly meetings, and maintaining order within those meetings. (Blackwell, 2003 (b))

THE COURTS

The third branch of Athens' democracy was its judiciary, which was democratic for two reasons:

It upheld the *democratic law*, proposed and approved by the people…

If someone wanted a new law to be adopted, they had to post it on a public whiteboard for everyone to see, petition the council to put it on the agenda for an upcoming assembly meeting, and then put it to the assembly itself. If the assembly agreed to adopt the new law, it was passed on up to the "Nomothetai"; a council of five-hundred Athenians, selected at random, who considered the law, rubber-stamped or amended it. This process, known as "Deliberative Democracy", is something we shall return to in Chapter Six. (Blackwell, 2003 (b))

The judiciary also took a *democratic form*...

Back in the days of Draco, the courts themselves possessed the sheen of democracy. Anyone could bring a case against anyone else. But the archons, who oversaw proceedings, were *aristocratic*. And the members of the Areopagus, who cast judgement, were *oligarchical*. They dished out fines, punishments and impeachments, without answering to the people.

In the wake of the Persian Wars, when Athens' poorer residents saved the city, a newfound sense of bravado took hold of the common people. Led by Ephialtes, they petitioned the council and assembly to create a people's court; wrestling power away from Areopagus, and placing it in the hands of the masses.

The Areopagus continued to prosecute murderers, but its power was fatally diminished. From that point on, every other case was put to the citizenry... (Blackwell, 2003 (a))

The people's courts were democratic to their core. There were no haughty-taughty judges in silly wigs, sitting on pedestals, treating their courtrooms like their personal fiefdoms. The archons ensured that things ran smoothly, but their role was secretarial. The power remained with the people.

Juries, picked at random, gathered on a mass scale. There were never fewer than five-hundred jurors. For serious cases, there could be thousands.

And so it began...

The plaintiff and defendant took to the stage, looked out at this mass gathering, and began to state their case. They were each given an equal amount of time to speak, as measured by a water clock.

When the water ran dry, the speakers were compelled to fall silent, and the people had their say...

Each juror was given two ballots - one for the plaintiff and one for the defendant. They approached a pair of urns, cast their vote in the bronze urn, and discarded their remaining ballot into the wooden one.

The votes were counted and the verdict was passed. The jurors, meanwhile, were paid half a drachma a day - a reward which reduced the incentive for jurors to take bribes. (Blackwell, 2003 (b))

ATHENS AND BEYOND...

So there we have it.

Athenian democracy was supported by three pillars: Every emancipated, adult male could attend the assembly, propose, debate and vote on legislation. Most of these citizens would have also been selected to sit on the council, where they would have overseen the day-to-day running of the region. And, should they get into trouble, they could appeal to a massive jury of their peers.

It may not have been as democratic as the previous systems we encountered, but Athenian democracy did support a nation which was bore a resemblance to modern-day nations; replete with law courts, a navy, personal property and public infrastructure.

It was not the first *democracy*, but it was certainly one of the first *democratic states.*

It was not, however, unique...

***

Athenian democracy was inspired by Sparta...

The Spartans defined themselves as "Homoioi" - men of equal status. Everyone was granted the same education, irrespective of their wealth and social standing. They could criticise, depose and exile their kings. Men aged over thirty attended the assembly, where they elected members of the legislature. (Pomeroy, Burstein, Donlan, Roberts & Tandy, 2011)

Ancient Greece contained around a thousand communities like Sparta and Athens. Most were feudalistic. But democracies also existed in places such as Argos, Megara, Corinth and Rhodes; and in colonies such as Syracuse in Sicily, and Metapontum in Southern Italy. (Dilouambaka, 2017)

***

Athenian-style democracy would also come to inspire the town hall meetings of New England, and the Landsgemeinde of Switzerland - a nation we shall visit in Chapter Five. (Kobach, 1993)

It also inspired Rome…

When the Romans emancipated themselves from Etruscan rule, they immediately installed a senate to advise their kings. When those monarchs were expelled, this council became the most powerful body in the city-state; electing the consuls who governed Rome.

This was no democracy. It was an oligarchical system, ruled by the patrician class. To sit on the senate, a Roman had to be a member of the landed gentry. (Dahl, 2019)

The plebeians grew restless. And so, in 451BC, the senate sent a commission to Greece, to report on Solon's reforms.

This visit inspired a chain of events, which led to the democratisation of Rome…

The next year, the "Comitia Centuriata" was formed. This military assembly included members of both classes, although the wealthy held sway. It had the power to declare war, pass legislation, elect officials and hear appeals.

The "Comitia Plebis", a civil equivalent of the Comitia Centuriata, was formed a century later. (Augustyn, 2018)

These two assemblies were not as powerful as Athens' Ecclesia. They could be overruled by the senate. But even the senate was eventually reformed. Members of the plebeian class did find their way into the gilded halls of this governing body.

So whereas Athens was more of a *direct democracy*, ruled by the people's assembly, Rome was more of a *representative democracy*, ruled by two representative assemblies and one representative senate. For this reason, some historians argue that modern nations have more in common with Rome than they do with Athens. (Dahl, 2019)

RISE AND FALL

All good things come to an end. Iroquois and Greek democracy were no exceptions.

They had to contend with *internal threats*…

Enfranchised adult men may have had an equal right to speak in Athens' assembly, but their ability to do so varied considerably. A great orator could bend the masses to his will; by dint of his personality, turn of phrase and psychological nous.

This was the case with Pericles:

"Whenever he saw them elated, he would with a word reduce them to alarm... If they fell victim to a panic, he could at once restore them to confidence... What was nominally a democracy, became in his hands government by the first citizen".

Such a character could compel the people to make rash, emotional decisions, as was the case in 415BC, when the assembly voted to invade Sicily. The mission was such a disaster, it made people question democracy itself.

Abandoning the assembly, Athens was briefly ruled by a "Council of Four Hundred". This was replaced by a "Council of Five Thousand", before democracy was eventually restored. (Blackwell, 2003 (a))

***

The Athenians and Iroquois also had to contend with *external threats*...

Iroquois democracy ultimately succumbed to European imperialism. After choosing the losing side in the American Revolution, the Haudenosaunee became secondary citizens in their own land; forced to live in reservations and follow Washington's laws.

Athenian democracy also succumbed to foreign invaders...

In 338BC, Philip of Macedonia defeated the Athenian army at Chaeronea. Within fifteen years, the city had been completely humbled. The harbour was filled with Macedonian forces, but the Pnyx lay windswept and hushed. (Blackwell, 2003 (b))

3. MASS CONTROL IN THE MIDDLE AGES

For hundreds-of-thousands of years, we humans lived in small, democratic societies. These groups united to form confederate democracies. But then things went awry...

In Greek, Hebrew, and some Native American tribes, power was delegated to a council of elders. Age was supposed to imply wisdom, and these councils could act with the group's interests in mind. They were *representative*. The elders represented their families and clans. But they were not *democratic*. These councils involved a minority group, who dictated policy from the confines of their exclusive circles. Democracy, the rule of the people, had given way to "Gerontocracy" - the rule of elders.

Another threat to democracy came from the medicine men and their successors: priests, sorcerers and prophets. And yet another threat came from the wealthy - those individuals who controlled land, slaves and livestock.

The biggest threat came from the militias...

Armed gangs subdued their neighbours, killed anyone who refused to bend to their will, invaded new territories, and subdued their inhabitants too. Gang leaders named themselves "Kings", surrounded themselves with knights and vassals, and secured the loyalty of those lackeys by gifting them with counties and boroughs. Declaring themselves appointed by God, with a divine right to rule, they secured their legacies by handing power down to their offspring. (Gillin, 1919)

This was the age of "Feudalism" and "Manorialism"...

Kings ruled over their lords, ladies, princes and priests. These nobles ruled over everyone else. They acted as chiefs of their manors; meting out justice, distributing strips of land amongst the peasantry, and taking enough of their produce to keep themselves flush.

At least, this is the over-simplified story of the Middle Ages. And it may be true. But it is not the *whole truth*.

Kings did rule their kingdoms, but they did not rule them *completely*. They did not have the same means of surveillance, communication or transportation, which governments can utilise today.

Lords did rule their manors, but they were far from omnipotent. Pastures, forests and fisheries were held in common and managed, democratically, by the peasantry. Craftsmen united to form democratic "Guilds", which united to form "Free Towns". And monks ruled themselves from within the confines of their monasteries...

BENEDICT'S BROTHERS

Benedict of Nursia was not a happy chappy. You could say he was rather miffed. This son of a Roman noble, with stony cheeks and heavy eyes, could not help but judge his society harshly.

Here was lawlessness. Here was moral laxity. Here was immoral behaviour. The people of Rome claimed to be Christians, but they did not seem to give two hoots for the teachings of their lord, Jesus Christ.

Benedict cast a lonely figure as he turned his back on this corrupt society. He left Enfide, navigated a long, gloomy ravine, and ascended the piercing mountains which rose up on either side.

Here, five-hundred metres above the shimmering waters of a distant lake, Benedict made a home.

He left, briefly, to join a monastery; only to return to his cave when the other monks attempted to poison him. But this time, the hermit would not be left in peace. Rumours spread of his miracles, people came to see what the fuss was about, stayed, learned from Benedict, and encouraged him to move. He returned to the lowlands, and established twelve new monasteries.

With these new monasteries came a new constitution, "The Rule of St. Benedict". And with this new constitution came a new democracy... (Ford, 1907) (Newton, 2013)

***

Benedict's rules ushered in a system of control which was democratic, albeit within the confines of some very strict parameters. These were, after all, rules for monks; people who were honour-bound to follow God's *undemocratic* laws. Benedict added to the holy law, prescribing instructions which governed everything from meal times to sleeping arrangements.

But within such parameters, each Benedictine monastery did rule itself; applying a mixture of direct democracy, representative democracy and economic democracy. It did this by applying two concepts which democratic systems still rely upon today: The principal of "One person, one vote", and the idea that anyone could achieve high office, no matter their background...

***

Benedictine monasteries were *direct democracies*, in which assemblies were convened to discuss pertinent matters.

Consider these two passages from "The Rule of Saint Benedict":

"As often as any special business has to be transacted in the monastery, let the Abbot convoke the *whole* community... Because it is often to a junior that the Lord reveals what is best".

And:

"Let not one of gentle birth be placed higher than one who was recently a serf".

So anyone could influence community meetings, if they were young or old, from a wealthy family or a poor one. This might not sound particularly revolutionary to the modern ear, but compared with mainstream Roman society, in which a class system was fully entrenched, it was pretty radical stuff.

In religious terms, however, it made perfect sense. The monks were all God's children, equal in the eyes of their Lord. It would have been blasphemous to treat another monk as if he were your master. For the monks, there was only one master: God himself.

***

For less significant matters, power was delegated to the abbot, who was elected by the monks. The abbot was first amongst equals. He had a duty to lead on behalf of the entire group, and ensure that no hierarchy could form.

In this regard, the Benedictine monasteries could be called *representative democracies*.

Whilst Benedict urged his monks to consider candidates' wisdom, age and experience; he made it clear that "Even the most recent one to join the community" could be elected abbot.

***

Benedictine monks were not allowed to own, "Neither book, nor writing-tablet, nor pen". Possessions had to "Be common to all".

Their monasteries, therefore, could be dubbed *economic democracies*, not unlike the economic democracies of the !Kung and the Iroquois.

Monks were expected to do their share of monastery work, be that in the kitchen, field or infirmary. They were expected to labour hard, to contribute to the physical wellbeing of their community. (Benedict of Nursia, 516) (Newton, 2013)

***

So why mention the Benedictine monks? After all, many other religious communities existed at the time. Some may have been *even more* democratic than Benedict's.

It is because the Benedictine monasteries began to multiply...

In 595, Augustine and forty companions headed for England, determined to take the Rule of St. Benedict to those distant shores. They influenced the monasteries they passed on the way, leaving copies of their rulebook wherever they went.

Their pilgrimage proved a resounding success. By the Ninth Century, almost every monastery in Western Europe, the Celtic nations aside, were Benedictine democracies. (Alston, 1907)

When feudalism took hold, and kings began to cement their power, they were faced with two options. They could destroy this large network of popular institutions, earning themselves enemies at home *and* abroad. Or they could allow those monasteries to govern themselves. Inevitably, they chose the latter option; granting the monasteries their independence, and even exempting them from tax.

These religious associations, meanwhile, inspired lay folk to form similar associations of their own: The guilds...

THE FREE TOWNS AND THEIR GUILDS

The origin of the guilds remains shrouded in mystery. Some may have formed organically. Many claim to have Roman or Byzantine roots. And of course, several were inspired by the religious brotherhoods in the Christian church.

The guilds were voluntary organisations which united local craftspeople. They might unite a town's fishermen, for example. Florence's "Arte dei Medici, Speziali e Merciai", included doctors, apothecaries and haberdashers.

To join, potential members had to prove their ability, morality, orthodoxy and loyalty. They had to pay membership fees. They could be expelled or leave at any time.

* * *

The guilds were based on two seemingly contradictory principles: hierarchy and equality...

Their members ran small, hierarchical workshops. Masters employed, trained and housed apprentices, who graduated to become journeymen. Within the guilds, this *hierarchy* was maintained. The masters remained in charge. But all the masters were considered *equal*. All the journeymen were deemed equal too.

When issues arose which affected the whole guild, an assembly was called to make collective decisions. In this sense, the guilds were direct democracies. But for everyday issues, power was delegated to elected officials.

These representatives, who never stayed in office for more than a year, had several roles. They acted as arbiters between quarrelling members, they represented their guild in disputes with outsiders, ensured that members followed their guild's rules, protected their guild's apprentices, examined the candidates for mastership, and oversaw their guild's pious works.

The electoral process varied from guild to guild, and from region to region. Officials were normally elected by masters, or by the "Electors" those masters selected. Sometimes, journeymen were also given a vote.

In Italy, nominees were selected in secret ballots. Several candidates were usually approved at any one time; far more than were actually needed. When this happened, the names of the elected delegates were written on tickets, which were placed in padlocked bags. Whenever a new officer was required, a priest or child would pick a ticket at random, to select the next official. Given time, everyone who had been approved by their peers would hold office.

In Arras, they did things a little differently. The masters all selected a ball of wax from an urn. Whoever drew the ball which contained the words "Jésus-Marie" became the guild's new boss.

* * *

The guilds all had banners, seals and archives. They could possess land, buildings, money and bonds. They could contract and bargain.

They were, in short, self-governing democracies. They even had law books, which took a similar form across the continent. Statutes relating to prohibition, for example, always started with the same words: "Let none presume or be so bold as to..".

Their main role was economic. They sought to protect their customers, members and communities...

Each member was honour-bound to provide top-quality products to their *customers*, thereby protecting the integrity of their craft. Dyers in Florence had to dip their cloth into a set amount of dye, a set amount of times. Jewellers could not use imitation stones, even if they declared them to be fake. Fishermen in Rome had to ensure the meshes in their nets were within the agreed limits. Parisian spinners could only make pieces of linen in pre-prescribed sizes. In Maine, a butcher could only display his beef if two witnesses had seen the cow brought in alive. It was forbidden to sell damaged meat, rotten fish, decaying eggs or pigs which had been fattened on diseased blood.

The guilds also had rules that ensured fair play between *members*, such that the great could not crush the small, nor the rich overpower the poor. Masters were obliged to treat their subordinates well, give them expert training, and help them to become masters themselves. Members could not buy all the raw materials, in order to sell them on for a profit. Nor could masters hoard workers: In Paris, leather-dressers who employed more than two men were compelled to lend one to a fellow craftsman whenever he required assistance. The guilds also fixed working hours, prices and discounts: In Florence, any innkeeper who offered free wine to a passing stranger, to win their trade, was issued with a fine.

These fines, along with members' fees and donations, formed a maintenance fund which was used to support the *community*. An early incarnation of the Welfare State, the guilds held funerals for their members, financed local hospitals, gave alms to the poor, and covered the cost of religious worship.

There sure were a lot of rules to follow. And the guilds sure did have a lot of fingers in a lot of pies. But their rules and activities were all approved by their members. Anyone who did not like those rules, was free to propose amendments or leave their guild at any time.

***

Few guilds stood alone. They were based in urban conurbations, near other guilds. This left them with a choice, not unlike that faced by primitive societies. They could stand alone, risking conflict and subjugation. Or they could unite, like the Iroquois, forging alliances with their neighbours.

This happened in places such as Boulogne, Siena, Bruges, Zurich, Liége, Augsburg and Cologne. The guilds united to form "Communes" or "Free Towns" - self-governing republics which had their own constitutions, armies, mints and budgets.

They were, in essence, confederate democracies...

In Florence, twenty-one craft guilds came together, nominating priors and magistrates to govern their city. Strasburg was ruled by delegates from twenty-five "Zünfte". In Ghent, the weavers, fullers and "Small Crafts" created a mini-state.

Taking the baton from the guilds themselves, the first role of the free towns was economic...

They controlled resources. In Rome, they owned the fisheries and fish-markets. In Florence, they held a monopoly on salt.

Special magistrates set the price of vegetables, fruits, oil and wine - keeping them at a level that everyone could afford. Limits were placed on the number of bottles of wine a family could keep in their cellar, to ensure it was not hoarded by the rich. In Florence, rules were put in place which forced peasants to plant a certain number of fruit trees per acre. In Pistoria, every shepherd was required to supply 20% of their lambs.

These measures protected the poor *and* the rich. Ensuring that food was plentiful and affordable meant that the poor did not go hungry. This prevented insurrections, thereby protecting the wealthy.

The free towns also had a judicial role...

Their leaders, who were elected by members of the guilds, judged criminal cases; expelling some miscreants, and reducing the ranks of others. They issued taxes, set foreign policy and declared war.

United, the free towns grew strong. They could defend themselves against the feudalists - absorbing the wealth and power of local bishops, and subduing would-be-nobles - forcing them to retreat or join a guild.

But where the guilds *did not* unite to form free towns, they proved to be easy-pickings for the feudal orders...

***

In most of France, in England, and for a long time in Rome, the guilds continued to play a key role in everyday life. Internally, they remained democratic. But externally, they came to be ruled by kings, lords and provosts, who maintained armies that could annihilate them on a whim.

The guilds now needed to be granted permission to operate. Thus, towards the end of the Twelfth Century, King Henry II of England sanctioned the tanners' association in Rouen. At the beginning of the Thirteenth Century, King Philip II of France sanctioned the weavers' guild in Étampes.

These guilds now had to follow their monarch's rules...

King John II of France dictated two-hundred-and-twenty-seven such edicts, relating to wages and maximum tariffs. The "Statute of Labours" enforced similar standards in England. The feudal authorities forbade work on certain days, and judged disputes between rival guilds.

The feudalists also imposed certain duties...

Guild members were expected to police the streets and defend the ramparts. Doctors and barber-surgeons were expected to care for the poor.

And they demanded money...

To be a napery-weaver in Paris, individuals had to buy the right from the king. Philip II may have sanctioned the weavers' guild in Étampes, "For the love of God", but that did not stop him from demanding twenty pounds of cloth from every weaver. Provosts were known to charge taxes on both imports *and* exports.

The kings, therefore, essentially used the independent guilds; taking the systems they had built and the cities they had enriched, uniting them into a nation, and ruling them from afar. The royals took a share of the guilds' produce in taxes, and called on their members to join the royal army whenever the need arose.

***

The free towns, meanwhile, maintained their independence from external control. But their democracies began to crumble...

The wealthier families became cocksure. Seeking to monopolise control, they issued laws which prevented members of the lower classes from climbing the social ladder.

Now, to hold office, potential candidates had to satisfy three requirements. They had to be a certain age, they had to have money, and they had to have significant social standing.

Wool-merchants, money-changers and goldsmiths began to monopolise power, not because they were more numerous, but because they had the means to buy their way to the top.

Once they had secured their rule at home, these oligarchs launched wars to open new markets. To fund such wars, they took out interest-bearing loans, which they repaid by levying regressive taxes. To stop dissent, they suppressed public meetings.

This story repeated itself across the continent...

In Beauvais, the money-changers nominated seven "Peers" to the municipal administration. The other twenty-one guilds could only elect six representatives *between them*. In Brussels and Louvain, seven families furnished all the aldermen. Similar oligarchies formed in Ghent, Florence, Amiens and Genoa.

By the end of the Fifteenth Century, the free towns were no more. They too had fallen to feudal powers. (Renard, 1918)

THE COMMONS

The feudalists may have seized control, but they were not in *complete* control. Lords may have owned the land, but it was the people who managed its use - pooling their resources and administering their regions together:

"Peasants combined their individual plots into open fields and common pastures, and farmed them collectively... Peasant councils were responsible for overseeing economic activity, including planting and harvesting, crop rotation, the use of forest and water resources, and the number of animals that could graze on the common pastures". (Rifkin, 2014)

It is hard to say when such structures came into being. Perhaps they had always existed, evolving from the sort of primitive democracies we met in the previous chapters. They might have existed in the Sixth Century, whilst Benedict of Nursia was walking the earth. They may not have appeared until the time of the guilds.

What we do know is that organisations for managing the *commons* did exist in 1435, when eighty-four farmers met outside Valencia's St. Francis monastery to pen a set of regulations. These specified who could take water from the Benacher and Faitanar canals, how that water would be shared in good and bad years, who would maintain the canals, how officials would be elected, and what fines would be dished out to anyone who broke the rules.

These were democratic rules, agreed upon by the local farmers, to help them manage the supply of water in a way which would benefit them all.

But just because these rules were formalised in 1435, is not to say they did not exist before. Oral rules may have existed for *a thousand years*.

They continue to be enforced today...

***

The Valencia region is semi-arid. The trees are a drab shade of green, as though their very verdancy has been eroded by dust. The fact that anything can grow here at all, seems to defy the laws of nature. From a distance, the ground appears to be made from hard-baked sand.

To survive, the locals had to build canals, to irrigate their land. But this could have been a recipe for conflict. The region is broken down into several small farms. 80% are less than a hectare. If a few farms took a lot of water, without leaving any for the farmers downstream, all hell might break loose.

And so the farmers work together, to ensure everyone gets their fair share. This is why they agreed upon a set of rules, up to a thousand years ago, and why those rules were formalised in 1435.

To this day, Valanecien farmers still elect a "Syndic" to manage their local canal. The syndic can levy fines and ration water when the supply is low.

The seven syndics who manage the region's seven canals come together to form a water court, the "Tribunal de las Aguas", which convenes outside Valencia's cathedral each week. This is a people's court, where anyone can file a complaint against anyone else, and members of the public are free to come by and watch.

After the court session is done and dusted, the syndics might also convene a tribunal, and deal with whatever issues happen to be affecting the region as a whole.

***

Such a system is far from unique. There are about thirty irrigation communities in Murcia, and another ten in Orihucla...

In Murcia, the syndics of each community come together to form a general assembly, once a year. They elect an executive committee, to oversee the day-to-day management of the region's waterways, and vote to approve taxes and budgets.

In Orihucla, the general assembly meets every three years to elect a water magistrate, their lieutenant and a solicitor.

Further afield, the Zatijera institutions in the Philippines have been run along similar lines for at least four-hundred years. The irrigators agree upon rules amongst themselves, elect officials, police their canals, and perform maintenance work together.

Elsewhere, *different assets* are managed in a similar fashion...

***

Törbel, a Swiss village with around five-hundred residents, grips tightly to the side of a steep incline. Pale green fields contrast with dark green foliage. Snow-capped mountains kiss the oceanic skies.

As in Spain, the local peasants maintain their own *private* plots. They grow grains for bread and hay for their cattle. This is no communist utopia, in which *everything* is managed by the group.

But a good chunk of the village's resources are managed collectively. The village's wastelands, irrigation systems, paths, roads, forests and pastures have been managed collectively since 1224, if not before.

***

Cheese production is a big part of Törbel's economy. To produce that cheese, the villagers must raise cows. But if they raise too many cows, there will not be enough grass to feed them.

So, in 1517, the people passed a law which is still enforced today:

"No citizen can send more cows to the alps than they can feed during the winter".

Such a law is democratic; made by the people, to help the people...

Any villager who owns cattle becomes a member of the village's "Association". They can attend its annual general assembly, discuss its rules and propose polices. They can also elect the officials responsible for maintaining the village's roads, paths, fields, corrals, huts and pastures...

To ensure the villagers do not exceed their quota, an elected herdsman counts the cows in and out.

Another elected official manages the village's forests...

Each year, the forester marks the trees that are to be harvested. Households that are eligible to receive a share of that wood form teams, cut the trees, haul the logs and put them into equal piles. A lottery then takes place to distribute the stacks amongst the various households.

Wood cannot be harvested at any other time.

***

Törbel is not alone...

Four-fifths of the Swiss Alps are managed, democratically, by the local peasantry - a practice that dates back to the Middle Ages. Some, like Törbel, are managed by all the local villagers. Others are managed by corporations or cooperatives.

Surprisingly similar practices can also be found in Japan...

During the Tokugawa period, from 1600 to 1867, twelve-million hectares of forests and meadows were managed using the Törbel model. Families farmed their own private plots, but united to manage their shared land. Bundles of dried grass were allocated by lottery, in just the same way that wood was distributed in Törbel.

Three-million hectares of Japanese land are still managed in such a manner today.

***

These incredibly similar systems have allowed people to manage their shared fields, forests, waterways and fisheries, without outside intervention, for centuries if not millennia. Commons associations have survived droughts, floods, wars, pestilence, economic and political upheaval.

To do so, they have had to adhere to a few core principles.

They have needed to stand up to external threats...

They have had to earn the respect of lords, monarchs and governments. When the state or the private sector has come into conflict with the village councils, the villagers have had to act quickly and effectively - accessing low-cost legal mediation and exerting their rights.

And they have needed to be democratic...

The locals must have a say in writing the rules *they* are expected to follow. These rules must state *who* is allowed on the commons, *when* they can access the commons, and *how many* resources they can take. The officers who uphold these rules must be chosen by the people, and must be held accountable by the people. Punishments must not be too harsh. There can be no lingering resentment once justice has been served.

***

Commons-based villages seldom rely on outsiders to do their policing. The villagers police themselves; electing officers from amongst their rank.

It is an intimate process. The shame one might feel, should they be caught infringing *their* community's rules, is a punishment in itself.

In Japan, most villages had "Detectives", who rode around the commons on horseback looking for rule-breakers. Other villages rotated this position amongst the males.

Anyone found guilty of breaking the rules could have their harvest, equipment and horses confiscated. In the most extreme cases, they could be ostracised or banished from the village.

Yet even though villages did have elected officials, and these individuals did have some authority, power ultimately lay with the people...

When one village headman did not open the forests early enough, the people entered them en masse; taking the wood they needed to make trellises and poles. They argued that if they did not do so, they might lose their entire crop. And, because so many people disobeyed their headman, there was nothing his detective could do!

***

Back in Europe, the fines imposed upon transgressors were tiny when compared to the gains that could be made from breaking the rules. Stealing water from a Spanish canal during a drought could save an entire year's crop. Taking more than your fair share of wood from a Swiss forest could enable you to build the nicest house in the village.

Yet despite the potential rewards, very few people broke the rules. The record books of one Castellan Huerta survive from both 1443 and 1486. They show that less than five-hundred fines were issued in each year.

People respected the rules because they were *their* rules. They benefitted from those rules. And they could change them at any time. (Ostrom, 1990)

4. THE RISE OF REPRESENTATIVE DEMOCRACY

The Middle Ages, therefore, were a bit of a mixed bag...

Peasants managed their day-to-day affairs, farming their own plots of land in whatever way they chose, and uniting to manage the commons.

The monasteries also maintained their independence. They secured the support of the local peasantry through their acts of charity, and they deferred to the Pope before obeying their monarch.

The nobles controlled the regions, and had armies of their own. Kings often exempted both the nobles and the clergy from taxation, in order to maintain their support.

And then, of course, we have the free towns. These sat alongside other corporations - the likes of the parish communities, royal towns and baronial jurisdictions - institutions which also had charters of liberties, rights and militias.

To get the troops he needed to fight a war, or the tax revenues he needed to rule, the king had to negotiate with these powerful groups. It was a two-way street. These groups could serve the king, validating his rule. But they could also hold him to account - vetoing his laws, auditing his taxes, or rejecting his choice of successor.

In time, this two-way relationship was formalised. Kings began to call representatives from these groups to form assemblies - the pre-cursor of modern parliaments.

This process first took place in Northeast Spain... (Møller, 2014)

***

Eleventh Century Aragon was not at peace. Violence was endemic and the land was awash with private battles. Some were mere scuffles. Others were more like outright wars.

By the turn of the century, the mayhem had reached Catalonia. Left unchecked, it could have engulfed the entire peninsula.

The king got to work. Declaring himself, "Guarantor of the national peace", he imposed law and order on his people. But he could not do it alone.

To make their voices heard, he and his successors convened a series of "Pre-parliaments". They invited the high and mighty from across the kingdom, wined and dined them, and secured their allegiance. Between 1100 and 1327, Catalonia hosted thirty-four such assemblies. Aragon hosted forty-one.

These early parliaments were convened by the king, for the king; to enshrine his laws and secure his choice of successor. They were top-down affairs.

But as they evolved, these assemblies gradually became more representative...

King James "The Conqueror" hosted the first *fully* representative court in Barcelona, in December 1228, when he wished to raise funds for his invasion of Majorca. In the following decades, he hosted similar assemblies to win approval for his conquests of Valencia and the Balearics.

His reign marked a distinctive shift. As well as discussing the succession and peace, almost a fifth of parliaments were now being called to set taxation, and almost a quarter were being used to plan wars.

With the support of his nobles, and an ever-growing kingdom, James's power ascended to new heights. But "The Conqueror" had unleashed a beast - an assembly which contained every nobles, from every principality - a united block of powerful individuals.

They were to prove an unstoppable force...

Angry that they had not been consulted ahead of Aragon's invasion of Sicily, and incensed at what they considered to be unlawful taxes, these powerful individuals confronted James's successor, King Peter III. They took up arms and were ready to attack.

To appease his restless nobles, the king granted two rounds of concessions. In 1283, Peter passed the "Privilegio General". Five years later, Peter's successor, Alfonso III, passed the "Privilegios de la Union". These forced the king to hold annual assemblies, and stipulated that taxes had to be collected by the courts.

The whole system had been turned on its head...

The assemblies, which had originally been convened by the king, to secure his rule, were now being convened by the nobles, to empower *them*, and *limit* their king's authority. (Møller, 2017)

* * *

A similar tale was unfolding elsewhere...

By 1450, similar assemblies could be found in Poland, Hungary and Scandinavia. By the end of the Fifteenth Century, representative institutions could be found across most of Latin Christendom. (Møller, 2014) (Stasavage, 2010)

YE OLDE BRITISH DEMOCRACY

The British parliament can trace its origins back to the "Witan" - an inner-circle of loyal royalists who advised the Anglo-Saxon kings. And the "Moots" - the county meetings which were attended by local lords, bishops, the sheriff, and four representatives from each village.

By the time of the Norman Conquests, in the Eleventh Century, the Anglo-Saxon nations had merged to form England, and the Witan had evolved into the "Great Council". (Parliament UK, 2019)

These early English assemblies were similar to those in Aragon. The first two were convened to settle a new king's ascension to the throne. Between 1216 and 1260, 16.5% of assemblies discussed taxation and 5% discussed war.

These pre-parliaments *did* hold the king to account, rejecting the taxes he proposed to fund wars in France. But they did not become *representative* until 1265, when knights and townsmen began to attend. (Møller, 2017)

So the Witan evolved into the Great Council. This formed an assembly, which would go on to become representative, and eventually form the basis of the present-day House of Lords. (Parliament UK, 2019)

The Moots, meanwhile, were united by Simon de Montfort, in 1265, when he called the knights and burgesses from each borough to form a parliament. Thirty years later, this institution expanded, forming the "Model Parliament" which included members of the lower clergy and the general citizenry. (Ellis, 2014)

This parliament, which would become the present-day "House of Commons", was hardly authoritative. When, in 1376, it sent Thomas de la Mare to complain about the Poll Tax, the king had de la Mare arrested! Nor was it particularly democratic. Men were only enfranchised if they owned forty shillings worth of land or a freehold property. Women could not vote at all. (Chivers, 2017)

This parliament did, however, give *some* people a voice.

Five years after de la Mare's arrest, the rest of the nation would find *its* voice. Launching the Peasants' Revolt, the people demanded that the Poll Tax be scrapped, that serfs be freed to work for whomever they chose, that they be given the right to sell their produce at market, and that land rents be reduced. Tens-of-thousands of common folk descended on Blackheath, asking "When Adam delved and Eve span, who was then the gentleman?" Then they marched into the capital, killed their enemies, and confronted the king with an assortment of weapons in hand.

Many of the rebels were slaughtered in the months that followed, and many of their demands went unanswered. But they did achieve one of their goals. The monarch was forced to succumb to the will of the people and abolish the much-maligned Poll Tax.

Even in the time of kings, the people retained the power to force change. It proved difficult, rare and bloody. But democracy could prevail. (Jones, 2014 (a))

***

The rebel spirit of the Peasants' Revolt bubbled away for the next couple of centuries.

It finally boiled over, in the 1640s, when another popular protest engulfed the nation...

These were a time of economic unrest. Following the "Discovery" of the Americas, silver had begun to flow across the Atlantic, and into the pockets of a new mercantile class. Reinvesting this silver in land, the early capitalists sought a quick return. Both they and the feudal lords raised rents, breaking a timeless covenant between landlord and tenant. Peasants who could not afford to pay these inflated rents were evicted from the fields their families had farmed for centuries. They were faced with an unenviable choice: Become employees, dependent on their bosses' wages, or vagrants, who would be "Whipped until their shoulders be bloody".

In the century leading up to the 1640 revolution, the real incomes of common Brits fell to less than half their previous level.

King Charles, meanwhile, continued to rule his nation in the interest of the landowning nobles - not the new, mercantile class, nor the general population. Rebellions broke out in 1549, 1607 and 1631. The crown attempted to stifle this dissent by banning political meetings, cutting off the ears of political dissidents, and raising arbitrary taxes. But such a heavy-handed response only served to unite the king's opponents; aligning traders and industrialists, who wanted capitalism to take the place of feudalism, with the downtrodden poor, who wanted to overturn the system that had impoverished them and their families.

The parliamentarians, led by Oliver Cromwell, formed a "New Model Army". They held political discussions, became convinced of their cause, and fought with the passion of true believers.

They charged, knee to knee, maintaining discipline, reforming and charging again. Their victory at Marston Moor gave them effective control of the north. Their victory at Naseby decimated the royal forces. (Hill, 1940)

**

They may have won the First English Civil War, but the parliamentarians were divided. At the Putney Debates, in 1647, most attendees agreed with Thomas Rainborough's famous plea:

"For really I think that the poorest he that is in England hath a life to live, as the greatest he".

But they disagreed about who, exactly, should be enfranchised...

Cromwell, representing the merchants, argued that the vote should only be extended to men who owned land worth forty shillings a year, and freemen of trading corporations. The Levellers, representing the peasantry, wanted votes for all men. Yet even here there were divides - some Levellers did not believe that servants and alms-receivers should receive the vote. (Kettle, 2007)

The debate was never resolved.

A Second Civil War broke out in 1648. As the parliamentarians headed for victory, they captured the king, conducted a hasty trial, declared him a "Public enemy", and chopped off his head. The monarchy was declared, "Unnecessary, burdensome, and dangerous to the liberty, safety and public interest of the people". The House of Lords was declared, "Useless and dangerous". Both were abolished and a republic was proclaimed.

But the commoners remained disenfranchised.

Feeling betrayed, the Levellers revolted. Their rebellion was quashed and their leaders were shot. Their movement disintegrated and their calls for universal suffrage were lost to the wind.

***

Cromwell maintained power in the years that followed. But Cromwell's successor, his son, could not continue what his father had started.

Exploiting parliament's weakness, Charles II returned home, pretended he had been king all along, and reached a compromise with the parliamentarians: The monarchy and the House of Lords would be restored, but they would no longer have the executive powers of days gone by. The kind of arbitrary taxation that threatened private property became a thing of the past. Monopolies were broken up, giving businesses free reign.

Real power now resided in the House of Commons, with its merchants and squires, and with the land-owning men who could elect those representatives.

It was democracy for rich, but not for the poor. (Hill, 1940) (Hill, 1958)

***

The Victorians continued the job the Levellers had started two-hundred years before...

As in the run-up to the English Revolution, living standards had crumbled in the early 1800s. In 1809, spinners were earning twenty-one shillings a week. A decade later, they were earning just twelve. Streets were left dirty, windows often lacked glass, and families were pawning their furniture. (Bates, 2018)

The people were restless...

At Spa Fields, in London, an audience of ten-thousand signed a petition that demanded universal suffrage for men, annual general elections, and secret ballots. But when Henry Hunt attempted to deliver that petition to Prince George, he was turned away, not once but twice.

A second meeting, held to protest Hunt's treatment, soon became heated. Leaving the protest ground, a band of burly sailors raided a gun shop and armed the baying mob. They headed for the Royal Exchange, where they were surrounded and arrested.

A parliamentary report from the time, declared that similar "Attempts have been made in various parts of the country". (Bloy, 2003)

Civil unrest was on the rise. Female reform societies were popping up across the nation, and Luddites were breaking their masters' looms. After the "March of the Blanketeers" and "The Pentrich Rising", Henry Hunt spoke again; calling for universal male suffrage at meetings in London, Birmingham and Leeds, before arriving in St. Peter's Field.

Sixty-thousand people, over half the population of Manchester, huddled in tight. Wearing their Sunday best, and holding banners marked "Taxation without representation is unjust and tyrannical", they sang patriotic tunes, laughed and cheered.

The authorities responded with violence. They charged into the crowd on horseback, killing eighteen peaceful protestors and injuring six-hundred-and-fifty more. (Bates, 2018)

But those protestors did not die in vain. Their calls were heeded when the "First Reform Act" passed through parliament, enfranchising one-sixth of adult men. (Chivers, 2017)

It was not enough.

When six *farm labourers* from Tolpuddle were arrested for attempting to assert democratic control over their workplace, a jury of *farm owners* found them guilty of swearing an illegal oath and sentenced them to seven years of slavery in Australia.

Demonstrations swept across the nation. Eight-hundred-thousand people signed a petition, and the government was forced to pardon the "Tolpuddle Martyrs"; paving the way for the trade union movement to flourish. (Chisolm, 2009)

Just seven months later, "The London Working Men's Association" was established. They published "The People's Charter", making six demands which would revolutionise Britain.

Supporters of this charter, the "Chartists", held meetings which were attended by hundreds-of-thousands of people, and submitted petitions which contained millions of names; uniting townsfolk and country-dwellers, the working and middle classes. They staged riots in Newcastle and Birmingham. And they gave their lives for the cause. Twenty-two Chartists were shot dead by soldiers at the Westgate Hotel. (British Library, 2019)

The last major Chartist protest took place in 1848. But their calls lingered on. After centuries of minority rule, five of their demands *were* enacted. People without property were allowed to stand in elections in 1858, secret ballots were introduced in 1872, constituencies were made equal in 1884, politicians began to receive salaries in 1911, and universal suffrage for men was granted in 1918. (Bloy, 2016)

***

Still, British democracy could not be called "Representative" if women were denied the vote.

Women *had* been involved in the Chartist movement from the get-go. They had formed Female Charter Associations, they had challenged Chartists to campaign for female suffrage, and they had published pamphlets to garner support. The utilitarian philosopher, Jeremy Bentham, went as far as to write a "Plan of Parliamentary Reform", calling for female suffrage, way back in 1817. John Stuart Mill presented the first women's suffrage petition to parliament in 1866. (British Library, 2019) (Chivers, 2017)

But progress was painfully slow...

Growing impatient, the "Women's Social and Political Union" committed itself to a policy of "Deeds not words". In 1909, they organised the biggest demonstration in British history. Two-hundred-and-fifty-thousand people marched from Hyde Park to Downing Street, where they threw stones, smashed windows and tied themselves to railings. (British Library Learning, 2018)

The next January, on what became known as "Black Friday", the state reacted with force. Three-hundred activists marched to Westminster, to protest the government's decision to shelve a pro-democracy bill. They were surrounded by the police, beaten and molested for several hours.

Attempting to bury the story, the Home Secretary, Winston Churchill, rejected calls for a public inquiry.

It was a turning point...

Before this negligent act, the campaign for women's votes had been dominated by the peaceful "Suffragists". But in the wake of Black Friday, and the attempt to cover it up, the violent "Suffragettes" came to the fore.

They organised a window-smashing campaign in London, before going national; conducting the biggest bombing and arson campaign in British history. They destroyed politicians' houses, railway stations, post offices and churches. (Ridell, 2018)

The authorities arrested scores of pro-democracy campaigners.

When those Suffragettes went on hunger-strike, the authorities force-fed them - restraining their arms and pouring food down their throats. When these tactics failed, the Suffragettes were given the "Cat and Mouse" treatment. They were released from prison, only to be re-arrested just as soon as they had returned to health. (Norris, 2019)

The Suffragettes were demonised, they were called "Terrorists", but they emerged victorious. In 1918, the "Representation of the People Act" gave some women the vote. Ten years later, all women aged twenty-one or older were enfranchised. (Jones, 2014 (a)) (Chivers, 2017)

***

So, what does this tell us?

Primitive democracy was crushed, first by the Roman conquerors, and then by the Anglo-Saxon kings. They used violence to establish and protect their undemocratic regimes.

Only when the people fought fire with fire did they re-establish a semi-democratic system: Representative democracy.

Tens-of-thousands of people died during the English Revolution. Everyday people laid down their lives at Peterloo and Newport. Pro-democracy activists were attacked, arrested and tortured by soldiers and police. But their efforts *were* rewarded. They secured the vote.

Two lessons emerge from this tale...

Lesson One: Soldiers and police protect the establishment, not the people. In the Part Three, we shall look at some ways through which we might turn this situation on its head, by establishing armies and police forces which actually *work for us*.

Lesson Two: Democracy is not handed to us as a gift from above. It must be fought for from below. Ideally, the fight should be peaceful. Regrettably, it can be a rather bloody affair...

THE FRENCH REVOLUTION

As in Britain, the French pro-democracy movement began in harsh economic times...

When France lost the Seven Years War, in 1763, it conceded most of its American colonies, along with the revenues those lands had brought. The campaign itself had taken a heavy toll. France's debts were astronomical.

When King Louis the Sixteenth ascended to the throne, his nation was in the midst of a financial crisis. But, rather than demand money from the nobles and clergy, he raised taxes on the nation's poor. France's population had grown by 30% in the previous century, it was struggling to feed itself, and so that tax hit hard.

Profiteers decided to hoard grain, the price of bread skyrocketed, and discontent began to spread.

***

These events took place at the dawn of a new political consciousness: The Enlightenment. People were beginning to think for themselves, demanding liberty and equality; challenging the aristocracy itself.

Maximilian Robespierre, "An eloquent speaker, with never a hair or a phrase out of place", questioned his monarch:

"Do you know why there are so many needy people? It is because your luxurious existence devours in one day the substance of a thousand men!"

Similar sentiments made their way onto clandestine pamphlets, which were passed around the nation, inspiring the starving poor to act. They rioted, raided bakeries, and lynched any shopkeepers they thought might be hoarding grain.

Attempting to restore order, King Louis convened the "Estates General". But this parliament was far from democratic. The peasants made up 97% of France's population, but their deputies could be outvoted by representatives of the other 3%. When they found themselves locked out of the palace, they sensed a conspiracy.

They were unfazed. They held an impromptu meeting on a sports court, where they declared themselves the "National Assembly" - the true government of France.

It was just a paper victory.

The king responded with force, sending thirty-thousand troops to Paris. But the people were up for the fight. They formed a national guard, raided the military hospital, distributed twenty-eight thousand muskets, and headed for the Bastille - that stony keep, the eternal symbol of tyrannical government, where enemies of the crown "Disappeared".

The people stormed the Bastille, tore into the soldiers with knives and pikes, dragged the governor out onto the street and beat him to death. They dismantled that fortress, brick by single brick.

Upon hearing of these events, King Louis asked, "Is it a revolt?"

"No sir", he was told. "It is a revolution".

It was, indeed, a revolution. And the people's demands were clear.

They wanted a constitutional monarchy, equal rights for all men, justice under reasonable laws, freedom of the press, and taxation for the aristocracy.

***

The next time Paris heard rumours of the army's approach, the people did not stay put. The "Fearsome Fish Ladies" of the central markets, known for their muscled shoulders and hardened personas, led the march to Versailles; scalers and knives in hand.

The most magnificent palace in Europe had been home to the French monarchy for a century. Built twelve miles outside the capital, to protect the king from his subjects, it had never seen scenes like these.

By morning, twenty-thousand people were trampling the palace's manicured lawns and defecating in its fountains.

Their numbers continued to swell.

"Remove yourselves from this opulent monstrosity", the masses demanded. "Come live alongside the people in Paris!"

Rather than answer, King Louis prevaricated.

The people grew restless. They charged, massacring the royal guards, before searching for the queen, Marie Antoinette, shouting: "Give me her entrails", "Give me her head", "I want a leg" and "I want an arm".

The people raided the royal stores, emptying them of grain, captured the royal couple, and marched them to a Parisian palace.

They were prisoners in all but name.

***

For two years, King Louis played the part of a constitutional monarch - signing paper after paper, each of which diminished his power.

His frustrations began to mount. And so, in June 1791, he and his queen disguised themselves as servants, snuck away in the midnight hour, and headed for Austria.

When they were captured, a few miles from the border, the news began to spread.

It did not take long for opinions to shift. These royals were not only superfluous, they were also traitors and cowards.

It was the beginning of the end for King Louis and his queen...

During another riot, in which eight-hundred people lost their lives, Louis held a vote to suspend the monarchy. The First French Republic was born.

The following April, Louis found himself atop the scaffold. His words drowned out by the sound of beating drums, his arms and legs tied, the sharp blade of the guillotine came thundering down; detaching his head from his shoulders, and detaching the French people from their monarchical past.

***

The years which followed were far from utopian...

France's army was forced to do battle with anti-revolutionary forces from Austria, Prussia and Britain.

Parisians broke into their city's prisons, raped and mutilated women, disembowelled priests, and hacked aristocrats to pieces.

Insurrections were put down with glorious, unflinching force. Police spies turned in anyone who uttered so much as a single word against the revolution. Rebels and priests were tied up and drowned. The guillotine fell with eerie regularity, slashing through flesh like a knife through butter.

Hundreds-of-thousands died.

Robespierre was unrepentant. He quite literally wished to "Terrorise" his enemies; to destroy every last remnant of the aristocracy, and anyone who might support it, so that the republic would have the space it needed to flourish.

He did not mince his words:

"Terror without virtue is disastrous. But virtue without terror is powerless".

***

The tides began to turn.

The French army, led by Napoléon, gained the upper-hand. They repelled attacks at the border and massacred anti-revolutionaries at home.

For Danton, it was time to end "The Great Terror" - to end martial law and establish a democracy. But Robespierre was in no mood to give up the fight. He rounded up Danton and his supporters, put them to death, and continued as before.

It seemed that there would only be one way to restore order. Robespierre would have to go.

When he appeared upon a hilltop, dressed in a toga, as though he believed himself to be a god, his opponents had the ammunition they needed. They declared him insane.

Robespierre was arrested, freed by his supporters, recaptured by the National Guard, marched up onto the scaffold, and made to suffer the same fate he had inflicted on so many others.

The man had died. But the rights of man lived on. (Shultz, 2005)

***

So what, exactly, was this new "Republic"?

It never did become the democracy the revolutionaries had envisioned. The Jacobin Constitution of 1793 did give every French man the right to vote, but Napoléon seized control before an election could be held.

The effects of the French Revolution were, however, significant. The revolution vanquished the aristocracy. It gave the world some fine ideals - those of "Liberty, fraternity and equality". It gave us the "Declaration of the Rights of Man". It created "The long-lasting foundations for a unified state, a strong central government, and a free society dominated by the middle class". (Wooloch, 1998-2000)

***

The following years were turbulent to say the least...

Napoléon declared himself emperor, but was banished by King Louis' younger brother, who returned to become king. Napoléon displaced the king for one-hundred-and-eleven days, before finding himself banished once more. The king returned to his throne, and passed his crown onto his younger brother.

Another revolution, in 1830, restored parliament's power. When King Louis-Philippe was overthrown, in the February Revolution of 1848, representative democracy took root.

The June Days Uprising brought about a second republic. The people elected Napoléon's nephew, Louis Napoléon. But, unhappy that he could only hold office for four years, he too staged a coup d'état; declaring himself emperor and destroying that nascent democracy.

A third republic was declared when Louis Napoléon was defeated in the Franco-Prussian War.

Women would have to wait another seventy-five years before they too could secure the vote. (Lee-Miller, 2018)

AHOY MATEY

At this juncture, it is worth taking a minute to consider the case for another group of people who also established their own democracies during this period. Those swashbuckling, wave-surfing, hook-handed, peg-legged tyrants of the Seven Seas: The pirates.

Like the groups we met in Chapter One, the pirates maintained a good chunk of their independence. And like those tribal peoples, they remained punctiliously democratic. Their "Floating societies" were, however, far larger than their land-loving cousins'. The average pirate ship had around eighty members. But Captain Blackbeard led three-hundred souls, and Captain Morgan commanded a squadron of ships with two-thousand mates. They show that primitive-style democracy can be scaled up...

The pirates elected their captain, and delegated power to him during battle - when snap decisions needed to be made, and there was no time for deliberation, disagreement or debate. The captain had to decide how to chase and engage a target, how to flee the authorities, and how to defend his crew from attack. In this regard, pirate ships could be said to be representative democracies. Their members elected a leader, who led them from on high.

But pirate ship captains did not have anywhere near the sort of authority that was granted to their counterparts in the merchant navy; men who were known to hit sailors in the head, dock their wages, and use the dreaded cat-o-nine-tails. Should a pirate attempt such acts, or should they show cowardice or poor judgement, their crew would hold a vote and boot them from office.

Furthermore, the captain only had one area of authority: Battle. The crew elected a second officer, the quartermaster, to oversee daily life aboard ship. It was the quartermaster, not the captain, who allocated provisions, selected and redistributed loot, adjudicated conflicts and administered discipline.

***

The captain and quartermaster may have received double or even quadruple the share of any booty their ship acquired. Theirs was no communist idyll. But it was relatively egalitarian nonetheless. In most instances, their lodgings, provisions and pay were the same as their crew's.

There was no deference whatsoever:

"Every man, as the humour takes him... (May) intrude (the captain's) apartment, swear at him, and seize a part of his victuals, if they like it, without his offering to find fault or contest it".

Pirate ships each had their own constitution, the "Articles of Agreement". These entrenched in law the right for pirates to vote on where they should sail, the shares of bounty each crew member would receive, and the compensation that would be paid out to anyone who was injured in battle. Such articles might include rules to prevent disorder; perhaps imposing a curfew, banning card games, or stopping the crew from bringing women aboard. They also set the bonuses which would be paid out in return for acts of bravery, and the punishments which would be dished out to miscreants.

Such constitutions, which tended to be remarkably similar, served a democratic purpose. They ensured that quartermasters did not become tyrants. The quartermasters did have power, given to them by their shipmates, but they could only use that power to uphold rules which had been written and approved by the group. They could not create new rules. If no precedent existed to deal with a specific crime, a jury would be called to decide the matter.

Pirate societies, therefore, featured three types of democracy, just like the Benedictine monasteries. They were *direct democracies*, in which the members wrote the rules. They were *representative democracies*, who elected quartermasters and captains to uphold those rules. And they were *economic democracies*, in which each member received similar provisions.

The system seemed to work...

The pirates did not need harsh discipline to maintain order. They were joint-owners of their vessels, who profited from their ship's success, so had a financial incentive to act in an orderly fashion.

This is how one observer described their societies:

"They perform their duties with a great deal of order, better even than on the ships of the Dutch East India Company. The pirates take a great deal of pride in doing things right".

And their work-ethic seemed to pay dividends:

"At a time when Anglo-American seamen on trading voyages to Madagascar were collecting less than twelve pounds sterling a year... The deep-water pirates could realise a hundred or even a thousand times more".

This is not to say the pirate's life was for all...

Pirates were outlaws, who risked being hung if they were caught. They murdered, stole and tortured. Their societies were *democratic*, but they were far from *righteous*. (Leeson, 2009) (Leeson, 2007)

TO INFINITY AND BEYOND!

Now let's get back on track...

We were charting the rise of representative democracy in Spain, Britain and France.

But why focus on these nations?

It is because they would go on to colonise almost half the globe; imposing their systems of governance onto the peoples they conquered.

This is how a member of the Lakota tribe described the transition:

"Before our white brothers came to civilise us, we had no jails. Therefore we had no criminals. You can't have criminals without a jail. We had no locks or keys, and so we had no thieves. If a man was so poor that he had no horse, tipi or blanket, someone gave him these things. We were too uncivilized to set much value on personal belongings. We wanted to have things only in order to give them away. We had no money, and therefore a man's worth couldn't be measured by it. We had no written law, no attorneys or politicians". (Deer, 1976)

The imperialist nations obliterated cultures like the Lakota's. They imposed things such as laws, jails, private property, money, markets, centralised government, taxation and representative democracy.

When they departed, they left these things behind.

***

Western imperialism generally followed one of two paths...

The first, known as *"Direct* Colonial Rule", was common in the Americas, Australia and New Zealand. Under such a system, the vast majority of the indigenous population were exterminated - the victims of starvation, disease and violence. The remainder were forced to assimilate or live on reservations. (Tully, 2008)

This is what happened to the Iroquois...

In 1750, the British settlers headed west, taking eight-hundred-thousand acres of Mohawk land. When the indigenous population fought back, they lost the war and were forced to cede yet more territory. Their conquerors burnt Iroquois villages, and gave their inhabitants smallpox-laden blankets - an early form of biological warfare that killed vast swathes of the population. The survivors were pushed into reservations, but even these were controlled from afar. In the early Sixties, for example, President Kennedy built a dam that flooded most of the Seneca's land.

The Cherokees, meanwhile, were pushed further and further west. Surrounded, they had no choice but to succumb to the white man's ways; privatising land, taking up professions, creating a written language, and even owning slaves. Their confederate democracy died a sorry death. (Zinn, 1980)

The colonisers marched ahead...

With the indigenous population removed, they settled their colonies - ruling them in much the same way as their homelands. Parliaments, land rights and prisons were exported from the old world to the new. Representative democracy was imposed on countries such as Canada, Australia and New Zealand.

***

The second form of imperialism, known as *"Indirect* Colonial Rule",* was common across Africa and the Indian subcontinent. Here, a small number of conquerors formed colonial administrations or trading companies, which they used to rule the indigenous people from afar.

The imperialists took local rulers, who had previously been *first amongst equals*, and recognised them as quasi-sovereigns. Using these proxies, they imposed Western-style laws on the native population. They replaced cooperative ownership, work and governance; with capitalist corporations, privatised labour and workplace discipline. The imperialists trained local militias, forming armies to protect property rights and trade. They made native customs illegal, and punished anyone who tried to preserve the traditional way of life. (Tully, 2008)

***

The path to democracy in the *settled* colonies followed a similar path to the motherland. The imperialists established representative parliaments, but not everyone had the vote. It took several protests, campaigns, riots and deaths to secure full enfranchisement...

The word "Democracy" does not appear once in the constitution of the United States. Thomas Jefferson, one of the founding fathers, went as far as to call it, "Nothing more than mob rule, where 51% of the people may take away the rights of the other forty-nine". (Mason, 2015)

Like Jefferson, the other architects of that revolution were members of the ruling class. George Washington was the richest man in the land. John Hancock was a prosperous Boston merchant. Benjamin Franklin was a wealthy printer.

They broke free from colonial rule because it served the interest of *their class*, not the majority...

In Maryland, for example, the post-revolution constitution required men to own property worth £5,000, in order to stand for governor, and £1,000, in order to stand for the state senate. The Jeffersons and Washingtons of this world would be represented, but 90% of the population would not. (Zinn, 1980)

The original American electorate only contained white men with property. White men without property would have to wait another eighty years before they could cast a vote. It took the suffrage movement to win votes for white women, in 1920, and the civil rights movement to win votes for all black people, in 1965. (Panetta & Reaney, 2019)

The first election in Australia took place in Adelaide, in 1840. But only six-hundred people were granted a vote. Representative governments were set up in several states, in 1850, but the people could only elect two-thirds of their politicians. The others were selected by the crown. Full male suffrage was introduced in 1856. *Some* women were able to vote in *some* elections as early as 1838, but it took the "Suffrage Societies" to win votes for *all* women in 1908.

***

Things were different in the lands subjected to *indirect* colonial rule...

In the British colonies, in particular, elections were held to quell potential revolutions. These prepared the native political elites to take over the imperialist system.

The Brits also handed control of their bureaucratic institutions to the local gentry. So when they did eventually leave, representative democracy was firmly entrenched.

The ex-British colonies, therefore, were more democratic than their Spanish and French equivalents, at the time of independence, although this disparity vanished over time.

Democratic nations can, after all, descend into tyranny. This happened in Nigeria, where the post-colonial government was taken over by the military, and in Malaysia, which became a one-party state.

The reverse can happen too. Undemocratic nations can become democracies.

As in Britain and France, the transition to democracy tends to begin when the people take to the streets… (Lee & Paine, 2016)

In the Philippines, for example, President Marcos's dictatorial reign was brought to an end by the "People Power Movement"…

When one of Marcos's most vociferous opponents returned from exile, he was assassinated as soon as he stepped off the plane. This malicious act sparked a revolution. Hundreds-of-thousands of Filipinos blocked Manila's main thoroughfare and refused to leave. When Marcos sent in the tanks to disperse the protestors, his officers disobeyed orders to fire into the crowd. Several nuns approached those vehicles, and handed flowers to the soldiers inside! On the fourth day, Marcos was forced to stand down. Representative democracy was restored. (McGeown, 2011)

A similar movement brought down President Shevardnadze of Georgia…

Desperate to cling on to power, his party rigged the 2003 elections. His supporters voted multiple times, whilst many of his opponents were unable to even vote once. Voter lists included dead people, but excluded thousands who were still alive. Ballots were not delivered to several polling stations, and the count was called into question by a team international observers. The exit polls put Shevardnadze's party in fourth place, yet somehow they managed to come out on top.

The president's opponents called for their supporters to take to the streets. Though their numbers were small, those protesters were determined. They stayed put, even when faced with snowstorms and icy gales.

After several weeks had passed, they marched on parliament. Unarmed, they each held a red rose aloft.

The ranks of uniformed police parted to allow them through.

Shevardnadze realised his time was up. He was hustled out through a rear door, leaving his tea by his chair, which his opponents picked up and drank ceremoniously, much to the delight of the crowd.

Shevardnadze resigned.

Fireworks illuminated the sky.

***

These examples show that popular protests can be as effective today, in the modern world, as they were in the days of the English and French Revolutions. They can bring down authoritarian regimes, and pave the way for representative democracy...

A year after Georgia's "Rose Revolution", Ukraine's "Orange Revolution" proceeded in a similar fashion. In 2000, the Otpor movement removed Slobodan Milošević from power in Serbia. In 2019, peaceful protests brought down President Bashir of Sudan and President Bouteflika of Algeria. The cases of Chile's Augusto Pinochet, Tunisia's Zine el-Abidine Ben Ali, and The Gambia's Yahya Jammeh, all show that protest movements can oust despotic regimes; preparing the ground for representative democracy to take root. (Ben, 2015) (Satell, 2015) (Chenoweth, 2013) (Spirova, 2008) (Robson, 2019) (Stephan & Gallagher, 2019)

IMPERIALISM FOREVER!

So representative democracy came to dominate the planet. In some cases, it was imposed by the imperialist powers. In others, the people campaigned for it themselves.

Whatever the case, the sorts of democracy we met in the first three chapters were almost obliterated. Top-down nation-states, with their centralised governments and market economies, were now the name of the game.

***

Representative democracy was never that democratic...

Even where representative democracies did spring up in the former colonies, they were hardly sovereign. Their strings were still being pulled from afar.

In place of the more traditional forms of colonialism came a new beast with several names - "Free Trade Imperialism', "Neo-Colonialism" and "Postcolonial Imperialism". The names were a mouthful, but the principle was simple: Nations could rule themselves at home, in a democratic manner, but they had to play by international rules, set by *undemocratic* institutions: The World Bank, International Monetary Fund (IMF), General Agreement on Tariffs and Trade (GATT), World Trade Organisation (WTO), United Nations (UN), and North Atlantic Treaty Organisation (NATO).

So-called "Democratic" nations were forced to privatise their assets, often against their people's will - opening up their land, labour and markets to international interests. Shorn of their wealth, they became dependent on economic support, military assistance and aid. They were subjected to bribes and sanctions, manipulated by voluntary and religious organisations, and gently swayed by legal, political and economic experts.

Where such "Lawfare" did not get the results that the big nations desired, they turned to their second-best tool: "Warfare". (Tully, 2008)

The United States, with over seven-hundred military-bases on foreign soil, took the lead - overthrowing any democratically-elected administration who refused to play by their rules...

In 1953, they ousted the democratically elected leader of Iran, Mohammed Mossadegh, when he tried to nationalise British Oil. A year later, they ousted Jacob Arbenz of Guatemala, when he tried to nationalise the United Fruit Company. In 1961, the United States forced Jose Velasco of Ecuador to resign, and assassinated Patrice Lumumba of Zaire - both of whom had been elected by their people. In the next few years, they helped oust the democratically elected leaders of the Dominican Republic, Brazil and Indonesia. I could go on, but I would not wish to bore you. I think I have made my point! (Kangas, 1997)

Of course, it would be wrong to single out the United States. Of the fifteen republics to rise from the ashes of the USSR, only Latvia, Lithuania and Estonia can be classed as genuine democracies. The others are still influenced by Russia - they may hold elections, but Moscow looms large. (Myre, 2014)

And then there are those nations that are not, and never have been democracies. The "Democracy Index", cited in the introduction, classed fifty-three regimes as "Authoritarian". Between them, these rule 35.6% of the world's population. (The Economist Intelligence Unit, 2018)

So representative democracy *has* spread. But it has failed to overcome several undemocratic regimes.

The transition has been supersonic...

According to the think-tank, Freedom House, just 29% of societies were "Free" in 1972, whilst 46% were "Unfree". By 1998, those figures had flipped: 46% were "Free", and just 26% were "Unfree".

Democracy does have the public's backing. Polls conducted in 2007 found that people on every continent considered democracy to be the best form of government. Between 68% and 86% supported democracy, regardless of their location, gender, religion and age. (Morris, 2015)

It may have the people's backing, but representative democracy remains deeply flawed. And it is not just because of the external threats we mentioned above. In representative democracies, we delegate power to a small group of representatives who seldom have our respect. A ComRes poll, conducted in September 2019, found that only 12% of Brits agreed with the statement, "Parliament can be trusted to do the right thing for the country". Representative democracy, after all, is not direct democracy. It is far from the people-first systems of the Utku and Iroquois. It allows us to choose our leaders, but it does not allow us to choose how they lead.

Still, hope springs eternal. People are trying to force change; to make their representative democracies a bit more *democratic*. In the next section, we shall see how...

PART TWO

MAKING REPRESENTATIVE DEMOCRACY A LITTLE MORE 'REPRESENTATIVE'

5. DIRECT DEMOCRACY NOW

Streaky marks drip without motion, submerged beneath the rubble, black but fading to white. The charred remains of this building, bombed and forgotten, remind us of this region's troubled past.

The rubble dissolves...

An ocean of wheat reflects the midday sun; swaying, ever so casually; glimmering, shimmering, forming a haze of a million hues.

If we look closely, we can see a mud-plastered house, or perhaps there are two. They also melt into the golden ether.

We see some sheep graze, meditatively, at the side of the road.

And we continue. On and on, diving deep into the heart of Rojava...

A RETURN TO CONFEDERATE DEMOCRACY?

We began this book by travelling the globe, visiting a collection of disparate groups who had one thing in common: Their democracy. Decisions were made collectively, usually during group assemblies, in which anyone could speak and everyone could vote.

There is a name for such a system: "Direct Democracy".

It has its limits. Most of the peoples we met in Chapter One live in small groups. Many contain just twenty or thirty individuals. Everyone can be heard.

But such a system could not possibly work in a modern nation with tens-of-millions of people. If we allowed everyone to speak, the discussions would last for decades.

How on earth could we cope?

In Chapter Two, we provided a solution: "Confederate Democracy". Peoples like the Iroquois operated direct democracies on the local level. But they also sent delegates to sit on regional councils, uniting their villages to form a nation.

Here, in Rojava, the Kurds are doing something similar *today*...

***

Rojava is comprised of three cantons in Northwest Syria: Cizîre, Kobanî and Afrîn.

Liberated from the Ba'athist regime, by August 2011 a dual system had formed. Around half of Rojava's Kurds had joined democratic councils - group assemblies which oversaw matters of justice, infrastructure and security. The state, meanwhile, continued to provide vital services - dealing with waste, sewage, water and traffic.

Beleaguered by the unremitting corrosion of war, the gears of state began to jam. And, as they rusted and groaned, the democratic councils stepped up to the mark...

When the state failed to collect rubbish, and garbage piled up in the street, the locals created "People's Municipalities", sourced trucks, hired personnel, and returned the streets to their former glory.

It was just the start. Before long, they were supplying drinking water, dealing with the sewage and organising traffic.

They had replaced the state.

There was just one problem. They had become a victim of their own success. Hundreds-of-thousands of people were flocking to neighbourhood meetings, but only a few lucky souls could fit inside the venues. (Knapp, Flach & Ayboğa, 2016)

To ensure everyone had a voice, the Rojavans created a tiered system...

At the base of the pyramid sit the "Communes". Each commune consists of a street or small village, containing between thirty and two-hundred households. These form the bedrock of Rojavan democracy. They are where decisions originate - where anyone can make a proposal, have a say, approve or reject a motion.

Meetings have been known to get heated...

One visitor was both startled and reassured when he witnessed a meeting descend into a minor fracas. A merchant had been accused of hoarding sugar, to inflate the price, and so the Asayîş (the local security force) had been called in to investigate. When the hall was told how the Asayîş had refrained from action, because they had not received clearance from their commanding officers, all hell broke loose. Papers were thrown, hands were waived and thunderous voices echoed from the rafters:

"Commanding officers? They work for us! This is exactly how bureaucratisation sets in!"

"So what do we have to do? Make up some kind of special hat? A big badge? Maybe that will impress them".

For the witness, this brouhaha made one thing abundantly clear. The communes really were authentic, decision making bodies. They were not just for show. Why else would passions become so inflamed? (Graeber, 2016)

**

Above the communes sit the "Neighbourhoods" - councils made up of delegates from between seven and thirty communes.

We should not confuse these *delegates* with the sort of *representatives* we see in national parliaments. Delegates are *duty-bound* to raise the issues which have been discussed in their communes. But they have no *right* to introduce topics of their own. They must act as humble servants of the people or they will be recalled.

The neighbourhoods send delegates to the "District", where they sit alongside members of social movements and political parties.

Finally, at the top of the pyramid, the "People's Council of West Kurdistan" (the MGRK) consists of delegates from each district. It represents the entire region.

**

Alongside each level of this pyramid are eight "Commissions". These deal with issues such as defence, economics, politics, civil society and justice. These commissions are also filled with elected *delegates* rather than *representatives*.

So, if someone has a suggestion, they will raise it at their commune meeting. If it is approved by the group, it will be passed sideways to a commission, to be implemented locally. It might also be passed upwards, to the neighbourhood, and rolled out across the region. (Knapp, Flach & Ayboğa, 2016)

**

Such a structure, whilst convoluted, solves the problem we mentioned above. It grants everyone a voice and a vote, in their commune, whilst uniting those communes to form of a modern nation.

The Rojavan system was inspired by the writings of the Kurdish rebel, Abdullah Öcalan; a man whose own worldview was inspired by the Iroquois and Cherokee.

Öcalan saw the emergence of top-down, state-based authority, as unnatural, "Enforced by the widespread use of violence and fraud". He claimed it had been resisted at every turn, and that people had a duty to overthrow it - to reinstate what he called a "Natural Society", without state violence, and with equal rights for women.

The Rojavans took him at his word...

Their system is powerfully feminist. Forty percent of the members of every council, commission, leadership position and court must be women. Fifty-five percent of municipal workers are female. "Women's Centres" educate the uneducated. Armed feminists have quite literally defeated the forces of patriarchy on the battlefield. Female soldiers go from door-to-door, encouraging women to attend neighbourhood meetings, and intimidating any abusive husbands who stand in their way.

In a region that is not known for women's rights, it is little wonder that the current system has garnered so much support from Rojava's female population. (Graeber, 2016)

***

Direct democracy is often criticised for demanding too much of the people. Yes, we would like a say in how our society is run, the logic goes, but we have too many other commitments. We do not have the time and energy to research and debate every issue.

Rojava provides a counterpoint to such a belief. The Rojavans are not, by their nature, more political than anyone else. Political participation was almost non-existent under the previous regime. Yet the Rojavans *became* political and now participate on a mass scale.

The power cuts helped...

"Once it was normal here for people to have the television on twenty-four hours a day", says Şirîn Ömer, a forty-five-year-old woman in Hilelî. "But then the electricity was shut off, and that left people's minds free to think about other things". (Knapp, Flach & Ayboğa, 2016)

The encouragement of activists, the opportunities for political education, and peer pressure also played a role. The obsessive emphasis on inclusivity remains important too:

"If a town of fifty-thousand has even one synagogue, attended by just fifteen Jews, Jewish representation is guaranteed on the assemblies. Every poster is translated, almost obsessively, into every language of every minority, however few people belong to it". (Jones, 2018)

***

So is Rojava a success? Does it provide a system to which the rest of the world should aspire?

It is certainly democratic. More democratic, perhaps, than any other modern society we shall visit.

But it is still early days. The council system has been tried before - in the Paris Commune, after the Russian Revolution, and during the German Uprising of 1918. None of those systems survived.

Each case faced both internal and external challenges...

Rojavan democracy will not last long if the people fail to defend themselves. Turkey seems hell-bent on destroying the Syrian Kurds, the Ba'athist regime wishes to reassert its control over the region, and another attack by Islamic State cannot be ruled out. Russia and the United States both have the power to crush Rojava. Let's not forget, the types of primitive democracy we spoke about at the beginning of this book did not fade away because the people rejected them. It was *outside invaders* who came, saw, conquered and crushed them. Likewise, the Paris Commune fell because it failed to defend itself against the French army.

Of course, just because the system is working well for now, does not mean it will work well forever. The Rojavan system is convoluted. Delegates at the top must communicate with the three levels beneath them. They must attend several lengthy meetings. Such people may very well evolve into a political class - the very thing the system was supposed to avoid. Indeed, this is exactly what happened in revolutionary Russia, where the democratic "Soviet Councils" became cogs within the machinery of Stalin's authoritarian state. (Graeber, 2016)

But the early signs *are* promising. About two-thirds of people in Cizîre, and over 90% of those in Afrîn, already attend meetings on a regular basis. The system has the support of over 70% Rojavans; a pretty outstanding feat when you consider that less than 40% of people are happy with the electoral system in Britain. (Knapp, Flach & Ayboğa, 2016) (Grice, 2015)

Rojava is under embargo, pretty much everything is in short supply. Things are tough. But the people seem resolute...

When the witness we met above was leaving, he apologised for not bringing any gifts.

The response he received was unequivocal:

"Don't worry about that... I have something that no one can give me. I have my freedom. In a day or two, you have to go back to a place where you don't have that. I only wish there was some way *I could give what I have to you*". (Graeber, 2016)

THE COMMUNAL STATE

Rojavan democracy was born of the Syrian Civil War - of blood-strewn streets, burgeoning graveyards, ashen buildings and smoky skies.

Whilst I expect many people would like to see a little more democracy in their lives, I doubt many would wish to endure such gory scenes.

This begs a question: How can we separate the means and the ends? How can we transform our centralised states, run from the top-down, *without* the bloodshed of war?

It has been tried in Venezuela...

***

The arboreal and the aqueous entwine. Rivers sliver through the rainforest. Damp air wafts across the plains.

These are the borderlands. One-hundred-and-fourteen-thousand hectares, where thousands of families can be found scattered across the meadows.

Beyond the horizon, we can almost see the Colombian sky. A haze of pastel shades cloak that foreign nation.

The people here are tenacious. They have faced down persecution, jail and even a hired killer. But this area, *their area,* the "Communal City" of Simón Bolívar, has inspired a nation... (Daboín, 2018)

***

Like in Rojava, the democratisation of Venezuela began with the people, who established "Neighbourhood Assemblies" back in the 1980s.

"We don't want to be a government", they said. "We want to govern". (Azzellini, 2013)

Unlike in Rojava, however, the Venezuelans were able to bring the state onside...

In 1999, the national government wrote a new constitution, which defined Venezuela as a "Participative Democracy". It passed the "Organic Law of Communes" and the "Popular Power Laws" to protect the neighbourhood assemblies. (Daboín, 2018)

This is not to say things were easy. The assemblies operated in the same spheres as the local authorities - representative bodies which had more power, more experience, and ultimate control of the purse-strings. In the face of such competition, the neighbourhood assemblies remained pretty ineffectual. (Jones, 2011)

That all changed when Hugo Chavez came to power. With 62.8% of votes, on a turnout of 74.7%, the podgy-faced, double-chinned man of the people had a mandate for change.

He set about his task, gradually replacing the top-down "Bourgeois State" with a people-powered "Communal State", offering financial support to the neighbourhood assemblies, and giving them the space they needed to grow.

Through a steady process of evolution, rather than revolution, it was Chavez's dream for the people to create a new system - a direct democracy, which would grow stronger each year, and eventually rule the nation...

***

The system begins with the "Communal Councils" - street parliaments which can contain anywhere from ten families (in indigenous areas) to four-hundred families (in urban conurbations). The communal councils can create committees, to manage things such as housing and healthcare, but these committees are only allowed to enact policies that have already been approved the people.

When enough communal councils are formed, they may come together to form "Socialist Communes". The people send delegates to attend such institutions, but can recall those individuals at any time.

By 2013, there were over two-hundred communes. They were managing projects, such as pipelines, which stretched across several neighbourhoods, and so were too big for a single communal council to run alone.

When an entire region has been organised into communes, they can come together to form "Communal Cities". So far, these have been established in more rural areas, where establishmentarian resistance is less prevalent. (Azzellini, 2013) (Wynter & McIlroy, 2006)

This brings us back to the Colombian border, and our friends from the communal city of Simón Bolívar...

***

The people of Los Picachos were unhappy:

"We were tired of working for the rich".

So they plucked up their courage and began to act:

"Fighting for the land... Rescuing the land".

They secured over a thousand hectares, formed Venezuela's first communal council, distributed ten hectares to each family, and tended the remaining land together; producing cassava, banana, passion fruit, papaya, pumpkin, chilli and lemon.

Several decades rolled by.

It was not until 2006 that the Los Picachos community united with its neighbours to form the Caño Amarillo commune - a group which represents over eight-hundred people.

But by this time, they had momentum on their side...

Through workshops and house-to-house visits, they engaged with everyone in the region; uniting thirty-eight communal councils into eight communes, which would go on to form the communal city.

They improved the road network, built communal housing and organised agricultural production. Believing they, the people, could manage their lives better than anyone else, they turned their sights on their traditional leaders. They challenged their representatives, whom they deemed inefficient, and held their mayors to account.

The communal city had evolved. It now consisted of delegates from every communal council, every commune, the Bolivarian militia, fisherman's councils, producers associations and food distribution committees. Almost three-thousand people attended assembly meetings.

Together, they established committees to oversee the sort of things which are normally managed by a top-down state: infrastructure, energy, water, education, culture, land, production and communication.

The evolution was almost complete. The state had been pushed into a corner. The people of the Simón Bolívar communal city had taken control of their lives. (Daboín, 2018) (Márquez, 2018)

***

What we have seen here should be an inspiration. Through a process of evolution, the people of Venezuela (with support from the national government) transformed a representative democracy, ruled by a political class, into a direct democracy, ruled by the people. If the Venezuelans could do it, then why not the British, Americans, Germans or Sri Lankans?

Of course, no system is perfect...

Participation is varied. Venezuelan women have been empowered, but many locals do not engage at all. The machinations of local government can be tedious. Many communities express an inherent distrust of the delegates they elect. The assemblies are contested spaces. They are still evolving, and they mean different things to different people. (Wilde, 2017)

When most people think of Venezuela, democracy is probably not the first thing that springs to mind. Indeed, all was not well in the nation whilst I was writing this book...

Venezuela was in the midst of an economic crisis. Its detractors blamed that crisis on Chavism itself, and on left-wing politics in general. Its supporters blamed it on Venezuela's overdependence on oil, falling oil prices, and economic sanctions.

But this is by the by. Venezuela's democratic system did not cause its woes. Nor is it the exclusive realm of left-wingers. The neighbourhood assemblies predate Hugo Chavez. They are backed by his opponents as well as his supporters.

The system has, however, been impacted. Enemies of Chavez's successor, Nicolás Maduro, have looted and burned venues used for commune meetings. With money tight, centralised funding for the communes has all but disappeared.

The system battles on, but it has been forced to do so alone. The Panal 2021 Commune, for example, has become self-sufficient. It owns and manages some bakeries, a textile factory, sugar packaging plant and food distribution centre. The profits from these operations are deposited in a communal bank, and reinvested in projects which the people select. (Fuentes, 2019)

Like the Simón Bolívar communal city, the Panal 2021 commune will survive. The state played its part, helping these groups to become established, and is no longer needed. Indeed, this was the plan all along - a sure sign that the theory can work. But it also highlights the system's vulnerabilities. Any commune which has not yet become self-sufficient faces a tumultuous future - vulnerable to the whimsy of fate, and the changing winds of national politics. For such a system to work, there must be a long-term commitment from a steady government - something that is entirely possible, but which can never be guaranteed.

* * *

So can we create a system which is both democratic *and* politically stable?

A little compromise might be necessary, but it can be done. Let's head over to Switzerland to see how...

THE STEADY SWISS

Direct democracy in Switzerland has a long history...

It all began in Schwyz, a small town surrounded by lakes and mountains, where every wall is white, and every rooftop looks a like a giant slab of milk chocolate. It was here, in 1294, that the first Landsgemeinde took place.

The Landsgemeinde was an annual open-air assembly; a spectacular affair, with over ten-thousand people in attendance. Folk would meet, make merry, and discuss the crucial issues of the day. Then they would raise their hands to approve or reject the decrees which had been proposed.

We should not paint an overly rosy picture. These cantons were dominated by a landed gentry known to be rough-handed with the peasantry. But the fact that the people were armed, skilled in battle, and had the Landsgemeinde on their side, meant that this small corner of Europe remained more democratic than its neighbours. (Kobach, 1993)

* * *

The first *regional* referendum in Switzerland took place at the beginning of the Fifteenth Century, in what is now the canton of Graubünden.

But Swiss democracy was almost crushed, in 1797, when Napoleon's troops marched on Switzerland; occupying their neighbour, and forcing it to become a nation-state.

The Swiss never forgot their democratic roots. They held their first *national* referendum in 1802; a rather strange affair, in which the new constitution was approved despite receiving just 44% of the vote. Abstentions were counted as votes *for* the proposed constitution, which tipped the balance.

When the French retreated, following their defeat at Waterloo, the Swiss reasserted control over their land; formalising a system in which referenda were used to curb the authority of their leaders... (Kobach, 1993)

***

Today's Swiss democracy did not require a Rojavan-style revolution *or* the sort of support we saw in Venezuela. It evolved over several centuries...

Five cantons still hold Landsgemeinde. In Appenzell, Inner Rhodes and Glarus, the people meet once a year to set taxes and vote for new laws. Other regions have their own democratic quirks, picked up throughout the years. Several cantons hold local and regional referenda. In some smaller municipalities, foreigners can be granted Swiss citizenship following a vote in the town assembly.

But it is Switzerland's love affair with the *national* referenda which has made it the darling of democracy-lovers worldwide. The Swiss have held over six-hundred nationwide votes since 1848. Over a third of all the world's national referenda have been held in this single nation. (Kaufmann, 2019)

The Swiss have three types of referenda...

The people themselves can suggest a policy - a "People's Initiative". In 2018, eight such initiatives were launched and six got the one-hundred-thousand signatures they needed to be put to the vote. One called for television licences to be scrapped, whilst another called for central banks to take control of the money supply. All six proposals were rejected by the electorate.

"Mandatory Referenda" take place whenever the government attempts to change the constitution, join a supranational community, or adopt laws which have been declared urgent.

And "Optional Referenda" take place if fifty-thousand people sign a petition to challenge a law which has been adopted or modified by parliament. (Nguyen, 2018)

***

So does this system lead to a raft of radical measures?

Well, actually, no...

Swiss-style democracy has proved so sturdy, for so long, because it has the support of both sides of the political spectrum. Liberals rose to power in many cantons by supporting the establishment of a referendum-based system. But conservatives soon latched on to the idea. They realised that large swathes of the Swiss working class were deeply conservative, with a fervent religious streak; empowering such people, giving them the power to vote in regular referenda, would help them to maintain the status quo. (Kobach, 1993)

The proof is in the pudding...

During the first seventeen years of this millennium, one-hundred-and-three people's initiatives were tabled. Of these, twenty-eight were withdrawn, sixty-five were rejected, and only ten were approved. In the vast majority of cases, the Swiss stuck with the tried and tested. (Lüscher, 2018)

This can even mean voting *against* measures to expand democracy. Swiss females were not enfranchised until 1971. When a referendum was held on women's suffrage, in 1959, the male electorate voted to maintain the status quo.

So why even bother with such a lengthy and costly process if, when all is said and done, life continues as before?

Well, some things *do* change. In 2019, the people voted to adopt a European gun directive, which made it more difficult for citizens to own semi-automatic weapons. An optional referendum was also passed, at the same time, which reformed pension finance.

But for the Swiss, the result is secondary. It is the *process* which matters. The people have a voice. They can table any motion they like. They can have their say on a raft of key issues every quarter. And so they feel the system works for them. The 2018 World Values Survey found that the Swiss trust their government more than any other people on the planet. (Langle, 2019)

***

Switzerland is not a direct democracy in the purest sense of the term. Napoleon made sure of that. Most policies do not originate with the people. They are penned by politicians in national institutions.

But the Swiss people *do* retain control. They can overrule their leaders' decisions. And theirs is a balanced system, with support from the left and the right. It has stood the test of time.

But can it be copied?

It would certainly require less of an overhaul to implement a Swiss-style system than a Rojavan or Venezuelan one. It should, in theory, be possible.

But we should not forget that Switzerland's democracy is hundreds of years old. It was created by the people, for the people, and has become part of Switzerland's cultural identity. No other nation has such a culture. It could take centuries for one to form.

Still, we may just be on the right track...

Around half the states in the USA do hold "Ballot Initiatives". Here, as in Switzerland, residents can pen their own legislation and have it written into law. They just need to create a petition, secure enough signatures, and then have their proposal approved in a referendum.

But no such system exists on a *national* level, and the results of these ballot initiatives can be pretty regressive. In California, for example, many votes have been held to *curtail* the liberties of minority groups, such as immigrants and homosexuals. But only one initiative has been proposed to *expand* such rights. That 1946 initiative, which sought to end racial discrimination in the workplace, was rejected by 72% to 28%. (Dyck & Lascher, 2019)

Elsewhere, many countries do have some provisions for direct democracy written into their constitutions. Since 1980, eight out of ten states have held nationwide referenda. The building blocks *are* in place. The real challenge, in the years to come, will be to expand the scope and scale of such referenda - to ensure that more people get to participate in them, that elected representatives are held to account more often, and that *national governance* becomes a little more democratic as a result. (Kaufmann, 2019)

In the next chapter, we shall look at ways in which *local governance* might also be democratised...

6. SORTITION 2.0

China might seem a strange place to visit during a tour of democratic systems. The country only has a single political party, the Communist Party. Party political elections cannot take place, and subjects such as Tibet and Tiananmen Square are strictly off-limits.

Yet it would be wrong to dismiss it entirely.

Let's begin with an analogy...

It is Friday evening, the end of a tough week, and you have decided to reward yourself with a meal...

At one restaurant, you can choose your chef, but not your meal. The chefs all make boastful claims about their cooking, and they all badmouth the other chefs. But whichever chef you choose, it will be them, not you, who will decide whether you will be eating beef or snails, gateaux or tapioca pudding.

In the second restaurant, you cannot choose your chef. They will be imposed on you by the management. You can, however, choose from a long list of dishes.

What restaurant would you frequent?

For the sheer extravagance of it, you may visit the first, and ask for your meal to be cooked by the chef who claims she can chop a carrot into a hundred pieces in five seconds flat. You may be enticed by the "Herb slinger of the East". The novelty value may appeal, as a one-off, but it is unlikely you would make this choice each week. After an allergic reaction, or one too many servings of gruel, the chances are you will revert to the a la carte option.

The first option is pretty crazy. Yet it is exactly what we do in representative democracies. We choose our leaders, our chefs, but we have very little say when it comes to the policies they cook up.

In parts of China, the authorities are trying the second option. They may not give their citizens much of a choice when it comes to choosing their leaders, their chefs, but they are giving locals a say when it comes to formulating public policy... (Leonard, 2008)

ZEGUO

Jiang Zhaohua faces a dilemma.

The Communist Party secretary for Zeguo has grand ambitions for his region. Some might say he is a little *too* ambitious. Jiang would like to start work on thirty infrastructure projects, including bridges, roads, parks and sewage-treatment plants. His budget, however, will only allow him to build ten.

Hard choices have to be made.

So what should Jiang do?

He fears that if he makes the decision himself, he may face allegations of corruption; of favouring one project over another in return for kickbacks. The public in neighbouring Huaxi have been known to riot. He does not want that to happen here.

So he selects two-hundred-and-fifty-seven locals, at random, to represent the Zeguo's two-hundred-and-forty-thousand inhabitants. They congregate in the lobby of a public school, giggle as they attach pink badges to their lapels, marking themselves as "Popular Will Representatives", and then take their seats in the auditorium.

These people - rich and poor, urban and rural, young and old - have already conducted a poll, ranking Jiang's thirty projects. Now they are quizzing the town's leaders, listening to opposing points of view, and debating the projects themselves.

By the end of the day, their views have evolved. Prestige projects, such as a park and some bridges, no longer hold the same appeal. Having digested the facts, they have changed their rankings and prioritised environmental programs instead.

Jiang has what he wants - a list of the ten most popular projects. His team don their overalls and get to work. (Jakes, 2005)

***

These events took place in 2005.

Deemed a success, Jiang's experiment soon became a regular staple of Zeguo life...

Each year, one-hundred-and-seventy-five residents are selected using a scientific process, to ensure they reflect the general population. They are briefed by experts with opposing views, given the chance to deliberate amongst themselves, and encouraged to ask questions.

After three days of intensive deliberation, the participants become experts on the subjects at hand. They have heard arguments from both sides, considered the facts, and drawn their own conclusions.

Final polls are conducted and decisions are made.

Unlike the original experiment, however, these representatives do not only choose between infrastructure projects. These days, the citizens of Zeguo decide how to allocate the town's entire budget!

"The public is very smart if you give it a chance", explains Professor James Fishkin. "If people think their voice actually matters, they'll do the hard work, study their briefing books, ask the experts smart questions, and then make tough decisions. When they hear the experts disagreeing, they are forced to think for themselves. About 70% change their minds". (Klein, 2010)

FISHKIN'S THOUGHTS

Fishkin is the godfather of modern "Deliberative Democracy" - a form of democracy we first met in ancient Athens...

Athenian democracy faced a challenge. Skilled orators could whip the electorate into a frenzy, persuading voters to support their proposals without considering all the consequences. On the back of one such vote, the Athenians launched the Peloponnesian War - a disastrous affair, which caused Athens to briefly descend into oligarchy.

When democracy was reinstated, the Athenians reformed their system. They created the "Nomothetai" - an assembly of five-hundred citizens, selected at random, who spent a day deliberating any motion which had been passed by the assembly, before it could be written into law.

The direct democracy of the Fifth Century BC had evolved into the deliberative democracy of the Fourth Century BC.

This was still people-powered politics, for the enfranchised population at least. And it provides us a lesson which remains relevant today...

Critics of Athenian-style direct democracy say it cannot be applied to the modern nation-state. You cannot fit tens-of-millions of people into a single venue, and have them debate key issues.

But mathematics tells us that we can accurately represent a large population with a random sample of its members. As long as the sample is big enough, and random enough, it *will* be representative, no matter how many people it has been picked to represent.

You cannot replicate the Ecclesia. But you can replicate the Nomothetai, on which it came to depend... (Fishkin, 2018)

***

Fishkin has put his theory to the test. And, as the Zegou example shows, it *has* achieved results...

Fishkin's first experiment began in 1996, in Texas, when the state asked the public what sort of electricity it would like to consume: gas, coal or wind. At the beginning of the process, only 52% of the population were willing to pay extra for renewable energy. After deliberation, that figure rose to 84%. The government of Texas heeded their people's calls, installing more wind turbines than any other state.

Deliberative democracy has been used in Japan, to consult the public about pension reform; in Bulgaria, to see if people would accept the desegregation of Roma-only schools; and in South Korea, to decide whether to resume the construction of two partially-built nuclear reactors...

The new administration was opposed to nuclear power, but was uncomfortable about abandoning projects which had already cost a substantial sum. So it let the public decide. And, after several days of deliberation, a sample of almost five-hundred Koreans chose to resume construction.

These examples are encouraging, but they have their limits. They have helped to make decisions on single issues, but they have not changed the nature of governance itself.

For that, we must visit Mongolia...

Since 2017, the Mongolian government has been obliged to convene a representative sample of its voters, selected by the National Statistical Office, whenever it wishes to amend its constitution.

When seven-hundred Mongolians considered eighteen such amendments, support for a second chamber fell by 31%, and support for six-year presidential terms fell by 21.5%. But support for a professional civil service and independent judiciary topped 80%. The people had spent a weekend considering the options, and had made their opinions clear.

The Mongolian parliament was left with a choice. They could

implement the proposals approved by the panel, or put the proposals to a referendum. One way or another, the people's voices would be heard. (Fishkin, 2018)

PARTICIPATORY BUDGETING

Deliberative democracy helps leaders to uphold the will of the people; allowing the electorate to choose their meal, even when they cannot choose their chef. It is by no means perfect. Getting people to participate can be a challenge. Focussing on annual budgets can cause administrations to overlook long-term investments. Deliberative democracy cannot be used to make the snap decisions which are needed in a crisis. But it can improve governance, in both democratic and authoritarian regimes.

Still, deliberative democracy remains a fledgling idea - tried sporadically, successfully, but not yet rolled-out on a global scale.

Another system, "Participatory Budgeting", has been far more contagious...

***

Dundee resident, Stefan Morkis, had done what any good comic-book fan might do. He had voted for Batman.

Morkis did not support any of the candidates who were standing for election, so he had written "Batman" at the bottom of his ballot, drawn a box, and put an X next to the name of his favourite caped-crusader. He had even given his reasons in the space below:

"Because none of these Jokers are good enough".

His was a common issue. He disliked every single party, he hated the choice he was being forced to make, and he felt his vote was inconsequential. (Morkis, 2018)

But that all changed when his town, Dundee, used participatory budgeting to allocate a portion of its infrastructure budget.

The year was 2018, and the council had £1.2m burning a hole in its pockets. So their staff gathered suggestions from the people, drew up a shortlist, and conducted a vote.

For eight weeks, any resident of Dundee aged eleven or over was able to rank the projects which had been proposed in their ward. Council workers took bags of tablets to schools and local "Voting Events". Some people voted online, from the comfort of their homes.

Their votes made a difference...

There would be dropped curbs, improved pavements, refurbished public toilets, an upgraded playground, new street lighting and more. Thirty projects had been selected by the very people who would benefit.

The people of Dundee had chosen how *their* taxes would be spent...

Over 10% of the electorate voted for the projects on offer. For 82% of those participants, it was the first time they had ever taken part in any form of community engagement. An overwhelming majority of participants felt it gave them a greater say in how their community was run, and were keen to take part again. (PB Partners, 2017-8)

***

Dundee was just the latest stop on a journey which had begun many years, and many, many miles away...

It all started with a typical conversation - the sort of scene repeated the world over, at one time or another. A workers' committee was making demands of their local government. An official was trying to appear sympathetic, but did not seem inclined to help.

He leaned back, shrugged, as if to say, "What can I do?", and took a deep breath:

"The municipal budget is like a short blanket. If pulled up, it would uncover the feet. If pulled down, it would uncover the head".

His statement was meant to be an analogy. But a textile worker took it rather more literally than was intended.

"I can make blankets myself", he said. "At the factory, we know the width, length and thickness of each blanket that needs to be made. But that blanket you are speaking about never passed through our hands. I suspect that if we could help, it would come out better".

The worker's idea was simple: Sometimes you can use the same resources and get better results. You just need a good dollop of ingenuity.

That is what happened...

The authorities of Porto Alegre appealed to the collective genius of their citizens, engaged them, and used *them* to make their limited budget stretch further than ever before... (Dias, 2004)

***

It was 1989.

A new government had just been elected in Porto Alegre, a Brazilian city known for its barbeques and strong tea. They wanted to put the people at the centre of politics. So they took to the streets, inviting residents to attend meetings in churches, gyms and clubs. (Gelman & Votto, 2018)

During the first round of meetings, government officials presented information about the municipal budget. Local citizens then discussed the ways they thought that budget should be spent. The administrators were essentially saying, "This is our wool", and the people were deciding the types of blankets that they felt should be made.

A second round of assemblies took place, during which each district elected two representatives. These met other representatives, from across the city, compiled a long list of all the projects which had been suggested, and then returned to their neighbourhood assemblies, which ranked the different projects. Those with the most support, across all the neighbourhoods, were selected. (Souza, 2001)

Underrepresented people came to the fore...

Women outnumbered men, the poor outnumbered the rich, and young people got involved in politics for the very first time. Up to forty-thousand Porto Alegrans contributed to the process each year. And they made a real difference - redirecting public investment towards the most disadvantaged districts. (Dias, 2004)

By 1997, sewer and water connections had increased from 75% to 98%, health and education budgets had more than doubled, the number of schools had quadrupled, and road building in the poorer neighbourhoods had increased fivefold. (Gelman & Votto, 2018)

***

Unlike deliberative democracy, participatory budgeting only focuses on one thing - a council's budget. It is voluntary, and so can attract politically minded activists, who might not represent the population as a whole. But it has achieved results, and it has spread across the globe. By 2013, two-thousand-seven-hundred municipalities had given participatory budgeting a go, including one-thousand-three-hundred in Europe, and eleven-hundred in Latin America. (Dias, 2004)

7. LIQUID DEMOCRACY

Like direct democracy, "Liquid Democracy" allows people to propose and vote on policies. But it also gives us the opportunity to *delegate* our votes.

It works like this...

You join a political party which uses liquid democracy, and find yourself voting on economic issues. Time after time, you realise that you are casting your vote in the same way as another member of the party. This person is an active participant, an economics expert who has built up a small following. It makes sense for you to allow that person to cast *your* vote, whenever an economic issue is up for debate, safe in the knowledge that you can take it back whenever you choose.

This frees you to focus on other issues. So you delve deep into legal policy. And, within a couple of months, you find someone else whose views match your own. You delegate your vote to that person - getting them to cast your vote, on your behalf, whenever legal issues are being discussed.

You continue to vote on policies which stir your passions, and you keep an eye on your delegates, to ensure they still represent your views. You feel that your voice is being heard, you are having a say on every issue that matters, but you can go for weeks without engaging with the system.

EARLY DAYS

Liquid democracy can trace its origins back to a paper written by Lewis Carroll, in 1884. But it remained on the fringe of political discourse throughout the Twentieth Century.

In 1912, William O'Ren called for the power of elected politicians to be weighted by the number of votes they received when running for office. In 1967, Gordon Tullock suggested that voters should be able to choose elected representatives to vote on their behalf, or have the right to vote themselves during live parliamentary debates. But it was only with the dawn of the World Wide Web that such ideas gained a practical footing. (Paulin, 2014)

Tech nerds and democracy hacks, whispered in the dark and dusty corners of cyberspace: "Wann das Liquid kommt?" *When will Liquid come?*

These prophets of democracy were waiting for their holy church - a web-based platform which would give politics back to the people.

But, as it stood, that was all they could do. Ask, "Wann das liquid kommt?" and wait for their messiah - some sort of techie upstart who would meander in from behind the firewall and lead them to the promised land. It was all a matter of blind, unflinching faith.

"We have this problem, but when Liquid comes it will all be solved", explained Andreas Nitsche.

He was to be a messiah...

Together with three co-conspirators, Nitsche sat down and began to code. It was a labour of love. These were volunteers, who did not have any financial backing. But they felt they could make a difference. The world needed them to create a system which would allow people's voices to be heard; without the need for mass moderation, without noisy minorities taking over, and without elected representatives ignoring the people's will.

Four months later they were done. They took their program, "Liquid Feedback", to the Berlin chapter of German Pirate Party, and asked them to give it a go. (Ramos, 2016)

THE DEMOCRACY SOFTWARE

Imagine the scene, if you will...

You have just returned from holiday and the memories are fresh in your mind. You reminisce about the splendid afternoon you spent in the park, reclining in the sweet afternoon breeze, whilst grass caressed your back.

The highlight of that day came when your cousin got out the coals, loaded up the public barbeque, and grilled some burgers. You washed your meal down with a few glugs of beer, sat around a fire-pit, and watched on as the sun began to set, roasting marshmallows and singing campfire songs.

Your local park may not seem as exotic as the one you experienced abroad. You have been there many times. But you do notice its beauty in the small things; in the way the butterflies balance on flowers, and the way the stream beats a rhythm of its own. Still, there is no picnic area, no barbeque, no fire-pit. You feel that the people in your town are being short-changed.

Why can't they have the same wonderful experience you had on holiday?

You behave like a good democrat, open your app, click "Create a new issue", and select "Proposal" from the drop-down menu. In the small box at the top of the page, you create a title for your campaign: "Picnic area in City Park". In the large box below, you set out your idea: "This initiative proposes a picnic area in City Park, with at least four tables, a fire-pit and two barbeques". You give your reasons in bold, adding three exclamation marks for good measure: "Picnic areas encourage friends and families to come together!!!" You add a diagram and drop a pin to show the exact location where you feel the picnic area should be built.

Thirty days are set aside for discussion.

Some people click the thumbs-up button displayed above your text.

One person makes an early suggestion: "The tables should be pink". Members' comments are somewhat mixed, as are the ratings. Some people click the "Should be included" option, but even more click "Should not be included".

Another suggestion, "The area should include recycling bins", gets more support. A clear a majority click the circle which says this amendment "Must" be included. You add it to your proposal and click "Refresh my support". An email is sent to anyone who has shown an interest.

You think things are going well, until other people begin to make alternative suggestions; clicking the "Competing Initiatives" button in the bottom-left corner of your page. One person calls for a similar project in a different location: "Picnic area in Garden Square". Another suggests a different project in the same place as yours: "Duck-pond in City Park".

When the thirty days are up, a fifteen-day moderation period is followed by fifteen days in which votes can be cast.

Three wide bars appear at the top of the screen - a green bar marked "Approve", a grey one marked "Abstain", and a red one marked "Disapprove". The three proposals appear in white boxes, which can be dragged beneath any bar, and ranked in order of preference.

You wait, nervously, counting down the days: Three. Two. One...

Your proposal wins! Not only have a majority of members placed it in the "Approve" section, they have also placed it in first position within that section.

You soon discover that three "Super Delegates" had made the

difference. Over a hundred members had asked those individuals to vote on their behalf, on issues relating to local planning. The super delegates had taken those members' votes, and used them to vote for your proposal.

Now you just have to hope that your party's elected representatives can convince the council to turn your idea into a reality. (LiquidFeedback.org)

THE BIRTH AND DEATH OF A DEMOCRATIC POLITICAL PARTY

In May 2010, the German Pirate Party decided to put Liquid Feedback to the test. Three-thousand members registered online, discussed hundreds of issues, and approved twenty-eight initiatives. (Swierczek 2011)

The software was only ever intended to *complement* representative democracy, not replace it. Politicians would still represent the party's members, and they would still retain the right to act as they deemed fit. Liquid Feedback simply held them to account, forcing them to justify themselves whenever they chose not to back an initiative. Should they do so too often, they risked being deselected. (Ramos, 2016)

The party's popularity peaked in 2011, when fifteen members were elected to Berlin's state parliament. These young radicals were just what the stuffy world of German politics was calling out for. Dressed in hoodies, shorts and overalls, they brought the political scene to life - opposing the censorship of video games, calling for greater government transparency, and campaigning for internet privacy. Before long, they held seats in another three state parliaments.

The Pirate Party's fall was just as rapid as its ascent...

When one of its representatives, Gerwald Claus-Brunner, told his colleagues, "You will have a minute of silence for me at the next plenary meeting", it is unlikely they took his words at face value. They should have done. Within three months, Claus-Brunner had murdered a young comrade, Jan Mirko L. By the time he had wheeled L's corpse through the street, and taken his own life, the German Party was dead on the floor. It had polled just 1.7% in the Berlin state elections and lost all its seats.

This is not to say that liquid democracy should be written off as a failed experiment. Whilst the German Pirate Party was being dumped into the dustbin of history, the Icelandic Pirate Party was coming third in the national elections. In 2012, Pirate Party candidates were elected in Austria, Spain,

Switzerland and the Czech Republic.

There are, however, lessons to be learned...

"Our biggest problem was that we let everyone in who wanted to join", says Stephan Urbach, a former Pirate Party activist. "Every political opinion was tolerated. I'd go to a party convention and there would be, like, holocaust deniers there". (Huetlin, 2016)

The German Pirate Party tried to be all things to all people, tore itself apart from the inside, and was unable to offer a clear message to the electorate.

But what if we took the Liquid Feedback software, and gave it to a group which *did* have a clear identity, with well-defined messages and goals? A group that needed to transform itself into a political party, in order to achieve those goals?

Things might be different, right?

YES WE CAN!

It was Spring 2011, and Spain had still not recovered from the Global Economic Crash. Unemployment was running at over 20%, youth unemployment stood at over 40%, homelessness was endemic, and political discontent was rife. So when a small collective of activists used Facebook and Twitter to promote their manifesto, "Real Democracy Now", people responded to their call.

They occupied thousands of squares in a single year. They distributed free food and water. It felt fresh, the beginning of something new. At its peak, 73% of Spaniards supported the protestors.

"Indignados" or "15-M" was democratic to its core - centred on public forums in which anything could be debated, anyone could have a say, and everything was decided with a vote.

In Madrid, they discussed ways to oppose cuts to public services. In San Blas, they concocted plans to brew and sell beer. They pitched their tents, debated electoral reform and women's right, raised their hands to show support, and crossed their arms in opposition.

Sometimes, they created projects which reached far beyond the movement. They stood guard outside the apartments of debt-ridden tenants, to save them from eviction. They created cooperatives through which people could exchange services without the need for money. And they inspired the "Occupy" movement in Britain and the States.

But their calls fell on deaf ears. The PP replaced the Socialists in the nation's parliament, but the government's policies remained the same.

***

Amongst the Indignados had been one Pablo Iglesias - a young professor with Jesus-esque hair, narrow shoulders, and an impish, almost feminine smile.

As the movement wound down, Iglesias's star began to rise...

He earned himself a cult following, as the host of the "Fort Apache" TV show; riding into people's homes on the back of a Harley Davidson, clad in leather and denim; hosting political debates and introducing musicians.

He began to appear on mainstream TV...

Slouching in his seat, one leg thrown across the other, he beat back the commentariat with a mixture of hard statistics and gentle condescension.

Iglesias had become a household name.

In January 2014, he and his students formed a new political party, "Podemos", *We can*. Their objective was simple - to transform Indignados from a protest movement, which could be ignored, into a political party which would have the power to bring about real change.

Podemos did not have much money. It did not have the organisational structure of the mainstream parties. But it did have the backing of a grassroots movement. It took the liquid democracy platform, born in Northern Europe, and gave it to that movement...

***

Organised through nine-hundred local "Circles", the magic happens on "Plaza Podemos" - a website which had half-a-million registered users at the time of writing. A liberal use of the colour purple and big, bold buttons give it a Twenty-First Century feel. Tens-of-thousands of people logon every day.

As with Liquid Feedback, the process is user-friendly. You simply give your proposal a title, type some text in a box, and click "Submit". Hey presto, your campaign is live.

Anyone with a valid ID can sign up, give feedback, and show support for your suggestion. If it generates enough interest, it will be put to the vote.

***

The party was barely established, but the EU elections were fast approaching and Podemos had high hopes.

Their circles had put forward one-hundred-and-fifty candidates, who had been ranked by tens-of-thousands of members, to produce a truly democratic slate.

With a month to go, the manifesto was complete. The people had spoken. They would nationalise the banking system, provide decent wages, improve pensions, end the privatisation of public services, stop fighting in imperialistic wars, and leave NATO. It was pretty left-wing stuff. Unlike the German Pirate Party, Podemos did have a clear, coherent identity.

There was just one problem. Only 8% of Spaniards knew who they were.

Half of Spain, however, had heard of Pablo Iglesias.

The party made a controversial move. They put Iglesias's face on their logo, to ensure they would be recognised in the booth.

It was to prove decisive...

Podemos convinced one-and-a-quarter-million Spaniards to vote for their new party, and grabbed five seats in the European parliament. Two years later, at the next general election, they took 24.5% of the vote and won over a fifth of the seats in Spain's Congress of Deputies. (Tremlett, 2015)

***

A clear identity and a celebrity leader helped put Podemos on the map. But it has not been all plain sailing...

Once in power, they were forced to compromise. Podemos had to build coalitions, which proved fruitful in the short term, but were always liable to fall apart. Iglesias's deputy, Iñigo Errejón, left to create a new party. Vox, a right-wing party, appealed to the same communities that had rallied behind Podemos - claiming that immigration, not austerity, was the source of their woes.

At the 2019 elections, Podemos lost twenty-nine seats.

So was this a nail in the coffin of liquid democracy?

Not really. Podemos still held 12% of the seats - a pretty impressive achievement for such a new party.

And other factors will always be significant...

Ideology, leadership, media coverage, allies and opponents all play a part when it comes to determining a party's success. The fact that a party's policies are chosen democratically means little to voters if they do not agree with those policies, or if another party has policies which better match their beliefs.

THEY ARE NOT ALONE

When discussing liquid democracy, it would be remiss not to mention "The Five Star Movement".

Founded by Beppo Grillo, a comedian and blogger with the same celebrity appeal as Iglesias, it uses an online platform called "Rousseau". Every couple of months, members are asked to logon and select five new laws from a list of about one-hundred suggestions. Around thirty-one-thousand people vote in each such referenda. (Berti, 2017)

The party's success has been staggering...

The Five Star Movement won a hundred-and-nine seats at the 2013 Italian general election. In 2018, it became the biggest party in both the Senate and the Chamber of Deputies, gaining over 35% of the vote. It has entered government, and even created a "Ministry of direct democracy".

In France, "La France Insoumise" has attracted half-a-million members. Despite only being formed in 2016, it secured seventeen seats at the 2017 French general election.

Yet whilst these examples are promising, they remain outliers. In most countries, democratic parties do not exist. Where they have been established, in place like Argentina and Australia, they remain on the fringes; lacking the supporter base, media contacts and reputation which traditional parties take for granted.

There is, however, an alternative...

Rather than create new political parties, which may struggle to break into the mainstream, we could always try to *reform* the parties that already exist. We could demand that their leaders, candidates and policies be chosen, democratically, by their members...

DEMOCRATISING THE BEAST

Feisty, young, and sharp of tongue; the then twenty-eight-year-old looked out into the flashing cameras and clasped her hands across her mouth.

"Oh my God, oh my God, oh my God", she whispered through the gaps in her fingers, before finally composing herself and addressing the crowd: "We met a machine with a movement!"

Alexandria Ocasio-Cortez, a social activist and part-time bartender, had done the unthinkable. She had taken on Joe Crowley - Washington high-ranker, darling of the establishment, next-in-line to be leader of the house *Joe Crowley*. And she had won. The people of New York's Fourteenth Congressional District had chosen this young upstart of Puerto Rican descent to be their candidate in the upcoming election.

It made headlines across the world. Winning a "Primary" against a standing representative is somewhat of a rarity. More often than not, once in office, a politician will retain their nomination for life. If they represent a safe seat, they will be re-elected ad infinitum, even if they are an unpopular or ineffectual politician.

But change can happen. Ocasio-Cortez showed us how.

Hers was a victory of people over money. Her rival's campaign outspent hers by a factor of ten-to-one. But her personality and policies outshone the power of the dollar bill; winning her 57% of the votes.

It was by no means the first upset New York had ever seen. In 1992, Nydia Velázquez defeated a veteran congressman in the same city. Two decades before, Elizabeth Holtzman unseated the chairman of the House Judiciary Committee.

But it was, undoubtedly, a victory for democracy. (Jacobs & Gambino, 2018) (Goldmacher & Martin, 2018)

***

So how common, exactly, are such primaries?

Back in Britain, it very much depends on the party involved...

Like Joe Crowley, MPs who represent the Scottish National Party and the Green Party must stand for reselection whenever a general election is held.

If members of a local Labour Party wish to challenge their sitting MP, however, they must vote to hold a trigger ballot, suggest another person to represent them, and then vote for that individual to be their candidate. It can be a rather long-winded and abrasive affair.

The Conservatives' policy seems even less democratic. To secure their party's nomination, a standing MP need only apply to their local executive council. In the vast majority of cases, this tiny clique will approve the MP's request, and keep them in place, without a vote taking place. (McGuire, 2018) (Casalicchio, 2019)

***

So much for deselecting incumbents. What about the process through which candidates are selected in the first place?

A study of eighty-three political parties, in twelve Western European nations, considered this very subject...

Researchers scored each party between one (authoritarian) and seven (democratic). Parties who allowed their leaders to select candidates, in a dictator-like fashion, received a single point. Parties got two points if their leaders delegated this task to a central office or national executive. They were awarded the maximum score of seven points if they allowed local members to select their candidate.

The average score, for the period from 1986 to 1990, was just 4.1. Worryingly, this was down from an average score of 4.8 in each of the five-year periods between 1945 and 1965.

There was, though, some positive news. Sweden scored 6.5, and Denmark scored 5.5. (Krouwel, 1999)

***

Even this may miss the point. Allowing members to choose their candidates may *appear* democratic, but it really depends on the size of a party's membership. We could still end up with a situation in which a hundred members choose the candidate who will go on to represent one-hundred-thousand constituents.

They may even rule the nation...

Indeed, when Britain's Liberal Democrats and Conservatives formed a coalition, in 2010, they appointed a twenty-six person cabinet. Between them, these individuals had been selected as candidates by just four-thousand local party members; a mandate of sorts, but hardly the strongest foundation on which to build a political system. (Hardman, 2018)

***

Then we have what is perhaps the most crucial role within a party: The leader.

These days, it might seem like standard practice for parties to allow their members to choose their head honcho. But this has not always been the case...

In the States, the Democrats and Republicans have been holding votes to select their presidential candidates for well over a century. Both followed the lead of the Anti-Masonic Party, who held a convention to select their presidential candidate way back in 1831. (Shafer, 1988)

It took several decades for the British to catch on. Individual members of the Labour Party were only allowed to vote directly for their leader in 1994. The Conservatives have only ever allowed their members to elect the party's leader on three occasions - choosing Iain Duncan Smith (2001), David Cameron (2005) and Boris Johnson (2019). In between, both Michael Howard (2003) and Theresa May (2016) assumed the top post unopposed.

***

That leaves the most important matter of all. Policy.

And yes, mainstream political parties do, on occasion, listen to their members and implement the policies they propose...

The British Labour Party has a rather convoluted process. The National Policy Forum works with two other committees to draw up proposals. These are then voted on at conference - a large affair, where around a thousand delegates from local parties, trade unions and socialist societies get to rubber-stamp proposals.

South Africa's ANC, and the Netherlands' People's Party, both follow a remarkably similar process.

Mainstream parties have also dabbled with the online world...

In 2007, Britain's Conservatives launched "Stand Up, Speak Up", allowing members of the public to read, debate and vote on proposals. The Liberal Party of Canada established something similar, called "As A Family", taking the most popular resolutions to the party's convention for one final vote. The Republican Party, in America, has its "Convention Without Walls".

Newer, more dynamic parties get a little closer to the sort of liquid democracy we met above....

The Canadian Green Party, for example, created their "Living Platform" in 2004. After inviting its *members* to suggest new policies, it asked its *supporters* to give their feedback on these propositions. No less than eight-thousand individuals had their say; choosing popular policies that helped the party to secure 6.7% of votes at the 2008 Canadian General

Election.

By 2012, the process was firmly entrenched in the party's makeup. They had found a halfway house - one part liquid democracy, and one part traditional party. Their *members* suggest the party's policies. But the party's *staff* manage the process - sorting suggestions into the appropriate categories. The members then have the final say - voting to approve or reject those policies. (Ashiagbor, 2013)

FINAL THOUGHTS

Liquid democracy is far from perfect. Super delegates can dominate proceedings. "Astroturfers" might infiltrate the party and corrupt its processes. Liquid democracy requires internet access, and thus excludes anyone who is not online. New democratic parties can struggle to break the mainstream, and existing political parties might resist democratic reforms.

Furthermore, whilst democratising political parties may force them to do more to represent their *members*, there is no guarantee that this will help them to serve the *wider population*. A 2017 study found that 51% of members of British political parties were university graduates, 80% were in the top three social classes, and 61% were male. They are far from representative. (Hardman, 2018)

This is not to dismiss the idea out of hand. Parties that use some form of liquid democracy are more democratic than those who do not. Liquid democracy is more practical than direct democracy. It may just be an idea whose time will come.

8. PEOPLE POWER

So you have given it your best shot through the official channels. You have written to your local representative, attended their constituency surgery, voted in several elections, joined a political party, and signed too many petitions to count. You may have even engaged with some of the methods outlined in this book. But your politicians have let you down. Your calls for change have been ignored.

Perhaps reluctantly, you feel you only have one option left. You have to take to the streets.

***

If this sounds familiar, you are far from alone...

In just two years, from the start of 2016, one-in-five Americans attended a political rally or street protest. One-in-four took part in a "Stay At Home" protest - volunteering for a campaign, joining a boycott or donating money.

These Americans were drawn from all corners of society. Women were just as likely to be involved as men, although there was a slight bias towards people who were white, wealthy, well-educated or suburban.

Together, they demonstrated about everything from women's rights to the environment, immigration, abortion, police shootings and gun law. (Jordan & Clement, 2018)

***

The numbers may be revealing, but the medium is nothing new. In the first section of this book, we looked at how popular protests helped to establish representative democracy itself...

In the UK, the Chartists won votes for men, before the Suffragists and Suffragettes won votes for women. The French Revolution began a long and bloody process, through which power was transferred from the monarchy to the French people. In the USA, the civil rights movement extended the franchise to all American citizens, regardless of their colour.

It is a trend that has continued in recent years - in the Philippines, Georgia, Ukraine, Chile, Tunisia, The Gambia, Sudan and Algeria. (Spirova, 2008)

In this chapter, we will take a look at how protests might operate *within* representative democracies; helping to hold the powerful to account, and ensuring they respect the will of the people...

THE BENTLEY BLOCKADE

Successful protest movements tend to have a few things in common. They develop over time - starting small, before achieving a critical momentum. They need people, resources and organisation. They require several different protests - some that last a few hours, and others that last months - some which involve a core group of true believers, and others that involve a democratic mass. Most suffer a string of setbacks, before achieving their ultimate goal.

To see this in action, let's consider the case of "The Bentley Blockade" - a protest against fracking in the Northern Rivers region of New South Wales. This is a land of national parks. A land of a million streams, which wind between deciduous trees, and babble over ancient pebbles, before plunging into the South Pacific Ocean.

It might sound like a paradise on earth, but this natural Eden was under threat. The price of gas had tripled across Asia, and businesses were looking to cash in - not to serve the Australian people, who already had an ample supply of gas, but to make money for themselves - fracturing the earth, extracting ancient methane from many kilometres beneath its crust, and selling it abroad at inflated prices.

Without consulting the community, their trucks arrived in 2010.

They rolled out their infrastructure at incredible speed, plunging rig after rig down through a flood plain, and drawing up plans for a pipeline that would have cut through the heart of an ancient forest.

It was a threat. Fracking can cause carcinogenic chemicals to be mixed into people's drinking water, the earth they walk on and the air they breathe. It can cause earthquakes. In the Northern Rivers, gas leaked into the streams, which could be set ablaze with a single match.

Yet the response was not immediate. Most people had never even heard of "Fracking". Many could not see a problem.

But for the few early movers that *did* see the threat, it was a patriotic cause:

"These barbarians are coming. They are coming with their bulldozers and their drill-rigs and their dump trucks... (But) I love this country and I'm prepared to fight for it!"

***

Their first task was simple - to unite the small groups that had popped up across the region; ensuring their members all had the skills, resources and organisation they would need.

It happened towards the end of 2011...

Ten experienced activists began training the newcomers, many of whom had never been part of a protest movement before. Having created a critical mass of well-trained individuals, they sent them into their communities, to win their neighbours' support.

They leafleted homes, distributed campaign information, shared DVDs, screened documentaries and surveyed local businesses. It helped that the gas companies were so visible. They were an obvious blight on the landscape. But this extra information helped to flesh out residents' fears. It was a perfect storm - a marriage of reason and emotion.

**

By the time they descended on Lismore, one of the biggest towns in the region, their voices had been heard. Seven-hundred people, over 2.5% of the population, turned up to a single meeting.

Within a week, those attendees had been put into working-groups and given projects to manage.

Momentum was beginning to build...

Campaigners visited every household, asking them a simple question: "Do you want your district to be gas-field free?"

The response was overwhelmingly positive - 94.9% of people said "Yes".

With a mandate to act, entire communities began to hold "Community Ceremonies" - party-style events, at which people of all ages and backgrounds came together in their local parks, wearing cheery smiles and brightly coloured clothes.

At the first such event, the mayor of Lismore Shire - a lady with short grey hair, a smart red blazer and cravat - declared the event the most "Spine-tingling" of her time on earth:

"We have, by an overwhelming majority, decided to declare our roads and lands CSG free!"

She called the people to step forward and populate the street-map which had been painted on the grass. Thousands of people responded with glee, skipping towards the line that represented the street on which they lived.

Standing side-by-side with their neighbours, they cheered and whooped as their road names were read aloud, before taking a "Frack Free Declaration", a scroll wrapped up in a red ribbon, and passing it along their line.

***

By April 2014, one-hundred-and-thirty-six communities had held similar events; denying the corporations the right to drill under their homes.

It brought the people together:

"It really helped people to feel empowered, not like victims. And this spread through the region. This belief that yes, we can take on the power-holders. This is doing democracy. This is what democracy *is*".

***

Other events complemented the community ceremonies...

The movement launched "CSG: The Musical"; mocking the fracking corporations, and raising AU$24k in just three nights. A series of concerts made even more. Seven-thousand people attended a single rally, in an area which was home to just forty-nine-thousand residents. Social media campaigns won support from near and far.

In September 2012, the Lismore City Council conducted their own poll, overseen by the Electoral Commission. It found that 87% of its population were opposed to the gas industry.

Yet still they refused to listen. Within days of the poll results being announced, the New South Wales government allowed Metgasco to begin production.

And so the protestors upped the ante. They staged their first blockade...

***

They were under no illusions.

"I know what it takes to run an activist campaign", one protestor explained. "I know you go broke. I know your earning capacity goes out the window. But I realised we had to act".

He headed for Glenugie - a small community, nestled in the trees, which had been earmarked for drilling.

It was Christmas 2012, and the activists arrived in a festive mood. One of them even inserted a Christmas tree into the proposed drill site.

Christmas decorations glistened in the midsummer sun.

But the newcomers were nervous.

It was understandable. The convoy of oversized lorries, sent in by the gas corporations, had the appearance of an invading army. They were accompanied by a battalion of marching police, dressed head-to-toe in black - in black caps, shades, shirts, belts and shoes.

When they received news of convoy's arrival, via a walky-talky, the activists got to work; blocking the roads which stood between them and the drill site.

A group of women, who dubbed themselves the "Knitting Nannas", knitted a yellow and black cordon, which they laid out across the lane. Others stood in the road, forming a human shield.

The police moved these protestors aside, and the trucks restarted their engines.

They did not get far. Another set of protestors had parked a vehicle across the road and removed the air from its tyres.

They shrugged when the police arrived, as if to say, "What can we do?"

Further down the road, another protestor had "Feinted".

When stunts like these were not bringing the convoy to a standstill, it could only move at a snail's pace. An activist was driving in front of the trucks at a couple of miles an hour. The roads were so narrow, they could not overtake.

***

When the convoy did eventually reach its destination, it was met by hundreds of activists singing Christmas carols.

The impasse did not last for long. Unable to disperse the crowd using peaceful means, the authorities turned violent...

Video recordings show the police ushering one protestor aside, dragging off three young ladies, and bundling an activist to the ground - falling on top of him as though he was the ball in a game of rugby.

In perhaps the most disturbing scene to be caught on camera, a woman was pinned to the ground. She screamed, with unrelenting anguish, as though she was being raped.

"It was vicious. It was brutal. And the police said, 'We will escalate'."

Yet the protestors, for their part, remained peaceful:

"We are practising the nonviolent principles of Ghandi and Martin

Luther King… We are doing this because governments have failed. And when governments fail, ordinary people have to become heroes".

It was a worthy sentiment. But it was not to prove successful…

At Glenugie, and at other subsequent blockades, the police eventually removed all the protestors. The gas corporations got their way.

Still, the activists took the positives. They realised that an operation which required twenty-four-hour policing was doomed to fail. It would cost too much money to sustain, and result in massive losses for the corporations.

It was early days. The movement just needed to a larger blockade. One with so many protestors, that no amount of police violence could break it…

***

The scale of the Bentley Blockade was unprecedented.

It created an unusual alliance between conservative farmers, local business owners, indigenous peoples, fire-service volunteers, health workers, local townsfolk, white-collar professionals and holidaying children.

The activists' calls had been turned on their head. No longer were they asking, "Please can you come to help us?" They were using social media to taunt their supporters, telling them, "Be sure you don't miss out!"

They attracted filmmakers, musicians, artists, comedians, priests, politicians and mayors. The John Butler Trio held an impromptu gig. A ten-year-old girl stood on a surfboard and recited a poem. People played guitars, bongos and didgeridoos. Children had fun with arts and crafts. Senior activists held courses in civil disobedience.

These activities drew the crowds. A thousand turned up on the very first day. And they continued to arrive in their droves, despite the unremitting fear, anxiety, stress, and police intimidation.

What they found was not so much a blockade, but a fully-functioning town…

"Camp Liberty" was perched atop some fields which had been donated by a local farmer. A main road ran along one side, and the proposed drill site could be found on the other. There were suburbs filled with tepees, campervans, tents, toilets and showers. A town centre contained a meeting hall, first aid hut, canteen, children's zone, café and sacred fire.

Free food was donated by local farmers and cooked by volunteers.

And then there was the blockade itself…

The gates were manned, twenty-four hours a day, by a roster of

"Simmos". With chains attached to their wrists, these activists were ready to lock themselves onto an array of objects whenever the frackers approached. Some devices were so large, a hundred protestors could bolt themselves on at once.

The Simmos were the first line of defence; a human-shield who would hold the fort whilst the protestors waited for reinforcements.

But theirs was not the *only* means of defence...

A "Greet the Dawn" ceremony protected the camp from raids by the riot police. Aerial drones were sent sky-high to spy on the authorities. And a concrete bunker, almost two metres underground, was occupied day and night.

Superintendent Greg Martin, the local police chief, called the Bentley Blockade, "The biggest public order exercise ever encountered by the New South Wales Police".

Yet he seemed unfazed. After four long months, his colleagues were planning an invasion...

***

Reports suggested that eight-hundred riot police were ready and waiting. "Operation Stapler" was going to be one of the biggest operations the state had ever seen, replete with water cannons, dog squads and horses.

A bloodbath was on the cards, and the authorities were nervous. State politicians feared the bad press that would come if anyone was killed or seriously injured. The blockade had made the national news, and the state government was feeling the pressure.

Representatives headed for Sydney with a message of caution:

"You can't send a thousand police to take on *five-thousand* protestors. It would be nothing short of a paramilitary invasion of a peaceful community".

The authorities had little choice but to back down.

On May 15th, the government suspended the Bentley drilling licence. During the next eighteen months, it rescinded every licence it had issued in the Northern Rivers area.

The campaign had become a monster. It had taken on the big corporations, the police *and* the government; and it had walked away victorious. (Shoebridge, 2016) (Kia & Ricketts, 2018) (Frost, 2014)

PEOPLE POWER!

So what does this teach us?

Well, there is good news. Protest movements can achieve their goals.

In this, the Bentley Blockade was not alone. Protest movements have helped to end slavery, wars and apartheid; win workers' rights and women's rights; reverse austerity and establish parties like Podemos.

We shall come across some other protest movements in this book...

In the chapter on democratic armies, we will look at the peace movement which ended the Vietnam War. In the chapter on policing, we shall see how Icelanders forced their government to imprison their island's rogue bankers. And in the chapter on the corporatocracy, we shall see how a mass movement forced Hamburg to re-municipalise its energy supply.

But the Bentley Blockade also teaches us that success comes at a price. It takes time, effort and money. There are sure to be setbacks along the way.

Such causes follow a fairly standard lifecycle...

They begin with a small group of true believers - passionate and dedicated activists who establish the campaign. In the Northern Rivers, these "Innovators" formed small groups in different towns, came together to unite those groups, and inspired and trained the first batch of "Early Adopters".

The early adopters, through their greater numbers, help to give movements the legitimacy they require to break into the mainstream. They might not be traditional activists. In the Northern Rivers, many had never been part of a protest movement before. But they believed in the cause, returned to their communities, talked to their neighbours, distributed information, and hosted the events that helped to build a critical mass. The "Majority" came on board.

The anti-fracking movement won the support of the majority fairly early on. When the activists surveyed residents, 94.9% said they wanted their neighbourhoods to be frack-free. Even most of the "Luggards", people who are usually wary of change, had been won over by the cause. (Barret, 2019)

In an effective democracy, this would be enough. The authorities would succumb to the will of the people.

In an ineffective democracy, however, some pressure may still be required. In New South Wales, the government refused to listen until its subjects staged a series of protests and blockades.

Ultimately, however, the government was forced to act.

This is no anomaly...

It used to be said that no government could survive if 5% of its people mobilised against it. New research shows this figure to be a little inflated. When looking at the data from every mass-movement of the Twentieth Century, researchers found the true figure to be just 3.5%. If about one-in-thirty people rise up against their leaders, their government is pretty much certain to fall. (Chenoweth, 2013)

This is not to be sniffed at. In the USA, 3.5% of the population amounts to around eleven-and-a-half-million people.

The Bentley Blockade only attracted a few thousand protestors. But then again, the protestors never intended to topple their government. They only wanted it to change its ways.

***

Movements can succeed even without inspiring millions to take to the streets. But it helps if they have *resources*...

They may have access to weapons or money. They may have allies in the mainstream political parties, unions, media, police or army. They may have leverage - the ability to threaten their rulers' wealth, move capital abroad, or mobilise mass-strikes. (Dahlum, Knutsen & Wig, 2019)

The Northern Valleys movement had some of these resources. It won support from local mayors, the business community and the national press. It raised the AU$5k-a-week it needed to run Camp Liberty.

***

But it is not enough simply to have people and resources. Movements need a *clear objective* and a *plan* that will help them achieve it.

Success cannot be guaranteed...

The Occupy movement hardly brought down capitalism. Its goal was too vague. It did not win mass support outside of the movement, and it did not have the resources it needed to take on the financial sector.

The tank-taunting protestor of Tiananmen Square may be the subject of several iconic posters, but his one-man show had little effect on the Chinese regime. He had no movement, resources or plan.

In the Northern Rivers, the activists did have a clear and simple goal - to stop the frackers. And they were organised. They built a fully functioning camp. They staged drills and training sessions. They had rotas for volunteers, surveillance systems and social media accounts.

It was a recipe for success - the perfect combination of people, resources, organisation and clear objectives. It is little wonder that it succeeded.

***

Success stories like Bentley explain why people continue to march, sit down, sit in, camp out, occupy, riot, loot, chant, sing, petition, lobby, hashtag, strike and boycott. Sometimes it works. And sometimes is better than never.

In the remainder of this chapter, we shall take a further look at a few of these forms of protest, before ending with a warning: When you take on the establishment, be prepared. The authorities are sure to fight back.

WE'RE ALL ACTIVISTS NOW

Let's begin with the good old-fashioned boycott...

Perhaps the most famous boycott in American history began when Rosa Parks was arrested for refusing to give her seat to a white man. The "Women's Political Council", the black churches and a young Martin Luther King, encouraged forty-thousand African Americans to abandon the city's buses. Just seven months later, a Montgomery federal court ruled that racially-segregated seating on the city's buses violated the Fourteenth Amendment. Montgomery's buses were desegregated by the end of the year.

A boycott of South African goods helped to end apartheid.

Boycotts of businesses have forced The Body Shop to ban animal testing, Burberry to stop using fur, HSBC to divest from an arms manufacturer, and Boots to reduce the price of its contraceptive pill. These last four campaigns all achieved their goals within the space of just three calendar years. (Shaw, 2010) (Livingston, 2018) (Carlile, 2019)

***

Strikes are another useful tool...

Before British dock and gas workers staged a series of walkouts, in the 1880s, they were forced to work for up to sixteen hours a day. Their strikes brought about the eight-hour day - a norm that was later enshrined in law.

When sewing-machine operators walked out of the Ford plant in

Dagenham, in 1968, they brought production to a standstill. The government paid attention; penning legislation that guaranteed equal pay for equal work, regardless of gender. (Stone, 2016)

But strikes need not be started by workers...

Back in the early 1600s, Iroquois women staged a "Sex Strike" - refusing to engage in coitus until they were given the right to veto future wars. Leymah Gbowee resurrected this centuries-old tactic in 2003, launching a sex strike that ended the Liberian Civil War. The tactic has helped to stem gang-related murders in Colombia, end political infighting in Kenya, and stop the feuding which had plagued Filipino villages. (Shaw, 2017)

Then we have the "Hunger Strike"...

These thrive on publicity. So it helps if the hunger-striker happens to be a famous, newsworthy name - a member of a well-established and popular movement, with connections in the media.

Hunger-striking Suffragettes helped to win women's rights in the UK. Mohandas Gandhi staged a hunger-strike, as part of his ultimately successful campaign for Indian independence. When Irish Republicans starved themselves to death in British prisons, they earned public sympathy in Northern Ireland *and* in Britain itself. One hunger-striker, Bobby Sands, was even elected to parliament whilst refusing to eat in jail! (Kohari, 2011)

***

We could continue in such a manner, considering cases where marches, blockades, petitions, tax resistance, community events and occupations have ultimately achieved their goals.

We could take a look at the "Tree Sitters of Pureora", who forced New Zealand's government to stop its policy of deforestation, by building tree houses and refusing to leave. We might focus on the mass marches of 1992, which forced the British government to abolish the Poll Tax. Or we might discuss the planned "Nurse-In" at Applebee's, which forced the restaurant chain to withdraw its ban on breastfeeding.

There have been so many protests, which have achieved so much, that it would be impossible to do them justice.

But before we move on, let's make one thing clear: Protests do not need to be dour affairs...

My first experience of a protest came as fresh-eyed sixteen-year-old, making my first visit to the Glastonbury music festival. Walking past the Jazz

World Stage, I came across two long-haired gentlemen holding placards marked, "Protest Naked". Needless to say, they were as nude as the day they were born!

Fans of the television show, "Jericho", once convinced CBS to commission a second season by sending them over twenty-thousand kilograms of assorted nuts. One can only speculate as to their reaction, when they saw their desk submerged beneath a mountain of salted cashews and roasted peanuts. (Martin, 1994) (Noble, 2011)

Then we have the humorous placards which can be found at almost every march:

"Jesus had two dads and he turned out fine".

"This wouldn't happen in Hogwarts".

"The people behind me can't see".

"Elves on strike".

"Our wives think we're at work".

"I'm so angry I made a sign".

It could be argued that protests *need* to be fun and entertaining to keep their members engaged. There was a reason the protestors in the Northern Rivers held concerts and shows: A happy movement is a healthy movement.

POWER TO THE PEACEFUL

So far, we have focussed on peaceful campaigns. But why stop here? Wouldn't a little violence help to move things along?

The evidence suggests it would not, at least when it comes to campaigns for regime change. When analysing every such movement, staged between 1900 and 2006, researchers found that nonviolent campaigns were "More likely to win legitimacy, attract widespread domestic and international support, neutralise the opponent's security forces, and compel loyalty shifts".

Fifty-two percent of nonviolent campaigns for regime change were ultimately successful. Armed struggles only achieved their goals 25% of the time. (Stephan & Chenoweth, 2008) (Chenoweth, 2013) (Barrett, 2019)

It is not hard to see why...

Violent resistance is physically demanding. Activists must be able to run, jump, dodge and dive. They may be hurt or arrested. They risk losing their jobs and even their lives.

For this reason, such struggles only attract a certain type of people: Dedicated activists who are physically strong, brave, and willing to take risks.

Nonviolent resistance is far simpler...

If a toddler does not want to eat the grape their parent is trying to feed them, they will clamp their lips closed. If they do not wish to move, they will sit with their arms crossed and wait to be dragged away. We are quite literally born with this instinct for nonviolent resistance.

Pretty much anyone can take part in a peaceful demonstration. And so they tend to welcome a fairly representative mixture of people, with different genders, ages, races, classes and political persuasions.

And because they attract more *types* of people, peaceful protests attract more people in total - around four times the amount as movements which have a violent element. These protestors are more likely to have contacts in government, business, the police and the media; and are therefore more likely to win support from those sectors. (Chenoweth, 2013)

Perhaps for this reason, peaceful campaigns are quicker than their violent equivalents. In the aforementioned study, successful nonviolent movements took an average of three years to achieve their objectives. Armed struggles took around nine years. (Stephan & Chenoweth, 2008)

***

The distinction, however, can be a little blurred.

Peaceful movements may attract a violent fringe....

The campaign to end the Vietnam War was almost entirely nonviolent. But members of the "Weathermen" did stage a "Day of Rage" - smashing storefronts and brawling with members of the police. They tried to wreak havoc during the "March of Death" - a thirty-six-hour event that attracted thousands of peaceful marchers. (Levering, 2017)

Other campaigns may be more evenly split...

The Civil Rights Movement fell into two distinct camps. The first, led by Martin Luther King, advocated for nonviolent direct-action and passive resistance. The second, led by Malcolm X, called for "Self-Defence" - meeting violence with violence.

***

The distinction may be even harder to see in what are being dubbed "Leaderless Movements"...

Pro-democracy activists in Hong Kong have held *spontaneous* rallies, roadblocks and sit-ins without any leaders calling the shots.

Extinction Rebellion is also a leaderless movement.

There is an up-side. Since such groups have no leaders, no leaders can be arrested. The power remains with the people.

But there is also a cost. Without a Gandhi-like figure to lead them, campaigners can fracture into disparate groups, each with its own tactics and ideals. When the police turn up in riot gear, some groups might respond with violence.

When France's "Yellow Vests" first stepped out of their vehicles, to demand higher wages and lower bills, they secured the support of 72% of French people. Yet when a small element turned violent - smashing shop windows, burning cars, defacing monuments and scuffling with the police - 85% of their compatriots disapproved.

Their acts of violence may have been more of a hindrance than a help.

Still, the Yellow Vests, violent and nonviolent, *have* achieved some of their goals. Within a month of taking to the streets, they forced President Macron to scrap his diesel tax. A year later, they forced the French government to discard its plans to raise the age of retirement. (Serhan, 2019) (May, 2019) (Donadio, 2018) (Mallet, 2020)

***

One of the most successful violent protests was led by Toussaint L'Ouverture and his spiky sidekick, Jean-Jacques Dessalines…

Born into slavery, toiling away as a farmhand in Haiti's relentless sun, Dessalines rise to prominence began with the slave rebellion of 1791, when he fought with such vicious intent that he was dubbed "The Tiger".

That rebellion left its mark. In 1793, France outlawed slavery.

Toussaint and Dessalines turned their attention to the eastern side of the island, which was controlled by the Spanish. Civil war ensued. Dessalines fought *with* the French, until they reinstated slavery, imprisoned and starved Toussaint. He then turned *against* that European nation.

His slave army, made up of both men and women, took the entire island. Dessalines rounded up thousands of French Haitians, had them slaughtered, and declared himself emperor.

The Haitian Revolution earned itself a place in history. It was the only slave rebellion that led to the establishment of a new, independent nation, controlled by its former slaves.

But the story does not end here...

Just two years later, in March 1807, the British government passed "The Slave Trade Act", which banned the transatlantic slave trade. Portugal followed suit in 1810, as did France in 1814, and Spain in 1817.

There is a school of thought which claims that it was the Haitians who pressured those governments into action - that they had watched on as France lost their slaves, slave owners and colony - and feared what might happen to *their* slaves, slave owners and colonies if they did not act fast. The history of slavery was littered with violent protests. The Haitians simply showed what such protests could achieve.

If such a theory is to be believed, the violent protests in Haiti not only ended slavery on that island, they also ended the slave trade across *several other nations*.

Indeed, something similar occurred a couple of decades later...

In 1832, sixty-thousand enslaved Jamaicans killed several slave owners and burnt down half the plantations on the island. Just two-and-a-half years later, slavery was made illegal in all of Britain's Caribbean territories.

I will leave you to do the maths... (Akala, 2015)

***

There may be a place for violence after all...

Let's not forget that the English, French and American Revolutions all involved their fair share of bloodshed.

Let's not forget that the democratic system we met in Rojava also required an armed struggle. We shall return to this topic in Chapter Eleven.

And let's not forget the anti-apartheid movement in South Africa, which bombed government buildings and the homes of government officials. Many scholars argue that those bombings, led by Nelson Mandela, did more harm than good. But Mandela did come out victorious. Apartheid was defeated in the end. (Kurtz, 2010)

***

Violence or nonviolence?

It remains a matter for debate.

THE RESISTANCE

We have seen that when all else fails, protests can succeed. They can force governments to respect the will of their people.

But the road to victory is laden with potholes and bumps. The authorities have a whole arsenal of tricks, which they use when stifling public dissent. And they have far more resources than most democratic movements.

***

The authorities can pass anti-protest *legislation*...

Responding to the Bentley Blockade, the New South Wales government introduced draconian laws which impinged the rights of protestors; threatening them with up to seven years in prison. (Shoebridge, 2016)

New Australian legislation, passed to criminalise Extinction Rebellion, means that anyone locking themselves to a fixed object during a protest can be fined AU$6,500 or sent to prison for two years. (Wahlquist, 2019)

In 1988, the British government passed the "Local Government Act", forbidding councils from boycotting goods produced in South Africa. The same legislation has been used to stop councils from boycotting Israel. (Hanna, 2016)

At the time of writing, France, Canada, and twenty-eight American states had passed similar laws. (Zerbisias, 2016)

***

Then we have the *underhand tactics* states sometimes employ...

Governments have been known to spy on their own citizens. In the UK, MI5 has even held files on Caroline Lucas - a democratically elected member of parliament. (Evans & Dodd, 2016)

States have also been known to infiltrate protest groups...

The FBI's Cointelpro program infiltrated black rights, feminist and anti-Vietnam War organisations - sowing the seeds of division between Malcolm X and Elijah Muhammad - controlling and disrupting those movements from the inside. (Martin, 1994)

And governments have been known to create fake, *pro-establishment* movements, to boost their credibility, or to reframe debates ...

The Russian government formed the "Nashi Movement", a youth-led antifascist cause. The Nicaraguan authorities have staged pro-government rallies, threatening civil servants who refused to take part. Government agents have even brawled with anti-government protestors, in places such as Lebanon and Hong Kong.

According to one study, authoritarian governments organise one counter-protest for every seven protests staged against them. That is a lot of fake protests! (Stephan & Gallagher, 2019) (Chenoweth et al, 2019)

***

Thirdly, governments can use *propaganda* - pretending to respond to people's call, even when they are not...

In response to the million-strong peace march of 1982, the American government launched a series of "Arms control initiatives" and "Strategic defence initiatives". These made no substantial difference whatsoever. America's nuclear arsenal remained intact. But they did give the *impression* that the authorities were responding to the people's calls, which was enough to dampen opposition.

Propaganda can also be used to attack individual activists - tarnishing them with disloyalty, accusing them of being agents of foreign entities, and branding them as the "Enemy within". (Martin, 1994)

And it can be used to smear entire movements...

Whilst I was writing this chapter, the British government released a "Counter Terrorism Policing Document", in which it placed peaceful groups such as Greenpeace and CND, alongside violent neo-Nazi groups such as National Action; smearing them by association. (Dodd & Grierson, 2020)

***

Fourthly, the establishment may use *threats of violence* and *violence* itself...

A person's job may come under threat if they speak out against their employer. Workers might be dismissed for attempting to form a union, complaining about conditions, or exposing their firms' unsavoury practices.

In the chapter on the media, we shall come across the case of Richard Peppiatt, a journalist who lost his job when he refused to write lie-ridden articles. And Chelsea Manning, who lost her job in the American military, when she exposed her organisation's heinous crimes.

It is understandable why people with jobs to protect might think twice before choosing to protest, and why movements can come to be dominated by students and the unemployed; people with far less to lose.

But it is not only jobs which can come under threat. A person's freedom may be jeopardised too...

History is littered with famous faces who have served time behind bars - the likes of Mohandas Gandhi, Nelson Mandela, Eugene Debs, Martin Luther King, Bertrand Russell, the Suffragists and conscientious objectors.

The state has a monopoly on violence. It can throw its opponents into small, poorly-lit rooms, for several years on end. And its police may turn violent during protests - using tear gas, batons and water cannons.

It can go further still...

Several members of the Black Panther Party, including its leader, Fred Hampton, were assassinated by the American police. They join a long list of activists, including the likes of Rosa Luxemburg and Malcolm X, who have been shot dead for making a stand, albeit not always by the state. (Martin, 1994)

There does not appear to be any sort of let-up. In 2019 alone, protestors were killed in Hong Kong, Lebanon, Chile and Iraq. (Serhan, 2019)

Freedom is not free. The price can be measured in blood.

LET'S WRAP THIS UP

Oscar Wilde called disobedience, "Man's original virtue". For Wilde, "It is through disobedience that progress had been made".

The Irish playwright may have had a point. When all else fails, disobedience can produce results. Although the risks are high, popular protests can force the authorities to respond to the people's demands.

Of course, a couple of questions must be asked: Does the cause have the majority's support? And do the people approve of its tactics?

It is understandable that nascent movements spend most of their time whipping up support, and that nonviolent movements, which are more likely to gain the people's backing, are also more likely to succeed.

But there are limits. People tend only to protest when they are *passionate* about a cause. Around two-thirds of Brits want their railways to be renationalised, but no major marches have been staged to demand this happens. Rail nationalisation does not pull at the heartstrings in the same way as things like peace and the environment.

We cannot rely on protest alone. And we cannot rely on politicians either.

In the next section we shall look at four areas of public life that affect us all: education, media, policing and war. We shall look at ways to democratise these spheres of control, with *or* without our leaders' consent. Because democracy cannot flourish without a well-educated, well-informed population. And it cannot survive if a nation's police and soldiers do not serve its people...

PART THREE

IN THE PUBLIC SERVICE

9. HEY TEACHER, LEAVE THOSE KIDS ALONE!

Let's begin with some personal anecdotes...

I must have been about seventeen when it happened. I had been predicted straight As, I was playing sport and doing plenty of charity work. You would think my school would be happy. But you would be wrong.

I had spent the previous couple of years going to music festivals. I loved their vibe - their culture of freedom, non-materialism and love. So it was perhaps natural that I did that hippy thing. I grew my hair.

My hair is thick and shiny, but it lacks any sort of natural order. It is not straight, nor is it curly. It does whatever it wants - forming random waves, popping up in one place, and then disappearing in another.

Normally, I would tie it back to keep it tidy. But this was forbidden at my school - a Hogwarts-like relic, which had begun life in a cathedral, moved across to the local jailhouse, and spent the next thousand years slowly sprawling down the hillside.

When my hair grew long enough to touch my collar, the school took action.

At first, a teacher with whom I had never conversed, asked me, "Don't you think it's time you had a haircut?"

I told her to mind her own business.

Then the deputy head was sent to smile, use his charm, and ask me to have a trim.

Finally, I was ordered to visit the headmaster. His words were clear: I would not be able to continue my studies until I cut my hair. Refuse, and I would essentially be excluding myself.

My grades did not matter. My hard work did not matter. My contribution to school life did not matter. My hair did not conform, and that could not be accepted.

In the end, I buckled. My father said he would fund a court case against the headmaster, so long as I cut my hair and concluded my studies first. The girls at the school were allowed to grow their hair, so I felt we could sue the head for sexual discrimination. But we never did go to court.

So why bring this up now?

Education, in its purest form, should give pupils skills and knowledge. It should teach them how to tell fact from fiction, and help them to discover themselves.

That is what I was doing. I was studying hard, getting good grades, and discovering myself. Growing my hair, standing out from the crowd, was a sign of my budding individuality.

But this was not "Education in its purest form".

My school did not want me to develop as an *individual*. It wanted me to *conform* to their standards, and it was prepared to punish me if I did not.

This brings me to my second anecdote...

I was eleven-years-old and had already been suspended several times. During a school assembly, I told the boy next to me that he was a "Bastard". Technically, I was correct. His parents were not married. I had just learned the meaning of this word and was keen to try it out. Of course, it was a nasty thing to say. I regret it now. And I was sent to the headmaster to explain myself.

I accepted the criticism that came my way. But one thing stuck in my craw. Why had the other pupil snitched on me? And why was the headmaster taking action?

"Oh", he said. "I'd do it for you too. If you ever have an issue yourself, just come and find me, at any time. I'll always be here to help".

A few days later, I had an issue. I found the headmaster outside my classroom and asked him to help.

"Not now", he said. "Can't you see I'm busy? I'm just about to do an assembly".

"But!" I protested. "You said I could talk to you at any time. *Any time!* You said you would help".

I was expelled for answering back.

Pupils, you see, were not allowed to challenge authority under any circumstances, even when they were right. *Especially* when they were right. It was the most heinous of crimes.

And now the third example...

I was nine-years-old.

I had lost my temper during class. Furious with the lesson, and the system, I had thought, "Enough is enough", stormed outside, ran to the perimeter fence and started to climb. I was finally going to be free.

It was all over before it began. I felt my legs being yanked down by a teacher. Head bowed, I was marched back to school.

***

These experiences sum up my experience of the British "Education" system...

You had to obey all the rules, no matter how bizarre; even when your behaviour, growing your hair, did not harm anyone else. You could not question authority, under any circumstance. And you could not escape. Whether you liked it or not, you were forced into this system for a full twelve years. People get less for murder.

Conformity. Compliance. Captivity.

These were the "Three Cs" of my education.

It was hardly "Democratic".

IT HAPPENED BY DESIGN

Sometimes it takes a comedian to sum things up concisely.

Over to you, George Carlin:

"(The establishment) don't want well-informed, well-educated people capable of critical thinking. They're not interested in that! That doesn't help them. That's against their interests. That's right! You know something? They don't want people who are smart enough to sit around the kitchen table and figure out how badly they're getting fucked by a system that threw them overboard thirty fucking years ago. They don't want that! You know what they want? They want obedient workers. Obedient workers! People who are just smart enough to run the machines and do the paperwork, but just dumb enough to passively accept all these increasingly shittier jobs with the lower pay, the longer hours, the reduced benefits, the end of overtime and the vanishing pension that disappears the minute you go to collect it".

Conformity. Compliance. Captivity.

***

Things used to be very different...

As hunter-gatherers, we had to acquire a vast array of knowledge and skills. We had to understand the habits of hundreds of different creatures, how to track them, how to make tools such as bows and arrows, and how to use them. We had to learn about hundreds of types of plants, where to find them, and how to process them. We had to know how to navigate, build huts, make fires, protect ourselves from predators, care for our young, negotiate with outsiders, and create harmony within our group.

And do you know what? We learnt these things without any sort of formal education.

Hunter-gatherers simply leave their children to play with the other children in their band - giving them the time and space they need to *educate themselves*. On occasion, they might ask an adult for help; initiating a spear-making lesson, for example. But in most things, it is enough for the child to simply *observe* such adults, and mimic them as they play:

"Boys who one day are playfully hunting butterflies with their little bows and arrows are, on a later day, playfully hunting small mammals and bringing some of them home to eat, and on yet a later day are joining men on real hunting trips, still in the spirit of play".

Children in hunter-gatherer groups have been known to copy the way adults build huts - constructing model villages of their own, and using them to act out scenes they have observed amongst the adults. They have been known to dig up roots, build fires, make music, tell stories, cook and care for infants:

"Because all this play occurs in a mixed-age environment, the smaller children are constantly learning from the older ones.

"Nobody has to tell or encourage the children to do this. They do it naturally because, like children everywhere, there is nothing that they desire more than to grow up and to be like the successful adults they see around them". (Gray, 2008 (a))

There is no coercion whatsoever...

When the Cherokee saw a child exhibiting their self-will, they did not consider it a bad thing. They did not discipline that child. They simply smiled, believing that the youngster was maturing into a strong, independent adult. Indeed, the Cherokee were hesitant to discipline their children in any way whatsoever, for fear of impeding their development.

The Iroquois, meanwhile, did teach their youngsters about their tribe's cultural heritage. Children were taught to show solidarity with each other -

to share their possessions and consider everyone else their equal. They were also taught to be independent, to *not* submit to overbearing authority - the very opposite of what happens in today's schools. In all other matters, however, Iroquois children were left to their own devices. Youngsters were allowed to wean and toilet-train in their own time. There were no harsh punishments. The "Three Cs" did not exist. (Zinn, 1980)

***

This changed when we became farmers...

Agriculture was not *skill-intensive*, like hunting and gathering. It was *labour-intensive*. It required everyone to work hard - ploughing, sowing, weeding and harvesting.

Children were forced to suppress their instinct for play, and toil in the fields with their parents.

Things got even worse under feudalism...

In one source, from the Fourteenth Century, a French count advises a noble's huntsman to, "Choose a boy servant as young as seven or eight... This boy should be beaten until he has a proper dread of failing to carry out his master's orders".

Today's schools were born of this authoritarian spirit...

Religious leaders saw education as a way of instilling Christian values; giving pupils the skills they needed to read and recite the scriptures. Capitalists saw it as a way of breeding efficient workers; encouraging punctuality, subservience, and a tolerance for long and boring work. Nationalists saw it as a means through which to build patriotism; to create a generation of soldiers who would believe in the glory of the nation-state.

The violence of feudal lords was brought into the classroom. One German schoolmaster even kept a record of the nine-hundred-thousand blows he administered with a rod, the one-hundred-and-twenty-thousand he dispatched with a cane, and the twenty-thousand he dished out with a ruler! (Gray, 2008 (b))

Things have mellowed a little since then, but the underlying ethos of our schooling system remains the same. Play is still discouraged in favour of hard work. We are still expected to be punctual - to obey the bell. We are still expected to follow orders, and respect our teachers, even when they have done nothing to earn our respect.

We take these lessons into adulthood - becoming *employees* who work hard, turn up to every shift on time, follow orders, and respect our bosses even when they do not deserve our respect.

We become smart enough to operate the machines, but not smart enough to question why.

And herein lies our problem. If we are not smart enough to question authority, how can we be smart enough to engage in a democratic system? Democracies only work when people hold authority figures to account!

For a democracy to function at full capacity, people must be able to understand key political issues which are seldom taught in school. They must be able to see through propaganda - to separate fact from fiction. They must *question everything*. And yet they are put through an education system which encourages them to blindly accept authority. To *question nothing*.

A democratic life requires a democratic education - one in which students hold their teachers to account. One in which the *pupils* set the rules, maintain discipline, decide what classes they will attend, and what topics they will study.

This is far removed from the education you most probably received. It is the polar opposite of the personal experiences I described above.

And yet "Democratic Schools" do exist. In the remainder of this chapter, we shall take a look at a few examples: The Summerhill School in Britain, the Sudbury Valley School in the USA, and the Santo Antônio do Pinhal School in Brazil.

EAST ANGLIA'S LITTLE GEM

Located in twelve acres of gardens and woodlands, the "Oldest Children's Democracy in the World" was established by Alexander Neill in 1921.

Writing in 1960, Neill explained that his aim, quite simply, was to give children the freedom they needed to be themselves:

"In order to do this, we have to renounce all discipline, all direction, all suggestion, all moral training, and all religious instruction".

Neill practised what he preached. He established a fee-paying boarding school, with under a hundred pupils, in which there were no room inspections or uniforms, where lessons were voluntary, exams were optional, and everyone had "The right to play".

In essence, he replicated the hunter-gatherer system.

***

Of course, given that classes were optional, students might choose not to attend any classes at all. Pupils who had just arrived from mainstream schools often vowed to, "Never attend any beastly lessons again".

On average, it took three months for such youngsters to come around. But when they did, they showed a genuine passion for learning. They were attending lessons because *they* wanted to study, not because someone else was forcing them. Nothing will keep a young Einstein away from his science classes, or a young Nina Simone away from her music lessons. They might skip some subjects altogether, but this is no bad thing. It simply frees up their time to focus on the things they love.

***

Even if a pupil chose not to attend classes, it did not impede their education. Neill cites the example of Tom, a boy who attended Summerhill for twelve years without attending a single lesson:

"His father and mother trembled with apprehension about his future. He spent much time in the workshop making things. He never showed any desire to learn to read.

"But one night when he was nine, I found him in bed reading David Copperfield.

"'Hullo,' I said. 'Who taught you to read?'

"'I taught myself'."

Neill continues:

"Some years later, Tom came to me to ask, 'How do you add a half and two-fifths?'

"I told him and asked if he wanted to know any more.

"'No thanks,' he said.

"Later on, he got work in a film studio as a camera boy. When he was learning his job, I happened to meet his boss at a dinner party, and I asked how Tom was doing.

"'The best boy we ever had,' the employer said. 'He never walks, he runs. And at weekends, he is a damned nuisance, for on Saturdays and Sundays he won't stay away from the studio'." (Neill, 1960)

***

When I first read Tom's story, it filled me with optimism.

"We don't need teachers to force literacy down our necks", I thought to myself. "We can learn to read and write, in just the same way that we learn to walk and talk: By imitating other people".

But then I began to have my doubts:

"Why then, doesn't *everyone* learn to read in such a manner? How do you explain the existence of illiteracy?"

The truth is, we do need the right environment. If we lived in a society without books, where no-one read or wrote, we would not become literate. But *within a literacy-friendly environment*, we do not need to be coerced. We will learn through a certain form of osmosis, through contact with the written word - on billboards, screens and Facebook - in text messages and emails. A literate child might read the text that appears in a computer game, whilst an illiterate child follows along - making sense of the symbols that their friend reads aloud. A family member may read the captions that appear on television. As a parent re-reads the same bedtime story, over and over again, their child will look at the pictures, and then at the words. They might memorise those words, and then repeat them out loud - pretending to read. In time, that pretend reading will slowly transform into real reading.

When circumstances demand that a youngster reads, the skills they have accrued through such activities will come to the fore...

Amanda tells the story of her daughter, who attended a democratic school:

"She had consistently told people that she didn't know how to read, until she made brownies this past November (at age seven). She asked her father and me to make her favourite brownies for her, but neither of us was willing to make them. A little while later she ran into the room and asked me if I would turn on the oven and find her a nine by eleven pan. (She said 'Nine ex eleven' instead of 'Nine by eleven'). I got her a pan and turned on the oven. Later she ran in and asked me to put the brownies in the oven. Then she said, 'Ma, I think I can read now.' She brought me a few books, then she read them out loud, until she jumped up and said, 'Those brownies smell done. Will you take them out now?'... Now she tells people that she knows how to read and that she taught herself how".

Lisa also sent her boy to a democratic school:

"He learned to read when he was four-years-old, as a by-product of trying to find free games on the computer. He would open the browser and ask me to spell 'Free', then 'Online', then 'Games'. All of a sudden he was reading".

Some children may be a little more proactive...

Kate's son "Taught himself to read" when he was nine. In a single month of self-study, he progressed from being a hesitant, poor reader, to a highly fluent reader, far superior to what was regarded as his grade level.

Indeed, learning to read when aged nine is not uncommon in democratic schools. Some youngsters teach themselves when they are just four, whilst others wait until they are eleven. But coming to literacy late does not impact these pupils' ultimate ability. Like Kate's son, when they do learn, they learn quickly. They are motivated. They *want* to learn.

Beatrice's daughter did not learn to read until she was eight. That is late by the standards set by mainstream schools. But at age fourteen, she "Reads hundreds of books a year", "Has written a novel", and "Has won numerous poetry awards". She is well ahead of her peers. (Gray, 2010)

***

Similar conclusions can be reached when we consider other subjects. Let's take computing as an example...

The TED Prize winning, moustachioed professor of education, Sugata Mitra, is best known for his "Hole in the wall" experiments. They began in Delhi, where Mitra cut a hole in his office wall, installed an outward-facing computer, and watched on as slum-dwelling children approached that machine, experimented with its touchpad, taught themselves how to move the cursor, and then click, and then type.

"Aha", screamed the critics. "Someone from your office must have shown them how to use it".

Undeterred, Mitra took his show on the road, setting up similar computers in several random locations.

His experiments achieved similar results...

In Shivpuri, a town in central India, where Mitra, "Was assured that nobody had ever taught anybody anything", the first child to approach the computer was a thirteen-year-old school dropout. He thought he was using some sort of "Interactive Television".

It only took that boy eight minutes to work out how to use the web browser. By the end of the day, seventy children had followed in his footsteps.

Mitra then headed to Madantusi, a village in northeast India, where there was no English teacher. He left a pile of CDs, because there was no internet connection, departed, and returned after three months.

He found an eight-year-old and a twelve-year-old playing a game.

"We need a faster processor and a better mouse", they told Mitra.

He was surprised:

"How on earth did they know all this?"

"Well, we've picked it up from the CDs".

"But how did you understand what's going on?"

"Well, you've left this machine which talks only in English, so we had to learn English!"

The children had taught themselves two-hundred English words - words like "Exit", "Stop", "Find" and "Save". They were even using these words in their day-to-day conversations.

**

Across all his experiments, Mitra found that he just had to supply one computer for six months, and three-hundred youngsters would learn how to use Windows, browse the web, paint, chat, email, play games, use educational tools, download music and watch videos.

They did not need teachers. They did no need adults. They did not need to be coerced in any way. (Mitra, 2007)

**

These examples should make one thing abundantly clear: We do not need to force children to attend classes. Schools can educate their pupils without resorting to authoritarian tactics.

But just because classes are voluntary at Summerhill, does not mean that the school is bereft of rules. Children are not allowed to climb on the roof, possess airguns, swim without a lifeguard, or cycle on the road alone. Anyone who is not in bed at the appointed time must pay a fine.

Rules do exist, but they are agreed upon collectively, at the "General School Meeting" - a weekly forum in which everyone has a voice, and the vote of a seven-year-old pupil has as much weight as the vote of the headmaster.

Pupils are not averse to disagreeing with their teachers, arguing their case and outvoting them, as Neill explains:

"I once brought forward a motion calling for swearing to be abolished by law, and I gave my reason: I had been showing a woman around with her little boy, a prospective pupil. Suddenly, from upstairs, came a very strong adjective. The mother hastily gathered up her son and went off in a hurry.

"'Why,' I asked at a meeting, 'Should my income suffer because some fathead swears in front of a prospective parent? It isn't a moral question at all. It is purely financial. You swear and I lose a pupil.'

"My question was answered by a lad of fourteen.

"'Neill is talking rot,' he said. 'If this woman was shocked, she didn't believe in Summerhill. Even if she had enrolled her boy, the first time he came home saying 'Damn' or 'Hell', she would have taken him out of here'."

The community sided with the youngster.

But this is not to say that minority groups are always outvoted.

Neill gives another example...

His work was being disturbed by the games of football being played in the lounge below his office. When he submitted a proposal to ban such games, his motion was rejected.

Neill raised the subject again and again. This showed the community that those games really were causing him a great deal of distress. And, in time, he won over the student population:

"This is the way the minority generally gets its rights in our school democracy. It keeps demanding them".

* * *

School meetings are self-governing. Each one is led by a different chairperson, who is appointed by their predecessor. Exhibitionists who make long and irrelevant speeches are regularly shouted down.

The *whole school*, in fact, is self-governing. Sports, dance and theatre committees are all elected, as are "Bedtime Officers", who enforce the curfew, and "Downtown Officers", who monitor off-campus behaviour.

If a student breaks a rule, they will be tried at the next meeting. Their guilt or innocence, and their punishment, will be decided by their peers.

Neill gives an example:

"Jim took the pedals from Jack's bicycle because his own bike was in disrepair, and he wanted to go away with some other boys for a weekend trip. After due consideration of the evidence, the meeting decided that Jim must replace the pedals, and he was forbidden from going on the trip.

"The chairman asked 'Any objections?'

"Jim got up and shouted that there jolly well were! Only his adjective wasn't exactly 'Jolly'.

"'This isn't fair!' he cried. 'I didn't know that Jack ever used his old crock of a bike. It has been kicking about among the bushes for days. I don't mind shoving his pedals back, but I think the punishment unfair. I don't think I should be cut out of the trip'."

After a "Breezy discussion", it transpired that Jim had not received his allowance for six weeks, rendering him penniless and unable to maintain his bike. His sentence was quashed and his schoolmates had a whip-round - raising the money Jim needed to repair his bike!

In most instances, however, pupils accept their punishments with "Docility". They respect their peers' decisions.

As for the punishments themselves, they are designed to fit the crime...

When three girls disturbed their classmates' sleep, they were made to go to bed an hour early. When two boys were found guilty of throwing clods at other boys, they were made to cart clods up to the hockey field. When four boys climbed a builder's ladder, they were ordered to climb up and down it for ten minutes straight.

Can you imagine those pupils voting to expel me for having long hair? It seems unlikely. Teachers do not bully their pupils at Summerhill. Nor do many pupils bully each other:

"The reason is not hard to seek. Under adult discipline, the child becomes a hater. Since the child cannot express his hatred of adults with impunity, he takes it out on smaller or weaker boys. But this seldom happens in Summerhill".

***

The grades achieved by Summerhill pupils fall below the national average. This is hardly surprising when you consider that exams are voluntary and lessons do not stick to the strict parameters of the national curriculum.

Summerhill does not aim to churn out *well-qualified* students. It aims to produce *well-adjusted* adults; people who are comfortable in their own skin, and free from fear:

"I emphasise the importance of this absence of fear of adults. A child of nine will come and tell me he has broken a window with a ball. He tells me because he isn't afraid of arousing wrath or moral indignation. He may have to pay for the window, but he doesn't have to fear being lectured or being punished".

A pupil who does not fear their teachers is unlikely to fear their bosses or political leaders. They will be well placed to participate in a democracy:

"I think of Jack, who left us at the age of seventeen to go into an engineering factory. One day, the managing director sent for him.

"'You are the lad from Summerhill,' he said. 'I'm curious to know how such an education appears to you now that you are mixing with lads from the old schools. Suppose you had to choose again, would you go to Eton or Summerhill?'

"'Oh, Summerhill of course,' replied Jack.

"'But what does it offer that the other schools don't?'

"Jack scratched his head.

"'I dunno,' he said slowly. 'I think it gives you a feeling of complete self-confidence.'

"'Yes,' said the manager dryly. 'I noticed it when you came into the room.'

"'Lord,' laughed Jack. 'I'm sorry if I gave you that impression.'

"'I liked it,' said the director. 'Most men when I call them into the office fidget about and look uncomfortable. You came in as my equal'."

Jack went on to become a highly successful engineer. (Neill, 1960)

***

So why spend so much time summarising a book which is over half a century old?

The truth is that Summerhill has barely changed since Neill put pen to paper. There are now "Ombudsmen" - child representatives who try to solve conflicts *before* they need to be raised at school meetings. Summerhill has had to adjust to social trends. I very much doubt the new headmistress will smoke with her pupils. But the overall structure remains the same.

Summerhill has passed the sternest test: The test of time.

Indeed, Summerhill has not just survived. It has inspired other schools around the world. Some have failed. Others have flourished.

In the United States, it was the Sudbury Valley School that first copied the Summerhill model. It, in turn, gave birth to a movement...

THE SUDBURY SCHOOLS

Sudbury Valley School can be found inside a Nineteenth Century mansion, in a rural corner of Framingham, Massachusetts. To the casual observer, it might seem more like a home than a school. Blackboards hide behind overstuffed couches. Bookshelves line the walls of several rooms, negating the need for an official library. A playroom is just as prominent as the science lab. A photography studio rubs shoulders with an art room.

Sudbury Valley admits children of any age. The majority of pupils have struggled in mainstream education. Some are rebels, who have clashed with their teachers. Others have failed to keep pace with their peers.

Its staff are predominantly part-time. They have included several businessmen, an editor, historian, musician, psychologist and priest.

***

Like all democratic schools, Sudbury Valley holds school meetings, in which rules are proposed, debated and set.

Let's consider the example of a new student whose jacket displayed a swastika. A motion was proposed that this jacket be banned, and a heated debate ensued:

"There were all sorts of people taking part, mostly teenagers and staff, but every once in a while, a young kid would say something too. And those who weren't talking were listening, rapt, learning about history, about Nazism, about why wearing a swastika might be exceptional, why it might be different, say, than wearing a hammer and sickle".

The meeting voted to ban the jacket. And, in time, the assembly created a new rule which banned hate speech altogether.

We can imagine a similar debate at Summerhill.

But the assembly meetings at Sudbury Valley go much further than at Summerhill. At Sudbury Valley, pupils and teachers also discuss the school's finances, its public relations, and the hiring and firing of staff. (Chertoff, 2012)

Sudbury Valley also has an additional institution: "The Judicial Committee". This panel is made up of a cross-section of the school community, selected at random, and rotated each month. It considers complaints, makes judgements and issues punishments. Pupils found guilty do have the right to appeal the decision at a school meeting, but most cases do not make it that far. This frees the assembly to focus on other matters.

***

The biggest difference between Sudbury Valley and Summerhill concerns the nature of education itself. At Summerhill, there are standard classrooms, with a standard timetable and orthodox teaching methods. At Sudbury Valley, there are not...

At Sudbury Valley, students must take responsibility for their studies; deciding what they would like to learn, how they would like to learn it, and the standards they would like to achieve. No authority figure will judge them. They must measure their progress themselves. (Gray & Chanoff, 1986)

In general, pupils begin their education whilst playing with older children. They learn to read by playing games which require reading skills, and they improve their powers of deduction by playing card games. The older pupils also benefit from this process. They learn to nurture and care for the youngsters, which helps them to mature. (Chertoff, 2012)

Through play, pupils usually hit on a subject that interests them, and then focus on it intently. They may spend their time fixing a car, programming a computer, practising the piano, or reading the complete works of a particular author. There are painters who paint, writers who write, and chefs who cook.

One student discovered his passion for photography when he was aged thirteen. He helped to build a darkroom and then spent half his time inside, perfecting his craft. When he graduated, he became a professional photographer. (Gray & Chanoff, 1986)

A Sudbury Valley teacher, Daniel Greenberg, cites another example:

"Richard practised the trumpet for four hours every day. We could hardly believe it. We suggested other activities, but to no avail. Whatever Richard did, and he did a lot at school, he always found four hours to play.

"It was not long before we discovered the virtues of the old mill house by the pond. Built of granite, nestled in a distant corner of the campus, the old neglected building took on sudden beauty in our eyes. And in Richard's. In no time at all, it was turned into a music studio, where Richard could practice to his heart's content.

"He practised for four or more hours a day, for four years.

"Not long after graduating from school, after completing further studies at a conservatory, Richard became first horn of a major symphony orchestra".

***

Some lessons do take place, but there is a twist...

At most schools, the authorities decide what subjects will be taught, when they will be taught, and the content that will be studied. At Sudbury Valley, where classes do exist, they are arranged by the students.

If pupils are unable to teach themselves, they will search for a staff member or a student to help them. If no teacher can be found, arrangements will be made for an apprenticeship outside the school.

Greenberg gives the example of a group of pupils who asked him to teach them arithmetic.

"You don't really want to do this", he told them. "Your neighbourhood friends, your parents and your relatives probably want you to, but you yourselves would much rather be playing or doing something else".

But the pupils kept on pressing. And so, reluctantly, Greenberg succumbed.

He was in for a surprise.

After attending a one-hour class each week, for twenty weeks, his pupils had mastered addition, subtraction, multiplication, long division, fractions, decimals, percentages and square roots. Subject matter which would have taken six years to study in a regular school, took just twenty hours at Sudbury Valley.

Greenberg told his story to a fellow maths teacher who was not at all surprised:

"The subject matter itself isn't that hard. What's hard, virtually impossible, is beating it into the heads of youngsters who hate every step. The only way we have a ghost of a chance is to hammer away at the stuff bit-by-bit, every day, for many years. Even then it does not work. Most of the sixth graders are mathematical illiterates. Give me a kid who wants to learn the stuff... Well, twenty hours or so makes sense".

This highlights another benefit of the Sudbury Schools...

So far, we have focussed on the pupils. But this shows that democratising the classroom can benefit teachers too. If their students attend classes of their own freewill, because they genuinely want to learn, the chances are they will be a pleasure to teach. Their teachers will not have to waste their energy keeping unruly youngsters in line. They will be able to get on with doing the thing they love: Teaching.

***

This just leaves one final type of education: The seminar.

If a teacher at Sudbury Valley has something interesting and informative to say, they might decide to host a lecture series. Usually, a crowd will turn up to the first one, to see what all the fuss is about. A few will drop out by the time the second seminar takes place. Eventually, the teacher will be left with a small but eager band who are genuinely curious about the subject. (Greenberg, 1995)

Many students choose to stay away altogether...

In a 1986 study, sixty-nine of the seventy-six students to have graduated from the school were interviewed. Of those who had enrolled at the primary level, 29% said they had not attended a single course or tutorial. For those who had entered at the secondary level, that figure rose to 56%.

The school seems unconcerned...

They only have one requirement: Students must defend a "Graduation Thesis" at a school meeting before they leave. They must show that they are ready to live their lives and contribute to society.

The evidence suggests they are...

In the aforementioned survey, half of Sudbury's graduates went to university, and a quarter completed an alternative form of further education. This is no mean feat considering most of them had left Sudbury Valley without any formal qualifications. They often had to study at less reputable universities, before proving themselves and moving on up to the top-tier colleges. They had to take entrance exams and attend interviews.

But they were motivated. They studied because they wanted to study. No-one surveyed had gone to university because, "It is the expected thing to do", or "To please my parents". And, whilst they lagged behind at first, they found that Sudbury Valley had given them the skills they needed to succeed. They were used to independent study and well-placed to get the most out of the university's academics.

This is how one Sudbury Valley alumni put it:

"I would hang out in the economics department, just as I would hang out in the office at Sudbury Valley. I'd just hang out and talk with professors. I always felt I had as much right to be there as anyone else. Most of the students felt a tremendous gap between themselves and the professors.

They weren't used to relating to the 'Enemy' in that way. But I didn't have that kind of feeling".

***

The best way to judge Sudbury Valley, however, would be to take a look at how its pupils fared in *later life*...

Half the pupils who had been at Sudbury Valley since primary school went on to have careers in the arts. Of those who arrived at secondary school age, four became social workers. There was a nurse, physical therapist, chiropractor, funeral director, silversmith, personnel director, building manager, sales manager, store manager, accountant, sales representative, receptionist, records clerk, hostess, waiter, bartender, computer technician, historian, pattern maker, baker, restaurant owner, cruise boat captain, automobile mechanic, carpenter, foreign service officer, product engineer, surveyor and stage manager. There was an oboe player for an orchestra, a lead singer in a band, a director of a children's theatre, a president of a small software corporation, a director at a tourism bureau, two homemakers, one unemployed person and several students.

The graduates had launched respectable, mainstream careers, with a slight bias towards the arts and caring professions. In many cases, they had begun their training whilst still at school:

"The two mechanics, for example, spent much of their time at Sudbury working on cars. The professional pattern maker spent much of her time sewing and developing new patterns. She was making all of her own clothes by age sixteen. The baker did a large amount of cooking at SVS, and this led to a cooking apprenticeship at a restaurant. The cruise boat captain spent as much of her time as possible working at a seacoast area where she could study navigation and sailing". (Gray & Chanoff, 1986)

ILLUMINATIONS

So, what is the catch?

Both Sudbury Valley and Summerhill are fee-paying schools. It has been argued that their pupils would have been successful wherever they had studied. They had supportive parents, willing to pay thousands of dollars for their education, and a middle-class background that could have opened doors.

These schools are certainly not unique...

The "Democratic Schools Directory" lists thirty-five Sudbury Schools in the USA. The "European Democratic Education Community" estimates that there are just over a hundred democratic schools on the continent. There are said to be two-hundred democratic schools in Korea, although students have to follow a fixed curriculum at each one. (Sadofsky, 2014)

Yet democratic schools tend to have less than one-hundred pupils. They are beyond the reach of most youngsters. And, where they do exist, they are liable to be challenged by the authorities at any time. Summerhill was taken to a tribunal in 2000.

Expanding beyond this small footprint is likely to be a challenge.

***

Let's briefly consider the case of the Risinghill School in Islington, North London...

Risinghill was never a democratic school. But its charismatic head, Michael Duane, did eschew the corporal punishment of his day. Loved by his pupils, who flocked to meet him in the playground, his school became infamous for the way he handled a minor theft...

When a lady complained that two Risinghill students had stolen her groceries, and that she would go hungry if they were not replaced, Duane encouraged the culprits to confess to their crime. Trusting their beloved head, two twelve-year-olds came to his office and admitted guilt. They said they had eaten the edible items, and dumped the rest of the lady's shopping.

Duane made his charges an offer which they were happy to accept. The two boys borrowed some money from their headmaster, returned to the market, did the lady's shopping, and delivered it to her home. They spent the following weeks doing chores to repay their debt to Duane.

It taught them a valuable lesson which traditional discipline could not, but it enraged the public. In the months that followed, a slew of fabricated stories made the school out to be a disorderly hell. Even though its pupils loved the school, and developed into respectable adults, it was closed down just five years after it had opened. (Newnham, 2006)

This begs a question. If such a modest form of non-authoritarian headmastery could cause such a brouhaha, what chance does an actual democratic school have? It is one thing to have a small, private democratic school in the countryside. Establishing a large, state-funded democratic school in the heart of a major city, would be another matter entirely.

Still, at least one state-run democratic school does exist. To find out more, we must head over to Brazil...

***

Nestled at the foot of the Mantiqueira Mountains, with a giant lawn that serves as its main classroom, the Santo Antônio do Pinhal School was not the *first* Lumiar School, but it was the first to go *public*. This elementary school is owned by the city and fully-funded by the state. With one-hundred-and-seventy students, it is as large as many of its peers.

The *original* Lumiar School was established by Ricardo Semler, back in 2002. Semler, a visionary entrepreneur who we shall meet in the chapter on workplace democracy, realised that Brazilian schools were not teaching initiative. This was proving to be a major issue for a man who was trying to empower his workers.

And so Semler took matters into his own hands. He established a democratic school in the bustling heart of São Paulo.

The Lumiar brand has since expanded. At the time of writing, there were ten Lumiar Schools. They are similar to the other schools we have met, but they do have their own individual quirks...

There are no lessons, walled classrooms, homework, examinations, fixed timetables or traditional teachers in the Lumiar Schools. Students study in mixed-age groups, in open spaces. They choose the projects *they* want to study. And can opt-out at any time - choosing to study independently or play instead. Indeed, a typical visitor might arrive to find the children playing tag, making necklaces from coloured beads, dragging chairs, or shouting out loud to their hearts' content.

Lumiar Schools employ two types of staff...

The first, known as "Mentors" or "Tutors", monitor the youngsters' progress, support them, and help them to select projects. They impart "Love, wisdom and values". But they do not teach.

As Semler puts it, rather succinctly:

"(We tell them not to) teach, because the little you know compared to Google, *we don't want to know*".

The second type of staff, known as "Masters", visit the school on a part-time basis to share their passion and expertise - teaching things such as piano, painting and Japanese culture.

Such courses are based on the Confucian principle: "I hear and I forget, I see and I remember, I do and I learn".

Doing is key. Through doing the things a child likes, they learn *other* important skills...

A child who enjoys music will probably choose to play an instrument of their own free will. They will have to learn some literacy skills, to read the sheet music, and some numeracy skills, to keep time. If they like reggae, they may go on the internet to learn about Jamaica, protest songs and black culture.

A child who signs up to design and make a bicycle, will inadvertently learn that Pi is 3.14. You cannot design a wheel without such information.

Fractions can be taught by a chef, who shows her young protégés how to divide a pile of sugar into thirds. Youngsters can improve their handwriting by learning about the World Cup, and creating lists of their favourite players.

Beneath such projects, the Lumiar Schools *do* follow a syllabus, and it *is* aligned with Brazil's national curriculum. Perhaps this is why, unlike the other democratic schools, they have broken into the public sector. They teach the skills *their government wants to be taught*.

But they do so in their own, democratic way...

The Lumiar Schools take the Brazilian curriculum, which is normally taught in a fixed, linear fashion, and break it down into six-hundred "Tiles". Pupils learn the same core competencies, but they do so in the order that is right for them, at the speed that is right for them, whilst completing the projects which appeal to their tastes. Unlike in most schools, where the curriculum dictates when a skill is taught, and the order that topics must be covered, in the Lumiar Schools it is the pupils who control the narrative.

***

Like Summerhill and Sudbury Valley, the Lumiar Schools are also run along democratic lines. Each day begins with a "Morning Meeting", in which students decide how to allocate the school's space and resources. Student representatives can be elected onto "Working Committees". And a weekly school council, "The Circle", provides a democratic space to discuss new projects, amend the rules, and deal with disciplinary matters. Attended by staff, students and parents - it also gives the community a chance to celebrate pupils' achievements.

***

Back at the Santo Antônio do Pinhal School, the circle was becoming tiresome for the members of Class 13. Aged just four and five, its pupils struggled to sit still for a full hour. Their minds wandered. Their fingers began to tap.

They petitioned their teacher, who patiently explained that the circle was *their* forum. Without attending, decisions that affected them would be made in their absence.

But still the complaints continued.

An extraordinary meeting was called, and the pupils of Class 13 explained just how tired they were.

Then one child had a brainwave:

"Why don't we have *two* circles, each of which lasts half the time?"

The idea was put to the vote and the motion carried. That five-year-old's idea changed the whole dynamic of the school.

***

From their very first days, pupils at Santo Antônio do Pinhal are encouraged to pen "Agreements" - rules which are discussed and agreed upon collectively. They decide which toys can be used outside, and which ones should be kept in the building. They are asked where they think the cutlery should be put after they have finished their lunch.

Because they have had a stake in making these rules, they are far more likely to follow them. The power resides with the pupils, as Semler explains:

"(Students usually come) up with the very same rules that we had, except they're theirs. They have the power. They can and do suspend and expel kids. So we're not playing school. They really do decide".

***

I apologise if you feel I am repeating myself. I appreciate that this system is similar to those we have already met. But there is a key difference. Santo Antônio do Pinhal is a *state-run* institution. It deserves special attention for this reason alone.

So why is it allowed to exist?

As we have mentioned, the Lumiar Schools *do* teach the skills mandated by the mainstream curricula. They aim to achieve the goals the state has set.

Their success *can* be measured, even though they do not hold examinations. Students are assessed on an ongoing basis, through observation, interaction and conversation. The results are recorded in a "Learning Portfolio".

The results speak for themselves…

The Santo Antonio do Pinhal School is *the best performing state school in the municipality*. It is little wonder the state government is happy to fund it. It gets a clear return on its investment.

More schools may follow. Nine Brazilian cities have already asked Semler to help them democratise their schools. Others are considering the idea.

This is not to say it will be easy. As of 2014, Semler had been trying for ten years to get state schools to adopt his model.

"I've found, very interestingly enough, that nobody wants it for free", he laughs. "So maybe we'll start charging for it and *then* it will go somewhere!"

Who knows? Maybe it will. (Semler, 2014) (Lumiar, 2019) (Hampson, Patton & Shanks, 2013) (Downie, 2004)

GOING MAINSTREAM?

This chapter began by highlighting the authoritarian nature of modern schooling. It then spent several pages introducing an alternative. Schools which are clearly democratic, but which remain rather niche affairs.

There may be a middle ground. Schools which are less authoritarian than the norm, but which do not attempt to be full-scale democracies. Unlike Risinghill, some such schools have survived…

***

Readers may be familiar with the Michael Moore documentary, "Where to Invade Next".

When Moore visits Finland, he finds a laid-back system in which pupils only spend twenty hours at school each week:

"Finland's students have the shortest school days and the shortest school years in the entire Western World".

They are not asked to complete any homework. Instead, after school, they are expected to play, spend time with their families or read.

When a school needs a new playground, the builders consult the pupils. Seven-year-olds take the subway to get to school, without adult supervision. Pupils are allowed to leave class and go to the toilet without a hall pass. There are no school uniforms.

Does this non-authoritarian system work?

You bet it does! According to the Global Education Rankings, Finland has the best-educated youngsters on the planet. (Moore, 2015)

***

But pupils do not have to wait until they are old enough to attend school to benefit from a semi-democratic education...

In Germany, there are over one-thousand-five-hundred state-funded "Forest Kindergartens", where three to six-year-olds are allowed to run free, out of sight of adults (but not out of earshot); climbing trees and skidding across frozen ponds.

Discipline is maintained through the carrot, not the stick...

Youngsters might eat in silence, for example, not because they will be punished if they make a sound, but because they hope a bird or deer might approach if they are quiet.

This is no idle experiment. The children often learn more through play than they would inside a typical nursery school. Counting leaves can improve a youngster's numerical capabilities. Building shelters can improve their teamwork. One study even claimed that graduates of forest kindergartens performed, "Better in cognitive and physical ability, as well as in creativity and social development".. (Gregory, 2017)

***

Other democratic elements have popped-up in schools across the globe...

At the Matthew Moss High School, in a deprived area of Greater Manchester, new pupils design and carry out a "My World" project, studying whatever topic they choose. They also organise and manage school trips, using the school's budget to make purchases.

The results speak for themselves. A higher proportion of Matthew Moss's former pupils end up in work or education than at any other school in the area.

At over a hundred "Big Picture Schools", in five different countries, each student is asked to create an individual learning plan. Parents are encouraged to get involved - attending meetings and acting as mentors.

Once again, these methods get results. At the sixty-seven Big Picture

Schools in the USA, all of which are non-selective, the graduation rate stands at 92% - way above the national average of 66%.

Sweden's Kunskapsskolan Schools also allow pupils to plan their education. Youngsters write their own schedules, study the curriculum at their own pace, and choose where to work - in class, in an open learning space, or at home.

The Kunskapsskolan Schools consistently outperform other Swedish schools serving similar demographics.

Then we have the Colegio Cardenal de Cracovia in Santiago, which educates over nine-hundred students who have been expelled from mainstream schools. Whereas the likes of Summerhill and Sudbury Valley might be considered *direct democracies*, this Chilean institution is more of a *representative democracy*. Each age-group elects representatives to sit on bodies such as the "Department of Health" and the "Department for Education". They elect a school president, and the school's "Police Force" - a body that holds trials and disciplines pupils found guilty of misdemeanours. The school even has its own constitution, cabinet, currency and bank! (Hampson, Patton & Shanks, 2013)

***

Many of the ideas we met in the previous section could also be applied to education. One already has...

In 2017, almost four-thousand pupils from five American high schools gave participatory budgeting a go.

Each grade made fifty suggestions, which were passed on to "Budget Delegates" - representatives who took this great mass of ideas and whittled them down. The surviving proposals were presented to the school. Finally, the students were asked to vote on how a part of the school's budget would be spent - choosing between fitness equipment, audio-visual equipment, art supplies and a garden. (Hall, 2019)

***

It is not hard to imagine how direct democracy might be incorporated into the classroom. Literature students could propose and vote on the books their class will read. History students could elect an era to study. Sports students could be given the choice between playing football and ultimate frisbee.

Nor is this unheard of. The Reggio Emilia approach to education is based on the premise that pupils should be able to exert some sort of control over what they learn. My university's student union hosted a weekly event, "The Union General Meeting", at which anyone could propose and vote on motions. University students, up and down the land, get to elect the people who will run their student unions.

***

Finally, as a last resort, students and teachers can always stage a popular protest. Such actions have been successful before...

When two-hundred students at Manchester's Myles Platting School went on strike, in the spring of 1968, even they could not have predicted the movement they would inspire. Determined to defend themselves against the use of the tawse, a pronged leather strap which their teachers used to beat them, the student union they formed would go on to be replicated by pupils in Swansea, Bristol and Cardiff.

Later that year, those unions came together to form the "Schools Action Union" - a group with six democratising demands: That schools be controlled by students and staff. That pupils be given the right to free speech and assembly. That uniforms be abolished. That schools be coeducational. That teachers receive better pay. And of course, the thing that inspired them all: That corporal punishment be banned.

On May the 17th 1972, the movement peaked. Ten-thousand pupils, from up and down the land, went on strike. They marched through central London, bringing that city to a standstill, holding banners marked "No to the cane" and "Democracy in schools".

Those pupils were met by the full force of the law. The police dispersed the crowds, arrested several children, and sent the remainder home.

The Daily Mail chirped that "Parent Power" had beaten "Pupil Power".

Indeed, several of the strikers *were* expelled from school for "Truancy". They were harassed by the press and disciplined at home.

But their calls echoed down the corridors of history. In 1974, corporal punishment was banned in all inner-London primary schools. It was banned in all state schools in 1986, and in all private schools in 2003.

British teachers can no longer get away with assaulting their pupils. And it is in a large part thanks to the actions of those meddling kids. (Emerson, 2020)

***

This student protest was far from unique...

In 1973, pupils at Birmingham's King Edward's High School staged a strike to demand higher student grants. And in 1977, members of Wanstead High occupied a part of their school in response to cuts to the education budget. (Foster, 2006)

More recently, children at Canada's Kennedy High took action when two beloved teachers lost their jobs, allegedly for being homosexual. They hoisted a gay pride flag up the flagpole, staged a mass walkout, and held a sit-in. (Lothian-McLean, 2020)

***

Sometimes evolution is more effective than revolution. Making small changes to the system, based on the ideas outlined at the end of this chapter, might not turn our schools into genuine democracies, but it would make them *more* democratic. It would reduce the impact of the "Three Cs".

If that means that the next generation of students can get on with their studies, without having to worry about jumped-up headmasters expelling them because they have long hair, well, it can only be a good thing.

10. THE FOURTH ESTATE

To make rational decisions when we vote, we need good information. We need to understand our society, its issues, and the policies which are up for debate.

All too often, however, our perceptions fall far from the mark…

In a poll conducted by Ipsos MORI, British people, on average, believed that the UK spent 19% of its GDP on healthcare, when it only spent 9%. Brits thought that one-in-six people in their nation were Muslim. The real figure was just one-in-twenty.

The difference was even starker in other nations. Americans believed that 17% of their compatriots were Muslim. The real figure was just 1%.

Brits' perceptions were *more* accurate than in thirty-eight of the forty nations surveyed. Only the Dutch had a better grip on reality. (Kentish, 2016)

On average, people in these countries believed that their nations spent 21% of their GDP on healthcare, when they only spent 8%. They believed that just 49% of people owned their homes. The real figure was 68%. They believed that the poorest 70% of people in their nations owned 29% of the wealth. They only owned 15%.

These findings might not surprise you. We cannot know everything, after all. Our perceptions were closer to the mark on other topics.

What was more concerning was the survey's conclusion:

"We are often most incorrect on factors that are *widely discussed in the media*". (Ipsos MORI, 2016)

If this is correct, the conclusions are stark: The more the media cover a topic, the *worse* our understanding of it becomes. The media, intentionally or not, spreads *misinformation* that could impede our ability to make rational decisions at the ballot box.

***

These distortions can be massive…

In another YouGov survey, the average Brit thought that 41% of welfare payments were claimed by the unemployed. The real figure was just 3%. Respondents overestimated the size of those payments and the length of time that people claimed them. They believed that 27% of welfare payments were claimed fraudulently, when the actual figure was just 0.7% - the equivalent of about £1.3b a year. (Jones, 2014)

Let's put this in context...

Brits *failed to claim* £13b of welfare payments - an amount *ten times greater* than the amount that was claimed fraudulently. Big businesses dodged at least £34b in tax - *over twenty-six times* the amount that was claimed fraudulently by welfare recipients. (Ryan, 2016)

***

It is easy to find the source of these misconceptions. We just need to look at the front-pages of some of Britain's most popular papers...

"Help Us Stop £1.5b Benefits Scroungers", screamed The Sun ahead of the 2010 General Election. "End the Something for Nothing Culture", yelled the Sunday Times.

The Sunday Express has led with "Mansions for Scroungers", "Scroungers on £85,000 a Year (in) Benefits", and "4M Scrounging Families in Britain". One front-page headline read, "Migrants Pay Just One Pound a Week in Tax". Several others have railed against Muslims and Gypsies.

I could not find a single edition of The Sunday Express whose front-page headline lambasted big firms for evading or avoiding tax.

With such headlines fuelling misconceptions, our very democracy can come under threat. People are more likely to vote for the parties which offer to tackle the relatively small issue of benefit fraud, than the parties which pledge to tackle the far larger issue of tax dodging. The first issue is drilled home via daily headlines. It incites our passions. The second issue, which receives very little coverage, barely registers. (Jones, 2014)

But how has it come to this?

CHOMSKY V MARR

In a classic TV interview, Andrew Marr attempts to grill Noam Chomsky...

Marr, that Glaswegian stalwart of the BBC, cuts an almost aggressive figure. His torso juts back and forth, jaggedly, hurriedly, whilst the corner of his mouth rises up the side of his cheek:

"How can you know that I'm self-censoring? How can you know that journalists are?"

Chomsky, wearing a cheap blue shirt, answers Marr with grandfatherly calm:

"I'm not saying you're self-censoring. I'm sure you believe everything you're saying. But what I'm saying is that if you believed something different, you wouldn't be sitting where you're sitting".

***

Most journalists do not set out to misinform the public. Marr himself believes journalism to be "A crusading craft" - a force for good.

But if a journalist was to regularly challenge her bosses, do you think she would keep her job? If her views did not tally with her employer's, do you think she would even be hired in the first place?

Chomsky argues they will not:

"There's a filtering system that starts in kindergarten and goes all the way through. It's not going to work 100%, but it's pretty effective. It selects for obedience and subordination, and especially I think..."

Marr interjects:

"So stroppy people won't make it to positions of influence?"

Chomsky maintains his cool:

"There'll be behavioural problems. If you read applications to a graduate school, you'll see that people will tell you, 'He doesn't get along too well with his colleagues.' You know how to interpret those things". (Marr & Chomsky, 1996)

***

There are, of course, a few exceptions to the rule - people who get through, even though they are not the "Right type".

They tend not to last for long...

A working-class lad, Richard Peppiatt got his big break when he was recruited by the Daily Star. But he was forced to leave his principles at the door; told to write bogus articles which scapegoated Muslims and asylum seekers for society's ills.

"If you don't write it, you get a bollocking", he later mused.

On one occasion, Peppiatt was told to camp outside the temporary residence of a family who had fled the Somali civil war:

"I remember going into the offices the next day, after no-one had come out of the house. The news editor called me over, opened a copy of The Sun, and went: 'Look, they've got a quote off the father of the refugees saying, 'I don't care, I'll take what I can get'.'

"I said: 'But he didn't even leave the house! He never said that!'

"The editor replied: 'That's not the point. You've got to be more canny'!"

***

The lies and deception took their toll:

"I felt I'd sold myself down the river. I hated what I was doing".

Peppiatt took to drink and, after consuming three-quarters of a bottle of Jack Daniels, he wrote an open letter to Richard Desmond, the billionaire media-mogul who owned the Daily Star.

Peppiatt knew he would lose his job. But he could not have predicted the barrage of abuse that was to follow. He received over one-hundred aggressive texts and calls a day. A man masturbated down the phone. A text message read: "You're a marked man until you die, we're going to get you, I'm outside your house now".

Peppiatt fell into a pit of despair and fear. He kept a baseball bat by the door, and could do nothing to stop his girlfriend from moving out. (Jones, 2014)

***

If, unlike Peppiatt, a journalist actually wants to keep their job in the mainstream media, they must toe the company line, as Anthony Bevins explains:

"(Having worked at) The Sun and the Daily Mail, I count myself as something of an expert on the insidious nature of the process. To survive and rise in or on the 'Game', you pander to the political prejudice of your paymasters, giving them the stories that you know will make *them* salivate". (Williams, 2019)

Those journalists who do last, and make it to the very top, are not necessarily the best journalists. They are the ones who fit the mould, whose views align with their bosses and their bosses' bosses - the billionaire barons who own the press…

THE BILLIONAIRE BARONS

So who, exactly, are these media moguls?

First and foremost, they are Rupert Murdoch and Jonathan

Harmsworth. Both are well-known known tax dodgers...

Murdoch's News Corp did not pay the British state a single penny in corporation tax between 1988 and 1999, despite earning £1.4b in profits. Harmsworth has based his holding company in Bermuda, in order to dodge corporation tax, and is non-domiciled in France, in order to dodge income tax.

Together with the Lebedevs, Richard Desmond and the Barclay Brothers, these billionaires control around three-quarters of Britain's press.

They also control the narrative...

Sir Harold Evans, the former editor of Murdoch's Sunday Times, has spoken of how he was often rebuked for "Not doing what he (Murdoch) wants in political terms", and how the two almost came to "Fisticuffs" when he printed an article by the economist James Tobin.

David Yellen, the former editor of The Sun, has admitted that "Most Murdoch editors wake up in the morning, switch on the radio, hear something that has happened and think, 'What would Rupert think about this?' You look at the world through Rupert's eyes". (London, 2013) (Bastani, 2019)

***

So, Britain's main newspapers are all owned by billionaires. These men tend to dodge tax. They tend to get their editors to print the stories *they* want to be published. They seldom punch *upwards*, at the rich and the powerful - the tax cheats, polluters, rogue landlords and dodgy bosses. It is not in their interest to expose people like themselves. Rather, they punch *downwards*; creating divisions within the democratic mass, by singling out immigrants, the unemployed, Muslims, Gypsies, trade unionists and striking workers.

The billionaire barons are motivated by money. They want to receive as much filthy lucre as they can. If they can benefit from some loopholes in the law, to save on tax, they are not going to promote the fact. They are going to run other stories, and demonise other people, to distract the populace.

This can affect the political arena too...

If a politician vows to keep the tax loopholes, the billionaire barons are likely to support and promote that politician in their publications. But if a politician promises to close the loopholes, break up their media empires, offer their workers shares in their newspapers, a place on the board and the right to unionise - well, all hell is likely to break loose. The billionaire barons are going to print article after article demonising that politician.

This is what happened in 2015, when Jeremy Corbyn - a scruffy, allotment-digging, jam-making, vegan teetotaller - became the leader of the British Labour Party. Corbyn wanted to *reverse* the cuts to welfare. He wanted to go after the tax cheats, dodgy bosses and billionaire barons.

The press was having none of it...

Academics at the London School of Economics studied eight major newspapers during the first three months of Corbyn's premiership. They found that well over half the articles concerning Corbyn were negative, including 25% which were "Antagonistic". Corbyn's views were absent in 52% of these articles, taken out of context in 22%, challenged in 15%, and only respected in 11%. Corbyn was subject to "Ridicule and Scorn" 30% of the time, and suffered "Personal Attacks" in 13% of articles.

The report concluded that:

"UK journalism played an *attack-dog* rather than a *watchdog* role. This is unhealthy from a democratic point of view and poses serious ethical questions as to the role of the media in a democracy, especially when it concerns the legitimate contestation of the government of the day". (Cammaerts, DeCillia, Magalhães, Jimenez-Martínez & César, 2016)

In the years that followed, Corbyn was mocked for sitting on the floor of a train, and for not bowing deeply enough at a remembrance service. He was called a Czech spy, anti-Semite, pacifist, terrorist sympathiser, communist and the Kremlin's stooge.

***

I appreciate this is a little partisan. Perhaps you believe Corbyn deserved all the negative press he received. Even so, it must seem slightly odd to see journalists putting so much more effort into attacking the opposition than the government itself.

It is significant because the written press can dictate the agenda for the rest of the media. Television and radio news bulletins quote the daily papers. They may lead with an in-depth "Newspaper Review", or feature a journalist who works for one of the billionaire barons.

Even when journalists do report the news objectively, they can swing perceptions through *intensity and absence*...

A terrorist attack at home is likely to be reported *intensely* for several days. Attacks on foreign soil, performed by our government's own soldiers, are often completely *absent*, even when they result in many more deaths.

Indeed, one study found that the American press gives at least one-hundred-and-thirty-seven times more coverage to the murder of what it considers "Worthy victims" in client states, than to the murders of similar figures in unfriendly nations.

Rather more subtle is the *pro-business bias* which can dominate the news. Trade unionists, representing millions of workers, are usually given less airtime than businesspeople, who only represent a handful of shareholders. Newsreaders report on share-price fluctuations several times a day, but tend not to have daily segments dedicated to changes in wages or workers' rights.

It is not hard to see why. News outlets rely on the advertising revenues they receive from businesses to stay afloat. They dare not bite the hand that feeds them...

Up until the mid-1960s, there were three left-wing papers in Great Britain: The Daily Herald, News Chronicle and Sunday Citizen. Between them, they had an average daily readership of nine-point-three-million. Surveys showed that Daily Herald readers, "Thought more highly of their paper than the regular readers of any other popular newspaper". But their readers were not big spenders, and their editorials could be critical of business. So firms did not advertise with those papers, they struggled to compete, and they ultimately ceased production. Today's papers have taken note. They know they must have a pro-business bias in order to secure the advertising revenues they need to survive. (Chomsky & Herman, 1988)

Governments can influence news outlets in a similar manner...

If they were to spend millions of dollars a year to air army recruitment ads, which brand soldiers as "Brave" and "Heroic", it is unlikely that those same stations would run reports calling soldiers "Cowardly" or "Murderous".

Governments may also try to influence the media *directly*...

We might expect this in authoritarian countries, but it also happens in democratic nations. At its peak, the CIA's "Operation Mockingbird" had influence over twenty-five American media organisations, including CBS, Time Magazine and the New York Times. By the 1950s, three-thousand CIA employees and sub-contractors were engaged in "Propaganda efforts" in the so-called "Land of the free". (Simkin, 1997)

Things are even worse elsewhere...

The 2020 "World Press Freedom Index" ranks the American press as the forty-fifth most free on the planet, dubbing it "Fairly good". Ranked below the States, the report considers press freedom to be either "Problematic", "Bad" or "Very bad" in one-hundred-and-thirty-three nations. (Deloire, 2020)

A STAR IS BORN...

There is good news. A democratic media *does* exist. It has done for many years.

And there is also bad news. The democratic media is frail, corruptible, and a tiny fish in a gargantuan ocean.

Still, giant oaks grow from humble acorns. Perhaps what little democracy we have may one day blossom, creating a media which serves the billions, not the billionaires.

For now, we will have to settle for the likes of Britain's "Morning Star", with its circulation of just over ten-thousand copies a day...

***

It was the "Enemy Within", or so its opponents would have you believe. The Morning Star was the propaganda wing of the Communist Party of Great Britain. When the paper fell on hard times, in the 1960s, it was Soviet Russia who came to the rescue, buying twelve-thousand copies a day, and providing the £3,000 a month the paper needed to keep its presses turning.

That was then.

When Mikhail Gorbachev rose to power, and the Morning Star's funding was cut, the paper faced an existential crisis. Unable to survive on its own meagre revenues, it found itself staring down the financial precipice.

There was only one way out. The paper looked to its readers for help. It became a cooperative, owned by its customers and workers, and run in their interests by the "People's Press".

Today, the People's Press is overseen by a committee that includes representatives from nine trade unions, which represent thousands of workers. But the paper's overriding strategy is set by its shareholders.

Anyone can become a shareholder in The Morning Star, by paying as little as a pound to own their small slice of the media pie. As shareholders, they can attend annual general meetings, in several locations across the nation. They can propose policies and vote on proposals. Like any true democracy, decisions are made on a "One person, one vote" basis. Owning thousands of shares does not give you thousands of votes. People who have been members for several years hold no more sway than a teenager who has just bought their first share.

***

These days, the Morning Star is edited by Ben Chacko - a long-haired Oxford graduate, who seems more comfortable in jeans than a suit and tie. If you were to pass him in the street, you might mistake him for a social worker. He does not look like your average media chief.

At the paper's headquarters, the air-conditioning unit, which once started an office fire, has still not been replaced. Sweat leaves its mark on the paper's thirty writers.

Red stars are embossed on the mirrors in the bathroom. A bronze relief of the paper's first editor, William Rust, can be found by the stairs.

Chacko calls his first AGM, "A baptism of fire... It was very clear that people were prepared to make a lot of sacrifices because the paper plays such an important role in their lives".

Those voices have certainly left their mark...

The paper may be the most left-wing daily in Britain, but it is no longer the communist propaganda rag of days-gone-by. It has been steered from the bottom-up, by its shareholder-readers, who come from a wide range of backgrounds.

"We have articles from people that at one time we would never have given the time of day to", says John Haylett, the paper's former editor. "(People) like the Welsh and Scottish Nationalists, the Greens and church people". (Platt, 2015) (Press, 2011)

***

The Morning Star is not alone. "Worker Cooperatives", in which employees run the show, flit around the fringes of our media...

Mexico's "Excelsior" was run as a workers' cooperative between 1917 and 2004. France's "Le Monde" operated as a workers' cooperative between 1944 and 2010. The New Internationalist Magazine, formed in 1973, is still going strong today. Owned and run by a trust, workers become trustees after they have completed a three-year probationary period.

Then we have the "Consumer Cooperatives", in which *customers* vote on policies, elect the board, hold them accountable, and receive a share of the profits...

The Cooperative Press was founded in 1871. Run by the Cooperative Group, with its eight-million shareholders, it still runs the "Cooperative News" today. The Bristol Evening Post also began life as a consumer cooperative, before falling into private hands.

Finally, we have "Multi-stakeholder Cooperatives", in which workers *and* consumers unite...

Ethical Consumer Magazine, founded in 1987, fits into this category. Established as a worker cooperative, it issued shares to its readers in 2009. Some of those customers sit on the magazine's board. (Boyle, 2012)

***

What we have here can be best described as a "Mixed Bag". Several publications have given democracy a go. A few are still going strong. They are often beloved by their readers. But they are small fry, with low readerships, who struggle to pierce the national consciousness.

The challenges are numerous...

The Morning Star must make £1.5m a year just to keep afloat. It cannot do this by selling papers alone, so must rely upon trade unions and customers to make sizeable donations.

Unlike the billionaire press, the Morning Star struggles to sell advertising space.

"The rich don't like us", Chacko explains. "They don't advertise with us".

And the problems do not stop here:

"We also have a problem with distribution because, even if we get there, the big sellers like WH Smith send the unsold papers back... We have no advertising budget... We distribute with a consortium of small-size publications, so we are subject to delays and holdups in a hostile sales environment". (Platt, 2015) (Press, 2011)

***

So, is there any reason to be optimistic?

Left to their own devices, media cooperatives struggle to compete in a market dominated by the billionaire press. But it does not have to be like this. We, the people, could always give them a helping hand...

Many nations already have a state-run media. Qatar has Al Jazeera. Germany has the ARD. There is France Télévisions, Radio New Zealand and the Canadian Broadcasting Corporation. The list goes on.

These organisations tend to be run from the top-down, by a nation's government. In Britain, for example, the BBC is controlled by the BBC Trust, which appoints a "Director-General". This individual works with "Audience Councils" to scrutinise the broadcaster's output.

But we could always turn this system on its head; selecting audience councils at random, in much the same way that we select juries, and asking these councils to select the trustees. We could implement a sort of representative democracy - giving every licence-fee payer the right to elect those trustees. We could even give direct democracy a go - allowing viewers to vote on how to divide the BBC's budget, on which programs to scrap and which ones to commissions, on maximum pay for star performers and minimum pay for the most junior of staff.

Indeed, it would be within the BBC's remit to do this. Their charter compels them to "Sustaining citizenship through the enrichment of the public realm". The cost would be minimal. Turning nationalised media outlets into cooperatives should not be a difficult thing to do. The effects for democracy, however, could be huge. (Boyle, 2012)

***

So much for the public sector. What about those billionaire barons?

In theory, readers and workers could unite to buy them out. In reality, this seems a tall ask. The papers' owners would be under no obligation to sell. It would require millions of readers and hundreds-of-millions of pounds to purchase a single publication.

We could ask the state to step in. But this could be deemed a little authoritarian.

Yet governments do *regulate* the media...

In the United States, that bastion of liberal free-markets, laws once mandated broadcasters to serve the *public interest*, not just their owners' *private interests*. The "Fairness Doctrine" required stations to "Present fair and balanced coverage of controversial issues", devoting equal airtime to opposing points of view. That legislation proved robust, seeing off challenges in the Supreme Court. But it fell out of favour during Reagan's laissez-faire regime, paving the way for today's partisan press. (Stefon, 2018)

The state can also intervene to prevent individuals from controlling large swathes of the media. The European Commission, for example, has a responsibility to ensure "Mergers in the media sector do not significantly impede competition". Their effectiveness could be questioned. But governments would have the power, in theory, to break up media empires, should the political will exist.

Such intervention may not be necessary...

Newspaper readership is falling. In 1983, over sixty-three-million papers were sold each day in the States. By 2018, that figure had fallen below twenty-nine-million. Between 2003 and 2016, German newspaper sales fell from twenty-two-million to sixteen-million a day. Across the twenty-eight European Union nations, penetration rates fell from 37% in 2012 to just 29% in 2016. (Barthel, 2019) (Fuller, 2019)

Of course, many readers have simply moved online - consuming those very same papers in their digital format. But the online landscape remains an entirely different beast. With low barriers to entry, almost anyone can publish articles on the web. It should, in theory, be a far more democratic place...

DON'T HATE THE MEDIA, BE THE MEDIA

The year was 1999. The air was filled with tear gas and rubber bullets.

People seemed to be materialising out of thin air, rising up through the pavements and walking out through the walls.

Outnumbered, the police panicked. They went "Full Robocop". Dressed in riot-gear, dark and mechanistic, they filled the streets of Seattle.

But the kids were unfazed. They formed a human-chain around the Seattle Convention Centre, brought the city to a standstill, and barred entry to the World Trade Organisation's conference.

World leaders, trade ministers and corporate executives had travelled the globe to take part in those antidemocratic meetings, which threatened workers' rights, the environment and indigenous peoples. The WTO was planning to impose food-safety standards on every nation on the planet, impose patents that would limit farmers' access to seeds, and make it illegal for farmers to save seeds. Its meetings were held in secret, away from the prying eyes of public scrutiny. Its decisions would be thrust on independent nations without their consent.

But the people were having none of it. With tear gas wafting up their nostrils, and rubber bullets rebounding off their torsos; they stood strong and they stood tall.

No Pasaran! They shall not pass!

The WTO's conference was cancelled, its plans for expansion were defeated, and its globalist vision never became a reality.

The undemocratic WTO was stopped by a democratic movement, as Michael Moore explained:

"This wasn't organised by any leader. It wasn't organised by any group. All right? It was organised by Monsanto. It was organised by Exxon and General Motors and Microsoft and all the other greedy bastards who have spent the last two decades trying to make as much money as they can at the expense of everybody here".

The movement was led by its members. Its victory was a victory for democracy. (Shiva & Wallach, 2019)

But why mention it now, when discussing the press?

The answer is simple. Those protests gave birth to a new form of democratic media: The "Indymedia"...

***

Amidst this civil war - insulated by chanting, engulfed by smoke - a central hub was going about its daily business. This was the "Independent Media Centre"; home to hundreds of chunky white computers, and hundreds of *volunteer* reporters, who were documenting events from within the heart of the battlefield.

They were sure of one thing. The revolution would not be televised, *by the corporate media*. The participants would have to broadcast live themselves.

When CNN claimed that no rubber bullets had been fired, the Indymedia released pictures of people holding up bullets for the world to see. Their website, Indymedia.Org, got one-and-a-half-million views - more than CNN itself. They released a daily paper, "The Blind Spot", and daily video reports.

Of course, the Independent Media Centre came under attack. Those

Robocop police, in their fork-tongued gas masks, called it a "Crime Scene", took a hose and smoked the place out.

But the citizen-journalists regrouped and marched ahead undaunted.

Theirs was one of the first ever "Open Publishing Platforms". Never before had independent journalists been able to upload content to a website without going through an editor. It was unprecedented. And it was just the start.

Anyone who arrived at the centre, looking to help, received basic media training. They returned home with all the skills they needed to set up media centres *of their own*... (Goodman & González, 2019)

***

Around one-hundred-and-seventy-five Indymedia sites popped up across the globe. Many of them were supported by Independent Media Centres of their own. Occasionally, they went to print. Brooklyn's "Indypendent Paper", a "Free paper for free people", still distributes thirty-thousand copies of each edition.

Most Indymedia sites, however, remained somewhat niche. They took a radical, anti-capitalist and anti-globalist line, which failed to engage the masses. But they did remain democratic... (Scherer, 2014)

They were supported by an army of hackers and coders, committed to "Open Source Software" - programs that could be used by anyone with an internet connection, wherever they might be. They used their own secure servers, rather than rely on servers which were controlled by corporations.

Operating on a shoestring budget, doing battle with armies of trolls, these pioneers kept the show on the road. In an era before social media and blogging, they paved the way for the internet revolution that was to follow.

Using pseudonyms, participants were able to speak freely - making un-moderated, anonymous posts - discussing contentious topics without fearing reprisals. Meetings were open to all. They reached out to marginalised peoples, such as the Aborigines, to give them the voice they had often been denied.

And so, they spread - to Atlanta and Austin, Argentina and Armenia, Andorra and Austria - on the internet, the radio and in print.

And then they began to contract... (Goodman & González, 2019) (Giraud, 2014)

***

The Independent Media Centres were never going to be in for an easy ride. The police attacks which began in Seattle, in a cloud of tear gas and smoke, continued unabated. Volunteer journalists and coders were arrested, imprisoned, maimed and even killed. Web servers were seized. Corporations filed lawsuits against the independent media and lobbied to have them banned.

They succeeded, forcing several Independent Media Centres to close their doors for good. (Anonymous, 2019)

There were internal problems too...

Maintaining a hub of talented individuals was always going to be a challenge, especially when the movement never really expanded beyond its radical roots. Contributors got weighed down in lengthy debates.

Today, only a few dozen Independent Media Centres remain active.

Yet all is not lost. Other civilian journalists *do* still have a voice. Some of them have been active for decades... (Giraud, 2014)

SOCIETY'S MEDIA

The people-powered "Citizen Media" was alive and kicking long before the internet revolution. Self-published zines, reprinted on busy photocopiers, burping and beeping, had been churning out faded pages for years. Whether it was a science-fiction magazine with its roots in the 1940s, an indie publication formed to publicize the punk-rock movement of the 1970s, or a sports club's supporter-written fanzine; these publications were made by the people, for the people. Like the Indymedia, however, they remained niche affairs. Most editions sold under a thousand copies.

Pirate radio reached a slightly wider audience...

In its heyday, back in the swinging Sixties, groovy DJs would sail out into the ocean blue, beyond the reach of the authorities, and broadcast whatever they wanted to play, whenever they wanted to play it.

The movement is not entirely dead...

In 2010, opponents of Fiji's military dictator began broadcasting from a Dutch-registered merchant vessel moored in international waters. The "Fiji Democracy Movement" defied the censor-friendly regime; pumping out "Facts" not "Propaganda", determined to give the Fijian population the information it deserved. (Maynard, 2010)

Community radio, meanwhile, continues to pull its punches in hospitals, student unions and community centres across the globe.

Then we have television...

In Canada, "Community TV" was, for a while, a great bastion of the citizen media. Produced to the highest standards, with the help of the professionals, local volunteers were given the means to make the programs their communities demanded. The big cable networks had little choice in the matter. The law *compelled* them to provide fully funded "Community Channels". In the Seventies, these networks were required to dedicate 10% of their revenues to their community stations. But that figure has fallen dramatically in recent years - to 5% in 1991, 2% in 1997, and to just 0.5% in 2016. (Gray-Donald, 2017)

The USA has travelled a similar path...

Not so long ago, American cable firms had to apply for licences within each state. Savvy politicians, with their electorate's interests at heart, often demanded that they give something back. They might be required to dedicate a channel to governmental meetings, to produce educational programming for schools, or to provide those good old community channels.

"Public Access Television" has trained thousands of citizen journalists. Even today, you could be flicking through the channels when there, on your screen, is your very own hairdresser, telling you about the toxins in your household products.

Alas, as in Canada, the heyday for public access television appears to be behind us. The corporations, led by AT&T, have gone from state-to-state, lobbying for business-friendly legislation that has freed them from their obligations to their communities. Public access television does still exist, but it is a shadow of its former self. (Rosenberg, 2010)

***

Perhaps the biggest opportunity, and the biggest challenge for citizen journalists, has come from Indymedia's offspring, "Web 2.0". This is the version of the internet that allows anyone to upload content - through social media sites, blogs, personal websites and video-sharing platforms.

Web 2.0 gives the power to the people. We no longer have to rely on the billionaire-owned press for news. We can report on it ourselves. We can discuss it on our YouTube channels and blog about it on our WordPress sites, before sharing our content on Facebook and Twitter.

Web 2.0 has spread with unprecedented speed. As of October 2019, Facebook had almost two-and-a-half billion users. YouTube had two-billion. Twitter looked like the poor relation, with its mere three-hundred-and-thirty-million accounts! (Clement, 2019)

Ahead of the 2017 UK election, the most popular article on Facebook, which was shared over one-hundred-thousand times, was written by Thomas Clark. Going by the moniker, "Another Angry Voice", Clark is a one-man show, "An independent blogger from Yorkshire... (with) no funding from corporations or political parties", who relies on "Pay as you feel" donations from his readers.

Clark wrote four of the twenty-five most shared articles ahead of that election. Other independent news outlets, The Canary and Evolve Politics, also made it into the top twenty-five.

It would be wrong to suggest that blogs such as these, written by the people, for the people, were stealing the show. During that election campaign, eighteen of the twenty-five most-shared articles came from the traditional press. The ten articles which received the most engagements on Facebook across the whole of 2017, regardless of their topic, *all* came from the mainstream media.

Anyone can open a Facebook account, free of charge, and use it to promote their blogs and videos. But reaching an audience remains a challenge. Half the stories posted on Facebook, in 2017, only received 0.03% of engagements. (Tackley & McAlister, 2018)

***

Perhaps we are missing the point. Citizen journalists do not have to dominate the media. They just need to be heard - to add independent voices into the media mix, inspire democratic thought, and influence the way people vote.

Bloggers like Another Angry Voice came to the fore when it mattered: At election time. We have already seen how social media powered the 15M movement, which led to the creation of Podemos, and how it rallied support for the Bentley Blockade.

Social media has also been credited with inspiring the Arab Spring...

***

It all began in Iran, where protestors were challenging the results of the 2009 election. Whilst returning to her Peugeot 206, a twenty-six-year-old tour guide, Neda Agha-Soltan, was shot dead by the police.

As tragic as it was, Neda's murder may not have proved significant if it had not been for the fact that two witnesses just happened to be filming.

One sent his video to a friend, who forwarded it to the Voice of America and The Guardian. The story made it into the mainstream press.

He also forwarded that video to a friend in the Netherlands, who posted it on Facebook. The video was copied to YouTube, as was the video which had been filmed by the second man.

With the power of social media behind her, Neda Agha-Soltan had been transformed. No longer an anonymous victim, she had become the face of a movement.

Hundreds of amateur videos were uploaded onto YouTube in the following days. Neda's name began to trend on Twitter. This revolution *would* be televised.

The Iranian state hit back - closing a part of the internet. But people found a way to get online. Their protests continued unabated. (Stelter & Stone, 2009)

They inspired the people of Tunisia...

In December 2010, Mohamed Bouazizi protested against police corruption by setting himself on fire. It would be wrong to suggest that social media alone turned this act into a mass movement. It was an emotional trigger. The people of Tunisia had long-standing grievances - they were sick of dictatorial rule, human rights abuses, poverty and unemployment. And they felt a sense of impunity. But the people did *unite* on social media, before taking to the streets, bringing down their President and overthrowing his regime. (Wolfsfeld, Segev & Sheafer, 2013)

They inspired similar protests across the Arab world.

When Facebook users were questioned, in both Egypt and Tunisia, 80% said that the platform was primarily being used to organise protests, raise awareness of domestic politics, and share news with the world. Only a small minority saw it as a platform for entertainment.

Indeed, over 88% of Facebook users said that they were receiving news of the civil unrest via social media - a much higher penetration rate than that achieved by the traditional press. (Salem & Mourtada, 2011)

Protesters used social media to organise both pro-government and anti-government demonstrations. They used sites such as Facebook and

Twitter to share images, stories and videos. They considered it a powerful, speedy and cheap tool for recruitment, fundraising, discussion and mobilisation. (Salem & Mourtada, 2011) (Wolfsfeld, Segev & Sheafer, 2013)

***

So social media can be used to spread the news, allowing users to share stories which have been written by people like them, as well as stories which have been written by the billionaire press. It can inspire mass movements which change the world, and spread information that can help us to make informed decisions when we vote.

A poll conducted by Pew Research, in 2018, found that 67% of Americans considered social media an important tool for "Creating sustained movements for social change".

But is it really the answer we are looking for?

We should proceed with caution...

Movements that spring up overnight, on social media, are likely to lack the durable, far-reaching foundations required to sustain them through good times and bad. This can leave them vulnerable when the authorities fight back. (Stephan & Gallagher, 2019)

When the revolt in Iran collapsed, the Iranian police followed the trails activists had left online - using their posts on social media to make thousands of arrests. It even crowd-sourced its witch-hunt - posting images of protestors online, and calling on snitches to report their neighbours. (Shanejan, 2011)

In Egypt, the authorities arrested three citizen journalists and closed Facebook's "Free Basics" - a service which had attracted three-million users in two months.

Turkey, meanwhile, continues to demand that Twitter removes any tweets of which it disapproves. (Hempel, 2016)

This phenomenon is by no means limited to the Arab world. Cyber-surfing police can use the net to research citizens' political views, habits and friends in any nation. They can also employ fake activists to steer public opinion...

In China, the authorities employ thousands of trained "Commentators", known as the "Fifty Cent Party", to make pro-government posts. In Russia, social media sites give pride of place to pro-Putin stories. During the 2019 EU elections, 6% of tweets came from bots - fake accounts, run by computers rather than humans. (Shanejan, 2011) (Chandler, 2019)

This phenomenon is known as "Astroturfing"...

Astroturfing is where government and corporate agents pretend to be grassroots activists, and establish *fake* movements on social media - publishing blogs, starting Facebook and Twitter accounts, writing "Letters to the editor", and posting comments in online forums.

Astroturfing is designed to confuse - to chuck so much conflicting information into the mix that you throw your hands up and give in. It can give the false impression that there is widespread support for an agenda where there is not. It can make you feel like a black sheep, even when your views are widespread.

Wikipedia has become fertile ground for astroturfing. It should be the people's encyclopaedia - a site on which anyone can add or edit pages. But the reality is a little different...

When investigators looked into the medical conditions described on Wikipedia, and checked those articles against peer-reviewed academic studies, it found that Wikipedia contradicted the medical research 90% of the time. Wikipedia had been co-opted by the pharmaceutical industry. The scientific community had been locked out. (Attkisson, 2015)

Furthermore, just because social media sites have been a boon for the democratic media in the past, does not mean they will continue to be so in the future. Unlike the Indymedia, these platforms are not owned and run by the people. Facebook's main shareholders include Mark Zuckerberg, whose net-worth was estimated to be $72.3b in November 2019; Eduardo Saverin ($11.1b), Dustin Moskovitz ($12.2b) and Sheryl Sandberg ($1.8b). These people have more in common with the billionaire barons than they do with you or I. (Maverick, 2019)

In January 2018, Facebook changed its algorithm, declaring "That friends and family (should) come first" - thereby relegating news stories beneath a sea of baby pictures and status updates.

The effects have been stark...

The aforementioned Thomas Clark, of "Another Angry Voice", says "I used to get ten to fifty-thousand hits on Facebook, and up to a million on viral articles during election time... Since Facebook altered the algorithm, below ten-thousand is the absolute norm, and the idea of going anywhere near a hundred-thousand, let alone a million, is a fantasy". (Dracott, 2011)

With a few minor adjustments to Facebook's code, the democratic media had the carpet pulled out from under its feet.

It is not hard to see why. Facebook is a profit-hungry business. But it does not receive a penny from bloggers like Clark. It can suspend or ban their accounts, hide or obscure their posts, without any repercussions. Big businesses and political parties, on the other hand, pay Facebook for advertising. It profits Facebook to put the needs of these organisations first.

Whilst Twitter banned all political adverts, in October 2019, Facebook actually encouraged them. It refused to subject them to any sort of fact-checking whatsoever.

The results were stark. During the 2019 UK election campaign, First Draft News found that 88% of the adverts posted by the Conservative Party were "Misleading". The Conservatives subjected hundreds-of-thousands of Facebook users to sponsored posts which were littered with unverified claims - suggesting that they would build forty new hospitals, when they had only set aside enough money to *upgrade* six - and promising to employ fifty-thousand new nurses, when eighteen-and-a-half-thousand of those nurses were already in position.

Democratic news articles, written by everyday folk, and shared by your average user, had given way to outright lies, written by the establishment, and given pride of place in return for cold hard cash.

This was not an isolated incident. During the Brazilian election of 2018, companies supporting the far-right candidate, Jair Bolsonaro, also spent millions of dollars on WhatsApp posts and adverts, many of which contained outright lies. (Chandler, 2019)

Like astroturfing, these "Dark Ads" can help to fuel misconceptions. Rather than solve the issues we met in the introduction to this chapter, Web 2.0 can actually make things *worse*.

Rather than rely on the mainstream media *or* social media, we might just have to take matters into our own hands and equip ourselves with the tools we need to tell fact from fiction...

THE WAR ON FAKE NEWS

When one thinks of Finland, certain things come to mind: Lapland, and its most famous resident, Santa Claus. The Northern Lights. Wife carrying.

Saunas. Pickled herring. Sautéed reindeer.

Readers of this book might have already added something else to the list: Finland's schools. In the previous chapter, we mentioned that the Nordic nation tops the Global Education Rankings. Despite only opening for twenty hours a week, its schools still find time to teach "Media Literacy"...

It all began back in the 1950s, when discussions were held both inside and outside of school - challenging the way films were affecting society - distinguishing between "Bad" propaganda and "Good" art.

Things have moved on since then...

These days, media literacy is considered a basic "Civil competence". It is taught to every pupil, from preschool up, as well as to the general public. Youth projects, libraries and governmental bodies all play a part; hosting events such as the annual "Media Literacy Week" and "Newspaper Week". There is also a "National Games Day", when adults and children play computer games together, before discussing their influence. (Aaltonen, 2013)

This rather extensive strategy has paid off. Finland tops the European "Media Literacy Index". According to research by the Open Society Institute, the Finns show more resilience to disinformation than citizens of any other European nation. The Dutch and Swedes, who also teach media literacy, come third and fourth in those rankings. (Charlton, 2019)

The lesson should be clear: Education is a vital weapon in the war against the billionaire barons.

It is not, however, the only weapon that can be used. Several nations have followed in Malaysia's footsteps and gone for the nuclear option - an outright ban on fake news...

Legislation in Singapore requires social media sites to carry warnings on any posts the government considers untrue, and to remove any comments deemed to be against the "Public interest". Failure to comply can lead to fines of up to $1m and ten years in prison.

Responding to Russian meddling in the 2017 presidential election, the French passed two bills to censure false information during election campaigns. Germany has passed a law requiring Twitter and Facebook to quickly remove hate speech.

Such measures are not without controversy. They are highly authoritarian. They could be used to protect governments from fair criticism, rather than to protect the people from untruths. (Ungku, 2019)

Furthermore, even if they are successful, they will only serve to block *misinformation*. They will not help to *spread the truth*.

Some websites do attempt to provide unbiased information…

"Electoral Compasses" have grown in popularity in recent years. These sites take users through a series of policy areas, such as housing and education, explain the main parties' ideas, anonymously, and then ask participants to select the policies they like the most. Once they have completed the survey, the parties whose policies they have selected are revealed.

This is pretty objective. The policies listed should be factually correct. And such sites have proved popular. Four-point-seven-million people used the Stemwijzer site ahead of the Netherlands' 2007 election.

But such sites do not always cut through. Almost half-a-million Brits completed the "Vote For Policies" survey ahead of the 2019 general election. The Conservative Party's policies were only chosen 18.6% of the time - far less often than the policies of three other parties. Yet on polling day, they received 43.6% of the votes - way more than those other parties.

Just 10% of people who used Stemwijzer went on to change the way they voted. The figures were even lower elsewhere - at 6% in Germany, 3% in Finland, and just 1% in Belgium. (Garzia & Cedroni, 2010)

It would seem that it is not enough to present factual information when elections roll around. By this point, our biases may be too entrenched to shift. We need honest, professional and brave reporters to hit us with the truth on *a daily basis*…

SAVE THE JOURNALISTS

You may very well have heard of the film, "Spotlight". It did win the 2016 Best Picture Oscar, after all.

Spotlight follows a team of investigative journalists at the Boston Globe. Working out of a cramped office, amidst stacks of paper on unkempt desks, the team investigated John Geoghan, a priest accused of sexually abusing children, and the Archbishop of Boston, who was alleged to have turned a blind eye. They uncovered a scandal, exposing eighty-seven paedophile priests in the Boston area alone.

This is journalism at its best. Working hard, for many months, a team of intelligent and dedicated reporters uncovered a dastardly truth and exposed it to the world. (McCarthy, 2015)

Of course, this is just a lone example. A Pulitzer Prize is awarded to investigative journalists every year. Between them, these wordsmiths have exposed a raft of scandals, including abuses in hospitals, spying by the police, and corruption in the lobbying industry.

Journalism can be a dangerous vocation. In 2018, thirty-four journalists were killed, two-hundred-and-fifty were imprisoned, and sixty went missing. We owe the profession a lot. (Schneider, 2018)

Yet it would be wrong to take it for granted. According to Pew Research, newsroom teams have lost 23% of their staff in just ten years. In today's fast-paced world, where click-bait rules supreme, we cannot rely on the mainstream media to fund investigative journalism forever. We must all be whistle-blowers now... (Moore, 2019)

***

The screen is a blur of grey on grey. A handful of individuals, only slightly darker than the road, appear to be minding their own business.

But this is no regular CCTV footage. In the centre of the screen is a marksman's target.

As the individuals cross the street, heading into the shadow of a narrow building, a crackly American voice vibrates through the radio:

"Hotel Two Six, this is Crazy Horse One Eight. Have individuals with weapons".

It is not possible to see any weapons on the screen.

"Yep, he's got a weapon too".

The camera pans around, before zooming in on a huddle of civilians who are standing on a street corner, having a conversation.

"Come on, fire!"

The *chuckety-chuckety-chuck* of machine-gun fire begins, but there is a slight delay. Only after a couple of seconds have passed, do the dust clouds rise; engulfing the group, who dive for cover.

"Keep shooting! Keep shooting!"

The images are a blur; all dust clouds, fire flashes and haze. But still the voice perseveres:

"Keep shooting! Keep shooting!"

When the smoke lifts, we can see people running in every direction. The camera follows them. The shooting continues:

"Clear".

Chuckety-chuckety-chuck.

"Clear".

Chuckety-chuckety-chuck.

"Clear".

***

These events, filmed from an American Apache helicopter, took place in Baghdad in 2007. Two of the men killed were journalists, employed by Reuters. Two children were badly injured during the attack.

The video, called "Collateral Murder", was uploaded onto the Wikileaks site by Julian Assange:

"Of course, the title is absolutely correct. It speaks about very specific incidents... A man is crawling in the street, completely unarmed, wounded, and he is killed by a thirty-millimetre cannon from the air".

Yet that war crime would not have been exposed had it not been for a whistle-blower, Chelsea Manning - an army intelligence analyst, based in Baghdad, who shared two-hundred-and-sixty-thousand confidential documents with Assange.

Assange then shared those files those with the world.

***

Whistle-blowers like Manning and Assange do democracy a service - exposing the horrific acts done in our name - providing us with the evidence we need to judge our politicians, before deciding whether to re-elect them or remove them from office.

But Manning was not received with a hero's welcome. She was arrested within seven weeks of this video going live. Assange was forced to seek refuge in the Ecuadorian embassy, in London. Like Manning, he was also eventually arrested. (McDermott & O'Brien, 2012)

***

Tales such as these are nothing new. Daniel Ellsberg leaked classified information during the Vietnam War, way back in the 1960s. Nor are they exclusively militaristic. Edward Snowdon exposed the American government for colluding with software companies to gather private information from millions of Americans' devices. A mysterious whistle-blower, known simply as "John Doe", leaked the "Panama Papers" - eleven-and-a-half-million documents which exposed corporate fraud and tax evasion.

Unfortunately, whistle-blowers continue to be attacked by the state. Under Barack Obama's presidency, more whistle-blowers were targeted, persecuted and prosecuted, than during every single previous American administration combined!

Whistle-blowers have also been attacked by the corporate press. NBS once held a panel which asked, "Why shouldn't you (Edward Snowdon) be charged with a crime?" The Washington Post ran an article calling for Snowden to surrender himself. One journalist for Time Magazine tweeted that he could not, "Wait to write a defence of the drone strike that takes out (Julian Assange)".

Yet all is not lost...

As ineffective as it may be, legislation does exist that is supposed to *protect* whistle-blowers. In America, it dates back to 1778, when Congress passed a law stating that, "It is the duty of all persons... to give the earliest information to Congress, or any other proper authority, of any misconduct, fraud or misdemeanour". The "Whistle-blower Protection Act" of 1989, and the "Protecting Whistle-blowers Directive" of 2012, were supposed to supplement this legislation. (Higdon & Huff, 2019)

If such legislation was actually enforced, if investigative journalists and whistle-blowers were given the platforms they deserve, if media literacy was improved, if we paid attention to electoral compasses, and if we supported the democratic press - well, we might just get the information we need to make good decisions at the ballot box. Democracy might have a chance.

11. THE PEOPLE'S ARMY

The 15th of February 2003. London. Great Britain.

A grey, condescending mist hangs from the heavens; falling in gnarly wisps, mocking the streets below. Leafless branches flutter in the breeze. Small birds perch atop ancient buildings.

The ground rumbles, jolted by millions of marchers, who stretch out from Euston to Parliament Square.

Turn up The Mall and we see them coming: Nuns. Toddlers. Archaeologists. Lecturers. Dentists. Walthamstow Catholic Church. The Swaffham Women's Choir. Country folk. Townsfolk. A hairdresser from Cardiff. A poet from Cheltenham. Girls with designer bags. Football fans with a banner marked, "Make Love Not War (And a win against Bristol City would be nice)".

This is the biggest political protest in the nation's history, and it is not an isolated event. Millions of people are marching through the streets of Barcelona, Rome, Baghdad, Sydney, New York and San Francisco.

They have the nation's backing...

An ICM poll, conducted three weeks earlier, found that only 30% of Brits support a war in Iraq. Only 10% believe it should start without support from the UN's Security Council. (Travis, 2003)

The people have spoken, in the polls and on the streets.

As Jenny Mould, a teacher from Devon, puts it: "I drove up last night. It took seven hours but it was definitely worth it. The government should, it must listen to the people. Otherwise, what's the point in democracy?" (Ferguson, 2003)

What *is* the point in democracy?

Despite this protest, and overwhelming public opposition, the government votes to invade Iraq. Rather than respect the democratic will of the people, it launches a propaganda blitz to persuade the public to support its unpopular war, *after* it has already begun.

The people of Iraq, meanwhile, do not come into the equation. No democratic undertaking asks them if they wish to be bombed, invaded or killed.

***

War represents a dilemma for a nation's politicians.

It is clearly good for business...

Arms dealers make billions by selling weapons to governments and rebel groups on both sides. After those weapons have been used to raze a country to the ground, contractors making billions more - winning lucrative contracts to clean up the mess. Investors often buy up the defeated nation's assets at rock-bottom prices. Banks might issue loans to fund those purchases, and charge interest on those loans.

But war is not so good for the people...

They must watch on as their loved ones are murdered, maimed and tortured – as their homes and businesses are turned to dust, and their homeland's culture is replaced by that of their invaders. We, the taxpayers, must foot the bill.

Politicians are faced with a dilemma. Do they serve the corporations? Or do they serve the people?

In Iraq, they chose to serve the corporations...

Lockheed Martin, the arms manufacturer, saw its share price jump by 145% on the back of the Iraq War. Halliburton was paid over $20b to build mini-towns for American troops on "Cost Plus" contracts which guaranteed them a profit. "Iraqis found themselves drinking water from Bechtel pipes, their homes illuminated by GE lights, their infirm treated in Parsons-built hospitals, and their streets patrolled by DynCorp-trained police". Two-hundred of Iraq's nationalised banks, factories, mines and oil companies were sold to foreign investors at bargain-basement prices.

And what about the people?

Five-hundred-thousand of Iraq's public-sector employees lost their jobs. Their nation was turned into a breeding ground for terrorists. Their homes and businesses were turned to rubble. Millions died. (Klein, 2007)

***

Yet despite the British government's decision to go to war, military intervention could have been avoided...

British soldiers had to choose sides. They could follow the orders of a few *hundred* politicians, or they could respect the democratic wishes of tens-of-*millions* of Brits. But they could not do both.

This is not as fanciful as it might sound. In the UK, such a choice really does exist. If a member of the armed forces does not believe a war is just, they are well within their rights to claim conscientious objection. A soldier who has joined the British army to serve the British people, is entitled to refuse to fight in a war that the British people do not support, and which might provoke retaliatory attacks *against* Britain.

Soldiers with democratic ideals do not have to fight in undemocratic wars.

Unfortunately, most soldiers are unaware of their rights. But even these individuals remain in control of their actions. It may not be legal, but they still possess the freewill necessary to reject orders, mutiny or abscond.

This was the case with Mohsin Khan, an air force reservist who went "Absent without leave". He did not know he had the right to conscientious objection, and so he was court-martialled for his stand. But he played no part in the Iraq War. (Parliament UK, 2011)

Had all the soldiers in the British and American armies followed Khan's lead, the Iraq War would not have started, and millions of lives might have been saved.

Most soldiers, however, were not as brave as Khan.

***

This tale is by no means a unique...

A Pew Research poll, conducted in March 2011, found that 77% of Americans were opposed to the bombing of Libyan air defences, and that 82% were opposed to sending American ground troops into that East African nation. Despite this opposition, the American government declared war that month. (Pew Research Centre, 2011)

As was the case with Iraq, American soldiers had to make a tough decision: To obey their government or to obey the people. And, as was the case in Iraq, they sided with their rulers.

But why?

The answer is simple: Most armies are not democratic. Their soldiers are not trained to serve the people. They are taught to follow orders...

WHY DID THEY GO?

In the comments section below his YouTube video, a viewer has written, "This guy is the most para looking para I've ever seen". Square-faced, with cropped hair, sideburns and an eleven o'clock shadow, Ben Griffin does have a steely demeanour. He might be wearing a polo shirt and jeans, but beneath the civilian attire it is easy to see a man whose grandfather, uncles and cousins, all had military careers.

Griffin had been keen to follow in the family tradition. He spent his early childhood watching war movies and reading commando comics:

"The soldiers were brave and plucky. They fought against evil soldiers: The Germans and Japanese".

When he turned thirteen, Griffin joined the army cadet force, wore a uniform, marched up and down, and relished the chance to prove himself. He listened to the tales of soldiers returning from missions abroad, smoked, drank and swore.

By the time left school, he had no desire to do anything else. He was, "An ideological recruit. A true believer".

***

So there he was, on his first day, sitting with thirty-four recruits.

A burly forty-five-year-old was addressing the room:

"Only eight of you are going to pass this course".

Griffin, a skinny nineteen-year-old, did not fancy his chances.

But it soon became apparent that it was not necessarily the biggest, toughest guys who were going make it. It was the people who could put up with stuff. "The people who could hack it".

The process began with military-drill...

A relic from times gone by, it may seem a little ridiculous to expect the modern soldier to march up and down, left-turning, right-turning and coming to attention. But there was method in the madness:

"One person stands out the front, screaming out commands, and the whole platoon, without thinking, immediately does what they're told".

Drill served a crucial purpose. It helped to mould the recruits into brainless automatons, who would obey orders without a moment's hesitation or thought.

Those orders extended well beyond the marching ground...

Sometimes they were contradictory. One minute, the recruits would be told to do one thing. A couple of minutes later, they would be told to do something else. They would have to stop the first task and respond to the new command.

If the word "Corridor" was shouted out loud, the recruits had to run into the corridor and stand in line. When they heard the word "Chins", they had to stick out their chins and wait for them to be punched. When they heard the word "Tongues", they had to open their mouths and wait for their tongues to be squeezed.

Once, as Griffin was turning the corner, he was asked, "Griffin! Where are you?"

"I'm on my way", he replied. It was a reasonable answer to a reasonable question, or so you might think. Only Griffin's officers were not looking for an answer. They punished him for "Answering back".

Punishments were an essential part of the training...

There were push-ups, sit-ups and "The Position" - a form of physical torture in which recruits were made to sit with their backs against the wall, but without any support beneath their thighs.

"You might have to run up and down a hill, carrying a mate for an hour, until you threw up. Or you might be kept out in the snow overnight, with no cover or sleeping-bag".

Those who were unable or unwilling to follow orders were punished so relentlessly that they were forced to drop out. But those who could blindly follow commands, made the grade.

Bearing this in mind, it is easy to see why such soldiers would go to war in Iraq. They had been conditioned to obey orders, without hesitation or thought. So, when they were ordered to go to Iraq, they packed their bags and left. It was as simple as that. A civilian might have considered options such as disobedience, desertion, conscientious objection and mutiny. A soldier would not:

"When we joined the army, we were still civilians. We were still people who had our own sense of right and wrong - our own sense of freewill and what we wanted out of life. Military training is about getting rid of that. It's about turning you from a civilian into a soldier".

**

This explains why soldiers did not rebel. But it does not explain why they wilfully ignored the wishes of the people they were supposed to be serving.

For this, we need to understand the gang mentality of a military unit...

The punishments outlined above were not only inflicted upon

individuals. The whole group could be punished for the indiscretions of a single recruit.

If this person was unpopular, he was ostracised, "To the point where he was beaten up when the screws weren't looking".

Such recruits soon dropped out.

But if the recruit was popular, their peers gave him their full support. This made him feel special. And, "As everyone else dropped out, he felt even more special, because he had survived".

It encouraged those survivors, "To be loyal to the gang, no matter what".

But it did not stop there. The respect they had for each other, as *insiders*, was entrenched by an even greater disdain for *outsiders*.

They did not care about the queen, their country, or even the army. Other soldiers were called "Crap hats". Civilians were called "Civvy cunts. Useless, disgusting human beings, who wouldn't even join the military. The lowest of the low".

The soldiers who went to Iraq ignored the democratic wishes of the British people because *they despised the British people*. Their loyalty was to each other, not to democracy. (Griffin, 2015) (Griffin, 2016)

THE POUM

So, what is the alternative? How can we transform our armies, such that they operate along democratic lines, and serve the will of the people?

It might sound like a tall order, but it has been done...

In the first section of this book, we mentioned that the Iroquois elected "Chiefs", and that pirates elected "Captains". Both were military leaders. Both could be replaced at any time, with a democratic vote.

Then we have the Germanic tribes, documented by Tacitus, whose military leaders were elected based on their valour. (Gillin, 1919)

We could return to the English Revolution, when members of the New Model Army elected "Agitators" - representatives who were sent to parliament, to demand their rights.

When the government was thinking of disbanding that army, two regiments staged mutinies; reminding their leaders that they, the people, were in charge. The government took note, reversing its plans and arranging a committee to meet with its disaffected men. (Smith, 1990)

Similar mutinies can be found among the Apache, who abandoned Geronimo when he acquired a taste for suicidal missions. And among the Yanomamo, who had a reputation for abandoning war-hungry chiefs. (Boehm, 1993)

But if readers of this book are familiar with just one democratic army, the chances are it is the "POUM" - the guerrilla militia made famous by George Orwell's book, "Homage to Catalonia"...

***

The year was 1936. General Francisco Franco had staged a coup d'état, seizing power from Spain's democratically elected government. But the Spanish people were fighting back. Democracy lovers from across Europe, Orwell included, had felt a "Thrill of hope". They had travelled from near and far to fight against Franco's thugs.

The "Democracy versus Fascism" narrative might be an oversimplification...

Franco was as much of a feudalist as a fascist. He was backed by the aristocracy and the church. And his opponents were fighting for something far more radical than representative democracy. Attempts were made to establish workers' governments, run by local committees, and workers' patrols were established to replace the state's police. The last vestiges of authoritarian control had been abolished. There was no "Boot-licking", no "Cap-touching", and no use of the formal "Usted".

Furthermore, the fight against Franco was not led by Spain's government, which was sorely underprepared. Rather, it was led by trade unions and individual political parties, who acted spontaneously; calling a general strike, seizing weapons from the public arsenals, and forming the militias which would hold the fascists at bay.

They were as rag-tag as you might expect...

Recruits could not train with guns, since the few weapons they had were needed at the front. Militiamen wore more of a "Multiform" than a uniform. They all wore red and black handkerchiefs, caps which displayed their party badges, corduroy knee-breeches and zipper-jackets. But some wore gaiters, whilst others wore leggings or high boots. Some jackets were made of leather, whilst others were made of wool. They had to make do with whatever could be produced in a hurry.

Yet despite their meagre resources, despite being unprepared and inexperienced, they managed to hold a professional army at bay.

How did they do this?

Let's take a look at their military structure:

"The essential point of the system was social equality... Everyone from private to general drew the same pay, ate the same food, wore the same clothes, and mingled on terms of complete equality. If you wanted to slap your general on the back and ask him for a cigarette, you could do so, and no one thought it curious. In theory, at any rate, each militia was a democracy and not a hierarchy... (There were) no titles, no badges, no heel-clicking and no saluting".

Orwell witnessed this on just his second day in Spain...

During instruction, he observed how hard it was to get the recruits to stand in line. These lads, many of whom were just sixteen or seventeen, refused to obey orders if they did not agree with them. Rather than submit, they stepped forward and argued with their commanding officer.

In an authoritarian army, such behaviour would result in harsh disciplinary action. But not here. The lieutenant, "A stout, fresh-faced, pleasant young man", would not have had it any other way. When one recruit addressed him as "Señor", he turned, a look of pained surprise on his face, and remarked: "What! Señor? Who is that calling me Señor? Are we not all comrades here?"

Of course, such a system was not without its annoyances. At first, Orwell had to argue for five minutes before his orders were obeyed. It took months for things to change. But, as Orwell was keen to point out, "It also takes time to drill a man into an automaton on the barrack-square".

Eventually, the militiamen pulled together:

"In January, the job of keeping a dozen raw recruits up to the mark almost turned my hair grey. In May, for a short while, I was acting-lieutenant in command of about thirty men, English and Spanish. We had all been under fire for months, and I never had the slightest difficulty in getting an order obeyed or in getting men to volunteer for a dangerous job".

Orwell uses this word, "Volunteer", at regular intervals throughout his memoir...

On one occasion, a request is made for fifteen volunteers to attack a fascist redoubt. In the blink of an eye, we find fifteen volunteers on the march. A few pages later, a comrade asks for five volunteers to search for a lost friend. Again, we immediately find ourselves in No Man's Land, confronting bullets and bombs, on a mission to find our man.

Whereas traditional armies use fear to keep soldiers in line - the fear of being disciplined, court-martialled or even shot - these militias appealed to class loyalty. Rather than punish a man, "You appealed to him in the name of comradeship".

Traditional army discipline *could* still be evoked. The POUM's soldiers could be shot for desertion. But such punishments were seldom needed:

"The workers could always be brought to heel by an argument that is almost too obvious to need stating: 'Unless you do this, that and the other, we shall lose the war'."

It is hard to imagine such an argument at work in Iraq. But these soldiers were committed to their cause. They marched to the front - cheering, happy and excited - because they believed "They were fighting for something better than the status quo".

This belief inspired some unlikely victories:

"Men and women armed only with sticks of dynamite rushed across the open squares and stormed stone buildings held by trained soldiers with machine-guns. Machine-gun nests that the fascists had placed at strategic spots were smashed by rushing taxis at them at sixty miles-per-hour".

This is not to say that such enthusiasm was always efficient. Many a bullet was wasted shooting at distant targets. Several comrades fell victim to friendly fire.

The conflict descended into trench warfare...

Endless days were spent in the mud, consumed by boredom, without sufficient firewood, coffee or tobacco. Very little land was ever gained. Very few people were ever killed.

It was here that the militiamen's enthusiasm helped swing the balance. Using megaphones, they "Shouted a set-piece, full of revolutionary sentiments, which explained to the fascist soldiers that they were merely the hirelings of international capitalism, fighting against their own class, and that they should come over to our side. This was repeated over and over by relays of men. Sometimes it continued throughout the night".

It had the desired effect. From his first days in Spain, Orwell observed a trickle of deserters coming across from the fascist ranks:

"If one comes to think of it, when some poor devil of a sentry, very likely a trade union member who has been conscripted against his will, is freezing at his post, the slogan 'Don't fight against your own class' ringing again and again through the darkness is bound to make an impression on him. It might make just the difference between deserting and not deserting".

***

This all sounds pretty encouraging, right?

A bunch of untrained, under-resourced and inexperienced youths had held the might of the Spanish army at bay. They had encouraged fascist soldiers to defect, and provided the Spanish government with the time it needed to organise. They had done this without coercion. It was enough that people believed in the cause. They were driven by the *hope* that they would create a more democratic nation, and by the *fear* that Spain might fall to the fascists if they were defeated.

Alas, the story does not end here...

Whilst internally sound, and successful when faced with a level playing field, the militias were unable to withstand foreign intervention.

The anti-fascist forces had always been a motley crew - a mixture of anarchists, socialists, trade unionists and different political parties. But it was the communists, on the authoritarian end of this spectrum, who had accrued the best weapons, thanks to their relationship with Stalinist Russia. They were the group who looked the most capable of winning the war, and so they were the group that amassed the most public support. They weaselled their way into a position of influence and encouraged the government to reform its army along authoritarian lines.

Differential pay rates were introduced, volunteerism was replaced with conscription, and a propaganda campaign was launched to destroy the public's faith in the militias. The POUM fighters, who had done so much to resist the fascists, were branded as Trotskyist traitors. Several were left to rot in jail.

The rest, as they say, is history. This new authoritarian army, lacking the enthusiasm of the POUM's militias, could not resist the fascists for long. Franco also had foreign support. His troops eventually triumphed.

Thirty-eight years would pass before the Spanish people could vote in another general election. (Orwell, 1938)

THE YPJ AND YPG

So far, so mixed.

We have discovered a democratic army, which had its successes, but which ultimately faced defeat. If an army is judged by the wars it wins, we cannot use the POUM as a benchmark, despite its democratic integrity.

The modern equivalents of the POUM, however, have a far better track record (at the time of writing, at least). In Rojava, the People's Protection Units (YPG) and Women's Protection Units (YPJ) have been fending off attacks from ISIS, the Turkish government *and* the Assad regime; despite lacking helmets and bulletproof vests, and despite possessing inferior weapons. It was their victories that led to the establishment of the democratic autonomy we spoke about in Chapter Five...

***

Kobanî. 1:00AM. The 19th of July 2012.

An eerie hush was on the brink.

A hotchpotch of scavenged weapons, hidden for years behind bookshelves and cabinets, under paving stones and floorboards, were about to be unleashed. People from almost every household, with little or no military experience, were tiptoeing forward, united, waiting with bated breath.

Here they were. Here at the centre of Kobanî. Here, at the centre of power for Assad's troops - massed, with guns in hand, and a loudhailer held high:

"If you give up your weapons, your security will be guaranteed".

Bullets loaded. *Click.*

Safety off. *Click.*

A tap for good measure. *Click, click, click.*

Assad's troops looked out across this great mass of people.

They were clearly outnumbered, outmuscled and outgunned. In the morning, they were out of town - allowed to flee to Turkey or Damascus.

Not blood had been spilt. (Knapp, Flach & Ayboğa, 2016)

***

Having gathered the government's weapons, the locals went on the march - liberating the region's villages.

"The people had no more fear", said Heval Amer. "Everyone joined in, many with only wooden clubs in their hands".

"In Dêrîk we tried to hold the people back", explained Hanife Hisên. "But they pushed ahead of us. We set up control points. The people said, 'Give us the weapons', and we distributed them. We went to the state security forces and surrounded them and told them to go. They got their things and left".

And that, it seemed, was that. The YPG and YPJ believed in "The theory of the rose" - to defend themselves, like that thorny plant, without initiating battles themselves.

And so they held onto the land they had liberated, but allowed the Syrian government to retain the rest of Rojava.

Then, in the Spring of 2012, the Ba'ath regime began to shoot, at random, into the Kurdish areas of Aleppo. The councils reacted, creating YPG units in the summer, and liberating the city in the autumn.

Some institutions, such as the airport, remained in government hands. But the war had already been won. (Knapp, Flach & Ayboğa, 2016)

***

So how, exactly, is the Rojavan army democratic?

It breaks the "Androcracy". Rather than being run by men, for men, it is run by both men *and* women. In Kobanî, half the fighters are women. In other areas, around a third are female.

It is people-powered. By 2014, over half of the women in Rojava had received weapons training. In Cizîrê and Afrîn, brief periods of conscription continue to expand this involvement.

The training they receive is the opposite of that experienced by Ben Griffin. Rather than stop participants from thinking, it includes lessons in history, politics, nature and society, which actively encourage the recruits to think for themselves.

Thinking leads to talking...

When they are not shouting at their enemies, engaging in the sort of psychological warfare we met in Catalonia, Rojavan troops can be found chatting amongst themselves.

"We read and discussed the roles women play in this war", said Çiçek. "Whenever anyone fell, we immediately talked about it, and about why they fought, so that morale wouldn't waver".

Like in Catalonia, Rojavan soldiers are upbeat. They sing. They feel part of the cause. They want to fight, without needing to be coerced. (Knapp, Flach & Ayboğa, 2016)

But in Rojava, they go further still...

Civilians and soldiers are united...

They attend commune assemblies together. When it comes to making military decisions, they all get a vote. They all elect representatives, who sit on the defence commissions, and ensure that their decisions are enacted.

If a soldier fails to obey a command, therefore, they will not just feel as though they have betrayed their comrades and their commanders. They will feel as though they have betrayed the democratic wishes of their entire community. (Graeber, 2016)

For sure, commanders do exist. But they are also elected, democratically, by the defence commissions. They do not hide in ivory towers. They can be found on the front line, leading by example. (Knapp, Flach & Ayboğa, 2016)

***

If my English readers are familiar with just one YPJ soldier, the chances are it is Anna Campbell...

The boyish blonde was always a bit of a free spirit. At primary school, she once saved a bumblebee from a group of older children. She was a "Dedicated bookworm, lover of insects, storyteller, and creator of everlasting childhoods".

Campbell found university life unfulfilling. Compelled to make the world a better place, she put her studies on the back-burner, became an activist, protested against the tripling of tuition fees, joined the Hunt Saboteurs, and travelled to the Jungle, in Calais, to protect refugees from the police.

It was only natural, then, for Campbell to be inspired by events in Rojava. She felt a duty to support the cause.

Like Orwell before her, Campbell packed her bags, waved goodbye to her family, and headed east.

***

Her diary shows just how welcome she felt...

Here she was, surrounded by like-minded souls, living in her dream society - a place that was humanitarian, ecological and feminist.

But Campbell wanted to do more than just exist. She wanted to contribute. Every single day, she would ask her senior commander, "Why aren't you sending me to fight?"

Her commander did everything she could to dissuade Campbell:

"I didn't send her. We have our rules and systems. Unless she completes all her training, she's not allowed to fight. We do our best not to send the international women to war".

Still, Campbell's desire was strong. In her diary, she wrote:

"I'm ready to fight for this land, and even die for it if necessary, although I'd rather not".

Campbell's commander had no choice but to give way to her subordinate's calls, and allow her to travel to Afrin, to defend Rojava from the Turkish army. Campbell even dyed her hair black, to pass for a Kurd, so she could make it through the Syrian checkpoints.

During her last ever video recording, she spoke of her excitement:

"I'm very happy and very proud to be going".

Campbell would never return...

On the 15th of March 2018, she was killed by a Turkish airstrike. Her body hit the dust; a pair of tatty white trainers on her feet, and an AK47 in her hands.

***

So why mention Campbell?

Her story is a tragedy. It is the tale of a young and happy individual, struck down in her prime. But scratch beneath the surface and one word permeates her tale: Democracy.

Like Orwell, Campbell went to fight for a democratic system. She did so of her own free will, because she believed in the cause. She was not a patriot, fighting for the country where she just so happened to be born. She was not cajoled by the authorities - coerced by conscription, persuaded by propaganda, or enticed by a paycheque. It was not her *commander* who sent Campbell to fight, it was Campbell who forced her commander to send *her*.

***

Campbell was not alone. Other foreigners have also headed to Rojava to do their bit.

Jamie Jansen fought against ISIS in Raqqa...

Jansen does not look like your typical soldier. He looks a little nerdy. The contrast between Jansen and Ben Griffin could not be starker.

He was a reluctant warrior:

"I'd always put off the idea of going to Rojava because I didn't want to pick up a gun and hurt people. I was always a nonviolent direct activist... It felt very strange to be holding a gun, thinking I could have to kill someone with this at any moment. I was hesitating, thinking, 'I'm going to actually fire at human beings.' Am I going to do it? And then I did it".

Jansen was arrested by the British authorities as soon as he returned to Britain. But he shows that it can be done. Anyone, from anywhere, can join this democratic army. And, unlike Campbell, most do survive to tell the tale. (Parker, 2019)

FIGHTING FOR DEMOCRACY

We have met a couple of democratic armies, who fought wars for democracy itself. Yet these ideas need not be linked. Authoritarian armies have also been known to fight for democracy...

World War Two, rightly or wrongly, has been branded as a war for democracy. The Allies fought alongside Stalinist Russia, which was no democracy. They enlisted support from their colonies - subjugated nations, which were seldom democratic. But they did defend the representative democracies of Britain and France, against the fascist dictatorships of Germany and Italy. In this sense, they *were* fighting for democracy. And some soldiers from the colonies did believe that by fighting in that war, they would hasten independence - a process that would enable their nations to become democraties. In this sense, they were fighting for democracy too. Still, the British and French armies were authoritarian beasts. They conscripted people, often against their will, dished out commands from on high, and expected soldiers to blindly follow orders.

Herein lies a problem. The soldiers in these wars may have been fighting for democracy, but had they been ordered to fight *against* democracy, they would have probably done as they were told.

Let's not forget that soldiers in state armies have been responsible for several genocides, including the Holocaust. They have bombed civil populations, dropped nuclear bombs, tortured prisoners, fired on unarmed protesters, invaded sovereign lands and occupied entire nations. When challenged, soldiers normally say, "I was only following orders".

What we need are moral soldiers who can think for themselves. Soldiers who would never follow such orders...

DEMOCRATISING OUR ARMIES

The POUM, YPG and YPJ give examples for other armies to follow...

Traditional armies could also allow their soldiers to elect their superior officers, or develop orders through a democratic process. Their soldiers could be given history and philosophy lessons, to help them to think for themselves and become moral warriors.

These things *could* all happen, but it seems unlikely...

Armies' top brass do not want free-thinking subordinates. They want automatons - soldiers who are skilled enough to fire the guns, but not righteous enough to question why.

Yet change need not come from above. Democracy is normally established from below, when the people stand up and demand it.

So how can this be achieved in an army?

I started this chapter by giving a few options: Soldiers can disobey orders, mutiny or abscond.

Whilst all may seem unlikely, in the present climate, it should be noted that such actions have been successful in the past.

Let's travel back to Christmas 1914...

World War One had descended into a stalemate. All was mud and slurry, frost and ice.

As the bullets flew overhead, something strange happened. The soldiers began to sing! Enemy soldiers soon found themselves standing face-to-face in No Man's Land, sharing brandy, showing each other pictures of their loved ones, shaking hands and playing football.

They did this of their own volition, much to the chagrin of their superior officers. They were punished for their mutiny. But their actions set a precedent which would ultimately end the war...

A year later, riots and demonstrations spread across Germany. The German arms industry was hit by strike after strike.

In 1917, almost half of France's units on the Western Front refused to obey orders.

In Pirbright, British soldiers organised their own voluntary training sessions. Royal Artillery units rioted in Le Havre, burning down several army depots. They went on strike in Etaples and Boulogne. At Shoreham, they absconded.

At Val De Lièvre, British troops elected a "Soldiers' Council" and called for a general strike. They descended on the army headquarters and seized control. Within days, their number had swelled to twenty-thousand, and they had formed a union that linked them to similar committees in other army units. (Tatchell, 2014)

But it was the Germans whose efforts proved decisive:

"Under the cover of seamen's yarns in the lower decks, in the lockers, the munitions rooms, even in the lavatories; an underground organisation was built... They took over the bridges, ran up red flags and pointed the guns of rebel ships at the hulls of those that did not rebel".

Thus, began the Kiel Mutiny.

A group of rebel sailors refused to embark on a suicide mission, turned their ships around, and headed back into Germany.

Jan Valtin, a participant, recalled what happened next:

"That night I saw the mutinous sailors roll into Bremen on caravans of commandeered trucks. From all sides, a sea of swinging, pushing bodies and distorted faces were moving toward the centre of town. Many of the workers were armed with guns, bayonets and hammers".

The Kaiser fell. (Mason, 2014)

A war which lacked the people's support, was stopped by the people. A democratic movement had infiltrated an authoritarian army and bent it to its will.

***

It would not be the last time that people-power ended a war...

Opposition to the Vietnam War might not have clicked into gear until almost ten years after it had begun, but it soon picked up a head of steam.

The movement followed a lifecycle like those we met in Chapter Eight...

First, there were the "True Believers" - the left-wing peace groups, opposed to the Cold War, and the college students, inspired by the Civil Rights Movement. These people trained and recruited activists, informed and educated the population, and held protests which helped to normalise opposition to the war.

The "Majority" came on board. In April 1967, half-a-million souls marched through New York City. It was the biggest protest in American history, and it would go on to inspire a draft-dodging movement. Young men, led by the likes of Muhammad Ali, refused to join the army on moral grounds.

Then came the direct action. Protestors broke through police lines, penetrating the Pentagon itself. Activists occupied army induction centres, impeded army training sessions, and blocked access to military recruiters. Religious leaders dumped blood on draft records. Hippies manipulated the media with attention-grabbing stunts.

The message began to shift.

"Hey, hey, L.B.J., how many kids did you kill today?"

Became:

"One side's right, one side's wrong, victory to the Viet Cong".

Even returning soldiers were getting in on the act; confessing to the atrocities they had committed, distributing anti-war pamphlets at military bases, and throwing their medals at the Capitol building.

In 1967, forty-seven-thousand soldiers deserted their posts.

In 1971, eighty-nine-thousand followed suit. Almost a fifth of recruits were listed as "Absent without leave".

Many who remained, refused to fight. Some even resorted to "Fragging" - killing their commanding officers.

By 1973, one in every five discharges was "Less than honourable".

It was all too much for the authorities to bear. In 1975, they heeded the people's calls and withdrew from Vietnam. (Zimmerman, 2017) (Zinn, 1980)

***

In both cases, it took time. The Vietnam War was twenty-years-old by the time it ended. And in both cases, it required civilian involvement. Most of the mutineers were conscripts with limited training. They were not professionals, like Ben Griffin, who had not endured years of indoctrination.

But it did happen. Authoritarian armies *were* forced to bend to the will of the people. And if it could happen then, it could happen now. We just need to learn our lessons...

We cannot simply stage a single march, before a war begins, and expect it to make a difference. We must march over and over again, for several years. We must take direct action. We must exert pressure on the soldiers who fight in undemocratic wars, as well as the politicians who launch them.

And to get the message through, we must ensure that those soldiers have a civilian conscience. To be *for* the people, they must be *of* the people...

CIVIL SERVICE

The Swiss army can call on one-hundred-and-forty-thousand troops. But of these, only ten-thousand are full-time soldiers, in the Ben Griffin mould. The remainder are civilians. They have completed their basic training and returned to Civvy Street, semi-automatic rifle in hand, ready to be called upon should the need ever arise.

Such a need did arise during World War Two. When Nazi Germany threatened Switzerland's borders, it quickly mobilised a guerrilla army that contained one-in-five of its citizens!

As I write, Swiss soldiers are being recalled from civilian life to combat the coronavirus epidemic. They are helping to guard the nation's borders, provide transportation services, and assist the healthcare profession - cleaning, laundering and offering nursing care in hospitals across the land.

***

Having such a civilian base helps to keep the Swiss army grounded...

It is hard to imagine a situation like that outlined at the beginning of this chapter, in which millions of Swiss people march through the streets of Bern, only for the Swiss government to turn around and call upon those *very same people* to fight in the war against which they had just protested.

Since 1815, the nation has had an official policy of "Armed neutrality". Its army does not interfere in foreign wars. It is only used for defence.

There is, however, a caveat. Such a large, civilian-centred army is only possible through conscription. The Swiss government *forces* its youngsters to undergo basic training, "Replete with tightly choreographed marching, target practice and crawling in mud... while being constantly yelled at by abusive sergeants".

That sounds rather authoritarian to me!

Still, whilst 65% of Swiss men do receive military training, only one-in-four are selected to serve, and those who do not wish to join the army can opt for civilian service instead.

The system *does* have the people's backing. In a referendum, held in 2013, 73% of people voted to keep conscription in place.

So the Swiss system does solve the issue raised at the beginning of this chapter. It provides an army that serves the people, not the corporations. But the means through which this is achieved, conscription, may not be everyone's cup of tea. (Artamonov, 2019)

***

Let's consider one final, rather less authoritarian solution...

Instead of having a professional army that serves the establishment, or a conscripted army recruited by force, a nation might choose to have *no army whatsoever*. A government cannot wage war, against the wishes of its people, if it does not have an army to fight!

Such a solution may appear far-fetched. But it has been tried...

Costa Rica decided to dismantle its army back in 1948, for political reasons. To ensure there would be no repeat of the civil war that had just engulfed the nation. And also for economic reasons. Its Defence Minister, Edgar Cardona, reasoned that the nation would be better off spending its military budget on education, healthcare and social security.

The results speak for themselves. According to the World Health Organisation, Costa Rica has the best healthcare system in Central America. The nation has a 98% literacy rate. It ranked twelfth in the 2017 World Happiness Index and came first in the Happy Planet Index.

But what about defence?

Costa Rica may not have an army, but it does have a well-resourced police force, armed with military-grade weaponry, and a professional coast guard. Between them, these groups defend the nation from attack.

In 2018, Costa Rica celebrated seventy years without an army. The system works.

Furthermore, since it does not pose a military threat, Costa Rica is free to play the role of peacekeeper. It played an integral part in the Esquipulas Peace Accords that ended years of war in Central America.

It has even inspired one of its neighbours to follow in its footsteps. In 1989, Panama also abolished its army.

They have a saying in Costa Rica:

"Blessed is the Costa Rican mother who knows her newborn son will never be a soldier". (Trejos, 1989)

Blessed indeed!

12. PROTECT & SERVE

The air filled with the sound of trumpets, trombones, drums, claps, cries, cheers and calls:

"What do we want? Living wages! When do we want them? Now!"

"Down with the rotten boroughs! Down with tariffs on grain!"

"Votes for all!"

A pasty-skinned, bristly-haired politician took to the stand. Arching his back, he paused to appreciate the scene, before fleshing out the slogans on a sea of banners:

Equal Representation.

Universal Suffrage.

Love.

At the front, the orator's words were well received. Further back, they were lost to the wind. Walls groaned, shutters clanged, and eighty-thousand protestors did not hear a single word he said.

Nor did they hear the raspy voice of a dog-faced magistrate as he leant through a window to read the Riot Act:

"Our sovereign lord the King chargeth and commandeth all persons, being assembled, to immediately disperse themselves".

Unheard, he was ignored.

He called for reinforcements.

Six-hundred hussars, four-hundred cavalrymen, four-hundred constables and two canons entered the scene. Then came the yeomanry - local business owners, incensed that their workers had gone on strike. Riding on horseback, with cutlasses and clubs in hand, they knocked a baby from its mother's arms and charged on through the masses.

For an eternal millisecond, the world stood perfectly still.

The silence was the loudest noise.

Then the panic turned outwards.

The yeomanry charged inwards, their sabres drawn, slashing their way through the flags.

"Drive them through", an officer bawled.

"For shame", another replied. "The people cannot escape!"

***

This is how I described the 1819 Peterloo Massacre in my fourth novel, "Money Power Love". A pro-democracy protest was quashed by the yeomanry in the most violent of manners.

The "Yeomanry" helped local magistrates to keep order in the days before there was a nationalised police force. It was comprised of local volunteers, but it was far from democratic. Dominated by the middle-classes, it served its own class, not the majority.

Yet rather than disband or sanction this ill-disciplined mob, in response to the atrocities they had performed, the government actually *rewarded* them - increasing their funding by 75%. (Hay, 2018)

It was a short-term fix...

The British establishment had a bigger conundrum to solve. Across the channel, the French Revolution had handed power to the people. In an attempt to stop a similar transformation at home, the British government had outlawed trade unions and banned public meetings of more than fifty people. But the populace was growing restless. It was breaking these laws at their leisure.

The government had two options. It could shoot the protestors down, thereby creating a number of martyrs. Or it could allow the protests to continue, and risk a revolution.

They needed a third way.

So what did they do?

They established a full-time professional police force, trained to inflict nonlethal violence upon crowds - dispersing their protests *without creating martyrs*.

When not disrupting people's protests, the Bobbies were on the beat. The eyes and ears of the state, their very presence intimidated would-be-activists. The intelligence they gathered helped to keep the pro-democracy movement at bay. (Whitehouse, 2014)

The Irish Constabulary was established just three years after Peterloo, to control the disenfranchised peasantry, who were fighting for their rights.

The Metropolitan Police Force was established in London soon after. Dressed in navy uniforms, its policemen looked like domesticated soldiers. And, like the army, they served the government - reporting to the Home Secretary, rather than their peers. (Kinna, 2015)

By 1856, a national police force had been established. There would be no turning back. (Reiner, 2016)

***

A similar story was unfolding in New York...

As in Britain, American craftsmen began their careers as apprentices - indentured servants who received bed and board in their master's house. After seven years, they became journeymen.

This was a hierarchical system. The master was in charge. But apprentices stood a good chance of becoming masters themselves, once they matured, and they shared a personal relationship with their boss.

That all changed during the Industrial Revolution. Increased competition forced masters to act like entrepreneurs - cutting costs, and asking their subordinates to work harder, for longer, in return for lower wages and worsening conditions.

Apprentices were no longer offered lodging in their masters' homes. They went out, mingled with other people, discussed their grievances, formed alliances, and began to fight back.

The riots began.

In the 1760s, New Yorkers agitated against the Stamp Act. In 1802, the city's sailors went on strike. Between 1801 and 1832, black New Yorkers rioted four times to prevent former slaves from being sent back to their masters. Between 1825 and 1830, riots took place on an almost monthly basis.

The establishment responded with violence...

When the riots hit the wealthier parts of town, on New Years' Eve 1828, the upper classes called for reforms to protect their wealth and status. They eventually got their way...

By 1845, New York had a large, well-paid, professional police force with a military chain of command. On hand day and night, they protected the powerful, by controlling the people. (Kinna, 2015)

***

These stories, from either side of the Atlantic, teach us a clear lesson. Governments did not establish police forces to control *crime*. They established police forces to control *crowds*. To control *us*.

These police forces were not democratic - created because the people demanded them. They were authoritarian - created to defend the elites.

***

Some things never change...

I recall my first political protest, "Reclaim the Streets", an anti-capitalist festival held on May Day 2000. When the police got bored of our presence, they surrounded us with interlocked arms, forming an impenetrable human wall. They began walking, forcing us out of Parliament Square, before dumping us a mile away. It was a highly efficient, anti-democratic operation that brought an end to the day's events.

Then there was the time I was arrested for protesting against a NATO meeting in Newport. It was a scary thing, being chased down the streets by a bunch of burly policemen. I was locked in a cell until I missed my coach back to London, then issued with the trumped-up charge of "Assaulting an officer". I had to return to Newport twice before those charges were dropped. It felt like they were trying to grind me down - to cause me so much stress that I would never protest again.

BUT WE NEED THE POLICE!

Today's professional, state-run police forces may have been invented to stop protests. They may still be used to break up marches, occupations and strikes. But we need the police, right? Without a police force to "Protect" us, people could get away with murder, rape and paedophilia.

Or so the logic goes.

The reality is a little different. We survived for hundreds-of-thousands of years without modern police forces. We did police ourselves in this period. We just did so differently. In many cases, we did so in a more democratic manner.

In the next section, we shall see how this was done - looking at various forms of democratic policing from both the past and present - the sort of policing that goes after real criminals, rather than political protestors.

This is a start. But it is not enough.

For a police force to be truly democratic, it should not only focus on small-time criminals. It must also defend the people from the *biggest criminals* of them all...

***

Although estimates vary considerably, the PLS Medicine Journal estimates that around half-a-million people died during the first eight years of the Iraq War. The General Secretary of the United Nations, Kofi Anan, declared that war "Illegal". Yet the police have still not arrested its architects:

Tony Blair and George W Bush. (Vergano, 2013)

Imagine if you or I killed half-a-million people! I think the police would have a thing or two to say. But Bush and Blair are members of the establishment. They get a free pass.

They are not alone...

The Global Financial Crash of 2018 was caused by the reckless gambling of a financier class, who repackaged and resold sub-prime loans that should have never been issued in the first place.

The consequences were catastrophic...

The American government spent $700b to bail out the banks. Then, through quantitative easing, it spent trillions more on bonds and mortgage-backed securities. The main beneficiaries were the rich - the sort of people who could afford to own financial assets. Millions of poorer citizens lost their homes. Thirty-million people lost their jobs.

The knock-on effects sent countries like Greece, Ireland and Portugal into a tailspin. (Cassidy, 2018) (Hoffman, 2015)

In the UK, the government responded with a policy of "Austerity" - a reduction in public spending which, according to the British Medical Journal, led to one-hundred-and-twenty-thousand excess deaths in just seven years. (Watkins, Wulaningsih & Da Zhou et al, 2017)

Yet despite these far-reaching, life-destroying consequences, only forty-seven bankers were ever sent to jail. Twenty-five came from Iceland. Only one American served time. (Noonan, Tilford, Milne, Mount & Wise, 2018)

***

We could go on...

Consider the polluters who put the very existence of the human species at risk: The oil drillers, coal burners, airline operators, meat farmers and state militaries. And now compare them to the environmental activists who are attempting to save us all.

Who do you think the police are arresting in greater numbers?

I will give you a clue: In April 2019, the Metropolitan Police arrested over a thousand environmentalists during a "Die-In" at the Natural History Museum. That is over a thousand people, at just one protest, in just one place. (Perraudin, 2019)

Can you name a time when a thousand polluters were arrested in one fell swoop?

I cannot.

***

Then we have tax crime...

The IRS estimates that tax dodging costs the American state $330b a year. Tax dodging costs the UK around £34b a year, according the government, and up to £122b a year, according to the tax expert Richard Murphy. (Ariely, 2008) (Reland, 2017)

Big businesses and billionaires are stealing our money, right in front of our eyes, and the police are turning a blind-eye.

***

Perhaps the most comprehensive book on the subject is Matt Taibbi's "The Divide". Taibbi spent a part of his youth studying in Soviet Russia, where there was one law for the rich and another for the poor:

"The teenage farsovshik (black market trader) who sold rabbit hats in exchange for blue jeans outside my dorm could be arrested for having three dollars in his pocket, but a city official could openly walk down Nevsky Avenue with a brand-new Savile Row suit on his back, and nothing would happen".

Taibbi feels that his nation, the USA, is headed in a similar direction:

"We've become numb to the idea that rights aren't absolute, but enjoyed on a sliding scale... In the villages of Pakistan or Afghanistan, we now view some people as having no rights at all. They can be assassinated or detained indefinitely outside any sort of legal framework... We very quickly learned to accept the idea that America now tortures and assassinates certain foreigners as a matter of routine, and have stopped marching on Washington to protest the fact that these things are done in our names... (Yet) our prison population is now the biggest in the history of human civilisation. There are more people in the United States either on parole or in jail today (around six-million) than there ever were at any time in Stalin's gulags. There are also more black men in jail right now than there were in slavery at its peak".

This is not a left-right, communist-capitalist issue. It affects governments of every hue...

Like the black-market trader, picked up for the smallest of crimes in Soviet Russia, American cops are super-tough on everyday Joes and Janes. In

2011, the NYPD stopped and frisked almost seven-hundred-thousand people. The following year, they issued six-hundred-thousand summonses for petty misdemeanours like carrying alcohol in public or riding a bicycle on a path. Between 2004 and 2009, more black and Latino people were arrested in New York than actually lived in the city! Taibbi gives the example of one poor soul, arrested for "Obstructing pedestrian traffic", when there were no pedestrians in sight. Another man was arrested for drawing graffiti which was *black*, on the basis that he was in possession a *yellow* highlighter.

Meanwhile, the biggest American criminals walk free...

In the lead up to the 2008 crash, one banking regulator estimated that a million cases of criminal fraud were committed on Wall Street *every single year*. There were several instances of larceny, falsifying records, accounting fraud, embezzlement and tax evasion. Yet no senior executive was sent to jail.

HSBC has laundered up to $7b for drug cartels, allowed Russian "Used car dealers" to deposit $500k a day in travellers' cheques, supplied over $1b to a bank founded by one of Al Qaeda's original benefactors, and disobeyed state sanctions to process transactions with North Korea, Iran and Sudan. The likes of UBS and Barclays fixed interest rates, in what came to be called the LIBOR Affair; impacting the price of trillions of dollars of financial products. Yet none of their employees went to prison.

Meanwhile, a single American county knocked on *twenty-six-thousand* doors *in a single year* - pre-emptively searching people's homes, going through their underwear drawers and private possessions - on the basis that they *might* have committed fraud when applying for a tiny amount of welfare.

The police clearly have the resources. They could go after the big criminals at HSBC, UBS and Barclays. But they choose not to. (Taibbi, 2014)

***

In the last section of this chapter, we shall look at some ways in which we might democratise this system - forcing the police to go after the *big criminals*, whose crimes impact the *majority*.

But let's begin at the beginning...

BEFORE THE POLICE, WE POLICED OURSELVES

In the chapter on primitive democracy, we met several groups who continue to exist without any sort of state-sanctioned police.

It is not hard to imagine why...

If you live in a small society of twenty or thirty people, if you have a close personal relationship with every member of that society, and if you rely on everyone else to survive, then it is unlikely that you would wish to commit a crime in the first place.

If you do something untoward, you may find yourself punished without being arrested or even tried. The !Kung would mock you. The Utku would ostracise you. The Nambikuara would abandon you and your friends.

***

The historian, Gary Nash, documented as much among the Iroquois:

"No laws and ordinances, sheriffs and constables, judges and juries, or courts or jails - the apparatus of authority in European societies - were to be found before the Europeans' arrival. Yet boundaries of acceptable behaviour *were* set. Though priding themselves on the autonomous individual, the Iroquois maintained a strict sense of right and wrong:

"He who stole another's food or acted invalourously in war was 'Shamed' by his people and ostracised from their company, until he had atoned for his actions and demonstrated to their satisfaction that he had morally purified himself". (Nash, 1970)

***

Things were more formal in Ancient Athens...

Three-hundred "Rod Bearers" were used to control crowds, guard public meetings, handle prisoners and make arrests. But they were more like security guards than modern police. (Tsolakidou, 2013)

Matters of justice were dealt with democratically...

The people wrote and upheld the law. Any citizen could raise a claim against any other citizen. Should they do so, they would have to do their own detective work and make their own case to a jury of their peers.

***

This "Do It Yourself" justice remained popular throughout the Middle Ages...

The "Hue and Cry" was a common practice across Europe. If someone witnessed a crime, they were obliged to cry "Thief" or "Criminal". Anyone who was present then had to chase the guilty party. Indeed, it was a crime *not* to act like an arresting officer once the alarm had been sounded.

In England, this was complimented by the "Tithings" system...

Men were put into groups of ten. If one committed a crime, the other nine were responsible for detaining him. If they were unable to locate him, a much larger search party, known as a "Posse", would be formed. Any man could be called upon to join the posses, which were also used to control riots.

As towns grew, monarchs began to appoint unpaid "Justices of the Peace", or "Magistrates", from the ranks of the local landowners. This was hardly democratic. But in most matters, law and order was maintained by the "Parish Constable" - an unpaid farmer or tradesman who patrolled the streets and taverns, made arrests, whipped vagabonds and impounded stray animals. Constables served for a year, before passing their responsibilities onto another member of the community.

In bigger towns, the constables were assisted by volunteer "Watchmen", who patrolled the streets at night. Every member of society was expected to perform this duty, although the rich often paid poorer people to cover their shifts. The watchmen only turned pro in 1663.

***

This sort of people-powered policing *has* survived into the modern era. But it is often dependent on a somewhat unexpected factor: Town planning.

Two schools of thought permeated the subject throughout the Twentieth Century...

The first, led by Le Corbusier, called for strictly planned cities, organised in grids, with separate roads for vehicles and pedestrians, and separate zones for housing, retail and commercial properties. Where such cities were built, in places like Brasilia and Chandigarh, they required a strong state to plan and lead construction. They were authoritarian beasts. They lacked any sense of community and so needed to be policed.

The second school of thought, led by Jane Jacobs, argued that towns should be mixed - a hodgepodge of the new and old, retail and housing, where rich and poor lived side-by-side. Jacobs championed a democratic sort of town planning. She believed that towns should be allowed to evolve - to become the sum total of the millions of small decisions made by their inhabitants.

For Jacobs, order in such towns need not be maintained from above, by the police. It could be maintained from below, by the people who shared its public spaces.

These people would unite through the sort of exchanges we might consider trivial - nodding "Hello", admiring a baby, or asking where someone bought their pears.

"But the sum is not trivial", Jacobs insisted. "The sum of each casual, public contact at a local level - most of it fortuitous, most of it associated with errands - is a feeling for the public identity of people, a web of public respect and trust, and a resource in time of personal or neighbourhood need".

The effect is cumulative. The more people there are in an area of town, the higher the probability that at least one of them will step in to stop a crime.

Shopkeepers often take the lead...

They have an incentive. If they ensure their streets are safe, more customers will walk those streets and visit their stores. They also have the means. They are on hand, observing their environment, throughout the day.

Jacobs once witnessed as much herself...

As she gazed on down from her second-floor window in Manhattan, Jacobs saw a man attempt to kidnap an eight-year-old girl. Before she could intervene, all sorts of people had surrounded that man. The butcher's wife, the deli's owner, a fruit vendor, a laundryman, and two customers of a bar all helped to thwart that abduction, without any assistance from the police.

***

Jacobs was on what she called "Sidewalk terms" with several members of her community. Several neighbours left their keys with a shopkeeper:

"A person didn't think twice about asking someone to hold one's seat at the theatre, to watch a child while one goes to the restroom, or to keep an eye on a bike while one ducks into a deli to buy a sandwich".

These small acts helped to maintain order, without the need for police. All that was needed was a strong community. (Jacobs, 1961) (Scott, 1998)

Such a community is unlikely to emerge in a planned city, where people are thrown together, or where retail and housing are kept apart. It is unlikely to exist where populations are transient. And it may struggle to gain traction in a world in which multinational stores have replaced independent shopkeepers.

Still, more formalised "Neighbourhood Watches" do operate today...

THE NEIGHBOURHOOD WATCH

When Kitty Genovese, a twenty-eight-year-old New Yorker, was stabbed to death in an apartment's foyer, the public was outraged. Thirty-eight eyewitnesses had watched on as the gruesome scenes unravelled, goggle-eyed, like a popcorn-munching audience at a Quentin Tarantino film.

The people were perplexed:

"Why had no-one helped? What on earth has happened to our sense of civic duty?"

The theory was simple...

If you or I were to witness a crime, alone, we would feel compelled to save the helpless victim. If lots of people were to witness that same crime, however, we would all stand back and wait for *another* person to play the hero. No-one would come to the rescue.

The reality was a little different...

Despite the newspaper headlines, the thirty-eight eyewitnesses did not actually exist. One witness called out, "Let that girl alone". Two others claim to have called the cops. A fourth ran to help Kitty and held her as she died. (Merry, 2016)

The sense of outrage, however, *was* real. New Yorkers felt compelled to unite - to police their communities together. And, in the early 1970s, the National Sheriff's Association provided them with the framework they needed. They formed the first ever "Neighbourhood Watch"...

***

Almost half a century on, the American neighbourhood watches are well established. They help locals to secure their homes, they put stickers in windows to let burglars know they are being watched, and they drive around in packs - patrolling the streets, looking for "Red Flags" such as newspapers piled up in front of homes, slow-moving vehicles, abandoned cars and broken lights.

This is how Frank Cotnick, the president of a New York neighbourhood watch, describes what he does on patrol:

"If there are any fires or medical emergencies, we report them to the proper authorities. If there is a car accident, sometimes we will direct traffic. If there is a big fire, we will work with the emergency services and help to keep other vehicles away... If it's two or three o'clock in the morning and you see a kid underneath an overpass and hear a paint can jiggling, the chances are he's doing graffiti. If you see a male on a bicycle circling a woman who seems scared, you know something is wrong". (Geberer, 2014)

***

The neighbourhood watches spread to Britain in the 1980s.

Within just five years, forty-two-thousand had been established, covering two-and-a-half-million households. They even spawned a sub-genre of community watchdogs - the likes of "Vehicle Watch", "Taxi Watch", "Pub Watch", "Boat Watch", "Shop Watch", "Caravan Watch" and even "Sheep Watch"! (Moores, 2017)

Things have plateaued since then, but membership remains strong. Neighbourhood Watch UK claims to represent two-point-three-million households, "Bringing neighbours together to create strong, friendly, active communities where crime and anti-social behaviour are less likely to happen".

***

So much for the past and the present. What about the future?

Let's take a trip to The Netherlands...

The land of tulips and windmills never did embrace the neighbourhood watches with the same gusto as their English-speaking brethren. Until, that was, the smartphone came along.

The invention of chat applications like WhatsApp, Telegram and NextDoor, enabled the Dutch to think about community policing in a whole new way. Now they could exchange warnings, concerns, advice and information without the need to pound the street or knock on doors. If they witnessed anything untoward, they just had to send a message to the other members of their watch. They could even post an update on their community's Facebook or Twitter page.

The commitment required fell dramatically. The Dutch had found a lazy person's alternative to the traditional watch - one which involved all the talking, but not so much of the walking.

And, unlike the original watches, theirs were often established and run by the people, without any support from the state. (Pridmore, Mols, Wang & Holleman, 2019)

* * *

You may have spotted a weakness at the heart of these watches. They are staffed by part-time volunteers. They can hardly be relied upon to deal with every issue, night and day.

In Whitehorse, Canada, the people have solved this dilemma. They have established *a full-time, professional watch*.

It all began when Brandy Vittrekwa was beaten and left to die on a snowy track, in 2014. Hers was not the first murder to take place in the town. Whitehorse's homicide rate was way above the national average. But Vittrekwa's murder was a tipping point. The locals came together to demand a citizens' watch. They secured funding from the state government, recruited four people *from among their number*, and provided them with training in everything from conflict resolution to mental health care. Those "Community Safety Officers" took to the streets in the spring of 2017.

These days, if a member of the community has an issue, they can call the police for help, *or* they can call these "CSOs". The choice is theirs.

It makes sense...

If some people you cared about were having a fight, you might not want the police to attend the scene. They could arrest your loved ones, press charges, and force them to serve time behind bars. But you might want someone to come and break up that fight, before anybody got hurt.

In Whitehorse, locals can call that "Someone" - their local CSO. *Their CSOs do not carry guns, make arrests or press charges.* They would not want to. It would alienate them from their community. What is more, they may very well intervene on behalf of the locals, *against* the police. When the police were called to deal with a complaint about a dog, for example, the CSOs explained that its owner was mourning the loss of a family member, and that it would be insensitive to arrest them. The police backed down.

The CSOs do some genuine policing. They break up fights, intervene in domestic assaults, take intoxicated teens back home, help people who have overdosed on drugs, and check in on people who are fighting addictions.

They also do some community work. They have been known to help tribal elders light their fires, distribute fresh deer meat, drive kids to ice-hockey, change light bulbs, chase bears and pick up hitchhikers.

The CSOs maintain the spirit of the neighbourhood watch, but they do so on a far-reaching, professional basis. (Keevil, 2019)

**

Whatever the means, the results have been fairly positive...

A 2008 study by the American Justice Department found that crime fell by 16% in areas with a neighbourhood watch. (Geberer, 2014)

Results have been even more impressive in the Netherlands. The thirty-five WhatsApp groups in Tilburg have helped to reduce burglaries by a whopping 40%.

Still, the schemes are far from perfect. In the Netherlands, the constant contact among members has led to an increase in, "Ethnic profiling, vigilantism and anxiety". (Pridmore, Mols, Wang & Holleman, 2019)

And in America, neighbourhood watches hit the news for all the wrong reasons when one watchman, George Zimmerman, shot and killed an unarmed teen, Trayvon Martin. (Geberer, 2014)

Perhaps this can be explained away. America's official police killed just under a thousand people every year from 2015 to 2018. It is a part of that nation's culture.

But this does highlight a risk. Neighbourhood watches, given too much power, could descend into vigilante-style mobs which are just as brutal as the state's police.

**

Are neighbourhood watches a solution to the problems we outlined at the beginning of this chapter?

In a word, "No".

They show that communities can police themselves, to prevent petty crimes and catch petty criminals. But they still work with state police forces. Many rely on state funding.

Neighbourhood watches were brought to Britain by Margaret Thatcher, who proudly declared, "Much of the work must come from citizens themselves. There comes a point when the government can't do anything more".

Her message was clear. The neighbourhood watches were supposed to help the police, reducing the burden on the state. They were not supposed to replace or reform the police, to protect protestors or police the powerful. (Moores, 2017)

So where next?

There are two options. We can give *representative democracy* a go, electing our police chiefs, in the hope they will represent the will of the people, and support the watches from above. Or we can go the way of *direct democracy*, empowering the watches to replace the police entirely...

REPRESENTING THE PEOPLE

The most famous sheriff in history, the Sheriff of Nottingham, was no people's champion. It took an arrow-slinging outlaw, Robin Hood, to stand up to that fictitious tyrant.

But the original sheriffs, in Ninth Century England, were nowhere near as despotic. Selected by the serfs, they were informal leaders who maintained harmony in their village.

The king, noting the sheriffs' popularity, decided to incorporate the position. All of a sudden, sheriffs had real powers and responsibilities. They were collecting taxes, maintaining jails, arresting criminals and issuing writs. But they no longer served the people. They served the crown.

Still, the memory lingered on. And, when the British conquered the globe, they took the concept with them; appointing Captain William Stone as Sheriff of Northampton, Virginia, in 1634.

Here, in America, the gears went into reverse. The position became *more* democratic. After eighteen years, the same shire *elected* a sheriff for the first time on American soil.

Like its British equivalent, the early American sheriffs were charged with collecting taxes, maintaining jails and making arrests. They also administered punishments such as flogging, banishment, and "Execution by choking".

These days, there are over three-thousand sheriffs in the United States, 98% of whom are elected by the people they police. (R. Scott, 2019)

Nearly every county, in forty-seven states, has an elected sheriff. Their authority has diminished, the cities now have their own police forces, but they remain powerful in rural areas, and across the South and West.

Sheriffs tend to be local people; elected by their constituents, to serve their local communities. And they tend to have their finger on the pulse...

According to Casey LaFrance, an associate professor at Western Illinois

University, "The sheriff's the one that's going to tell me I'm getting divorced if I don't know it, or tell me I have eight days to leave my house". (Powers, 2018)

***

Things went full circle, in 2012, when Britain introduced elections for "Police and Crime Commissioners". According to the police's website, commissioners must deliver "The kind of policing you want to see". They must engage with the public, manage budgets, and appoint chief constables.

Theresa May, then the Home Secretary, described the introduction of these commissioners as, "The most significant democratic reform of policing in our lifetime". She claimed it would wrestle control of policing from the central government and give it to "The people". Assuming, that is, "The people" have the massive amounts of money which are required to run a successful campaign for office. (Reiner, 2016)

***

So what, exactly, do these elected police chiefs do?

Let's visit Florida, to see one in action...

THE PEOPLE'S POLICEMAN

From the sky, the Apalachicola National Forest has the appearance of a green, patchwork quilt. Longleaf pines stretch out as far as the eye can see. Semi-barren roads stitch the landscape together, disturbed only by the odd cow, Baptist church and confederate flag.

People are a rarity here. And so, when Sergeant Hoagland noticed a red pickup truck drifting off the road, two hours into his shift, he did what any upstanding officer would do. He pulled the vehicle over.

Two Chihuahuas yapped with excitement.

The driver stepped out of his truck, revealing a bulge in his pocket. The man was concealing a handgun. The safety was turned off and there were bullets in the chamber. The driver did not have a permit for the gun, and so Hoagland transported him to the county jail.

***

Whilst the arrest was taking place, the county sheriff, Nick Finch, was on his way to Dirty Dick's Crab House.

Elected at the second attempt, just three months before, Finch never did have his crab dinner. Instead, the blue-eyed former military man headed straight for the jailhouse, where he met the county's most recent detainee.

The prisoner stated his case: He had chronic lung disease. If he ever felt woozy, he fired his gun to alert his partner, who would run to his assistance. He normally left the gun at home, but he had forgotten to remove it from his pocket.

Finch nodded sympathetically:

"Fortunately for you, young man, I'm a believer in the Second Amendment... I know what law rules the day, and it's the U.S. Constitution".

He un-cuffed the suspect, unbolted the cell, and allowed the man to walk free.

***

The state was not pleased.

Considering Finch a threat to law and order, they hauled the sheriff up in front of court - accusing him of misconduct in office and the falsification of records.

But Finch, the democratically elected sheriff, had the people's backing. By the time his trial took place, his supporter-base reached Australia. His Facebook page had more likes than there were residents in Liberty County. Three rallies had been held in his name.

A crowd welcomed Finch to court, waving flags and raising placards:

"When injustice becomes law, resistance becomes duty".

"Protect our constitution".

"Nick Finch, the people's sheriff".

Finch marched up the steps and entered the courthouse. With an American flag pinned proudly on his lapel, he made his case, waited an hour for the jury to reach its verdict, and walked out a free man.

He was reinstated as sheriff and awarded more than $160k in compensation.

Democracy had won the day.

***

Sheriff Finch had not acted alone.

Shortly after the story hit the news, he was contacted by Richard Mack, the founder of the "Constitutional Sheriffs and Peace Officers Association".

The CSPOA believes that sheriffs should have the right to choose which laws they enforce. Many choose not to arrest jaywalkers. In theory, they could choose not to arrest activists - marchers, occupiers or blockaders. The CSPOA just so happens to focus on gun laws.

Finch survived because the people were on his side, whipped up into a frenzy by Mack and his supporters. He had a democratic mandate to be lenient on gun crime, and so the state could not oust him. Only the people could do that...

Six weeks before the next election, one of Finch's acquaintances got into a drunken altercation. He grabbed his gun, shot and killed his assailant.

The incident did not play well with the electorate. The gun-friendly sheriff was booted out of office, receiving just 6% of the vote (Powers, 2018) (Harte, 2016)

***

This is a clear case of democratic policing...

The people elected a gun-friendly sheriff, with a mandate to be lenient towards anyone found in possession of an illegal firearm. When that sheriff *was* lenient, there was nothing the state could do. The people had his back. But when he lost the people's support, he was given his marching orders.

In theory, this is revolutionary.

But in reality, most American sheriffs tow Washington's line. The CSPOA works with hundreds of sheriffs to protect Americans' right to bear arms, but there do not appear to be any similar organisations to push other agendas.

Almost every sheriff in America is a white man. They have an average tenure of twenty-four years. Several allow their prejudices to influence their work. (Powers, 2018)

Furthermore, the rural places where sheriffs are most active, tend to be different from the urban places where the neighbourhood watches proliferate. The idea of a democratically elected police chief protecting a democratic watch is a nice one, but not one that occurs too often.

American city-dwellers can elect prosecutors and judges. They can elect their mayors, who might guide their city's police. But in reality, such figures rarely change the system. (Bandyopadhyay, 2013)

Back in Britain, Northumbria's first elected police chief, Cara McGuinness, promises to "Focus on fighting crime and keeping communities safe". Her counterpart in North Yorkshire, Julia Mulligan, promises to

"Protect the vulnerable". It is worthy stuff, but it is rather bland. These figures have the potential to solve the problems described in this chapter, yet such issues are absent from their agenda.

Still, it is early days. Things can always change.

DIRECT DEMOCRATIC POLICING

So, if we cannot rely on sheriffs, even when they are elected, we will have to consider the alternative: Empowering communities to police themselves.

This happened in the 1960s, when the Black Panthers attempted to police the police. Wearing uniforms, carrying guns; they trailed the cops, documented their misdemeanours, and cited the law to any officer who attempted to violate their constitutional rights. (Bloom & Martin, 2013)

***

Whilst black communities were defending themselves against the police, Jewish communities were defending themselves against neo-Nazis...

Up and down America's east coast, the likes of Kavod and Hashkivenu have recruited "Community Safety" teams - training and coordinating them to protect their synagogues during the high holidays. (Haft, 2019)

My childhood synagogue, back in England, also asked members to guard the gates - protecting the congregation inside.

***

Then we have the Occupy movement, in which disruptive individuals were shunned, ignored and even expelled.

Similar tales can be found in housing collectives, in which members who do not pay their rents are sometimes evicted, and in social centres, which have used the internet to name and shame rule-breakers. (Tamblyn, 2019)

We have already mentioned the democratic schools, in which pupils and teachers write and enforce the rules together, holding trials during school meetings and voting to reach a verdict.

There is nothing stopping us from implementing such a system in our workplaces, social clubs, streets and towns. The crucial factor is *consent*. At democratic schools, every pupil *consents* to the system. They can always move to another school if they are unhappy.

This is also the case with the "Beth Din" - the court of the Jewish people. This institution has no innate power. It gains its authority from the people it judges, who consent to its ruling before proceedings begin. Only then does its verdict become legally binding - protected by the national law.

The Beth Din typically rules on disputes between Jewish-owned businesses, and between partners in Jewish divorces.

It provides a means of *civil arbitration*. Acting as a neutral bystander, it considers the facts and then enforces a resolution. It just so happens to apply the Jewish law. But a Muslim court could very well apply Muslim law. A street, neighbourhood or town could also agree upon its own set of rules, and create its own civil court, protected by the national law. (Tarry, 2008)

***

Such a system would hardly defend us from *every* type of crime...

Crime, these days, can be a technical issue. Experts are needed to solve murder cases, track down paedophiles on the dark web, and stop attacks before they happen.

Perhaps it would help if we elected our *entire police forces*, not just their chiefs; maintaining the right to recall officers at any time.

And so we return to Rojava...

***

Each commune in Rojava elects a delegate to join the ranks of the HPC and HPC Jin - the men's and women's self-defence forces. These forces operate across the city. But their members are directly accountable to the communes which elected them. If they fail to follow their neighbours' commands, they will be recalled.

Once elected, members of the HPC and HPC Jin undergo an intense training regime; learning about self-defence, feminism, weaponry, tactics and ideology. Combined with the experience they get on the beat, this equips them for life in the police.

But their terms do not last forever. The goal is to allow absolutely everyone in Rojava to serve in the HPC, at one time or another.

And so, to prepare members for their turn, the current members of the HPC train their neighbours, even before they take office. They also stand up in front of their peers, criticise themselves, and allow others to criticise them; a process which keeps them humble, and helps them to become better public servants. (Austin, 2008)

***

The HPC is democratic, it protects the community and attempts to replace the state's police. But it fails in the last regard. It sits alongside the Asayish - a region-wide force that conducts investigations into issues such as sexual violence and rape. It is hard to imagine the short-term, amateur delegates in the HPC having the skills required to investigate such crimes. (Argentieri, 2016)

And yet, in most regards, they do not need to...

According to Ciwan İbrahim, "Crimes like murder, prostitution or drug abuse are practically non-existent". (Jindar, 2016)

If you live in a community where *you* propose, debate and set the rules - then why would on earth would you break them?

The democratic process makes Rojavans feel valuable and fulfilled. And people who are happy and fulfilled are far less likely to commit crimes in the first place.

***

Rojava is not unique...

When the women of Cherán, Mexico, lost patience with the armed loggers who were roaming their town - demanding payments from small businesses, killing and kidnapping the locals - they rose up, blockaded the loggers' trucks, and took some of them hostage. The standoff was intense. But they eventually got their way. They drove those criminals out of town. They also expelled their police and politicians, who had been protecting the loggers all along.

The people began to police themselves...

They established armed checkpoints on the three main roads into town, staffing them with local men and women. To this day, every vehicle is stopped, to ensure the loggers do not return.

The locals also arrest and punish any members of their community who are found guilty of minor offences, most of which involve alcohol.

The system works...

Cherán is located in a state which is known for its violence. There were one-hundred-and-eighty murders in Michoacán, in July 2016 alone. Yet during that same year, there was not a single murder, kidnap or disappearance in Cherán.

What is more, unlike in Rojava, the people of Cherán have secured the support of the national authorities. The Mexican government still provides it with funds. Its ban on political parties had been upheld by Mexico's courts. (Pressly, 2016)

***

Systems like these can solve the first problem outlined above. Members of Occupy camps tend to not go after democratic protestors. They tend to be the democratic protestors.

In theory, they could also solve the second problem. They could go after the warmongers, rogue financiers and climate criminals.

But then again, so could anyone else...

THE BIG CRIMINALS

We have the power! We can all make "Citizen's Arrests".

Such arrests remained the norm, even after Peterloo. The state's early police forces remained small. They depended on the people's assistance.

As late as 1894, "Perhaps the most celebrated mass murderer of the century", H. H. Holmes, was caught thanks to the detective work of a private citizen, Frank Geyer. The entire Philadelphia Police Department only had fifteen detectives. They relied upon people like Holmes to get the job done. (Soniak, 2013)

But as police departments grew, this need diminished.

These days, we can still be called for jury duty, to decide a suspect's fate, but most police forces would rather we left everything else to them.

Still, we do retain the right to make arrests...

In Britain, the "Police and Criminal Evidence Act" gives us the right to arrest anyone committing an act of theft, criminal damage or assault, so long as no police officer is capable of detaining the criminal. It is, however, a risky business. The arrested person may press charges against *you* for assaulting or kidnapping *them*. (Myers, 2011)

Likewise, in the USA, citizens retain the right to make arrests. But the law varies from state to state. You need to be an eye-witness and again, you could get in trouble if things get messy. (Perry, 2019)

Still, the very fact that we can make a citizen's arrest, means we do not have to rely on the state. We can take matters into our own hands, and arrest the big criminals *ourselves*...

A TRAM SHED, A DEAD COW AND A MASS MURDERER

Twiggy Garcia looks like a session musician. His Jimi Hendrix afro is trendy and chic, as is his crimped goatee. His eyes almost purr. He seems placid - hardly the sort of person you would expect to find in a brawl.

Neither does the Tramshed restaurant seem like the sort of place you would expect to see such a ruckus. At the centre of this industrial building stands a work of art produced by Damien Hirst - a tank of turquoise formaldehyde, in which a cockerel sits atop a cow. Long tables and exposed bricks surround this tank. It is a gentrified mishmash; confused, controversial, and perfectly at home amidst the messy brilliance of Shoreditch.

Garcia's heart began to pound.

The barman had become aware of an eerie presence, but he could not determine its source.

Finally, after several moments, he followed the eye-line of the security guards who were perched at the bar. Only then did he notice the mass-murderer in their midst. Tony Blair, a man responsible for hundreds-of-thousands of civilian deaths, was tucking into his meal.

Garcia's friends said he should not do it. But he felt compelled to stand up for this tyrant's victims.

He shivered. His feet ricocheted as he walked, barely making contact with the ground. He was overcome by doubt and trepidation.

But Garcia's mind was clear. The man before him was responsible for the mass slaughter of innocent people. He was responsible for launching an illegal war - breaking articles thirty-one and fifty-one of the UN Charter.

"He needs to be tried at The Hague", he thought. "Why should only Nazis and African warlords be brought to justice?"

Garcia took a deep breath, composed himself, placed his hand on Blair's shoulder and declared:

"Mister Blair, this is a citizen's arrest for a crime against peace - your decision to launch an unprovoked war against Iraq. I am inviting you to accompany me to a police station to answer the charge".

Blair attempted to placate the citizen-turned-policeman, struggling desperately to justify his crimes, whilst his son went to fetch the security guards.

Garcia could sense the writing was on the wall:

"I've had a few run-ins with the police and it never ends well. They have no respect for the laws they are supposed to uphold".

He left the building, never to return. His stand had cost him his job, but his integrity remained intact. (Whitfield, 2014)

***

Garcia was by no means the first civilian who had attempted to arrest Blair...

In 2010, Grace McCann, a thirty-five-year-old charity worker, called for Blair's arrest as he was giving evidence to the Chilcot Enquiry. The former prime minister was not even in the room. Yet McCann was bundled out of the building by the state's police.

Two months later, an Irish journalist attempted to arrest Blair at the European Parliament. He got a little closer; placing his hand on Blair's shoulder, before a bodyguard pushed him away.

When Kate O'Sullivan told Blair she was placing him under arrest, during a book signing session, the warmonger did not even look up. He simply smiled, signed O'Sullivan's book, and allowed the security staff to act. They grabbed O'Sullivan, pulled her away, restrained her arms, and told her to "Shut up" as she listed the ways in which Blair had breached the Geneva Convention.

And when a fourth man, David Lawley-Wakelin, attempted to arrest Blair in 2012, *he* ended up in court. He was forced to pay a £100 fine and £250 in costs. (Laughland & Saner, 2012)

***

So, whilst we retain the right to arrest these big criminals, *we* can be prosecuted when we try to exert that right. The criminals, meanwhile, walk free.

All is not lost...

The individuals mentioned above have one thing in common: They went it alone. Outnumbered, they could be easily brushed aside.

In Iceland, however, the people acted en masse...

ICE ICE BABY

Deregulated in the early 2000s, Iceland's three main banks played hard and fast. They borrowed €14b in 2005 alone; a massive amount for an island with just three-hundred-and-thirty-thousand inhabitants. Then they lent that money out at inflated rates, pocketing the profits and embarking on an orgy of consumption - hosting private parties with pop stars, buying up trophy assets, and filling the streets of Reykjavik with the latest Range Rovers to hit the market.

By 2008, the banks' assets were ten times greater than their nation's GDP. But their empire was built on debt.

Along came the Global Economic Crash. The banks lost their funding, could not service their debt, defaulted, and went bust. (Robinson & Valdimarsson, 2016) (Milne, 2016)

The Icelandic Króna lost half its value, inflation hit 18%, a quarter of Icelanders lost their savings, and a large chunk of the population was forced to emigrate.

Those who remained were angry...

A thousand people took to the streets on the day the last bank was declared insolvent. Regular meetings, filled with speeches and songs, took place in front of the national parliament each week.

Then came the "Citizens' Meetings" - organised talks, including a televised panel in which the government was quizzed by the people.

The meetings grew...

In November 2008, six-and-a-half-thousand people gathered outside Iceland's parliament. Some of them covered that building with a poster which read, "Sold. IMF".

By now, the "Usual Suspects" had been joined by people from all corners of society - young and old, political and apolitical.

A corporate flag was raised above the parliament. Missiles were launched at the police.

When an activist was arrested, five-hundred protestors marched on the police station and demanded his release. The police acquiesced!

***

The protests died down a little during December's festivities. But small protest groups did manage to storm the parliament, occupy a bank, and interrupt Iceland's end-of-year television broadcast.

The police reacted with pepper spray and handcuffs, but the protestors were riding a wave. When an officer asked an activist, Hörður

Torfason, to step away from the parliament, because he was disturbing the politicians, Torfason had a brainwave. He told his fellow activists to "Polish their pots and pans".

They heeded his call…

At the next protest, people used their kitchenware to make one of the biggest rackets Iceland had ever known. Spoons and spatulas were transformed into drum sticks. Battered old saucepans emitted a dullish squeal. Blackened frying-pans added a clunky baseline.

The cacophony was enough to make one's ears bleed.

It was too much for the politicians inside Iceland's parliament.

But it was not too much for Iceland's police. Dressed in riot-gear, they were ready to march into battle.

The people were ready too. They sang, chanted, and banged their pans. And, as the peaceful majority stood back, an active minority stepped forward; throwing eggs, paint, stones and dirt.

Twenty-one activists were arrested, but the survivors were not deterred. The next day, they returned with wind instruments in hand. Benches were burned and a large Christmas tree was toppled.

The police responded with tear gas, pepper spray and batons. But the protestors battled on.

That night, the governing party held a meeting. Within a week, their coalition had crumbled. The people had forced an election.

A quarter of Iceland's population had taken to the street, the government had fallen, and a new one was about to emerge… (Bernburg, 2016)

***

Olafur Hauksson is a large man. During the course of a single interview, with the Financial Times, Hauksson helped himself to sushi, salad, chicken, noodles, salmon, potatoes, mushrooms, some more chicken, some more sushi, a selection of desserts and a coffee. He has the build of an old-fashioned rugby player and the face of The Simpsons' Chief Wiggum.

After graduating from law school, Hauksson joined the Icelandic police. He became the chief of a sleepy Icelandic town, collected taxes, issued parking fines and broke up drunken brawls. His biggest case involved an attempted murder.

From there he became the nation's "Special Prosecutor", a position no-one else wanted. Hauksson only had three members of staff. "No computers, no phones, nothing".

That all changed with the "Pots and Pans Revolution". The people had spoken. They wanted justice. They had forced an election and elected a government who were responding to their calls, supplying Hauksson with one-hundred-and-six new investigators.

His team got to work, telling junior employees at Iceland's banks to dish the dirt on senior staff, or face the full weight of the law themselves. Gradually, they worked their way up to the top.

Hauksson's first major conviction came in December 2012. Larus Welding, the former CEO of Glitnir Bank, was convicted of fraud. His conviction was overturned, but he returned to prison in 2015, when he was found guilty of a "Breach of trust".

Hreidar Mar Sigurdsson, the chief executive of Kaupthing Bank, and Sigurjon Arnason, the chief executive of Landsbanki, soon joined Welding behind bars. Convicted of market manipulation and fraud, they were sent to the Kviabryggja prison, on a cold, windswept corner of the island.

Hauksson was the only person in the West to have jailed the boss of a big bank. And he could not have done it without a popular protest that forced the authorities to sit up and listen to their people. (Robinson & Valdimarsson, 2016) (Milne, 2016)

***

Other nations could have reacted in a similar manner. They could have prosecuted staff at the ratings agencies who gave subprime loans a Triple-A rating - a fraudulent act. They could have gone after the politicians who ignored the warnings of economists such as Steve Keen, and financiers like Michael Burry - a dereliction of duty, equivalent to the "Breach of trust" for which Welding was imprisoned.

They had the tools. They chose not to use them.

Or, rather, they were not *forced* to use them.

No other protest hit the scale of the Pots and Pans Revolution. 15-M and Occupy were large, but they did not welcome a quarter of Spaniards or Americans.

Still, other protests have borne fruit...

We started this chapter with a summary of Matt Taibbi's book, "The Divide", in which the author juxtaposes the leniency offered to the big financial criminals, whose crimes *affected the majority*, with the NYPD's "Stop and frisk" policies, which *harassed the majority*.

Here, there has been progress. Taibbi concludes his book by stating that, "A federal judge named Shira Scheindlin handed down a ruling *against* New York's stop-and-frisk policies".

Why did Judge Scheindlin feel a need to brand stop-and-frisk "Unconstitutional"?

"The ruling came at the end of a long and well-coordinated campaign by groups like the Centre for Constitutional Rights". (Taibbi, 2014)

A people-powered campaign forced the American police to change their ways, just as happened in Iceland. There is hope after all!

PREVENTION IS BETTER THAN CURE

So where does this leave us?

It is no good democratising the police if we do not democratise the judiciary. We might elect our judges, abolish diplomatic immunity, provide more legal aid to the poor, and place limits on the amounts the rich can spend on lawyers.

We must also democratise the law - ensuring it is proposed, debated and approved by the people.

With such reforms in place, we might form a neighbourhood watch, to police our communities ourselves. We might elect police chiefs to protect these patrols, enabling us to make citizen's arrests. Or we might empower those watches, as in Rojava and Cherán.

In the meantime, we can always take to the streets; forcing the authorities to listen to our demands.

Still, need we go this far?

The very act of democratising our societies may reduce the need for police. If we have a say in how our communities are run, if they operate in our interests, why on earth would we turn to crime? Liberated, happy people are far less likely to need policing.

There is even a school of thought that claims we would have less crime if we had *fewer* police. This theory was first tabled by Elinor Ostrom, the Nobel Prize winning economist, who noted:

"(Smaller police departments) consistently outperformed their better trained and better financed, larger neighbours".

When police forces are small, citizens are more likely to step up to the mark and police their communities themselves. Smaller police forces are more likely to be in touch with local residents. They have to reach out to them for help on a regular basis, a process that can help to build trust. Smaller forces are less likely to be weighed down by bureaucracy. And because they cost less to run, they free up funds which can be invested in things like youth centres and sports courts; giving youngsters things to do with their time, thereby ensuring they do not grow bored and turn to crime.

Indeed, this is why the Black Lives Matter movement is asking us to, "Defund the police". They believe the police budget would be better spent *preventing crime* rather than policing it. (Vansintjan, 2020)

Prevention, as they say, is better than cure...

Several studies have shown that crime is lowest in areas with settled populations. When neighbours have a shared background, and when they all depend on each other, there is less need to coerce them into behaving well. (Scott, 2019)

Inequality is another determining factor. Amongst Western nations, those with lower rates of inequality also have smaller prison populations, fewer murders and more liberal judiciaries. It costs far less to police such nations. (Wilkinson, 2011) (Reiner, 2016)

In Sweden, young men are 32% more likely to commit a crime after completing their compulsory military service. The long-term unemployed, and people who lack job security, are also more likely to turn to crime. (Hjalmarsson & Lindquist, 2019) (Ellis, Beaver & Wright, 2009)

If we wish to reduce crime, and therefore reduce the need for police, it follows that we should do whatever we can to reduce inequality, scrap conscription, and find secure jobs for the entire workforce.

This is entirely possible. But it involves stepping from the judicial and into the economic.

Which brings us to the final section of this book...

PART FOUR

ECONOMIC DEMOCRACY

13. DEMOCRATIC CONTROL OF THE WORKPLACE

Tony Benn, the pearly-haired pipe-smoking politician, had a simple rule of thumb:

"If one meets a powerful person - Adolf Hitler, Joe Stalin or Bill Gates - ask them five questions: 'What power have you got? Where did you get it from? In whose interests do you exercise it? To whom are you accountable? And how can we get rid of you?'

"If you cannot get rid of the people who govern you, you do not live in a democratic system".

Now take a minute to ask yourself these same questions of your *boss*...

Does your boss have power over you - the ability to tell you what to do and when to do it? Was this power given to them by someone other than yourself, such as your company's chief executive? Are they exercising that power in other people's interest, perhaps a group of shareholders? Are they accountable to someone other than you and your teammates?

Can you get rid of your boss?

If not, your workplace is not democratic.

I know mine never were!

***

Before finishing my first book, I returned home from the Himalayas, where I had been living a frugal existence - writing full time, and living on a diet of rice and dhal. With barely two pennies to rub together, I was forced to take a second job, working in the kitchen of a chain of pubs known for its cheap fare; chucked into deep fryers, microwaves and grills.

I enjoyed the cooking and I liked my workmates. But neither I nor my colleagues had any say over the work itself. We could not choose the menu, amend the dishes or decide what chores should be done.

Indeed, this was not my first time working in such a pub. As a barman, aged eighteen, I recall being made to polish the brass every night, even when it was sparkling. It was servile work. Whenever I complained, I was told that it was the company's immutable, inflexible policy - unchangeable and non-negotiable. I had two choices: Do it or quit. So I did it. And as for the brass? Well, it became dirtier each night - submerged beneath an ever-thickening layer of creamy polish.

Back in the kitchen, things were just getting started...

The rota was only announced at the beginning of the week, and I never had the same shift pattern twice. I asked for the management to change this, but was told it would be impossible. It was the "Company's policy" after all.

This meant I could not make plans for my life outside of work. I could not take advantage of early-bird deals, when buying coach tickets to visit friends, nor could I commit to family events. When I asked for certain evenings off, I was assured I would get them, only to find out that I would have to work.

The workplace itself was cramped. We had to get changed in a busy hallway, between two open cupboard doors, whilst other people squeezed by. We were not paid for the time we spent getting changed. We were not paid for half our breaks, which we were forced to take, even it meant sitting around, twiddling our thumbs. Nor were we paid for the extra time we spent working at the end of our shifts, if the kitchen was still busy.

When accounting for this, our salaries fell below the minimum wage.

And this is *before* you take into consideration that we had to buy black trousers and shoes with *our own money*. We were not reimbursed the money we spent when commuting into work, nor were we compensated for the time those journeys took.

When it came up in conversation, it was clear that my colleagues were aggrieved. But there was nothing they could do. They had no voice. And when I asked about forming a union, to give them that voice, their response was simple: Such talk would get us the sack.

I quit that job within three months.

***

Other people have it far worse...

Female staff at Sports Direct, for example, have been asked to perform sexual favours in order to earn permanent contracts. Workers at the company's Shirebrook warehouse are verbally abused over the loudspeaker if they do not move quickly enough. They are fined fifteen minutes wages if they clock-off one minute early, and they are punished for crimes which include "Time wasting", "Excessive chatting", "Horseplay", "Using a mobile phone" and "Wearing branded goods". To show compliance with this final rule, they are required to endure a partial strip-search, during which their socks and underwear are checked.

Workers are so scared of being docked wages, they come into work when they are ill. Ambulances visit the site on a regular basis. On one occasion, a pregnant lady was so scared of getting into trouble, she did not even leave work when she went into labour. She removed herself to the restrooms and gave birth on the toilet! (Goodley & Ashby, 2015) (Wright, 2016)

***

I did not begin this chapter with a personal anecdote because my own experiences were particularly bad. Workers at places like Sports Direct have clearly suffered far more than I ever have. People in sweatshops, in the Global South, have things even worse. I did so because my experiences, however gruelling, were not particularly extreme. They are often the norm...

In 2009, a global survey of ninety-thousand workers found that only 21% considered themselves "Highly engaged". The other 79% were sleepwalking through their days; physically present, yet far from content. (Hamel, 2009)

A 2016 study, conducted in the USA, found that just 33% of employees had complete faith in their management team. Hardly a ringing endorsement. (Lee, 2017)

And when polled in 2008, 25% of American workers considered their bosses to be outright dictators. Less than half believed their workplace fostered creativity. (Adelman, 2008)

***

Work dominates our adult lives. The average person spends the equivalent of thirteen years and two months in the workplace. They spend several more years commuting to work, thinking about work, recovering from work, and dealing with emails from home. (Belli, 2018)

This begs a question. If work dominates our lives, and our workplaces are authoritarian beasts, can we really say that we live in a "Democracy"?

Perhaps not.

But does it have to be this way? Need we be pushed from pillar to post by our bosses? Couldn't our workplaces be a little more democratic?

THINGS USED TO BE DIFFERENT

Such an idea is not as absurd as it might sound…

In primitive societies, no individual has the right to tell another what they can hunt. No chief can dictate where or when they can forage.

Big game *does* have to be hunted collectively. And both natural talent and random circumstances can divide the group, giving different roles to different members. One person might just happen to spot a wild beast. The fastest individuals might be asked to chase that animal. The best spear-thrower might naturally assume the role of marksman. But this does not cause a hierarchy to form.

If anyone tried to behave like a manager in a typical business, the chances are they would be mocked, shunned or even ostracised.

The power remains with the people. And the people must cooperate…

An ape living in a dense rainforest could, in theory, survive by searching for fruits and nuts on their own. But the early humans, living on the Great Plains, had to travel in groups for protection. They needed to work together to hunt big game. They had to cooperate to survive.

As Charles Darwin put it in "The Descent of Man":

"Those communities which included the greatest number of the most sympathetic members would flourish best and rear the greatest number of offspring".

Human evolution followed a model of "Survival of the most cooperative". The democratic workers survived. The authoritative bosses were left for dead. (Johnson, 2013)

***

In Chapter Three, we saw that a diminished sort of workplace democracy did survive into the Middle Ages…

Whilst masters could tell their journeymen and apprentices what to do, such people did sometimes have a vote in their guilds, where they could pass rules to stop their masters from being *too* abusive. Monks worked collectively in their monasteries, peasants convened councils to manage the commons, and pirates held meetings to decide where to sail.

***

This spirit survived the Industrial Revolution…

In Britain, by the 1850s, workers had formed trade unions in most factories. In metalwork and engineering, in particular, skilled craftsmen retained most of their former autonomy.

Toronto's barrel makers went one step further. Their union actually *set the wages*. They presented a price list to their bosses, who had to either accept it or face a lockout. The workers controlled their work. They owned their own tools, controlled access to apprenticeships, and restricted output when demand was low, in order to keep their wages high. (Mason, 2015)

These examples are encouraging. But they are of another time.

So let's turn our attention to a democratic workplace that is still alive and kicking today...

IS IT A BIRD? IS IT A PLANE? NO, IT'S SEMLERMAN!

Ricardo Semler's face has a weather-worn appearance. His receding hairline is fast approaching the bald patch atop his crown. His eyes could belong to a Buddhist monk. He seems wise, but old; ready for retirement, like a football manager, respected for his former glories, who can no longer outwit his younger rivals.

Appearances can be deceiving.

Semler is still full of beans. He continues to champion the Lumiar Schools we met when discussing education. And he never was a brawler. He never could be.

Semler fell ill soon after taking over his father's company, Semco Partners - a Brazilian firm that manufactures everything from commercial dishwashers to digital scanners. He lost consciousness at all the wrong moments, struggled to sleep at night, and then fell asleep for days. His headaches felt like a plague.

After visiting several doctors, one finally cracked the code:

"You have nothing whatsoever, Ricardo... But you are suffering from an advanced case of stress. The most advanced case I have ever seen in a person of twenty-five".

It was not hard to see why.

The year was 1982, and Semco was a mess. The threat of bankruptcy loomed large. Senior managers were spending most of their time running from bank to bank, searching for new loans, just to keep the company afloat.

They worked hard and they worked long, toiling through the night to search for forgotten contracts, and travelling the globe to win new business.

But their real problem lay closer to home.

Semco was autocratic. The powerful ruled from up high, and the wise obeyed their commands. There was no wriggle-room, no opportunity for people to do things *their* way, no space for their creativity to shine. On some occasions, the staff even had to ask permission to go to the loo!

Senior employees kept basic information close to their chests, as if it were a tightly guarded secret.

The effects were there for all to see. People felt crushed, as though they were mere cogs, lost amidst a gargantuan machine. They sat down, performed their tasks, and counted down the minutes. It was little wonder that productivity was so low.

Something had to change.

***

The first step was simple. Semler split his factories into small units, placing his workers into teams of one-hundred. This allowed people to form a personal relationship with everyone else in their team.

Semler removed the clock which had been used for punching in and out. It was a show of trust - his way of telling his staff that he believed they could manage their time.

He began to involve his workers in the decision-making process. Starting small, employees were allowed to choose the colour of their uniform, fix problems in the cafeteria, and set compensation for the days between Christmas and New Year.

The results were almost immediate. Within twelve months, sales had doubled, inventory had fallen by two-thirds, and the company had unveiled eight new products. Their rejection rate had fallen from 33% to under 1%, and productivity had increased by almost a half.

***

Semco's days of financial woe were behind them, but the democratisation process was only just getting started. Before long, the firm was also asking its employees to make the *big decisions...*

When they needed a new plant for their marine division - which makes compressors, propellers and pumps - they did what any normal business might do. They went to their estate agents and asked them to find a site.

After months of trying, their estate agents came up short.

With nothing left to lose, Semco turned to their workers. And, in the space of a single weekend, those individuals found not one, but three potential venues. The firm stopped production for a day, piled everyone into buses, and visited each building in turn. Then they held a company-wide vote; asking their employees which site they preferred.

It left Semco's management with a dilemma…

The factory their employees had chosen stood opposite a Caterpillar plant which experienced regular strikes. Semco's managers were keen to avoid such a hotbed of labour agitation.

Still, they were committed to empowering their workforce. So they took a punt, bought the site, and allowed their staff to design its layout. Their workers installed a flexible manufacturing system, and hired one of Brazil's leading artists, who painted almost everything, inside and out, including the machinery itself.

"That plant really belongs to its employees", Semler explains. "I feel like a guest every time I walk in".

But the results were clear. In 1984, when Semco moved to its new facility, the average worker was generating $14,200 a year for the company. Four years later, that figure stood at $37,500, and Semco's market share had risen from 54% to 62%.

***

The company's philosophy had performed a one-hundred-and-eighty degree turn. But for Semler, their new management style was just plain common sense:

"Workers are men and women who elect governments, serve in the army, lead community projects, raise families, and make decisions about the future. Friends solicit their advice. Salespeople court them. Children and grandchildren look up to them for their wisdom and experience.

"But the moment they walk into the factory, the company transforms them into adolescents. They have to wear badges and name tags, arrive at a certain time, stand in line to punch the clock or eat their lunch, get permission to go to the bathroom, give lengthy explanations every time they're five minutes late, and follow instructions without asking a lot of questions".

Semler was having none of it:

"We hire adults, and then we treat them like adults".

Any rule which could be abolished, *was* abolished. Company norms, manuals and regulations hit the dust.

These days, Semco does not have a dress-code. There are no complex rules on business expenses, no security searches, storeroom padlocks or petty-cash audits:

"(It's) not that we wouldn't prosecute a criminal act... We just refuse to humiliate 97% of the workforce to get our hands on the occasional thief".

And those schedules?

Completely gone! People can come and go whenever they like.

At first, this presented a dilemma. One worker wanted to begin his shift at 7:00am. But when he arrived, he could not get started. He needed the forklift operator to bring him parts, and that person had chosen to begin work at *8:00am* - an hour after our friend.

It did not take long for the workers to find a solution. Before Semco's managers knew what had happened, their employees had *taught each other* how to use a forklift truck!

In fact, most of Semco's people can now do several different tasks. They have trained each other, of their own volition, without any managerial interference.

***

The system functions because workers are judged by their output - by the quality and quantity of the things they produce or sell. They are not judged by the time they spend working:

"So, we'd say things like, let's agree that you're going to sell fifty-seven widgets per week. If you sell them by Wednesday, please go to the beach. Don't create a problem for us, for manufacturing, for operations. Then we'd have to buy new companies, we'd have to buy our competitors, we'd have to do all kinds of things because you sold too many widgets!"

It works both ways...

If a team fails to achieve its targets, which it sets for itself, its members take responsibility - working day and night to catch up.

***

Semco's system saves them a fortune in administration. Since the workers manage and administrate themselves, there is little need for dedicated managers and administrators. Semco do not employ a single assistant or secretary, and they only have a few clerks:

"(We told our people) we don't want to see your expense report, we don't want to know how many holidays you're taking, we don't want to know where you work.

"We had, at one point, fourteen different offices around town, and we'd say, go to the one that's closest to your house, to the customer that you're going to visit today. Don't tell us where you are. And more, even when we had thousands of people, we (only) had two people in the HR Department, and thankfully one of them has retired".

***

The chain of command, from the president down to the newest employee, is just four levels deep.

"Factory Committees" and a "Women's Committee" speak up for the people they represent, ensuring that managers provide them with fair pay and conditions.

If they do not, it is unlikely will not retain their authority for long...

Every six months, workers submit anonymous appraisals, rating their bosses' performance. If their managers score less than 70%, they will lose their leadership position, and return to the rank and file.

In practice, such events are rare. Managers are not hired or promoted until they have been interviewed and accepted by *all* their future subordinates. The chances are, they will be attuned to their needs.

Even the top brass are kept humble:

"Our board has two seats open, with the same voting rights, for the first two people who show up. And so we have had cleaning ladies vote at board meetings, alongside a lot of very important people in suits and ties. And the fact is they kept us honest".

***

Semler has created an environment of openness and transparency...

Back in the Eighties, he put a computer in the canteen - allowing everyone to see how much they and their colleagues were being paid, how much profit they were making for the company, and what they were spending on expenses:

"When we held the first large meeting to discuss these financial reports, the first question we got was, 'How much do division managers make?' We told them. They gasped. Ever since, the factory workers have called them 'Maharaja'.

"But so what? If executives are embarrassed by their salaries, that probably means they aren't earning them. Confidential payrolls are for those who cannot look themselves in the mirror and say with conviction, 'I live in a capitalist system that remunerates on a geometric scale. I spent years in school, I have years of experience, I am capable, dedicated and intelligent. I deserve what I get'."

***

Semco's openness serves a purpose...

In the previous section of this book, we looked at ways in which education and the media establish a basis for democracy - providing people with the information they need to make good decisions at the ballot box.

Semco give their *workers* this sort of information.

Workers can set their own targets, because they can calculate how much they will need to produce or sell to cover their wages and make their firm a profit.

In some cases, Semco even allows its workers to set their own salaries. They have all the tools they need, after all. They can see what similar workers are getting for similar work, how much they are making for the business, and what the firm can afford to pay them.

Semco's staff also receive a share of their company's profits...

Twice a year, the firm calculates the post-tax profit achieved by each unit and hands 23% back to its employees. They normally vote to divide it equally among themselves. If there are a hundred workers in a unit, each will receive 1% of the dividend, be they the cleaner or the boss. But there are exceptions to the rule:

"One division chose to use the money as a fund for housing construction. It was a pretty close vote, and the workers may change their minds next year. In the meantime, some of them have already received loans and have begun to build themselves homes".

***

The point of all this should be apparent by now. Workplace democracy works, at Semco at least, because it benefits both employees *and* shareholders...

In the two decades Ricardo Semler was in charge, Semco's revenues rose from $4m to over $160m. That is a growth rate of over 20% a year. The company now operates in four countries and makes a third of its income by helping to run operations for firms such as Carrefour and Walmart.

At the same time, management associations, labour unions and the press have all named Semco as the best firm to work for in Brazil. Annual employee turnover remains under 1%.

***

Perhaps we should leave the final words to Semler himself:

"At Semco, we try to respect the hunter that dominated the first 99.9% of human history. If you had to kill a mammoth or do without supper, there was no time to draw up an organisational chart, assign tasks or delegate authority. Basically, the person who saw the mammoth was the 'Official Sighter'. The one who ran the fastest was the 'Head Runner'. Whoever threw the most accurate spear was the 'Grand Marksman'. And the person all others respected most was the 'Chief'. That's all there was to it. Distributing little charts to produce an appearance of order would have been a waste of time. It still is.

"What I'm saying is, put ten people together, don't appoint a leader, and you can be sure that one will emerge. So will a sighter, a runner, and whatever else the group needs. We form the groups, but they find their own leaders. That's not a lack of structure, that's just a lack of structure imposed from above".

And what is the key factor that keeps the show on the road?

Profit-sharing...

"Getting back to that mammoth, why was it that all the members of the group were so eager to do their share of the work - sighting, running, spearing, chiefing - and to stand aside when someone else could do it better? Because they all got to eat the thing once it was killed and cooked. What mattered were results, not status". (Semler, 1993) (Semler, 2014) (Borges, 2019) (Semler, 1989) (Downie, 2004)

ONE STEP AT A TIME

If the Semco model was so great, you might expect every firm to jump on the bandwagon. You would be wrong. Semco remains an outlier - an oasis of democracy in an ocean of authoritarian workplaces.

Let's not forget that Semco only became a workplace democracy in a last-gasp effort to avoid closure. It was a final throw of the dice, when all else had failed.

Businesses that are not faced with such challenging circumstances, are not likely to make the changes Semco made. They will probably stick with the tried and tested.

Still, other firms have democratised their workplaces *a little*...

***

Happy Computers is the only firm in the UK to be shortlisted for the "IT Training Company of the Year Award" every year for more than a decade. There is a good reason why. Henry Stewart, Happy's founder-owner, has imported the Semco model to Britain:

"Imagine a workplace where people are energised and motivated by being in control of their work. Imagine they are trusted and given freedom, within clear guidelines, to decide how to achieve results. Imagine they are able to get the life balance they want. Imagine they are valued according to the work they do, rather than the number of hours they spend at their desks.

"Wouldn't you want to work there? Wouldn't it be the place that enabled you to do your best work?"

It all sounds good in theory. But how does it work in practice?

Well, Stewart gives his workers "Pre-approval" to make whatever changes they choose, without asking for permission, so long as they operate within certain parameters - respecting the company's branding, ethos and budget.

So, when Happy wanted a new website, a member of staff was given a few criteria to fulfil, relating to keywords and design, and then left to her own devices. She took ownership of the website, launched it on her own terms, and watched on as it shot up the Google rankings.

When a receptionist wanted to redesign Happy's reception, she got to work and made the changes she felt were necessary.

These people did not need to ask their boss for permission. Their decisions had been *pre-approved*, even before they had been made.

***

Happy also allow their reception staff to set their own hours:

"We set the parameters, stating that the company needed two people on the phones every day from 9:00am to 5:30pm, and one person on reception from 9:00am to 11:00am. Also, everybody should be in on

Tuesdays, to enable a full staff meeting to take place. But within these parameters, the team can agree their hours (amongst themselves).

"The compressed week is popular, as is going home early on Fridays. But overall, everybody gets more or less what they want".

***

As at Semco, Happy's staff elect their supervisors. But at Happy, people can also move between teams, to find the best boss for them:

"It makes sure everybody gets to choose who is best able to support and challenge them".

***

Finally, Happy allow their employees to see how much everyone earns:

"Even if salaries are fair, people will often assume they are not fair if they are kept secret. They will imagine that people have got rises because they stay late, go to the pub with their manager, or are simply somebody's favourites. This is not good for morale and, sadly, without transparency those rumours are often true".

Indeed, such a policy is not as unusual as it might appear. In Norway, *everyone's* income is published online.

***

Similar policies have even been adopted by famous brands such as Gore Tex, Pret A Manger, and Netflix…

Netflix has no vacation policy whatsoever. When it comes to expenses, their policy is just five words long - "Act in Netflix's best interests". And as for travel, well, the "Rules" are just as simple - "Travel as you would if you were spending your own money".

As at Semco and Happy, Netflix seems to have abandoned the traditional, top-down approach to management. They allow their employees to manage themselves.

It seems to work…

"There is also no clothing policy at Netflix", one manager explains. "But no one has come to work naked!"

***

Minimising rules does not maximise disorder. It simply gives people the space they need to act like responsible adults.

Take the case of Tom Tribone. Soon after he became manager of a chemical plant, Tribone noticed something peculiar. Output doubled on the weekends, when he was not around. His presence was actually *impeding* production:

"The most effective direction I could give my people was simply to log the orders that came to the plant and convey that data... These folks know how to run the plant. If they knew what the customer wanted, and didn't have too much interference from me, they got it done".

You do not need to force good ideas on good employees...

When Marion Janner released her "Star Wards" brochure, introducing seventy-five ideas to improve mental-health wards in British hospitals, she had no authority whatsoever. She could not *make* those hospitals adopt her suggestions. Yet within eighteen months, half the mental-health wards in the nation had done just that. Their patients were managing their medication, bringing their pets onto their wards, and creating in-house events. Those wards adopted Janner's proposals because they were good ideas. And good ideas do not need to be imposed from above. They only need to be suggested.

Of course, to really inspire people, it helps if *they* get to do the suggesting...

At the Brighton-based software firm, Brandwatch, the development teams are given such an opportunity on "Funky Fridays", when they are set free to work on whatever new idea takes their fancy. Brandwatch has reaped the rewards, launching twenty "Funky Friday" projects in a single year. (Stewart, 2013 (a))

***

So much for minimising top-down control. What about that mainstay of democracy, the election?

They are more common than you might think...

When the chief executive retired at W. L. Gore, the firm behind the Gore-Tex brand, its staff nominated the individuals they felt would make a good replacement, and then voted for their preferred nominee.

The winner, Terri Kelly, called her election a "Surprise". Kelly has no business training, she is an engineer by trade, but she was good at her job and respected by her peers, who gave her a mandate to lead.

Once in office, Kelly stuck with the culture that earned her this big promotion:

"We believe that rather than having a boss or leader tell people what to do, it's more powerful to have each person decide what they want to work on... Once you've made your commitment, however, there's an expectation that you'll deliver. So there are two sides to the coin: The freedom to decide and a commitment to deliver on your promises". (Caulkin, 2008) (Stewart, 2013 (a))

***

Elections need not only be held to select leaders. They can also be used to decide *policy*...

Back in 1999, when Total Renal Care was teetering on the verge of bankruptcy, they took the radical step of handing control to their workers. Their "Citizens", as they became known, voted for a total rebrand; renaming the healthcare business "DaVita", and deciding to prioritise things such as "Service Excellence" and "Accountability".

Democracy remains an ongoing process...

The company unites, every six to eight weeks, to get feedback and ideas from its citizens. In between these "Voice of the Village" meetings, staff can make suggestions online.

"Democracy rules", explains Kent Thiry, DaVita's Mayor. "There have been numerous issues where I've disagreed with the outcome of a vote, but the vote had prevailed".

It all sounds very well and good in theory. But does such a system actually, you know, work?

The proof, as they say, is in the pudding...

DaVita's revenues have soared, jumping from $1.5b in 2001 to $12.5b in 2015. Their stock returns have regularly been in the top 3% of all the firms listed on the S&P 500. (Blakeman, 2015) (Stewart, 2013 (b))

***

Holding votes such as these can help a workforce to feel empowered. They give every member of staff an equal right to dictate their company's direction.

But is it wise to give every employee a vote on every decision? Would such a process not distract people from their work?

It is a question we have already posed. And it is a question we have answered, when introducing liquid democracy - the system which allows people to *delegate* their votes.

Liquid democracy has already been trialled at Google...

Using "Google Votes", on their internal social network, "Googlers" made three-hundred-and-seventy proposals in the system's first three years. They decided the direction of "Googleserve", Google's volunteer program, and "Googlestore", its internal shop. They selected several t-shirt designs, named Google's buildings, and set company-wide standards for the company's programming language.

The most popular vote to be hosted on Google Votes followed on from a food fair held at the company's California headquarters. Googlers were invited to taste an array of yummy snacks and meals, before voting online - selecting their favourite choices in up to twenty-five different categories. Tens-of-thousands of Googlers seized the opportunity. And their choices were respected. Every first choice food item was subsequently stocked in Google's micro-kitchens.

It is still early days. Liquid democracy needs to expand into more areas of operation, and delegation remains low. Just 4.7% of votes were delegated in the previous example. But the system does have potential. One Googler, for example, was delegated fourteen votes. They branded themselves an expert on vegan food, won the trust of their fellow vegans, and voted for vegan dishes on their behalf. (Hardt & Lopes, 2015)

***

Now let us consider the hiring process. Usually the preserve of the human resources department, or a cabal of senior staff, employees tend not to choose their teammates.

It does not have to be this way...

Under "Collaborative Hiring", workers get the final say. For sure, applicants may be screened or interviewed by the high and mighty. But to be employed, they must also complete a trial shift. At the end of that shift, employees are asked about the candidate's performance: Could they do the job? Did they get on with their teammates? And would they fit into the company's culture? Applicants are only employed if they get the nod from existing workers.

Collaborative hiring is on the rise...

At Pret A Manger, the sandwich shop which has branches in nine different countries, workers vote to approve or reject candidates. Pret stores can be high-pressure environments, especially during the lunchtime rush.

The staff who already work there, know what it takes to survive. They are well-placed to judge candidates before hiring them for good.

At Able & Cole, the organic vegetable box delivery company, drivers are consulted before the company employs their new boss. (Stewart, 2016)

***

Finally, let's turn our attention to two of the most important elements of workplace democracy: Profit-sharing and boardroom representation.

Perhaps the most famous workplace democracy, in the United Kingdom at least, is the John Lewis Partnership - the organisation behind the John Lewis department stores and Waitrose supermarkets. I may have a biased perspective when it comes to this organisation - my auntie worked in one of their stores. But the company is, "The UK's largest employee-owned business", according to its website:

"We started as an experiment in industrial democracy... We're more than employees, we're owners. That's why we're called 'Partners'."

The John Lewis "Experiment", which began in 1929, has certainly stood the test of time. But is it a true democracy?

Its "Partners" do elect representatives to its "Partnership Council" and board. Its partnership council provides a structure through which complaints and ideas can filter up to the board. It can change the firm's constitution and can even remove the company's chairman.

But John Lewis do not go as far as some of the previous examples. Managers *are* expected to listen to their subordinates and act in their best interest. Yet, at the end of the day, their subordinates are still expected to fall in line and do whatever their managers ask. Managers demand loyalty and respect, as they would do in a traditional firm.

This same paradox occurs when it comes to profit-sharing. John Lewis's "Partnership Bonus" adds, on average, an additional 15% to employees' wages. But that bonus is not split evenly. Employees who are paid higher salaries, also receive higher bonuses. Employees who receive lower wages are not given a say in the matter.

Still, it is an encouraging start. Workers do receive a share of the profit they help to produce.

Blackwell Books, Wilkin & Sons (a jam-maker) and Scott Bader (a manufacturer of polymers) are among over a hundred British companies which also have "Significant employee ownership", according to a study by the Employee Ownership Association. These organisations contribute more than £25b to the British economy each year. (Cathcart, 2013) (Wood, 2012)

Employee representation is even more common...

As of 2015, only ten of the twenty-eight states in the European Union did *not* have legislation which compelled firms to include workers on their boards.

The legislation varied from nation to nation...

In Spain, for example, some state-owned firms were compelled to include two workers on their boards. Private firms were not. In Sweden, any firm which had over twenty-five members of staff was obliged to dedicate a third of the seats on their boards to its workers. In Germany, firms with over five-hundred employees had to hand a third, and firms with over two-thousand employees had to hand a half of the places on their boards to their employees. (Fulton, 2015) (Major & Preminger, 2019)

THE WHOLE HOLACRACY

Let's recap...

We began with Semco, who transformed themselves from a top-down organisation, into a genuine worker democracy. We then looked at a selection of other firms who democratised parts of their businesses.

Perhaps, given time, these will continue their *evolution*, and end up like Semco. Or perhaps they will stabilise, as partial democracies, like the John Lewis Partnership.

We have not, however, come across any firms who have undergone a democratic *revolution* - throwing their traditional management structures to the wind, and becoming full-on democracies overnight.

We have not yet encountered "Holacracy"...

***

So what, exactly, is holacracy?

Imagine you want to drive somewhere. It is highly unlikely that you will hot-wire a random car, drive on the wrong side of the road, or spend the entire journey in reverse. There are rules. You know these rules, and you follow them, without a boss sitting beside you, telling you what to do. Still, you can drive your car anywhere you want, at any time you like. You retain a large chunk of control.

This, in a nutshell, is holacracy.

As an employee in a holacratic firm, there are a few rules you have to follow. You cannot infringe upon other people's projects or abandon your own responsibilities. An accountant cannot redesign the company's website, without the website controller's blessing, any more than she can hot-wire a random car. As an accountant, she will be expected to complete the company's accounts. But so long as employees follow these basic rules, agreed upon by their peers, they will retain the freedom to do what they want, whenever they want, without any bosses getting in their way.

Holacracy bins the traditional, pyramid-shaped chain of command; with a single chief executive at the top, a handful of senior managers one rung down, several junior managers, and bucket-loads of standard employees at the base. Instead, it operates with "Circles". There may be separate circles for operations, accounts and marketing. Within the marketing circle, there may be smaller circles for telemarketing and social media. Some people may belong to several different circles. Some circles may elect delegates to represent their interests within other circles. But there are no command structures *within* these circles. No individual holds any power over anyone else. Everyone must be a leader, suggest improvements, agree and amend the rules together. (Robertson, 2015)

"(In a human body), you don't have a boss cell telling the other cells what to do", holacracy's inventor, Brian Robertson, explains. "Every cell has its own self-organising process. And yet, they're kind of grouped together into an organ that integrates them and acts as a whole entity".

Holacracy takes this "Body" model and imports it into the workplace.

***

Does it work in practice?

The jury is out.

According to the Holacracy.Org website, "There are over a thousand holacracy-powered organisations worldwide that are moving faster, adapting to change, and scaling up without losing their entrepreneurial culture".

But at the most famous brand to give holacracy a go, the results have been mixed...

***

Zappos, the online shoe store, has always had a zany culture. Long before it became a holacracy, the California-based outfit held mass-meetings featuring comedians, live music, themed costumes and llamas. Yes, you read that correctly. *Llamas.*

Do take a minute to let that sink in.

Llamas.

Then the chief executive, Tony Hsieh, had his eureka moment. He discovered that when a city doubles in size, innovation increases by 15% per capita. But when a firm doubles in size, innovation per capita falls.

"We need to make Zappos less like a firm, and more like a city", he concluded.

And so he got to work, trialling holacracy within his HR department.

The trial did not last long. After just six weeks, Hsieh sent an email to his staff, announcing that the *entire company* was to become a holacracy.

"Embrace self-management by April 30", it concluded. "Or we'll give you a three-month severance package to leave".

Within a month, two-hundred-and-ten employees, about 14% of the company's staff, had taken up Hsieh on his offer.

***

Cleansed of the naysayers, power was returned to the people...

"In the old world, many decisions would have to come to me for final approval", Hsieh explained. "Under holacracy, authority and decision-makers are distributed throughout the company, in multiple roles and circles".

"Self-Management" and "Self-Organisation" were the name of the game. People were defining their duties themselves, albeit with their co-workers' consent. They were dabbling in different functions, and creating far-out job titles such as "Time Sorcerer" and "Agent of WOW".

Hiring and firing decisions were handed over to committees. Disciplinary issues were raised at governance meetings. And tactical meetings were held to ensure that everyone was reading from the same script.

***

The transition was tough, at first, for Zappos' HR director, Hollie Delaney. A company veteran, who had worked her way to the top, she found herself with no title, no job description, and none of her former power. She felt she had no "Real" job at all.

Delaney did not remain in limbo for long...

Within a year, she had amassed more than thirty roles and joined fifteen different circles. She was the "Lead Link" of the "People Operations Circle", the "Adviser Sensei" of the "Employee Relations Circle", a "Compensation Philosopher" for the "Compensation Circle", and the "Dopamine Driver" of the "State Of Mind Circle".

Because she did not have any subordinates, she did not have to "Babysit" those workers. She could put her skills to use and take part in a more diverse range of operations than was ever possible before.

Delaney's job titles may sound a little crazy. Some employees have expressed concerns about how they might appear on their CVs. But the fact that Zappos could create almost five-thousand roles, in almost five-hundred circles, means that every individual can tailor-make a role that is perfect for them. The work finds its way to the worker. (Feloni, 2015) (Feloni, 2016)

***

The system was in place. But did it work? Had Zappos created an "Entrepreneurial culture"? And had it encouraged "Innovation"?

Some members of Zappos' staff are certainly enjoying their newfound freedom...

Over in the call centre, Jacqui Gonzalez once spent an hour and a half helping a customer, going the extra mile to deal with that person's needs:

"We don't have to put someone on hold and ask permission... We don't have a manager that you need to be transferred to. How refreshing is that?"

Gonzalez and her colleagues can even send gift baskets and thank-you cards to the clients they have helped, without fearing what their boss might think. No such bosses exist! (Noguchi, 2015)

One of Gonzalez's call-centre colleagues, Tyler Williams, was spotted by Zappos' marketing department, invited to join their circle, and given a budget to plan the company's internal events. It was Williams who instigated a scheme that allowed dog-lovers to bring their four-legged friends into work:

"Under the old system, you would get everyone, from human resources to health and safety, saying that it couldn't work. With holacracy (the tables are turned). They have to prove that it can actually *harm* the company".

A consultation process was launched, allowances were made for employees with allergies and phobias, a set of best practices was penned, and Williams's idea became a reality. (Coleman, 2016)

This was by no means a unique example...

"Zappos Adaptive", which creates shoes for people with special needs, was launched at the behest of an employee whose role had nothing to do with product development, but who saw an opportunity and was keen to see it to fruition. (Tomasian, 2019)

The list goes on.

***

Holacracy has certainly empowered workers at Zappos, and this *has* led to innovation. The effects on the company's bottom line have been encouraging too. Zappos' profits rose by 78% to $97m in the year it became a holacracy.

But it would be wrong to suggest that the Zappos experiment has been an unmitigated success...

Around 18% of staff left the company within twelve months of Hsieh sending his email. Many felt that the transition process was rushed, that support was lacking, and that the new system was imposed from on high, in an undemocratic manner. Whilst some managers enjoyed their newfound freedom, others were unhappy at having their authority torn from their grasp. "Resistance" and "Frustration" were rife during the weekly coaching sessions which accompanied holacracy's rollout. Some workers even missed the security of having a boss to watch their back, and felt that they were "Drifting" without direct supervision. Others felt unmotivated without a company ladder to climb.

Furthermore, the very bureaucracy that the new system was supposed to avoid, soon became a mainstay of operations. Staff were forced to attend countless meetings, which all followed a fixed format. Workers were no longer ruled by a boss. They were ruled by something far worse: A book.

A few years down the line, things still appear to be in flux...

There are now "Lead Links", responsible for assigning roles and representing their circles - managers in all but name. On the Glass Door website, where workers can rate their workplaces, Zappos has an average rating of 3.6. Glowing reviews juxtapose with scathing remarks.

Holacracy is democratic, it does have its supporters, but it is not everyone's cup of tea. Revolutions seldom are. (Feloni, 2015) (Feloni, 2016) (Coleman, 2016)

THE ELEPHANT IN THE ROOM

You may have noticed something peculiar. The workplace democracies we have discussed so far, were all imposed by senior managers. I am talking here about the likes of Ricardo Semler, the former chief executive of Semco; John Spedan Lewis, of the John Lewis Partnership; and Tony Hsieh, Zappos' head honcho.

Elsewhere, employee representation on boards has been mandated by parliamentary legislation.

The results may have been democratic, but the means were not.

There is a reason to focus on such examples. They are less antagonistic. If you can get a firm's top dogs to buy into the process, you may just be on to a winner.

But there are also limits to such a strategy. What if your company does not have a Semler, Lewis or Hseih? What if your nation does not have a worker-friendly administration?

In such circumstances, you may have no choice but to go it alone; to establish a worker cooperative, or to stage a takeover, *against* your bosses' wishes...

* * *

Set amongst a verdant industrial park, in the Provençal village of Gémenos, the Elephant Tea factory's two administrators left the staff to their own devices. Thus liberated, the workers took it upon themselves to tinker with production - streamlining the system whenever they spotted an opportunity for improvement. There was a tacit understanding between worker and boss. A share of the increased profits, generated by the workers' innovations, would be redistributed to the workers themselves. The staff, management and shareholders were all in this together.

But the factory was a victim of its own success. After a series of mergers and acquisitions, it was bought by Unilever - the world's largest producer of tea.

The staff began producing Unilever's "Lipton" brand alongside their own, churning out billions of tea bags a year - each crammed full with carefully cured leaves, and flavoured with lemon, mint, linden and verbena.

They continued to tinker. By the 1990s, they had sped up production by over 50%. They were generating more profits than ever before.

"Did they give any of that money to us?" one worker asked. "No. Did they use it to hire more workers, or new machinery, to expand operations? No... What did they do? They hired more and more administrators.

"When I started working here, there were just two of them - the boss and the HR guy. It had been like that for years. Now suddenly there were three, four, five, seven guys in suits wandering around. The company made up different fancy titles for them, but they all spent their time trying to think of something to do. They'd be walking up and down the catwalks every day, staring at us, scribbling notes while we worked. Then they'd have meetings and discussions and write reports. But they still couldn't figure out any real excuse for their existence. Then finally, one of them hit on a solution - 'Why don't we just shut down the whole plant, fire the workers, and move operations to Poland'?"

It came to pass...

In September 2010, Unilever announced they would be shutting down operations, which had been ongoing since 1896, and move abroad. (Graeber, 2018)

***

The workers, it would be fair to say, were not best pleased. Backed by the CGT Union, they did the only thing they could. They occupied their workplace.

Unilever waited patiently, sure that the furore would blow over. But they had underestimated their workers. Whilst some did fall by the wayside, seventy-six held strong for over three-and-a-half years.

"It was hard", noted Xavier Imbernou, who now works in quality control. "We went months without pay, digging deep into our savings. Whole families suffered. But we had such support, from around the country. Our struggle became symbolic".

A dream kept them going, holding the fort and maintaining the machinery. A dream that one day, in the not too distant future, they would have *their* plant back, and this time *they* would be in charge.

***

Unilever offered their former employees no fewer than four

redundancy packages. They even invited them to continue their careers in Poland, for a much-reduced wage.

Each offer was rejected by an employment tribunal in Marseille.

Indeed, it was those law courts that would eventually come to the workers' rescue, invalidating Unilever's attempts to close the factory and forcing it to pay €177,000 in severance pay to each of its former employees.

The local government played its part too. Keen to preserve jobs, it bought the factory from Unilever and handed it to their former employees.

Those workers had everything they needed. They took a chunk of their severance pay and used it to transform their factory into a workers' cooperative.

***

The people had taken on the corporate machine and emerged victorious. But whilst the war had been won, the peace had not…

"You have to realise, we did production", explained Gerard Cazorla, the first elected president of new the "Scop-Ti" cooperative. "Purchasing, transport, marketing, sales and distribution; all of that was Unilever's responsibility".

The learning curve was steep, and disagreements were common…

The idea of working with France's big supermarket chains did not go down well with the purists. The idea of recruiting sales staff, on a commission-only basis, led to some serious soul-searching and debate:

"We have to be pragmatic. Sometimes I have to take my union cap off. We have a big factory to run and sixty salaries to pay. We're not going to change society. There's still going to be capitalism. But we try to do what we're doing as best we can, according to our values".

Those "Values" have held sway…

Roles are now decided democratically, by an elected eleven-person board, and at regular "General Assemblies". Big salary differentials have become a thing of the past. Supervisors only earn €70-a-month more than their staff. To support the community, the cooperative uses local and organic ingredients wherever it can.

***

The product is flying off the shelf.

Scop-Ti has established an upmarket brand, "1336", named after the number of days its members occupied their workplace. They are supplying supermarkets, under those supermarkets' own labels. And they are bringing the region's linden orchards back to life.

Revenues are up. In its first five years, Scop-Ti's turnover grew from €460k to €4m. Forty-two people who worked for the old company still have jobs, and twenty-four have retired with full pensions.

But the cooperative has yet to return a profit, at the time of writing, and the banking sector has been unwilling to help.

Scop-Ti has gone to the people - crowdsourcing almost €300k in one fell swoop. They expect to break even in 2020. (Azzellini & Ressler, 2018) (Henley, Kassam, Letsch & Goñi, 2015) (Calvetti, 2019)

THEY ARE NOT ALONE

The Scop-Ti story is inspirational...

Despite the efforts of their former bosses - and a multibillion-dollar, multinational behemoth - its workers stood strong, stood tall, and turned their factory into a fully functioning democracy.

It is by no means a freak example. Several thousand worker cooperatives have been born on the back of similar struggles...

Workers at RiMaflow, in Italy, also occupied their workplace; not once, but twice. When it seemed as though the game was up, and they would never produce cylinders again, those workers repurposed their factory. They used it to recycle computers and electronic devices. They opened a bar and cafeteria, organised a flea market, and hosted community events. (Azzellini & Ressler, 2014)

Other tactics have produced similar results...

When Spain's Mataró Music School was on the brink of closure, following the Global Economic Crash, its students took to the streets to demand that the authorities save their beloved institution.

A compromise was reached. The school would remain open, but its management would be privatised.

With nothing left to lose, its teachers threw together a bid for the contract. And, before they knew it, they had been handed control of their school!

It came as a bit of a surprise...

"We went from being teachers to being members in a co-op", said

Sánchez de la Blanca. "All of a sudden we had to think about how we were going to organise ourselves (and) manage our finances".

The first year "Involved a lot of swearing" and a very real cost. Salaries fell by 30%.

But a democratic process was introduced, centred on monthly meetings, at which anything could be discussed. And, slowly but surely, things began to improve. The school now teaches two-thousand pupils in seven municipalities. It has taken on forty new teachers. Wages are still 12% lower than they were at their peak, but they are on the rise.

***

Takeovers such as these are never easy. Workers with little experience of industrial action must commit themselves to lengthy negotiations, occupations and court cases. They must make tough business decisions, maintain expensive and outdated machinery, and seek out markets in harsh economic times. But their cooperatives can flourish. And they can provide a democratic alternative to traditional firms.

The numbers speak for themselves...

Following the "Great Depression" of 1998, around fifteen-thousand Argentinians took control of more than three-hundred businesses - running everything from a chain of barbeque restaurants to a petrol storage facility.

Around five-hundred new worker cooperatives popped up in Europe following the Global Economic Crash, including about thirty a year in France. (Henley, Kassam, Letsch & Goñi, 2015)

But it is in Spain where things have really taken off. There are no fewer than eighteen-thousand cooperatives in the Mediterranean nation, many of which are several decades old.

The poster child of them all is named after the village in which it was formed - "Mondragon"...

***

Established in 1956, Mondragon has been dubbed "The world's largest worker cooperative". It would be more accurate, however, to call the Basque-based group a *family*. Mondragon is an umbrella organisation which includes two-hundred-and-sixty cooperatives, and one-hundred-and-fourteen subsidiaries.

These include what might appear to be regular businesses - the likes of Fagor Industrial, Spain's largest manufacturer of domestic appliances -

Eroski, Spain's largest chain of supermarkets - and the Caja Laboral credit union, Spain's ninth-largest bank.

Together, these employ over seventy-thousand people in thirty-five nations. They generate €12b a year, which puts them on a par with the likes of Kellogg's and Visa.

***

Mondragon's members all own an equal share of their cooperatives. But outsiders, who have never worked for one of Mondragon operations, cannot buy these shares. Takeovers, like the one we saw at the Elephant Tea factory, can never take place.

Members have the sort of job security that other workers can only dream about. They receive a share of the profits they help to generate. They can vote for policies at their own cooperative's general assembly. And they can elect delegates to represent them at the "Cooperative Congress", where decisions are made that affect the group as a whole.

Perhaps for this reason, Mondragon's members all receive a respectable wage, whilst executive pay packets are kept in check. The highest-paid members receive no more than nine times the salary received by the lowest.

***

The 2008 economic crash hit Spain hard. Unemployment reached 25%, and over half the nation's youth found themselves out of work. But pretty much every one of Mondragon's members kept their job, and pretty much every one of its cooperatives stayed in business.

The reason?

Whilst other firms were busy shedding workers, Mondragon's members were voting to give themselves a 5% pay-cut, and to forgo dividend payments for as long as the recession continued.

It worked. Mondragon did not make any redundancies. If a cooperative ended up with too many workers, it simply moved them across into one of the group's other organisations.

***

It would be wrong to paint Mondragon as some sort of workers' paradise. Since going global in 1990, a decision which was backed by a democratic vote, Mondragon have opened over a hundred subsidiaries, mainly in developing and post-communist nations. The *workers* in those firms do not enjoy the same benefits as Mondragon's original *members*. In China, Mondragon subsidiaries have been exposed for mistreating staff and paying them poverty wages.

Even in the Basque region, the group now employs a significant number of temporary workers. Across the board, only a third of Mondragon's employees are full members, with democratic rights.

This should serve as a warning. Just as authoritarian firms may become *more democratic*, so might democratic firms become *more authoritarian*. The process of change is a two-way street.

***

So why mention Mondragon? The Spanish group might just seem like a larger version of the sorts of cooperatives we have already met.

Its history, however, is somewhat different...

Mondragon was created *as a cooperative*, by the students of a Catholic priest, José María Arizmendiarreta. A Republican, on the same side of the Spanish Civil War as George Orwell, Arizmendiarreta was jailed by Franco's troops. Upon his release, he returned to Mondragon, which was just a small village at the time, and fashioned himself into a community priest - acting the activist on behalf of his parishioners.

Arizmendiarreta ran a technological college, to educate his congregation, and encouraged his graduates to form cooperatives. A handful did just that - occupying an abandoned factory, producing paraffin heaters and cooking stoves - forming the organisation that would become Fagor Electrodomésticos.

Their forward-thinking approach and commitment to research helped the movement to grow - spinning off new organisations in several industries and expanding into many different nations.

In 1984, these cooperatives united to form the parent group - Mondragon.

This is why Mondragon deserves a place in these pages. It provides an alternative route to workplace democracy - one which does not require a firm to go bust, an economic crisis, or a Semler-type figure. Mondragon show that worker cooperatives can be founded *as cooperatives*, stand the test of time, grow to the size of a multinational giant, and succeed on several fronts - all whilst sticking to a fairly democratic model. (Kasmir, 1996) (Kasmir, 2016) (Mathews, 2012) (Tremlett, 2013)

ONE STEP BEYOND

Let's recap...

We have seen firms like Semco and Zappos hand control to their workers. And we have seen workers take control for themselves - democratising their firms and creating their own cooperatives. We also noted that governments can play a role - compelling firms to give employees a place on their boards.

Such paths to democracy may work in a world dominated by factories, schools and shops. But where does leave people who work remotely, without fixed contracts or personal contact with their peers?

It is early days, but "Platform Cooperatives" are being formed online...

There is Lyft - a ride-share app, not dissimilar to Uber, which is owned and run by its drivers. Plans are afoot to create "EthicalBay" - a cooperative version of eBay. Workers at Amazon's Mechanical Turk are attempting to create, run and own a crowdsourcing platform. Loconomics, a task marketplace, aims to give freelancers a platform cooperative of their own.

Only time will tell if these are a success. Many may fail. They are challenging rich and powerful firms, after all. But some might just survive, taking workers' cooperatives into the digital age. (Gorenflo, 2016) (Schneider, 2014)

***

Then we have the self-employed individual. Such people live free from coercive bosses. In essence, they are one person, mini democracies.

Becoming self-employed can be a liberating experience. When I quit my job to become a writer, I used to look at myself in the mirror, whilst cleaning my teeth, and think "Yeah, I'm happy now. I'm free".

It is a pretty common route to escaping the big bad boss. In the European Union, 15.3% of workers are self-employed. (OECD, 2019)

Yet, without institutional support, or a guaranteed paycheque, things can be tough for the self-employed. I had to leave my home and loved ones to launch my career. I struggled for several years before my third novel began to sell.

With great freedom comes great risk.

***

We could always call on our governments to reduce that risk, perhaps through some sort of tax break. Whilst we are at it, we could also demand that our governments pass legislation to give workers more rights, force firms to pay a living wage, or provide subsidies to new cooperatives. (Schneider, 2014)

Such policies can benefit both workers *and* firms...

Having surveyed over six-hundred-thousand workers, across the globe, the HR consultancy Tower Perrins concluded:

"(The operating income of) companies with high levels of employee engagement, improved by 19.2%... (But for) companies with low levels of employee engagement, it *declined* by 32.7% over the study period".

Firms who treat their employees well are also likely to see their share-price increase at a faster rate...

The Financial Times found that an investment of £100, in April 2001, would be worth £166 by 2006, if it had been used to buy shares in the FTSE 100 companies that made it into the UK's "Best Workplace" rankings. The same £100 would have only been worth £132, had it been invested across the board.

Firms that treat their staff well can also expect to find recruitment easier, see improved customer satisfaction, lower staff turnover and reduced sick leave. (Stewart, 2013 (a))

We do not have to take an *us-and-them* approach. Businesses and workers can democratise their workplaces and reap the rewards *together*.

14. DEMAND AND SUPPLY

Let's begin, as all good discussions should, with a classic scene from Monty Python's Life of Brian...

Reg, the character played by John Cleese, is sitting in the dark, lecturing a motley band of rebels:

"They've bled us white, the bastards! They've taken everything we had, not just from us, but from our fathers and from our fathers' fathers".

Stan, sitting to Reg's left, echoes his comrade's words:

"And from our fathers' fathers' fathers".

"Yes".

"And from our fathers' fathers' fathers' fathers".

"All right, Stan. Don't labour the point... And what have they ever given us in return?"

One of eight masked activists raises his hand, somewhat tentatively:

"The aqueduct?"

"What?" Cleese's character responds abruptly. It appears he had not expected his question to be answered.

"The aqueduct".

"Oh yeah, yeah they gave us that. Yeah, that's true".

Another masked man chips in:

"And the sanitation".

Reg's sidekick agrees:

"Oh yes, sanitation. Reg, you remember what the city used to be like?"

"All right, I'll grant you that the aqueduct and the sanitation are the *two things* the Romans have done".

"And the roads".

"Well, yes, obviously the roads. The roads go without saying. But apart from the aqueduct, the sanitation and the roads..."

"Irrigation!"

"Medicine!"

"Education!"

"Health!"

"Yes, all right, fair enough".

"And the wine".

"Oh yes. True".

"Yeah, that's something we'd really miss if the Romans left". (Jones, 1979)

THE CHICKEN AND THE EGG

Cleese's character asks a valid question. "What have the Romans ever done for us?"

The answers he receives, however, go spectacularly awry. They focus solely on *supply*. The Romans *supplied* us with aqueducts, sanitation, roads, irrigation and wine. But were they supplying these things *for us*? Were the Romans helping to satiate a pre-existing *demand*?

As with all such hypothetical questions, it is nigh on impossible to reach a firm conclusion. For sure, King Verica, who ruled the region around the River Thames, did like the Roman lifestyle, did covet Roman trinkets, and did call upon the Romans to defend his lands from other kings. The Romans responded to King Verica's entreaties, landed on English soil, took over English land, and built aqueducts and roads.

But what of the various kings who ruled the rest of the land? Did they want the Romans to arrive, form an allegiance with their enemy, and conquer their territories?

And what of everyday English folk? Before the Romans arrived, do you think those people were sitting around, saying, "Our roads are rubbish. What we need is some of those Roman roads"? Or do you think they were happy with their traditional paths and tracks? You know, the ones they had used for millennia, whilst making pilgrimages to Stonehenge and looking for places to hunt.

And what about the wine? Do you not think the good old folk of the British Isles were happy with their own water, ale and mead?

Were the Romans really supplying these things *for us*, because we demanded them? Or were they supplying things we had never demanded, because they wanted to create a new market for *their goods*?

***

This may be a partially fictitious example. The Life of Brian was a film, after all. But the Roman occupation of Britain was real, and this is far from a unique example.

I recall a family dinner at which one of my cousins proudly boasted that, "We (the British) were pretty good colonialists. We gave India the railways".

I could not help but ask myself, "Did the Indians want the railways?"

The British did not build the Indian railways to enrich Indian lives. In 1600, when the East India Company was established, India was an economic powerhouse, responsible for producing 23% of the world's GDP. It was wealthy enough to build railways without the help of Britain; a nation that was only producing 1.8% of the world's wealth at that time.

According to Governor-General Lord Hardinge, the British built the railways for "Commerce, government and military control". The railways were not built to transport Indian people, although that was a by-product of their construction. Indians *were* allowed to travel in cramped, third class sections, whilst their conquerors travelled in white-only first-class cars. Rather, the railways were built to transport Indian resources, such as iron ore, coal and cotton - taking them to the ports, so they could be shipped back to Britain.

The age of the British Raj enriched Britain. Its share of global economic output rose fivefold. But it was a disaster for the Indian people. By 1940, after a couple of hundred years of foreign rule, India had become a third world nation. Ninety percent of Indians were living below the poverty line. Tens-of-millions had died as the result of man-made famines.

But, as my cousin once said, we had given them the railways. (Tharoor, 2017)

***

This is not even the most blatant example of the British Empire pushing the *supply* of a good for which there was little or no *demand*. For that, we will have to travel to China...

It was the Eighteenth Century and the Europeans had acquired a taste for luxury Oriental goods - primarily for tea, but also for porcelain and silk. There was just one problem. The Chinese had no incentive to trade these items with the Europeans. China was a wealthy, self-sufficient nation. There was no Chinese *demand* for anything the Europeans could *supply* in exchange for their tea.

The Portuguese came up with a solution. They supplied opium.

Opium was by no means a new product. It had been introduced to China in the Sixth Century. But it had only ever used in limited quantities. *Demand* for opium was virtually non-existent.

The Portuguese turned opium into a mass-market good - flooding China with the addictive drug, and getting the locals hooked. They *created a new demand* for their product.

The British came onto the scene in 1773, establishing a poppy-growing monopoly in Bengal and recruiting a team of private traders to ship it to China. Other nations followed in their footsteps.

Back in 1729, the Chinese were only importing two-hundred chests of opium a year. But by 1838, they were importing forty-thousand.

The sale of that opium generated the revenues the Europeans needed to buy the Chinese tea, porcelain and silk they had coveted for so long.

But opium addiction was disastrous for China. It led to chronic health problems, caused several premature deaths, and inspired two Opium Wars, both of which China lost. (Pletcher, 2015)

***

In each of these examples, *supply* was pushed where there was very little *demand*. A few European traders did very well for themselves, but the people of India and China suffered immensely.

I do not wish to labour the point too much. But I will include an example from the other side of the Atlantic, so my American readers do not feel abandoned...

***

It was the 1890s.

The latest economic depression had hit hard. American people were tightening their purse-strings. American firms were struggling to sell their wares.

In 1897, Senator Albert Beveridge declared: "American factories are making more than the American people can use. American soil is producing more than they can consume. Fate has written our policy for us. The trade of the world must and shall be ours".

William McKinley put it even more succinctly: "We want a foreign market for our surplus products".

There was very little hiding from the fact. The United States launched the Spanish-American War for one key reason - to impose its products on foreign peoples.

The mission was a success. America conquered Puerto Rica, Guam and the Philippines. American businessmen and politicians that raised their champagne flutes in celebration. The Typographical Union celebrated too. They believed they would win more work, printing books for export to America's new colonies. Glassmakers believed they would export more glass. Railway worked predicted a boom.

But very little thought was given to the people of those conquered nations. (Zinn, 1980)

DEMOCRACY VERSUS CORPORATOCRACY

We have shown that *states* can push supply where there is little or no demand. More often than not, however, it is private *businesses* that play this game...

***

The year was 1870, and an almost never-ending supply of diamonds had just been discovered near South Africa's Orange River. Supply was increasing, prices were tumbling, and investors were worried.

And so they merged, in 1888, forming the De Beers cartel. They restricted the supply of their stones, to perpetuate the illusion that diamonds were scarce and therefore special.

Still, this only solved half of their problems. They had stopped the price of their product from falling, but they still had masses of diamonds in their vaults. To sell those gems, they needed to push demand.

They recruited the N. W. Ayer advertising agency, in 1938, and headed for Hollywood, where they gave actors and actresses diamonds to wear both on *and* off the screen. They liaised with newspapers and magazines, sending them photographs which showed those gems on the fingers of Hollywood's leading lights, and stories which stressed the size of those stones.

The advertising agency encouraged fashion designers to talk about the "Trend towards diamonds". They persuaded the British royal family to wear the jewels. They held lectures in American schools, which "Revolved around the diamond engagement ring". And they established the "Diamond Information Centre", in order to whip up stats and facts that would imbue their press releases with a greater sense of authority.

Above all, they created a brand. These were not stones. Oh no! These were an essential ingredient for love. "A diamond is forever", after all. If you wanted your marriage to succeed, and last forever, you better buy a stone that lasts forever too.

It was baloney. Diamonds are not "Forever". They can be shattered, chipped, discoloured and incinerated. But the fiction was more important than the fact. In just three years, American diamond sales increased by 55%. Today, around three-quarters of American brides wear a diamond. On average, they cost a cool $4,000.

The De Beers were just as successful in Japan...

In 1967, less than 5% of Japanese brides wore diamond engagement rings. Just fourteen years later, after an advertising campaign in which diamonds were promoted as a sign of "Modern Western values", that figure had risen to 60%.

In both nations, one thing was abundantly clear. The *supply* of diamonds had most definitely led *demand*. (Epstein, 1982)

***

Big corporations have a whole arsenal of tricks up their sleeves, when it comes to manipulating demand. One such trick is the dummy "Alternative", designed to make a product look good *relative* to other items on the market...

When Williams-Sonoma released the first ever bread-maker, they were disappointed to say the least. They had invented a fantastic new machine, but sales were pitiful. There was simply no demand for their gadget.

What did they do? They created *another* bread-maker - one which was a little bit bigger, and a lot more expensive.

Did that bread-maker sell?

Of course not! Why would it?

But that did not matter. The first bread-maker was flying off the shelves. People were seeing it, comparing it to the second bread-maker, and concluding that it was a bargain. It was only a little bit smaller than the newer option, yet it was two-thirds the price! (Ariely, 2008)

***

This is a common move...

The Economist magazine lists three subscription options: A digital-only package for $59 a year, a print-only package for $125, and a print-and-digital combo, which also costs $125. No-one in their right mind would go for the print-only package, when they could get the print *and* digital editions for the same price. So why offer it?

In an experiment at MIT, one-hundred students were given these three options. As you might expect, no-one opted for the print-only deal. But eighty-four students, the vast majority of the class, went for the $125 combo.

When the print-only option was removed, these numbers flipped. Just thirty-two students went for the more expensive package.

The print-only option was not supposed to sell. It was supposed to make the combo deal look great *by comparison*. And it was clearly doing its job, encouraging fifty-two of the respondents to shift from the digital-only option, to one which cost them $66 more. (Ariely, 2008)

* * *

Businesses also create demand out of thin air by seducing us with a dirty little four-lettered f-word: "Free"...

You may have been to a conference where you gathered all the free pencils, magnets and notepads you could, only to drag them home and leave them in a cupboard to gather dust. You may have clipped coupons for things you had never previously desired. Or perhaps you have been back to the breakfast buffet one too many times, simply because you could do so without spending a dime.

We do irrational things when we are enticed by things which appear to be free. It is a fact that corporations use to their advantage...

Amazon offers free delivery. But there is a catch. A customer must spend a certain amount before they qualify for this deal - $25 in the United States, at the time of writing.

Now imagine you have put a book in your basket. This book is going to cost you $15. You are happy with that, it is the only thing you want, but you notice that you can have it delivered for free if you spend another $10. So you search around for $10 books, find one, and add it to your basket. You have saved a $5.99 on postage, but you are spending $4.01 *more* in total. Amazon has encouraged you to buy a book you had not intended to buy, by luring you with something which appeared to be "Free".

The appeal can be huge. When Amazon first offered free shipping, it generated extra sales in every country bar one - France. Upon further investigation, it turned out the Amazon France was not, in fact, offering free shipping. It was charging one franc, a measly $0.20, but this charge was enough to reduce the offer's allure. When the charge was removed, sales on Amazon France increased in line with every other market.

The allure was not with "Cheap" - $0.20 shipping was still a steal. It was with "Free". "Free" bewitches us like nothing else. (Ariely, 2008)

***

Let's consider one last way in which corporations encourage us to buy things we never really wanted - "Product placement".

Firms often pay top-dollar to get their products placed where customers will see them: On the table of books you have to pass as you enter a bookshop, at the end of an aisle, or at eye-level on a supermarket shelf.

Indeed, a visit to the supermarket is laced with this subtle sort of economic warfare...

As you step inside, your senses are accosted by a vibrant array of fruits, vegetables and flowers. The colours and scents put you at ease, relaxing both you and your purse-strings.

You meander along at a casual pace, dictated by the smooth music coming through the supermarket's speakers, turn a corner and voila! You smell freshly baked bread and roasting chicken. Can you resist? And, even if you can, does the smell of rising dough not encourage you to go and buy some other baked items? Does the smell of roasting chicken not make you amenable to the treats on offer in the poultry aisle?

As you pick up the beers you had planned to buy, you spot some nuts and crisps on the same shelf. You had no intention of buying these snacks, but you cannot help but think that they would complement your beverages. Why not pick up a packet?

And this twelve-pack! Buying in bulk has to save you money, right? But do you even check the prices to be sure? Many customers *assume* they are getting a better deal, and so pick up the multipack, even when it offers *worse* value for money. (Kendall, 2014)

SUPPLY VERSUS DEMAND

I guess you might be scratching your head right about now, asking

JOSS SHELDON | 289

yourself, "What on earth has any of this got to do with democracy?"

Let's answer that question...

You see, the supporters of free-market economics like to think that *supply follows demand*. If this were true, it would be a truly beautiful thing...

Imagine an economy in which lots of people want ice-cream, but no firms produce this yummy snack. A business person has a brainwave.

"Eureka", they scream. "I will give the people what they want".

They buy some land, build a factory, source some cream and begin production.

Everyone wins. The people's democratic cries, to be supplied with ice-cream, have been answered. The heroic entrepreneur, who rode to the rescue, is rewarded with oodles of lovely profit.

Great, right?

But what if the original premise is incorrect? What if nobody wants ice-cream? What if nobody has even heard of ice-cream? What if the people are quite happy, living as they have done for centuries, enjoying desserts such as apple crumble and sticky toffee pudding?

Along comes our plucky entrepreneur.

"Eureka", they scream. "I will give the people what *I* want to give them".

The businessperson buys some land, builds a factory, sources some cream and begins production.

But no-one buys their product.

So, supported by venture capital, they operate at a loss for as long as is necessary. They give out free samples, pay for their product to be displayed at the end of supermarket aisles, send food trucks to community events, plaster posters across billboards, sponsor sports teams, and take out advertisements on social media, radio and TV.

It works. People get a taste for ice-cream, begin to buy it on a regular basis, and the entrepreneur makes lots of money.

***

In the first situation, where supply followed demand, corporations were forced to respond to the democratic will of the people - giving them the products *they* demanded. This could be called an "Economic Democracy".

But in the second situation, where demand followed supply, this relationship was reversed. Corporations, driven by a selfish desire for profit, imposed their products on the people. Here, it was the people who were subservient to corporations. We had a "Corporatocracy".

***

Back in the real world, we have a little of both. We certainly demand things like food, without which we would die. Corporations *do* respond to these demands, supplying us with things like vegetables and meat.

But governments and corporations also try to sell us things we do not want or need. They try to *drive* demand, using us to further *their* objectives.

This may not always be a bad thing. There might not have been a democratic movement that demanded the creation of bread-makers, but we can still benefit from their invention. I use one myself. It saves me time *and* money.

Sometimes the results can be unclear. The people never united to demand the World Wide Web. Back in the 1980s, if my friends wanted to talk, we did not send each other emails or Facebook messages; we met up in person, and that was fine. Still, the internet *has* brought certain benefits - it allows us to make plans, meet new people and discover new information. The internet also comes with certain costs. If we refused to use it, we might lose contact with our friends or struggle to progress in our careers. We are compelled to use the internet, whether we want to or not.

It can be a trap. We have to go to work, often for the sort of corporations that supply bread-makers and internet connections, just so that we have enough money to buy things like bread-makers and internet connections! We have to pay for internet subscriptions, every single month, and replace our devices every couple of years, even though we never spent a penny on these things in the past. Like a gambler, glued to fruit machine, we can end up chasing our losses forever.

***

In a pure economic democracy, there would be no grey areas. Corporations and businesses would only produce the things that people demanded.

Is such a system possible?

Once upon a time, it was not just a possibility but a reality...

According to one school of thought, small tribal bands represent the "Original affluent society". They live close to nature, enjoy a massively varied diet, and have a leisure-based existence that only involves a few hours of work per day. They have no call for things such as computers or cars, because they have no idea that such things exist.

If the goal of economics is to abolish scarcity, to create a world in which everyone has everything they desire, then these guys are the champs. When they want something, like a berry or an apple, they go and get it. No demand is left unsated. (Sahlins, 1968)

But can we, born into consumption-based societies - surrounded by cars, buildings and gadgets - ever return to such a state of Eden-esque innocence?

It seems unlikely.

So what, exactly, can we do?

We can tackle the issue from several directions...

We can reduce our reliance on governments and corporations; choosing to lead non-materialistic lifestyles, or to share things rather than own them. We might outlaw advertising. Or we might seize control of production; forming consumer cooperatives that put people before profit...

RAGE AGAINST THE MACHINE

So how do we stop the big guys from manufacturing demand?

We can take to the streets, to oppose wars-for-markets. We can elect pro-peace administrations. If we become the victims of corporate occupations ourselves, we can form democratic armies to resist them.

We can resist big businesses too...

On an individual level, we can stick two fingers up at the machine, go and live with a tribal group, or relocate to a cabin in the hills.

This might seem a little extreme, but moderate alternatives do exist. I, for one, have moved to Bulgaria, where property is significantly cheaper than in my native Britain. I have been able to buy my own home, without getting a mortgage. So I have not had to take a job with a corporation, to repay such a debt. I have bought some chickens and bees, planted some fruit trees, and created a vegetable patch - thereby reducing my reliance on supermarkets for food. Still, I am not completely isolated. I do require money to heat my home, run my car and enjoy some leisure activities. I rely on corporations to print and sell my books. It is a balancing act. I call it, "Semiself-sufficiency".

Still, even this might not seem practical for many readers. So let's consider an even more moderate example...

***

It would be fair to say that James Hong, the founder of the "Hot or Not" website, is fairly well off. He is a multi-millionaire, after all. But he too is downsizing in his own, relative way. He has sold his Porsche Boxster and replaced it with a Prius:

"I don't want to live the life of a Boxster, because when you get a Boxster, you wish you had a 911, and you know what people who have 911s wish they had? They wish they had Ferraris".

Hong lives a very different life to me. I cannot afford a Porsche, so I could never trade one in for a Prius. I cannot even afford a Prius.

But the lesson Hong teaches is one we can all learn from. Buying a Porsche will not make you happy. If you owned one, you would probably compare yourself to the people who owned a Porsche *and* a Ferrari.

The more you have, the more you end up wanting. The challenge is to break the cycle. (Ariely, 2008)

Of course, this is easier said than done, especially when you are trying to go it alone. So why not join a club?

***

When I was growing up there was a magical place my mum used to take me. No, not the sweet shop. I am talking about a much healthier place. Somewhere you could peruse, read or borrow tens-of-thousands of books for free - the library.

Okay, technically libraries are not free. We pay for them with our taxes. But they are free at the point of use.

As I grew up, my library began to diversify - lending out cassettes, and then CDs, before finally installing desktop computers with internet access. These days, libraries can have reading programs, career resources, and production studios. They can be the first stop for immigrants, a place for parents to teach their children to read, and a space for the socially isolated to gain some precious human contact. Staff at a few libraries have even been trained to administer Naloxone to people who have overdosed on opioids.

The system is a game-changer...

Without libraries, if one-hundred people wanted to read a book, they

JOSS SHELDON | 293

would have to buy one-hundred copies. Businesses would have to use lots of electricity, paper and ink to print those books. Anyone who could not afford to buy books, would have to go without.

With libraries, however, we might only need to print a couple of copies. The benefits would be the same. One-hundred people could still read that book. But the costs would be much lower. Because we would be producing ninety-eight fewer books, we would we need less paper and ink, fewer printing presses and less labour. We would need less storage space to store those books, and fewer vehicles to transport them.

Our reliance on corporations would be reduced dramatically, as would our carbon footprint.

***

Libraries not only underpin *economic democracy*, they also support *political democracy*. The majority of places which have strong library cultures also have stable representative democracies and free speech.

Libraries reach right across a population...

In 2017, seventeen-million people visited New York's public libraries - more than visited every museum and every sporting event in the city. They are one of the few democratic, non-commercial spaces left in our communities - secular gathering places where people from all walks of life may come into contact. They have no political affiliation. They give access to ideas that span the entire spectrum of history, genre, gender and race. (Roy, 2019) (Anderson, 2018)

But libraries have their limits. They can be closed down by miserly administrations, and by authoritarian leaders who do not wish to be challenged by a well-informed population. They may provide us with democratic access to books, but they do nothing to satisfy our other demands. For these, we must still rely on corporations.

Or so you might think...

***

If you were walking through Toronto, you might not take a second glance at the storefront marked "Library of Things". The blue-and-white façade helps blend this store in with its surroundings. The record shop next-door, a novelty in Twenty-First Century Canada, is far more likely to catch your eye.

But give it a second glance and you might just be surprised. This

"Sharing Depot" is no ordinary shop. The things on these shelves are not for sale.

Memberships, which start at CA$55 a year, about $40 or £30, allow locals to borrow tens-of-thousands of dollars' worth of items - saving them a small fortune, and giving them access to things they might not have otherwise been able to afford.

Hosting a party? Great. Come on in, borrow some wine glasses, foldable chairs and a popcorn maker.

Going to a festival? Super. Grab yourself a tent, a camping stove and some sleeping bags.

Having the grandkids over? Cool. Borrow some games they have never played before. You can get them a different game every time they come to visit.

The Sharing Depot even has a sister, the "Toronto Tool Station", where DIY-ers can borrow the sorts of tools they might need once or twice a year, but do not need to own outright - things like hedge-trimmers, decking tools and concrete mixers.

***

By 2017, just four years after opening its doors, Toronto's Tool Library and Sharing Depot had attracted over two-thousand members. On the grand scale of things, this is a drop in the ocean. Still, according to the store's founders, there are about eighty other tool libraries across the globe. Universities and farms are also beginning to share their equipment. The movement is small, but it appears to be growing. (Strauss, 2017)

Things are even bigger online...

Sites such as Green Piñata Toys, send parents a new set of sanitised toys through the post each month. Their children use those playthings, return them, and receive a different toy the next month.

Clothes-sharing websites, such as Rent the Runway, give women the chance to dress up in the latest designer outfits, handbags and jewellery; before exchanging them for a new set of clothes.

ThredUP allows parents to send off the clothes which no longer fit their kids, earn store credit when those clothes are sold, and then use that credit to buy new clothes which actually fit their children.

These sites are all corporations. But non-profit equivalents do exist...

As of 2014, the Freecycle Network was home to five-thousand groups in eighty-five countries. The site's premise is simple. Members list their unwanted items online, other members see them, like them, and then pick them up for free. (Rifkin, 2014)

Sites such as Gumtree and Facebook Marketplace also allow users to list items they would like to give away.

***

Perhaps the most famous example of sharing comes from the automobile industry...

In North America, car-sharing organisations typically charge members a refundable deposit of between $300 and $500, a dollar or two for every hour they use a vehicle, and between twenty-five and forty cents for every mile they drive.

Compare this to car *ownership*...

Buying, insuring, taxing and maintaining a car can cost many thousands of dollars. But once you have paid for these things, each journey is relatively cheap - around $2 for a fifteen-mile trip. Car owners might therefore feel a need to chase their losses; making several cheap journeys, to justify their initial investment. They might over-consume.

With car-sharing, however, the only upfront cost is a refundable deposit. But a fifteen-mile trip may cost around $10 - five times as much as before. It is in car-sharers' interest to *limit* their consumption.

The results speak for themselves. Car-sharers drive between 40% and 60% less than car-owners. They temper their demand.

The effects do not stop there...

Eighty percent of people who owned a car before joining a car-sharing network, sold their car after becoming members. Before joining such a club, members owned 0.47 cars per household on average. After joining, they only owned 0.24 vehicles per household.

Because around eight to fifteen members share each car, fewer vehicles need to be produced - saving us work, protecting the environment, and leaving more car-parking spaces on our streets.

The system is by no means perfect. It only works in areas where lots of people live close together. It is still being rolled out across the world. But it does have a significant base. By 2016, five-point-eight-million people were using car-sharing services in Europe alone, according to research by Deloitte. And this number does not include the people who were using *bike-sharing services*. Several cities now rent out bicycles on an hourly or daily basis.

Whilst car-sharing may rely upon private corporations, and bike-sharing may require government intervention, people-led alternatives do exist. Relay Rides is a peer-to-peer car-sharing service that allows car owners to share *their own vehicles*. Sites like BlaBlaCar bring commuters together - allowing drivers to give a lift to anyone who wishes to make the same journey they plan to make, so long as they pay for some of the fuel. (Litman, 2000) (Rifkin, 2014)

***

These things can all help us to resist the big corporations, and retake control of our spending. But it is only a tiny piece of control. Most people do not sell their sports cars and replace them with smaller alternatives, move to countries where the cost of living is low, join a library of things or a car-sharing scheme.

So should we go for the nuclear option, and introduce an outright ban on advertising?

It might sound a little extreme, but it has been tried...

RECLAIMING THE STREETS

Gaze out at the glitzy screens which hover above São Paulo's streets, and you will be sure to see several public announcements. But you might find the experience a little strange, and it might take you a few seconds to work out why. Unlike in downtown London or New York, there are no corporate messages here - no ubiquitous logos, no adverts of any kind.

It was not always this way. At the turn of the millennium, São Paulo had been choking under a smog of signage.

Led by the mayor, Gilberto Kassab, the people fought back - passing the "Clean City Law", removing fifteen-thousand billboards and three-hundred-thousand storefront signs.

Scaffolds were left hollow where adverts used to soar. Logos were scrubbed from the outside of factories and silos. Shop names were removed from storefronts. Wooden frames appeared on the sides of apartment blocks, surrounding the spaces where corporate messages had once stood tall. (Mahdawi, 2015)

The policy proved incredibly popular. Five years after the city was cleansed of its corporate branding, 70% of Paulistanos said the clean laws had been "Beneficial".

This is not to say it was a total success. Corporations simply turned their focus elsewhere - using guerrilla marketing, advertising online and on social media. Rather than pay for illegal billboards, General Electric commissioned eye-catching murals which engulfed the sides of entire blocks - beautifying the city with its artwork, whilst subtly promoting its brand. (Falk, 2012) (Handley, 2012)

When Kassab left office, and a pro-business mayor took his place, the legislation was relaxed. The city allowed corporations to run thirty-two big screens, so long as they painted, cleaned and illuminated the city's bridges. (Wentz, 2017)

Nothing lasts forever.

Nor did São Paulo ever issue a complete ban on *all* forms of advertising. They only ever banned *public* signage; a single form of the medium which Kassab dubbed "Visual pollution". (Mahdawi, 2015)

It is easy to understand why...

When we buy a magazine, listen to a radio station or watch a television channel, we consent to receive whatever messages those outlets decide to air. But when we are outside, in what should be *democratic spaces*, places for the people, we have no choice. We have corporate messages imposed on us whether we consent to it or not. (Hellpern, 2016)

Even David Ogilvy, the godfather of modern advertising, was against the format.

"Man is at his vilest when he erects a billboard", Ogilvy once wrote. "When I retire from Madison Avenue, I am going to start a secret society of masked vigilantes who will travel around the world on silent motorbikes, chopping down posters in the dark!" (Mahdawi, 2015)

We cannot be sure if Ogilvy was ever true to his word.

One contemporary organisation, however, is going further than even Ogilvy could have imagined. *Brandalism* is not merely "Chopping down posters". It is actively replacing them.

The results are as entertaining as they are thought-provoking...

On one billboard, the words "Just Loot It" appear in place of Nike's slogan, "Just Do It". On another, four giant words consume a white background - "Man Crushed Under Success". A third shows a worker in a hazmat suit, holding a McDonald's happy meal on the end of a pole; offering it to a cartoonish image of a child.

In December 2015, Brandalism crossed the channel to expose the corporate green-washing of the Paris Climate Conference, plastering more than six-hundred pieces of art across the city. On one, David Cameron was seen wearing a racing driver's overalls, covered in logos from the likes of British Gas and Shell.

"(We challenge the) corporate control of the visual realm", Brandalism's Robert Marcuse explains. "(We challenge the way) those with the most amount of money can put their messages in front of everyone, without our permission".

Marcuse insists that brandalising is simple. You just need a high-visibility jacket, an Allen-key and a piece of artwork. But that is not to say it is always effective...

Brandalism once targeted the biggest advertising firms in London: Ogilvy, BBDO and J. Walter Thompson. It encouraged their workers to "Switch sides".

Over one-hundred people replied! They did not like the firms who employed them. Given a free choice, they would have done the same sort of work for Brandalism. But their jobs paid them the money they needed to survive, whereas Brandalism could not afford to pay them a penny.

They were essentially faced with a stark choice: Your money or your integrity. They had to forgo their dreams and take the money, just to stay alive.

Such is the corporatocracy. (Hellpern, 2016)

***

So far, we have considered two very different solutions to the same problem. In Brazil, the authorities banned public advertising from the top-down. In London, a grassroots movement attacked it from below.

In France, the two sides appear to be meeting in the middle...

Parisian activists are also challenging the commercialisation of public spaces, using paper and sticky-tape to cover the screens that flash at passers-by.

And politicians are doing their bit too. In the French parliament, François Ruffin has already tabled his "Pee in Peace" motion, which seeks to ban video advertising above urinals. Since 2015, over two-thousand such screens have colonised toilets in twenty-five French towns. Ruffin asks a simple, but pertinent question - "Who doesn't enjoy that rare moment of calm: Having a piss?"

His colleague in Grenoble is one step ahead. Erice Piolle, the mayor of that alpine city, has already replaced more than three-hundred signs with trees or community noticeboards. (Chrisafisi, 2019)

In 2011, Paris made plans to remove a third of its advertising hoardings. Two years before, Chennai also banned the erection of new billboards. Vermont, Maine, Hawaii and Alaska are all billboard-free. (Mahdawi, 2015)

***

It is a start, but there is still a long way to go. Around fifty-million new adverts are produced every year in the USA alone. The average American is exposed to a thousand such messages a day.

Marketing is big business. In 2002, American firms spent $237b persuading people to part with their hard-earned dosh. The sector consumes 2.3% of America's GDP. (Nelson, 2004) (Boddewyn, 2015)

But we need not attack the whole industry at once. We can pick our battles - waging war with the corporatocracy on a sector-by-sector basis.

Let's take smoking as an example...

On the 1st of July 1975, the Norwegian government passed a bill which banned the promotion of tobacco-related products. It was a democratic act, supported by 81% of the population. And it was a success. In 1975, the year the ban was introduced, the average Norwegian adult consumed two-thousand-one-hundred grams of tobacco a year. By 2002, they consumed just twelve-hundred grams. (Bjartveit, 2003)

Norway was not alone. When Iran banned tobacco advertising, 14.6% of Iranians were smokers. Five years later, that figure had fallen to 11.7%.

The results were even more profound in Thailand. Just nine years after banning tobacco adverts, the proportion of Thais who smoked had fallen from 35.2% to just 22.5%. (World Health Organisation, 2003) (Chitanondh, 2003)

Advertising bans do work. They allow people to retake control of their desires and reduce their consumption. The data speaks for itself.

***

The effects are by no means limited to the tobacco industry...

According to Anne Lappé, founder of Food Myth Busters, "Food corporations spend roughly $2b a year on ads targeting children and teens". Most of the products they push are unhealthy - filled to the brim with sugar and fat. Diet-related illnesses are on the rise.

But the fight-back has begun.

In 1980, Quebec became the first place to ban junk-food advertising to children. Since then, spending on fast food has fallen by 13% in the Canadian state, which has the lowest child obesity rate in the nation. Countries such as Chile, France, Norway and Ireland have all followed suit. (Tsai, 2016)

***

So we can ban public advertising, and we can ban adverts for items such as tobacco, junk food and alcohol. Such legislation does get results.

Nothing is stopping us from taking on other products - banning adverts for cars which pollute our environment, beauty products which make us hate the way we look, and gadgets which need to be replaced on a regular basis.

We, the people, might also create our own peer-to-peer reviews, to crowd-out the corporate ads. I am talking here of the personal recommendations you might give to a friend, the comments you might see at the bottom of an Amazon page, and the homemade videos you might find on YouTube. (Rifkin, 2014)

Will this be enough?

Perhaps not.

Even if we banned advertising completely, businesses would still try to whip up demand through pricing tricks, the power of "Free", and product placement. We could create some sort of corporate police, to monitor these activities, but that would be pretty authoritarian.

Thankfully, we have one more tool at our disposal...

CONSUMER CONTROL

Fans of the free market like to tell us that private firms are always efficient, they always serve the people, and we would live in the best of all possible worlds if we just left them alone to their own devices.

I have tried to draw a more nuanced, less idealised vision of the world - one in which there are both *democratic businesses*, which supply the people with the things they demand, and *undemocratic businesses*, which stir up demand for the things *they* wish to supply.

A good business will serve all its "Stakeholders". It will pay dividends to its *shareholders* and taxes to its *government*. It will provide its *workers* with good pay and conditions, treat the *environment* with respect, host *community* events, and supply the products its *customers* demand.

In many cases, however, businesses focus all their energies on generating short-term profits for their *shareholders*. They fail to consider the needs of their other *stakeholders*. (Freeman, 1984)

This is anti-democratic. A firm's shareholders represent a tiny minority of the overall population. In the UK, 81% of people do not own any shares at all. The vast majority of shares traded on the London Stock Exchange are owned by corporations, not by individuals. And whilst many people do own shares *indirectly*, through their pension funds, this does not endow them with voting rights. (Jefferies, 2015)

There is, however, a solution. Combine your stakeholders. *Make your customers your shareholders*, and give them a voice...

MORE THAN A CLUB

They call Futbol Club Barcelona, "More than a club". It represents both the region of Catalonia *and* its dreams of independence. It runs amateur and professional teams in thirteen different sports. And its football team is a global player, one of the most identifiable brands on the planet, twenty-six times winners of Spain's La Liga and five-times winners of the European Champions League.

But it is not just more than a club, it is also more than a corporation. It is a "Consumer Cooperative", owned and run by hundreds-of-thousands of its fans. (LaSalle, 2012)

***

Round-faced, tanned, a cheeky grin never far from his face; Joan Laporta is staring earnestly into a camera:

"If I become the president of Barcelona again, I'll make sure we keep winning, I'll revive La Masía, and I'll lay the foundations for another decade of success. With me as president, (Lionel) Messi will always be happy and UNICEF will return to the shirt".

His hands underline each pronouncement:

"That's why I'm asking for your vote. Thank you very much. Visca Barça y visca Catalunya!"

***

The campaign to become Barcelona's next president is as intense as any political election. There are regular polls. The nation's main newspapers dedicate several columns to each of the candidates' campaigns. There are even televised debates.

At Laporta's campaign headquarters, there are giant prints, busy TV screens, and tables covered in badges and flyers. There are five-hundred volunteers, a "Media Enquiries" team, and a "Director of Communications".

It is all very reminiscent of an American political drama.

But the drama, in this campaign at least, is thin on the ground. The fans are happy. Their team has just won the treble. Why would they oust the incumbent, Josep Bartomeu?

Well, someone has to challenge the throne, right? Democracy needs dissenting voices, to keep elected officials on their toes.

Laporta is picking his battles...

Unlike most clubs, Barcelona refused to place a corporate logo on its shirt for over a century. It was more than a club. Its shirt was more than a shirt. It represented something greater than nylon thread and coloured dye. It represented a dream, an ethos - the space which touched the players' hearts.

But Bartomeu had sold that space to Qatar, pocketing €45m, and slapping the name of a human-rights abusing nation on this sacred shirt.

Laporta is calling him out. He is promising to reclaim Barcelona's soul; to remove the corporate stain from Barcelona's jersey, and replace it with the name of a children's charity - UNICEF.

But will this gesture be enough to win him the election? (Lowe, 2015) (Berlin, 2015)

***

FC Barcelona resumed life as a democratic institution upon Franco's death, in 1978. But their elected president, Josep Núñez, came to be seen as regressive and corrupt. So a group of supporters established "L'Elefant Blauto", to campaign for *more* member democracy. And, in 2003, they got their man elected to the hotseat. Joan Laporta became president of FC

Barcelona.

Laporta recruited a management team, made up of Barcelona's *supporters* - people who genuinely cared about the club. Together, they built a global brand - boosting the club's revenues from €123m to €308m and laying the foundations for the most trophy-laden period in the club's history. They proved beyond any doubt that a business run by its customers could be a success. (Hamil, Walters & Watson, 2010)

Laporta left the club in 2010 to pursue a career in politics. But now he is back, ready to reclaim control.

Will the supporters remember his previous contribution, and re-elect him? Or will they retain his successor?

***

The club has done everything it can to encourage its members to vote...

In the conference hall next to its stadium, the tables are filled with free food and drink. Fans can have their picture taken with the trophies the club won the season before. There are activities for children.

The doors open. Members trickle in, cast their votes and leave. Fourteen hours pass, voting closes, and the ballots are counted. (Berlin, 2014)

Does Laporta win?

Unfortunately, for him, he does not. He secures around a third of the vote, but Bartomeu wins by quite some margin.

It is not the result Laporta would have wanted, but it is a victory for democracy nonetheless. It is hard to imagine the biggest sporting clubs in the UK or the USA giving their supporters the chance to remove their corporate chiefs. It is even harder to imagine the likes of General Electric or Disney allowing their customers to boot their CEO from office. But here, in Catalonia, we do not have to imagine such a thing. Barcelona's customers, their fans, are given such an opportunity every six years.

***

What we have described so far has all the hallmarks of a representative democracy. But fan-power does not stop here...

As well as electing the club's president, the club's members also elect its board. The board, in turn, is held to account by "The Assembly of Delegates" - a body of three-thousand members, most of whom are selected at random.

It is the assembly that selects the club's charitable projects. It votes on membership and ticket prices, as well as motions relating to marketing and merchandising. (Hamil, Walters & Watson, 2010) (La Salle, 2012)

At the 2019 assembly, for example, "Socios" voted to approve the 2018-19 fiscal report and the 2019-20 budget. They voted to revoke the three medals awarded to General Franco in the 1970s - a proposal which had been raised by several members, and which passed by six-hundred-and-seventy-one votes to two. But one member-proposed motion, to introduce electronic voting, was rejected. It gained 59.9% of the votes, but came up short of the two-thirds majority it required. (FC Barcelona, 2019)

***

It would be wrong to paint FC Barcelona as a paradigm of virtue. It is a democratic institution, but it is hardly squeaky clean…

The club's image took a blow when it partnered with Qatar. It was accused of evading taxes, when it under-declared the amount it had spent to sign Brazilian star, Neymar Junior. And it was banned from signing new players as a punishment for signing minors from abroad. (Berlin, 2015)

Even the club's democracy has its limits. When standing for president, a candidate must secure a bank guarantee which covers 15% of the club's budget - around €77m when Laporta ran in 2015. It is a rich person's game. (Lowe, 2015)

Nor is the Barcelona model secure from political threats…

In the past, almost every football club in Spain was supporter-owned. But in 1990, the Spanish government passed a law which forced any club that made a loss in the 1985-86 season to open themselves up to private ownership. Only four professional clubs in Spain are supporter-run today.

Still, these are joined by plenty of other clubs in other countries. The majority of clubs in Germany, Argentina and Turkey are also run by their fans. (Hamil, Walters & Watson, 2010)

***

It is when we look at ticket prices that the effects of member democracy really come into view…

According to The European Football Index, in the 2018-19 edition of England's Premier League, the cheapest season ticket cost £299. That was at Huddersfield Town, a relatively small club who were relegated at the end of the campaign. The cheapest season ticket at Arsenal cost £891! Across all twenty clubs, the cheapest season ticket cost £516 on average.

But across all the clubs in Germany's Bundesliga, the cheapest season ticket cost just £159 on average. At Bayern Munich, Germany's most successful club, season tickets were available for just £125. At Real Madrid, which is also supporter-owned, you could buy a season ticket for just £218. And at FC Barcelona you could grab one for £149. (My Voucher Codes, 2018)

The numbers speak for themselves.

When clubs are run democratically, by their customers, they put their customers first - charging them reasonable prices to attend games. When they are run as corporations, those prices become obscene.

Yet those higher ticket prices do not bring about success on the field. No club has won more European Champions League titles than Real Madrid. Nor does it result in greater fiscal success. According to Deloitte's 2019 "Money League", of the four clubs which had the highest revenues in world football, three were supporter-owned democracies.

Clubs run by their fans can be more successful than clubs run as corporations in every way. They can win more trophies, charge lower prices, *and* generate higher revenues.

TAKING THE SHOW ON THE ROAD

Traditionally, we have been given a somewhat binary choice. An industry or organisation can be nationalised or it can be privatised. It can be run by the state or by private corporations.

Both systems have democratic elements. If we do not like the way a nationalised industry is run, we can vote an administration out of office, and elect a party that will manage it differently. If we do not like the way a private business is run, we can vote with our feet, and take our custom elsewhere.

In reality, the alternatives might not be much better. Few elections are won or lost because of the way a party promises to run a single nationalised industry. And when it comes to natural monopolies, such as the railways and water supply, there tends to be very little competition in the private sector. When alternative suppliers do exist, they tend to offer an incredibly similar service for incredibly similar prices.

Whether they are nationalised or privatised, such industries tend to be ruled from the top-down. Be they headed by a minister or a chief executive, be they managed by a team of bureaucrats or a board of directors, they are likely to serve their masters, their parties or their shareholders, rather than their customers.

It does not have to be like this. FC Barcelona show that we do not have to nationalise *or* privatise. We can take organisations into *customer ownership*, and manage them democratically, from the *bottom-up*.

It might work something like this...

A government could take an industry, perhaps the railways, and give it to the people; issuing a single *citizen-share* to every person in the nation. These would not be normal shares. It would be impossible to buy or sell them. But they would entitle their owners, the people of the nation, to vote on key issues.

We could give our citizen-shareholders the right to vote for the chief executive and board; holding elections, like the one we saw between Laporta and Bartomeu. We could select a general assembly at random; compelling individuals to attend meetings, just as we compel people to attend jury service. We could even use a process of direct democracy, to give everyone in the nation the right to propose and vote on motions.

With such a structure in place, we could force the people running our railways to keep fares low, in much the same way that supporters of FC Barcelona force their club to issue cheap tickets. We could demand that they invest in their product, to provide us with a speedy and punctual service, in much the same way that FC Barcelona has invested in its team. We could even demand that they focus on making a profit - paying a citizen's dividend to every person in the nation.

If FC Barcelona can do it, why can't we?

We can. *It has been done*, in the energy sector, in countries such as Denmark and New Zealand...

***

It is as though they are watching you. Standing on the Copenhagen shore, looking out to sea, you are confronted by twenty wind-turbines, spaced at equal distances, like spectators in a theatre's front row. Gentle ripples add texture to the ocean's aquamarine surface. A trawler draws near.

When it was built, in 2000, the offshore windfarm here at Middelgrunden was the largest in the world. But this oceanic power-station was not met with public opposition. It was built with the public's support.

It began with a consultation...

Fifty-thousand residents had their say, telling their government what they wanted to be done. Their views determined everything from the position of the turbines to the content of individual contracts.

Some locals even backed up their words with cold hard cash. Eight-and-a-half-thousand Danish citizens invested €23m in the project - half the total budget. In return, they were issued shares in a consumer cooperative, which owns and manages half the turbines.

***

The Danish cooperative movement is nothing new. Several Danish banks, dairies and food shops are run as cooperatives. Danish communities have been funding their own *individual* turbines since the 1970s. It was the scale of Middelgrunden that set it apart.

The venture is run in a similar manner to FC Barcelona...

Every member of the cooperative has one vote, regardless of the number of shares they own. They all have an equal say when it comes to electing representatives to manage their turbines.

"(It's) about learning, and empowering our citizens", says Justin Gerdes, an energy expert and local resident. "It's also a great way to avoid the conflicts that sometimes arise when projects are proposed near where people live".

It generates an income too. The initial citizen-investors have made all their money back. They are now making an annual profit equivalent to 7% of their original outlay.

"It is much better than having (money) in a bank", says Christian Sørensen. "You are doing something positive for the environment... Not by killing the power, but (through) sustainable growth - creating bright, green jobs".

Put simply, the cooperative serves *all* its stakeholders...

The *shareholders* are *consumers* and members of the local *community*. Together, they produce green energy, which is good for the *environment*. The Danish *government* is on the cooperative's side. It has decreed that all new wind farms must be 20% community owned. Between them, these new wind farms are creating jobs for thousands of *workers*. (Martin, 2017) (Hoeschele, 2018)

***

There is an obvious flaw with the Danish model. Its cooperatives do not give a vote to *every* local consumer. They only enfranchise those citizens who invest in shares. In Middelgrunden, that amounted to eight-and-half-thousand members - about 1.4% of Copenhagen's population.

Whilst it would be almost impossible to force every *individual* to buy a stake in an energy cooperative, we can always force our *governments* to buy into such enterprises on our behalf.

This happened in Hamburg...

Inspired by a popular protest against nuclear energy, in which protestors formed a 120km long human chain, the people of Hamburg demanded a referendum.

It was tough. The electricity firms did everything they could to silence the people's calls, plastering Hamburg with their corporate propaganda.

Ultimately, however, the people's calls were answered. Their energy supply is slowly coming into public ownership.

The new model is partially democratic...

It is overseen by an "Energy Advisory Board", made up of consumers, scientists, business people, energy executives, local politicians and activists. This board is accountable to the local government, which is elected by the people. Its meetings are open to the public. Consumers are free to attend, ask the board questions, and submit proposals. Consumers can also keep track online, checking to see if their energy supplier is achieving its targets, and holding it to account if it is not.

These targets no longer focus on maximising profits. They focus on the common good - investing in green energy to reduce pollution. (Petersen, 2016) (Hoeschele, 2018)

It is a start. It shows that people can unite to take energy into citizen-control, on a scale which is much greater than that achieved in Denmark. But the level of consumer involvement is much lower than in Scandinavian.

What we really need is a system which is as democratic as Middelgrunden, but as far-reaching as Hamburg. And for that, we must head down-under...

***

The electricity supply in Auckland was free of corporate control from the get-go. The council built the city's first-ever power station to fuel

Auckland's trams. But it was a small-scale operation. In 1909, it had less than two-hundred private customers. In 1917, at the opening of a new substation, one councillor boasted, rather quaintly, that "After the war... electricity would be in every house".

Five years later, the council formed the "Auckland Electric Power Board" - a body which was owned by local consumers, who elected its management team. The AEPB maintained its structure for over seventy years, although its focus shifted during this time - from producing electricity to managing the energy grid.

In 1993, the AEPB was rebranded as "Vector" - a business-like organisation, which is compelled to compete in the free market. But to this day, over 75% of Vector's shares continue to be owned by "Entrust" - a body owned by its customers - a mass of well over three-hundred-thousand households and firms.

These customers can cast their ballot and have their say, every three years, to elect Entrust's trustees. Any Entrust customer can stand for election, and all of its trustees are customers themselves.

Entrust's customers are *all* paid a dividend. In 2019, bill-payers were handed NZ$360 each - about US$240 or £180.

Entrust literally takes the money earned by Vector, and hands it back to the people who have been buying their electricity *from Vector*. If the power company was to charge excessive rates, to inflate its profits, its customers would be compensated with a supersized dividend. It is impossible for Vector to act like a fully-fledged member of the corporatocracy, putting its shareholders before its customers, because its shareholders *are* its customers. (Daniels, 2005) (Hoeschele, 2018)

GOING GLOBAL

Like any type of organisation, not all consumer cooperatives are successful. The Google reviews for the Peace River Electricity Cooperative are truly abysmal. A slew of one-star reviews accuse it of offering a terrible service for an inflated price. But consumer cooperatives can work, and they do offer a democratic alternative to corporate rule.

The movement is going global...

EcoPower started with just thirty members in 1990. By 2013, it had forty-three-thousand members and was supplying 1.2% of Flemish households with green energy. One-hundred-and-sixty-seven new green energy cooperatives were established in Germany in 2011 alone. Basin Electric, a cooperative based in North Dakota, serves almost three-million customers in nine American states. (Rifkin, 2014)

* * *

It is not in the remit of this book to go into such depth for other industries. But it should be noted that the energy sector is not alone...

The first *modern* consumer-cooperative was established in Rochdale, in 1844, when twenty-eight locals scraped together whatever capital they could find and established a cooperative shop. They sold wholesome food at reasonable prices, before returning their profits to their members.

The "Rochdale Pioneers" established seven "Cooperative Principles", including the "One Member, One Vote", "Open Membership" and "Sustainable Development" principles. Since then, these principles have been adopted by over a billion members of consumer cooperatives, in over a hundred different nations.

* * *

Retail cooperatives remain the face of the cooperative movement...

In the UK, The Co-operative Group is the nation's fifth biggest food retailer, with over two-thousand-five-hundred outlets. It is the UK's biggest funeral services provider, a major insurer, and a provider of legal services. Seven-million customers have become members, without paying fees or buying shares. They can vote on motions at the Co-operative's Annual General Meeting, stand to become one of a hundred council members, and elect other members to that management council. They also receive a share of the Co-operatives' profits.

The Co-operative cares. It was the first British retailer to introduce degradable plastic bags, ban pesticides from fresh produce, outlaw animal testing, and introduce Fair Trade products.

But whilst its grocery stores may remain the face of the consumer-cooperative movement, they are far from the biggest show in town. Credit unions, banks run along cooperative lines, are the most widely used type of consumer cooperative in the USA, where they have over ninety-million members.

Housing cooperatives also operate on a mass scale. There are a hundred-thousand in India alone. Housing cooperatives manage three-and-a-half-million dwellings in Poland, and over a million properties in America.

The models they use can vary. They might take the form of an apartment block, in which each tenant owns their apartment, as well as a share in the block itself. Or they might consist of an area of communal land, with private plots for members' houses. But they are all owned by their members, and managed using the "One member, one vote" principle. (Doherty, 2020)

In the UK, the "Go-op" group is attempting to establish a new train line, running from Westbury to Birmingham, which will be owned and run by its passengers. The Phone Coop already provides home broadband and mobile phone connections. As of July 2018, there were sixty cooperative pubs, many of which were saved from destruction by local residents. (Bibby, 2013) (Hadfield, 2018)

There is no reason why similar cooperatives could not be formed to supply water, collect refuse or deal with sewage. The potential is immense.

THE ENEMY WITHIN

We began this chapter by looking at the threat corporations can pose to democracy. They can drive *demand*, to make money for a minority group, their shareholders, when they should be *supplying* the things for which there is a genuine, democratic demand.

We then looked at some solutions to this dilemma: Individual self-control, sharing collectives, advertising bans, and consumer cooperatives.

In an economic sense, these all provide solutions to the original dilemma. But corporations do not only attack our democracy *indirectly*, through the market. They also attack it *directly*, through lobbying…

***

Lobbying is a relatively new phenomenon. Back in the 1970s, very few firms employed a single lobbyist. But today, in the States, several employ *over a hundred*. In 2008, there were ninety-thousand lobbyists in Washington City alone.

It is big business. As of 2015, $2.5b a year was spent on lobbying - way more than the $1.18b that was spent to actually fund the House of Representatives, and the $0.86b that was spent to fund the Senate.

Politicians have come to rely on lobbyists to raise funds for their re-election campaigns. Some even hire lobbyist to run those campaigns!

But lobbying has a distinctly corporate bias...

Of the one-hundred American groups that spend the most on lobbying, around ninety-five tend to represent business. These corporations, which serve a small number of shareholders, spend thirty-four times more on lobbying than the trade unions and public-interest groups which represent *hundreds-of-millions* of Americans.

The result has been a corporate stitch-up. Lobbyists have successfully campaigned to kill off labour-law reform, tear up market regulation, and lower corporate tax rates.

At the turn of the century, for example, corporate lobbyists successfully pushed "Medicare Part D" - a program that forbids consumers from forming buyers' clubs to make bulk purchases at discounted rates. This was great for corporate profits, but terrible for the democratic mass, whose medical bills increased by $20.5b a year. (Drutman, 2015) (Frank, 2008)

But then lobbyists do not care much for democracy.

Paul Wyrich was a co-founder of "The American Legislative Exchange Council" (ALEC), a think tank that lobbies on behalf of big business. Speaking in 1980, Wyrich made it quite clear that he loathed the democratic process:

"I don't want everybody to vote. As a matter of fact, our leverage in the elections quite candidly goes up as the voter turnout goes down".

ALEC was the force behind the "Three Strike and You're Out" legislation, which gives life-sentences to any American convicted of three minor felonies. Why? Because ALEC represents CoreCivic, a prison operator that profits when prison populations increase.

ALEC also produces form-based legislation that can be copied from state-to-state, helping the likes of Walmart to pass legislation that permits them to sell more guns. (DuVernay, 2016)

The British equivalent of ALEC might just be the "Institute of Economic Affairs" - a think tank with links to fourteen members of Boris Johnson's first cabinet. The IEA, which does not disclose its funders, has lobbied for a US-UK trade-deal weighted heavily in favour of corporate interests, against helping Ford workers in Bridgend, and against a ban on junk-food advertising. (Lo, 2019)

Lobbyists often employ these sort of think tanks to write media-friendly reports, host Westminster parties, secure face-time with politicians, and get supportive letters published in the mainstream press.

Corporations also try to stifle dissent...

BAE Systems, Shell and Nestlé have been caught infiltrating the likes of Greenpeace, Amnesty International and PETA - employing divide-and-rule tactics to silence opponents of their corporate agenda. Others have created fake blogs, in an attempt to push opposing voices down the Google rankings. (Cave & Rowell, 2014)

Then we have what should probably be described as "Bribery through the back door", whereby corporations reward politicians for serving their interests, by giving them cushy positions *after* they leave the public sector.

Let's take the example of Patricia Hewitt...

As the British Minister for Health, between 2005 and 2007, Hewitt was responsible for a multibillion-pound budget. When she left office, several businesses who received a share of that public money were quick to reward her. Alliance Boots, a firm that makes about 40% of its income from Britain's National Health Service, appointed Hewitt as a "Special Advisor", paying her £300 an hour. Cinven paid her £500 per hour to perform a similar role. Bupa and British Telecoms both made her a director. (Jones, 2014)

It gets worse. Some politicians are even willing to take the corporate buck *when still in office*...

Whilst writing this book, it emerged that the Home Secretary, Priti Patel, was being paid £1k an hour by Viasat - a Californian company that was bidding for a £6b defence contract Patel would help to award! (Sabbagh, 2019)

Yet it would be wrong to single out Hewitt and Patel. Between 1996 and 2012, *three-thousand-five-hundred* diplomats and military officers stepped away from Britain's Ministry of Defence to work for arms manufacturers. The problem is so widespread, it can be pretty hard to see where the corporatocracy ends and our so-called "Democracy" begins. (Cave & Rowell, 2014)

***

So, what should we do?

Many solutions have been suggested. Not so many have been tried...

We could impose an outright ban on lobbying, lobbying firms and lobbyists; imprisoning anyone who tries to corrupt the democratic process.

Alternatively, we could introduce a tax on lobbying - making the corporations who lobby the most, pay the most. We could even pass the revenue that tax generates on to the public-interest groups who lobby on behalf of the people.

We might also employ a "Name and Shame" approach; letting the whole world know who is trying to buy our democracy, what they are doing, and why they are doing it. Lobbyists like to hide in the shadows. We could force them into the light. (Zingales, 2014)

A less confrontational solution would be to increase the wages of congressional staffers. Because of their low salaries, these people tend to be young and inexperienced. Turnover tends to be high. All too often, politicians become dependent on lobbyists for information, because they cannot afford to do their own research in-house. If they were given a sufficient budget, however, they could invest in their own research teams, thereby removing the need for outside help. (Drutman, 2015)

Finally, we could pass legislation to ban elected representatives from taking second jobs in the corporate sector. A 2015 YouGov poll found that 54% of Brits supported such a ban, whilst only 28% opposed it. But when a motion was put to the Commons that year, it was defeated comprehensively. The people's representatives were clearly not listening to the people. (Shakespeare, 2015)

***

Whatever solution we choose, something must be done to challenge big business's grip on our democratic institutions. The war against the corporatocracy must be fought on two fronts - in both the political and economic arenas.

15. SPENDING POWER

Economic democracy has the potential to be far more democratic than political democracy. In the political sphere, if one party wins 51% of votes, it might gain 100% of the power. The 49% of voters who did not vote for that party will remain voiceless. Whereas in the economic sphere, if 51% of people prefer pears, and 49% prefer apples, businesses can supply 51% of people with pears and 49% of people with apples. They can ensure that everyone's voice is heard.

If the political system operates under the principle of "One person, one vote", then the economic system operates under the principle of "One dollar, one vote".

Roll up, roll up! Spend your money! Cast your vote!

But for this to be truly democratic, for people to have the same number of "Economic Votes", they must have the same disposable incomes. If some people have more money, they will have more *economic votes*, and more of a say when it comes to distributing resources. We will no longer have an economic democracy. We will have a "Plutocracy".

***

Let's explain this with an example...

One-hundred-and-one people reside on Fruit Island.

One person, Lord Fruity, possesses most of the island's wealth. He has $900 in his weekly fruit budget, which he decides to spend on pears.

The other one-hundred islanders can each afford to spend $1 a week on fruit. They would all like to buy apples.

Thus $900 is spent on pears and just $100 on apples.

In response to this demand, fruit farmers put 90% of their resources (their land, labour and capital) into the production of pears, even though less than 1% of the people prefer that fruit. Just 10% of resources are allocated to the production of apples, even though over 99% of people desire apples, because just 10% of the money is being spent on that fruit.

This is the "Plutocracy Problem".

If one person has 90% the spending power, they will be able to dictate the way in which 90% of resources are allocated. If that person wishes to spend all their money on pink wigs, then 90% of the economy's resources will be used to manufacture pink wigs. It does not matter if no-one else likes pink wigs. They do not have the economic votes.

***

The examples I have just given are purely theoretical. Fruit Island does not exist. I do not know of any economy in which 90% of resources are allocated to the wig industry.

But the plutocracy problem is real. Resource allocation *does* react to spending. The rich do use their spending power to unduly influence production, regardless of what the majority might like to see produced.

Let's take a look at the UK's financial sector...

In 2017, this sector gobbled up 6.5% of the UK's economic resources - £119b of GDP. It enticed one-point-one-million people, 3.2% of the workforce, to labour in its various institutions. (Rhodes, 2018)

In contrast, the agriculture sector consumed less than 1% of Britain's GDP. It could only afford to employ 1.5% of the nation's workforce. (DEFRA, 2018 (a))

Are financial services almost seven times more important to British people than food? Would Brits really prefer to have a good portfolio of shares than a hot meal each night?

This seems unlikely. We need food in order to stay alive. People might like to hold stocks and shares, but nobody *needs* them.

Of course, the agricultural sector should not have to dominate an economy. In an ideal world, farming would be efficient enough to feed everybody, without requiring too many resources. This would free us to spend our incomes on *other* things, such as bonds and shares.

We do not live in an ideal world...

Research from the Food Foundation found that four-point-seven-million Brits regularly go a whole day without eating. More than eight-million people, 12% of the population, struggle to put enough food on the table each day. (Butler, 2016)

We do not produce enough food, at prices which people can afford, to feed the nation. Despite this, we allocate less than 1% of our resources to the production of food. (DEFRA, 2018 (b))

At the same time, we allocate over 6% of our resources to financial services.

Rather than allocate resources democratically, to satisfy a need for food held by 100% of the nation, we allocate resources undemocratically, to enrich a wealthy minority - the 19% of Brits who own shares. (Jeffries, 2015)

I can hear my critics scream:

"Oh, but the financial sector pays billions in tax, which is redistributed to help the hungry!"

"Stockbrokers' spending keeps local businesses alive!"

This is true. But it is not the whole truth. The finance sector does contribute to the economy. But it is bloated. The economy would be more efficient if the financial sector were smaller, because it hoards resources which could be put to better use elsewhere.

The UK economy missed out on £4.5t of growth, between 1995 and 2015, because it allocated too many resources to the financial sector. That is the equivalent of £67.5k per British person.

It inspired a "Brain Drain"...

In thirty years, starting in the mid-1980s, employees in the financial services sector were overpaid by around £280b, when compared to workers in other professions who had a similar level of education. By offering higher wages, financial firms enticed highly-skilled people, such as scientists and engineers, who would have contributed far more to their nation's wellbeing had they stuck with careers in science and engineering. (Baker, Epstein & Montecino, 2018) (Cecchetti & Kharroubi, 2015)

Had some of those people gone to work in agriculture, it is unlikely that so many people would have ended up in food poverty. Had the starving millions been given the £4.5t of lost growth, caused by the bloating of the financial services sector, they would have been able to feed themselves.

This did not happen.

Why?

The top 10% of British households have incomes which are six-point-eight times greater than the bottom 10%. They have six-point-eight times more economic votes than their impoverished peers. (Partington, 2018)

In 2016, the richest 10% of Americans and Canadians received around 47% of their nations' income. They had almost half of their nations' economic votes.

Things get even worse if we judge the planet as a whole...

In 2018, 82% of the world's new wealth ended up in the hands of just 1% of the world's population. Almost all the new economic votes went to a tiny plutocratic elite. (Alejo, Pimentel, Aymar & Lawson, 2018)

***

Like Lord Fruity, this elite use their economic votes to dictate resource allocation. They might spend some of their money on consumption - buying things such as food, housing and holidays. But what about the remainder? Well, if you have too much money to spend, the chances are you will invest it in financial assets and use it to make *even more money*.

This explains why the financial sector has grown so large. It serves the plutocratic class - the people with the most economic votes.

Poorer people, meanwhile, do not have so many economic votes. They do not have the spending power necessary to shift resources towards the production of life's essentials.

∗∗∗

The plutocracy problem is not a theoretical problem, confined to Fruit Island. It really does crush economic democracy in the real world.

It affects other forms of democracy too...

Take the issue of democratic policing. Should a well-meaning British law graduate choose to go into criminal law, to protect the everyday person on the street, they could expect to earn about £12k a year as a starting salary, £25k after three years, and £56k at the peak of their career. But should they choose to go into commercial law, to serve a small clique of plutocrats, they could expect to earn many times more. The average pay for partners in commercial law firms stands at around £1.5m a year. (Cohen, 2018)

The plutocrats use their spending power to lure lawyers away from the sorts of roles which would serve the majority, and into roles where they serve the minority. Their gain is democracy's loss.

RADICAL ANSWERS

We have defined the problem. In a democracy, the power is held by the *majority*. But our economies are not democratic. A plutocratic *minority* has more spending power than everyone else.

So, what is the answer?

It should be simple - give everyone the same amount of spending power!

But how?

There are three obvious methods...

We could give everyone the same income. We could make everything free. Or we could hold votes to distribute resources.

These solutions are not without their issues. They are pretty radical. The first two have a distinctly left-wing bias - they are not the sort of politically neutral policies that might appeal to the majority. The third solution is likely to be laborious, convoluted and messy.

But it is worth introducing these ideas, because we can extrapolate from them to find more moderate solutions. Solutions that are so moderate, in fact, that they are already being applied as a matter of course in most modern-day nations...

DIRECT ECONOMIC DEMOCRACY

Imagine you receive an e-ballot every year. Down the left-hand side of the screen are listed all the major industries in your country: Finance. IT. Construction. Healthcare. Retail...

There are three more columns, titled "Land", "Labour" and "Capital".

You are asked to allocate 100% of each of these resources. You may, for example, choose to allocate 30% of land to agriculture and 10% of labour to education.

The current figures appear in the boxes. The system may tell you that we allocate 1% of our land to healthcare. You just need to decide if that is too much or too little. You might want to nudge it up to 1.1% or knock it down to 0.9%. You might choose to reduce the amount of labour we allocate to the production of coal and divert it into the production of solar energy.

Once the ballots are in, averages are taken, and resources are allocated according to the will of the people.

Everyone has had their say. The poorest members of society have held as much sway as the richest. The plutocracy problem has been solved.

Great, right?

Well, not exactly.

This would invoke the same issues we encounter in any direct democracy. Even if we made voting compulsory, it would be almost impossible to make people do the research, overcome the propaganda, and become experts in resource allocation. Some might spoil their ballot. Others might not consider the facts. A system based on liquid democracy might achieve better results.

At least the current system works organically. Resources simply follow the money.

And, even if a vote-based system was introduced, it would be difficult to enforce the results...

Say the population voted for 2% of labour to be allocated to medical research, but only 1% of the nation was qualified to do such work. Would you force unqualified people into this profession? And what if 3% of labour was supposed to be allocated to agriculture, but only 2% of people were willing to do this work. Would you make workers move home and do a job they loathed? Would you really want to repurpose factories or reallocate land on an annual basis, knowing you might have to reallocate it again in a year's time?

***

Direct democracy does solve the plutocracy problem in theory. In reality, however, it might be impossible to enforce.

Let's not give up just yet.

What if, rather than ask *everyone* to vote on how *all* our resources are allocated, we just ask *some* people to vote on how *some* resources are used?

This is not unheard of.

In the second section of this book, we introduced deliberative democracy, through which a representative group was selected, educated, and asked to choose between different projects. And we met participatory budgeting, through which members of the public made suggestions, and locals then voted on their proposals.

We can go further still, not just voting on how to spend a council or government's budget, but also voting on the *size* of that budget. We could hold referenda to approve or reject proposed changes to tax rates. We could ask each of the major parties to propose a budget, and then hold referenda to select whichever one we prefer.

This would democratise resource allocation in the public sector. But it would hardly solve the plutocracy problem. It is in the private sector where a wealthy minority wields undue influence...

In the UK, an Opinium Poll found that 71% of Brits opposed "The promotion of arms sales to human rights abusing regimes". Yet, despite this opposition, the UK continues to sell billions of pounds worth of weapons to such regimes. If a few rich and abusive dictators are prepared to spend money on weapons, businesses will use British land, labour and capital to produce them, regardless of what the British people might want. (Smith, 2017)

In the USA, a Gallup Poll found that six-in-ten Americans supported "Dramatically reducing the country's use of fossil fuels". But in 2018, the supply of natural gas and petroleum actually *increased* by 4%. A few rich people and businesses were prepared to pay top dollar for fossil fuels, so businesses dug them up. (McCarthy, 2019) (Irfan, 2019)

In both examples, the spending power of a tiny minority overpowered the majority's wishes. But things would change if people were given a vote...

If there were a referendum, 60% of Americans would outvote the plutocrats, ensuring that fossil fuel production was reduced. Brits would outvote the arms dealers.

Individual referenda could be held to ban industries entirely, to ban the production of certain goods and services, to stop the sale of products to certain countries, and to tax or subsidise production.

This is not a flight of fancy. Such referenda do take place in Switzerland...

In 2017, 58.2% of voters backed the "Energy Strategy 2050". This will ban the construction of new nuclear power stations, subsidise hydroelectric utilities, and promote renewable energy. And in 2014, Swiss voters decided that no more than 20% of houses in any commune could be holiday homes. (Geiser, 2017) (Schuler & Dessemontet, 2012)

Even without such referenda, governments do sometimes ban the sale of certain goods, such as weapons or drugs. They tax things such as plastic bags. But they can be slow to react, and they might not act at all.

***

Before we move on, it is worth mentioning one more way we can vote - with our time...

Let's head over to South London, to the land of strawberries and cream, Pimms, and the ping-pong, grunt-grunt of lawn tennis. Yes, you guessed it: Wimbledon.

Watched by a global TV audience of millions, only a select few can squeeze into Centre Court's bottle-green seats. Under normal circumstances, prices would be ramped up. The plutocrats, the people who can afford to pay top dollar, would keep them to themselves.

Indeed, expensive Centre Court tickets are available. In 2019, a handful of five-year debentures went on sale. The price? A cool £80k. About £1,230 per day of tennis. (Friend, 2019)

But Wimbledon also holds some tickets back for the general public. These tickets are by no means cheap, they start at £64, but they are set at the sort of prices which many Brits can afford, as a special treat, and which keen tennis fans are often happy to pay.

At these prices, Wimbledon could sell out many times over.

So how do they ration their limited resource - these moderately-priced tickets?

Well, some tickets are allocated by a general ballot. Anyone can enter, and everyone, rich or poor, has an equal chance of being selected.

Some tickets are distributed to tennis clubs, who hold ballots of their own. The people who show their love of the game, by actually playing it, are rewarded with an extra opportunity to buy.

The remainder are sold on the gate. People turn up, often days advance, and camp out in rain and shine. They may not be rich enough to buy the debentures, but they show their desire for tickets by braving the elements and waiting in line, *voting with their time*.

These methods are democratic. Anyone, rich or poor, can enter a ballot or camp out in a queue. But can this method of resource allocation be applied to other areas of the economy?

Certainly, it could be applied to other sporting events. The right to buy tickets is already allocated by ballot at some international competitions, such as the Olympics and World Cup.

When celebrity chef, Heston Blumenthal, temporarily relocated his restaurant to Melbourne, two-hundred-and-fifty-thousand people applied for seats. Blumenthal could only serve fourteen-thousand punters in his time down-under. So he held a ballot, giving each of those foodies an equal chance of securing a seat of one of his much-coveted tables.

It is unlikely a house would be sold to a family that is prepared to camp outside its door for six months, if another family is prepared to pay a higher price. But if a government or housing association was to build some houses, and sell them on at cost price, it could hold a ballot, or create a waiting list to which everyone had equal access.

People queue at Wimbledon to prove they *desire* tickets. In other areas, people can be asked to prove their *need* for a good or service. When healthcare is nationalised, and free at the point of use, operations are often allocated to those with the greatest need. University places are allocated to those who have worked the hardest to get the best grades.

Neither system is perfect. Rich people can jump the queue by paying for operations. They can send their children to private schools, in the hope they will get better grades, and therefore gain access to the top universities.

But both systems offer hope...

Perhaps one day we will have a system whereby we do not only allocate healthcare to those people who need it the most, but also food, water and housing. Perhaps people will be able to take tests to prove their desire for cars. Perhaps they will queue to show their desire for holidays.

EQUALITY!

Now let's consider the second solution to the plutocracy problem - giving everyone the same income, and therefore the same number of economic votes.

When we talk about equal incomes, it is easy to think of communism. And when we think of communism, it is easy to think of Soviet Russia.

But Soviet Russia was no economic democracy. It was a planned economy. Even if everyone had the same income, which they did not, their spending could not be considered "Economic Votes", because supply did not react to demand. It was fixed by the state. If lots of people wanted apples, the shops would sell out of apples, and some people would be left unsatisfied. If not many people wanted pears, lots of pears would remain on the shelves.

To create an economic democracy, free from the plutocracy problem, we would need to give people equal incomes *and* keep a market economy, or at least some sort of economy in which supply reacted to demand.

I do not know of anywhere this has been tried.

***

So, is there a more moderate solution?

Well, rather than give everyone the *same* income, we could always tax the rich a little bit more, and redistribute that money to the poor - thereby ensuring that everyone has a *similar* income.

Such a practice would not create a *pure* economic democracy, based on the principle of "One person, one economic vote". But it would make our economies *more* democratic.

What is more, such a policy would have a democratic mandate…

When Oxfam surveyed seventy-thousand people, across ten countries, nearly two-thirds thought "The gap between the rich and the poor needs to be addressed". (Alejo, Pimentel, Aymar & Lawson, 2018)

And when the OECD asked twenty-two-thousand people in twenty-one nations, "Should the government tax the rich more than they currently do, in order to support the poor?", a majority of people said "Yes" in *every single country*. (Scarpetta, 2019)

***

Another solution, in the same vein, would be to issue *quotas*, limiting the amount that people can spend on certain items. We could, for example, limit the amount that anyone could spend on financial services.

You might recall that something similar was enforced in Florence, back when it was a Free Town. Limits were placed on the number of bottles of wine a rich family could keep in its cellar. The wealthy could not hoard this precious resource. It remained on the market, for the majority to consume. (Renard, 1918)

***

Alternatively, we could introduce a maximum income, to limit the number of economic votes held by any one individual.

A maximum wage was introduced in Egypt, in July 2014, when it limited public servants' pay to thirty-five times the minimum salary; ensuring that no state employee earned more than the president. (Safi, 2015)

Elsewhere, a law passed in 2010 meant that no Venezuelan public official could earn more than twelve times the salary of someone on the minimum wage. Legislators could only earn eight times the minimum salary, mayors up to seven times, and general public officials up to five times that amount. (Pearson, 2011)

***

Finally, we could introduce a *minimum income*, to ensure that everyone has at least a handful of economic votes, even when job opportunities dry up…

It is thought that two-point-seven-million American truck drivers will be replaced by driverless lorries by 2040. Vending-machines are already taking the place of some shops, and self-checkout terminals are taking the place of some cashiers. Two-million jobs were lost in human resources, finance, information technology and procurement following the Global Economic Crash. Half were never replaced. New search software means a single lawyer can now do the legal research that used to require five-hundred lawyers. There are far fewer secretaries, file clerks, telephone operators, travel agents and bank tellers than in the past. New technology has rendered them redundant. (Rifkin, 2014)

With fewer jobs on the market, we may find ourselves unemployed or underemployed - working part-time, on zero-hour contracts, doing whatever work we can find in the gig economy. We may have next to no spending power at all.

This is where "Universal Basic Income" might save us. *UBI* gives everyone in a nation a guaranteed income, without asking for anything in return. It ensures we all have a certain amount of spending power, no matter what happens in the job market.

The idea has its roots in antiquity...

The Roman authorities used to give free bread to its poorer citizens. Their motivation was far from altruistic. Their "Bread and circuses" were designed to keep people's minds busy and their bellies full, thereby preventing any sort of uprising. But the "Cura Annonae" did democratise the market for grain. The rich could not hoard that precious staple. It had to be distributed amongst the people. Nor could the rich monopolise the land, using it to build luxury villas and country retreats. A good portion of the land had to be set aside for farming, to grow grain for the people. (Beard, 2012)

Several experiments have tested the effects of a UBI in recent times...

The results from one of the original trials, conducted in Manitoba, showed that it can certainly affect the allocation of one resource - labour. Critics had argued that if people did not have to work, to earn money, they would stop working altogether. This never happened, perhaps because the experiment was only run for a limited period. It gave households at least CA$3800 a year, for a period of five years. But it did affect two groups. Youngsters spent more time at university, and mothers spent more time with their children. (Howgego, 2019)

Is this outcome democratic?

It is hard to say. We would need to ask the people if they wanted more full-time mothers and educated youngsters.

What about land and capital?

The theory states that if people had a guaranteed income, they would be more likely to start new businesses. Their guaranteed income could sustain them in the early years, allowing them to dedicate themselves to their enterprise, without needing to work a second job. It would also provide them with a safety net if their business failed.

There is some evidence to suggest the theory is correct...

In Alaska, profits from oil and gas extraction are shared amongst the population, giving each Alaskan a dividend of between $846 and $2000 per year. With such an income to fall back on, even if things go bad, Alaskans formed 16% more firms than would be expected for a state with its demographics. (Feinberg & Kuehn, 2019)

Not everyone is a fan of Universal Basic Income. Its critics argue that it is costly, inflationary, and that it makes people dependent on the state. But it does give everyone a guaranteed number of economic votes. And it can affect the allocation of labour, land *and* capital.

MONEY TO BURN

There is a third solution to the plutocracy problem. We could abolish money, and make everything free.

Let's return to our hunter-gatherer friends...

If one-hundred of them want apples, the chances are they will get together and spend the day walking to the nearest apple tree. If one of them wants pears, they may head off alone to get what they want.

Everyone has an equal resource - their ability to walk to a fruit tree and pick some fruit. Everyone has equal rights - the right to pick whatever fruit they find. A minority cannot laud it over the majority, using their money to buy all the fruit, *because there is no money*.

There is no plutocracy problem. Everyone has an equal number of economic votes - zero.

***

So, can we just go back to being hunter-gatherers?

Perhaps. But there does not appear to be a democratic mandate for such an idea.

Could there be an alternative in the future?

Perhaps. It is the case in the (fictional) Star Trek universe:

"The Federation have replicators which can instantly convert energy into almost any matter, form or material they desire... You don't need to trade because almost anything you desire can be produced, for free, at the touch of a button. And, if you don't need to trade, you don't need money". (Lamehdasht, 2017)

The system works because scarcity is not an issue. But we can also operate economies, without money, when scarcity *is* an issue...

***

The Black Rock Desert is a barren, rocky expanse of elephantine earth, squirting geysers, and skyscapes that seem to stretch on forever. Due east of California, it sits in the very heart of the capitalist world - the United States of America. It has seen two successful land-speed record attempts, and some not-so-successful attempts at amateur rocketry.

Oh, and it is home to "Burning Man"...

Burning Man is a weeklong festival of "Self-expression" and "Self-reliance". Each year, around forty-thousand people gather together, form a temporary society, build a giant wooden statue, and then burn it to the ground.

But what makes Burning Man so unique, is its rejection of market norms. Money is not accepted in this pop-up community. It operates a "Gift Exchange Economy". You give what you have to others, on the understanding that they will give whatever they have to you or someone else, at some time in the not-too-distant future.

Chefs might cook a meal. A psychologist might offer counselling sessions. Those with water offer free showers. Masseuses massage. Random citizens of this temporary city dish out drinks, homemade jewellery and hugs to anyone who shows an interest.

Dan Ariely, a professor at the Massachusetts Institute of Technology, made some puzzles and challenged people to solve them:

"At first this was all very strange, but before long I found myself adopting the norms of Burning Man. I was surprised, in fact, to find that Burning Man was the most accepting, social, and caring place I had ever been. I'm not sure I could easily survive in Burning Man for all fifty-two weeks of the year. But this experience has convinced me that life with fewer market norms and more social norms would be more satisfying, creative, fulfilling and fun".

***

Burning Man solves the plutocracy problem in two ways. Since there is no money, the rich cannot use their money to distort markets. But even if there was, it would not make a difference. Each individual chooses to supply the goods and services they wish to supply *before* they arrive. *The people allocate resources*, independently of others' demand.

***

So what, exactly, are the "Social Norms" of which Ariely speaks?

He is talking about the sort of things you might give to someone else, because it is the custom to do so, without expecting any money in return.

Say you knock on your neighbour's door and ask for some sugar. Do you think your neighbour will ask for payment, demanding a dollar or a pound? Do you think they will start to barter, asking for some flour? Or do you think they will smile, ask about your day, make you a cup of tea, and hand you a cup of sugar?

Most people would hand over the sugar without asking for payment.

If you hold a lift for someone who is rushing towards the closing doors, it is unlikely you will charge them a fee for the service, blocking their entry if they refuse to pay. When you wash your children's clothes, I doubt you will present them with a bill. The idea of your partner paying you for sex might very well disgust you. If someone asks you to pass the salt, during a meal, you *could* ask for payment for the product, the salt itself, and also the service, the act of passing that salt. But it is unlikely you would do so.

These acts are by no means altruistic. Your neighbour helps you with the sugar, on the tacit understanding that you might help them in the future. Perhaps they will go on holiday and ask you to feed their cat.

Whether you realise it or not, you are taking part in the same sort of "Sharing Economy", free from money, that underpins Burning Man. You may very well be doing it several times a day.

***

Then we have the voluntary sector...

When the American Association of Retired Persons (AARP) asked lawyers to provide discounted services to needy retirees, those lawyers overwhelmingly said "No". If the pensioners did not have the spending power to secure their precious labour, they would have to do without!

But when the AARP asked those *same* lawyers to donate their time, not for $30 an hour, but for $0 an hour, a majority said "Yes". It turned out that people want to help others *for free*. (Ariely, 2008)

Volunteers help out at sports clubs, youth clubs, charities, food banks, soup kitchens, religious and cultural groups. They provide goods and services worth billions of dollars without asking for a cent in return.

Like at Burning Man, the rich cannot just splash the cash and monopolise these services. They are spread across the nation and across the democratic mass.

COMMON WEALTH

It is not just services which can be free...

Let's take the air as an example. People do not pay for the air they breathe. A rich person cannot buy more air than a poor person, monopolise the world's air supply, or divert resources away from the production of air.

In the past, the same could have been said of drinking water. Anybody could have gone to a stream and taken as much as they liked. In some places, this is still the case. But today, much of the world's water is too dirty to drink. We must pay for it to be cleaned. Some bodies of water are located on private property. We do not have the right to take it.

A similar tale could be told when it comes to land. In Chapter Three, we visited Valencia, Törbel and Japan - places where land was held in common. Anyone could use it, but it was no free-for-all. Members of the local community agreed upon schedules and punished anyone who took liberties. There was shared-responsibility for that shared-land, which no-one owned, and which no-one paid to use. (Rushkoff, 2019)

These days, free-access land does still exist. In many nations, we can still walk through national parks and visit the beach without paying for the privilege. But if you wish to raise livestock, and need pasture, you will probably have to pay.

Perhaps air will go the same way. Ninety-one percent of the world's population already live in places where the level of air pollution exceeds

World Health Organisation guidelines. Over four-million people die annually as a result of breathing dirty air.

In the future, we may very well have to pay for companies to clean the air we breathe, just as we have to pay them to clean our water. Perhaps the atmosphere will be sold off to the highest bidder, just as land was privatised in the past.

The trend has been fairly negative. Once upon a time, everything was free, and everything was held in common. There are tribal groups for whom the same could be said today. But most people, in most places, must now pay for land, water and food. In my lifetime alone, a charge has been introduced to use some public toilets, parking meters have popped up on residential streets, tuition fees have been introduced for university education, and major sporting events have moved from free-to-air channels to subscription services.

Yet some things do remain free - *The Commons* - "Assets over which a community has shared and equal rights".

Take the example of a national gallery that does not charge for entry. A poor person can spend just as long looking at a painting as a rich person. They have the same right to stand in a corridor or sit on a bench. (Barnes, 2006)

Examples of commons include the community-owned forests in Nepal and Romania, the lobster fisheries in Maine, the pastures in East Africa, journals published by the Public Library of Science, the Helsinki Time Bank, local currencies, and open-source microscopy. (Monbiot, 2017)

In general, the commons can be sorted into three groups. "Natural Commons", such as air and water, as well as things like the oceans, national parks, airwaves and solar energy. "Community Commons", such as some national museums and galleries, as well as streets, playgrounds, holidays, calendars, markets, laws and libraries. And "Cultural Commons", such as language, religion, knowledge and music. (Barnes, 2006)

These things are free to everyone. They cannot be hoarded by a plutocratic class.

The battle *against* plutocracy, therefore, could be seen as a battled *for* the commons - doing what we can to preserve and expand the range of goods and services we can access for free.

Indeed, most developed nations already offer free access to

healthcare, education, policing, fire rescue, parks, roads and libraries. For twenty-five years, Turkmens were given a free allocation of electricity, gas, water and salt. (Putz, 2018)

Housing, land and information, might also be included in the commons...

***

At the time of writing, there were over two-hundred-thousand empty houses in the UK. *Three-hundred-and-twenty-thousand* Brits, meanwhile, found themselves homeless. This is the plutocracy problem writ large. The people with the most spending power were hoarding the nation's houses. (Kollewe, 2019) (Butler, 2018)

There is one clear and obvious solution. "Squatters Rights" - a democratic right which allows absolutely anyone to take an empty building and make it their home.

In the UK, squatters can claim ownership of a building if they can prove they have been squatting there continuously for ten years, acted as owners for the whole time, and did not have the owner's permission to live there in the first place.

Squatters' rights return economic power to the people. A plutocrat may be able to buy up lots of houses, but they will not be able to live in them all at once. Squatters take a far more democratic approach - "One person. One property". Anybody can squat.

But squatters' rights are a challenge because the squatters can be evicted at any time. They can even be fined for squatting.

A more moderate alternative was the "Couchsurfing" website, which allowed travellers to sleep on the sofas of local hosts, all across the world, without paying that host a penny. The site soon became popular amongst backpackers, who benefitted from the free accommodation, and hosts, who met new people from a variety of backgrounds. But its fall was as sharp as its rise. The IRS refused to consider it a charity and forced it to operate like a normal business. Its users abandoned ship. (Schneider, 2014)

***

What about land?

In the Fruit Island example, Lord Fruity used his spending power to encourage farmers to grow pears. But why rely on farmers? If the people of Fruit Island really wanted apples, they could have planted some trees and grown that fruit themselves. They would have only needed one resource - land.

"Allotments" give anyone in a nation, rich or poor, the right to such land. Yes, there is a nominal cost involved, but it tends to be small enough for almost anyone to afford.

There is just one problem - excess demand. There are one-hundred-thousand people on waiting lists for British allotments. On average, they must wait for three years. In some places, they must wait for forty. (Wallop, 2009)

An alternative has been tried...

In 2009, Hugh Fearnley-Whittingstall created "Landshare" - a matchmaking website which connected people with empty land, to locals who wanted land to farm. It was an overnight sensation. Twenty-thousand people signed up in the first few months. Many were given access to land for free. Others repaid the favour with a share of their produce. In Lancashire, for example, a hospice gave eight plots to local residents. They, in turn, gave a quarter of their crop back to the hospice.

The Landshare website went offline in 2016. They did not have the staff to keep it going. But by then, the "Food Is Free" initiative had already sprung up in Texas. It has since gone global, turning roundabouts, roadsides, and random patches of grass into crop-filled spaces. The "SharedEarth" project, which was also formed in Texas, turned twenty-five-million square-feet of unused garden space into shared agricultural land in its first four months. (Crae, 2016) (Rifkin, 2014)

***

Let's just consider one more case - information technology...

In the early days of the home computer, Microsoft developed an operating system, "Unix", which they owned and ran for profit.

Richard Stallman, the straggly-haired, beardy author of "The GNU Manifesto", was having none of it.

"Information wants to be free", he screamed from the rooftops.

He wrote his own equivalent of Unix, GNU, distributed it for free, and invited enthusiasts to improve his program on the "Collaborative Commons".

Whereas software like Unix was protected by "Copyright", GNU was protected by "Copyleft". People had the absolute right to reproduce, adapt and distribute the software. It could not be sold. *It had to be free.*

Coders from across the globe responded to Stallman's call, donating their time and skills, driven by a desire to create the sort of software which everyone could use, regardless of their spending power.

Thus was born "Open Source" software.

It became a phenomenon...

The Android system, used by 70% of smartphones, is open-source. So is the Firefox browser, used by 24% people on the web, and Linux, which runs the ten fastest supercomputers on the planet. The very basis of the internet is open-source - the underlying operating system, the webserver and programming language are all available for free.

Whilst we must normally pay for devices and internet connections, many cities do offer free WIFI in public places, as do some libraries.

Free internet looks set to become a common phenomenon...

America's Federal Communications Commission issued a report in 2013, proposing that free "Super WIFI Networks" be introduced across the States. Britain's Labour Party offered free internet in their 2019 manifesto. (Mason, 2015) (Rifkin, 2014)

Once online, most websites are free to use...

Using the web, any person can share information with anyone else, wherever they may be. The rich have no right to create more webpages or send more emails than the poor. Anyone can create their own website, blog, Facebook page, YouTube channel or email account. On Twitter, the profound thought of a suburban housewife can get more traction than the opinion of a billionaire. (Jeffries, 2014)

***

When I was a kid, if I wanted to find some information, I would have to buy a book or visit library. Now I can get that information on Wikipedia, for free, with a single click.

Wikipedia receives over eight-billion page views a month, making it the sixth most popular site in the world. It has twenty-six million pages, produced by twenty-four million registered contributors. If the site were run for profit, it would generate an estimated $2.8b a year. But it is not run for profit. Everyone can use it, rich or poor. Anyone can contribute to it. And that, in a nutshell, is economic democracy. (Mason, 2015)

***

The internet is also helping to provide further education for free...

It all began when Professor Sebastian Thrun of Stanford University taught an online course on artificial intelligence, back in 2011. Thrun had expected a couple-of-hundred students to login. So he was blown away when *one-hundred-and-sixty-thousand* people watched his lecture from the comfort of their sofas. Thrun had created the biggest classroom in history. Twenty-three-thousand students would go on to complete his online course.

Enthused, Thrun created an online university called "Udacity". The logic was simple. Setting up a course might require a lot of time, effort and money - experts had to create reading lists, host lectures, create assignments and write exams. But once these things had been done, the marginal cost was almost zero. An additional student could go online and watch a lecture without it costing the lecturer a cent. Classes could be free as well. It just needed students to organise themselves into online forums; to ask and answer each other's questions. Thrun's students even marked each other's work.

Once the initial costs are covered, such courses are free to produce, and so can be given away for free. In the past, you might have had to pay $50k to study at Stanford. You either had to be very rich or have access to a large amount of credit. But *anyone* can enrol at online universities like Udacity, no matter their spending power. Indeed, six-million people had already signed up for "Massive Open Online Courses" by 2014. (Rifkin, 2014)

***

Is the web perfect?

No way!

It is home to paedophile rings, revenge porn, cyberbullying, the spread of racist ideas and spam emails. Sites such as Facebook and Twitter hoard massive amounts of personal data, which they allow third-parties to use. Even Wikipedia, whose virtues I have just extolled, has a dark side. It has been corrupted by the pharmaceutical industry, as we saw in Chapter Ten.

But let's not throw the baby out with the bathwater. The web can be a democratic force for good.

Still, it is under threat. The corporations are coming...

Google Adverts might be open to everyone, but they are not free. Those with the ability to pay the most, stand the greatest chance of being seen. Anyone can comment on a Facebook post, but only the rich can afford to employ big teams of astroturfers to infiltrate discussions.

The American authorities have already rescinded "Net Neutrality" legislation...

Net neutrality democratised the internet, making it illegal for service providers to discriminate between users, content, websites or devices. Without such legislation, service providers have already begun to discriminate against customers on more basic packages - limiting the bandwidth they can use to stream videos and access certain apps.

In the future, some premium websites might be placed off-limits for anyone who is not wealthy enough to afford the more expensive subscriptions. Telecoms networks may very well provide access to their in-house sites, but not to the likes of Google or Facebook. (Finley, 2018)

Commons do not last forever. They need to be protected.

***

So the war for the commons needs to be fought on two fronts...

A defensive war is needed to protect the plutocracy-free zones which still exist. We must defend squatters, the internet, and the free status of our roads, air and museums.

We must also stage an offensive war to expand the commons - to make more land available for allotments and increase access to free WIFI. We might attempt to resurrect long-lost commons from the past. Or we might use technology to create new commons in the future...

CAPITALISM'S GLORIOUS VICTORY

If this chapter has read like a lefty manifesto, there is hope for those on the right. Pro-market ideology asserts that *competition between firms* will naturally drive down prices to the point at which everything become free...

My firm will undercut your firm's prices, to entice your firm's customers. Your firm will respond in kind. We will both be forced to innovate, to reduce costs, so that we can reduce our prices even further, and entice even more customers from each other. In time, we will reduce these costs so much that we will be able to produce our wares for next to nothing, and sell them for a price approaching zero.

According to this theory, we just need to be patient, allow markets to do their thing, and the price of everything will eventually fall to zero.

Everything will be free. The plutocracy problem will solve itself, without any need for intervention.

***

In some industries, such a theory has almost become a reality...

According to research from Deloitte, the cost of a one megabit broadband connection fell from $1,000 in 2000 to $23 in 2015. In just ten years, the cost of printing a million transistors fell from a dollar to six cents, and the cost of one gigabyte of storage fell from a dollar to three cents.

The cost of reading one-million base pairs of DNA has plunged from $100k to just six cents in recent years.

Such items are already *almost* free. (Mason, 2015)

***

The idea that competition between firms can eliminate all costs, and therefore make everything free, was proposed by Jeremy Rifkin in his book, "The Zero Marginal Cost Society".

Rifkin believes that each great step forward requires progress in three key areas - *communication, energy and transportation*.

We have already examined the internet, which has revolutionised communications - supplying a good chunk of the world's knowledge for next to no cost. Let's now take a look at the other two factors which make up "The Internet of Things" - energy and transportation...

***

Throughout our history, we humans have had to go out into the world to gather our energy - collecting wood to burn, extracting coal to fuel power stations, and tracking down uranium to create nuclear energy. Such endeavours have required blood, sweat and tears. Or, to use the economic jargon, they have required *resources*.

In recent years, however, we have seen a shift to renewable energy. It has been a game-changer. Now we can allow our energy *to come to us*:

"The sun collected on your rooftop, the wind travelling up the side of your building, the heat coming up from the ground under your office, and the garbage anaerobically decomposing into biomass energy in your kitchen are all nearly *free*".

By 2013, Germany was already producing 23% of its energy using renewable sources. So much solar and wind power was flooding Germany's grid, that supply outstripped demand. To shift the excess electricity, prices did not just fall to zero. They turned *negative*! The German grid was essentially paying people to take its electricity.

This phenomenon is by no means limited to a single nation. It has also been seen in places like Sicily and Texas.

Even the cost of producing the capital required to generate such energy is falling towards zero. In 1976, silicon photovoltaic cells cost $60 for every watt they produced. By 2013, the cost had fallen to just $0.66 per watt.

Individuals are already investing in their own solar panels, and consuming the electricity they produce. Nature contains a superabundance of energy; enough for everyone to take as much as they desire, regardless of their spending power. We just need the equipment to harvest it.

***

What about transportation?

We have already mentioned that truck drivers are set to be replaced by driverless trucks. Delivery personnel may very well be replaced by drones. Labour costs could very well fall to zero.

But what about capital costs? What about the money it takes to produce those driverless trucks and drones?

This is where 3D printing enters the equation.

It works something like this...

Anyone with a computer and a 3D printer can create an object to print, or download a design from the creative commons. They insert some sort of input into their printer - it could be melted plastic, melted metal, or some other sort of feed. The printer then builds the physical item, layer by layer - creating a fully-formed object with moveable parts.

3D printing is like the replicator in the Star Trek universe. Only it exists, right now, in the real world.

3D printing has already been used to create a car, Urbee, which runs on solar and wind power, and which can reach speeds of forty miles-per-hour. It is not unreasonable to suppose it might be used to produce the drones and driverless lorries of the future - making transportation all but free.

3D printing could even be used to print the solar panels that will allow us to harvest free electricity.

People are currently 3D-printing everything from jewellery to airline parts and human prosthetics. Researchers have used 3D printers to build small homes, using nothing more than sand, rock and some discarded waste material. 3D printers can even be used to *print other 3D printers*!

This is economic democracy in action...

In the future, we will be able to download designs from the creative commons, for free, import them into our 3D printers, and run those machines on free renewable energy; producing whatever we want *ourselves*. We will all be "Prosumers" - the producers *and* consumers of the things we want. This will not be *mass production*, as the likes of Taylor and Ford would have had it, with a mass of people combining to create a single item for other people to buy. This will be something far more democratic - a Gandhi-esque, *production by the masses*, with a massive number of individuals each producing the things they want to consume themselves. It will take the means of production from the minority, the people who run governments and businesses, and give it to the people.

Of course, we cannot be entirely certain that it will come to pass...

The theory requires lots of competition between lots of firms. But many industries are dominated by a single monopoly or a group of large firms, like Pepsi and Coca Cola, who are more likely to resort to branding wars rather than pricing wars. Furthermore, resources such as land are naturally limited. We cannot produce more land for free, driving down its cost, and so we cannot rely on markets to make it free.

But if Rifkin is right, if competition does drive prices down to zero, and the Internet of Things does replace the market, then the plutocracy problem will have been solved. We will all be plutocrats, producing and consuming whatever we desire. (Rifkin, 2014)

A FOURTH WAY?

Before we move on, it is worth considering a fourth solution to the plutocracy problem - "Collectivised Demand".

Everyday Joes and Janes, acting as individual consumers, may not have the spending power they need to influence production. But if they unite, form a customer union and spend their money *together*, businesses will have little choice but to sit up and listen to what they have to say...

***

If you have only ever heard of one customer union, it might just be the

"Dallas Buyers Club", made famous by the 2013 film in which Matthew McConaughey played the part of a real-life drug-runner, Ron Woodrof.

Woodrof had been diagnosed with HIV and given just weeks to live. Unable to afford the life-saving medication he needed, he took matters into his own hands - smuggling cheap medication into America.

On one occasion, Woodrof drove home from Mexico disguised as a parish priest. On another, he flew back from Japan with his medicine packed in dry-ice. His luggage was marked "Smoking".

The real Woodrof, unlike the version played by McConaughey, was just a "Little, well-groomed, cursing man who was shuffling papers, placing calls and working a calculator... (A man who) just wanted to live another day".

His was one of a handful of buyers' clubs, across the States, that served a desperate demographic - people who needed medicine, but lacked the spending power to get it. Their clubs were not legal, but they did save lives, and they did solve the plutocracy problem - ensuring that supply reacted to the people's demand. (Minutaglio, 2014)

***

Buyers' clubs are popping up across the UK today...

When patients with cystic fibrosis heard that Vertex Pharmaceuticals had developed a drug that tackled the underlying cause of their disease, they were delighted. Until, that is, they discovered the price - a whopping £104k a year - about four times the average salary of someone in full-time employment. When the National Health Service offered £100m a year for the drug, Vertex rejected the offer.

And so a collection of parents and patients formed a club. They met representatives from Argentina, where Vertex had failed to secure a patent, and struck up a deal to buy a generic version of the much-needed medication. Gador, the Argentinian manufacturer, were willing to supply their drug for £23k per patient per year, but offered to drop the price to £18k per year if the buyers' club could secure five-hundred customers.

The "Cystic Fibrosis Buyers Club" is not alone...

Similar clubs support people with hepatitis c, pulmonary fibrosis and some cancers; often with support from National Health Service doctors. (Cohen, 2019)

Together, they are giving normal people the sort of spending power that was previously only held by the plutocratic class.

PROBLEM SOLVED?

We started by defining a problem. Our economies are not democratic. They are not based on the principle of "One person. One economic vote". The rich have more spending power than the poor, and they use it to tilt production in their favour, regardless of what the majority might want.

We provided three absolute solutions - voting to allocate resources, equalising incomes, and making everything free.

We then discussed some more moderate policies. Ideas that are so moderate, they already exist today: Participatory Budgeting. Deliberative Democracy. Referenda. Taxing the rich. Subsidising the poor. Protecting and expanding the commons. Allowing markets to drive down prices. Creating customer unions.

We could add another solution - consumer control. Consumer cooperatives attempt to serve *all* their customers, without bending to the will of their richest clients.

Are these ideas enough?

Perhaps.

Perhaps not.

These measures only combat *indirect* plutocracy, through which the rich use their spending power to control markets. They do not tackle *direct* plutocracy, through which the rich use their money to buy our politicians.

Such a phenomenon is by no means new...

Wealthy citizens were reported to have bribed the judiciary in ancient Egypt, a full five-thousand years ago. Bribery existed in ancient China and in ancient Greece, where the Alcmaeonid family bought the Delphi priestesses a marble-clad temple in order to win their support. (Biswas & Tortajada, 2018)

Bribery bought the American dream...

"Thomas Edison promised New Jersey politicians $1,000 each in return for favourable legislation. Daniel Drew and Jay Gould spent $1m to bribe the New York legislature to legalise their issue of $8m in 'Watered stock'... (And the Central Pacific Railroad) spent $200k in Washington on bribes to get nine-million acres of free land and $24m in bonds". (Zinn, 1980)

Bribery remains an issue across the planet today. The World Bank has estimated that $1.5t is spent on bribes each year. That is about one-fiftieth of all the money on the planet! Other estimates suggest it is higher still. (Biswas & Tortajada, 2018)

The need for a democratic police force, to protect the people from the rich and corrupt, remains as great as ever.

16. SHOW US THE MONEY!

In my economics lessons at school, my classmates and I were told a beautiful fairy-tale…

Once upon a time, the people bartered to exchange their goods. If you had a cow, but you wanted chickens, you would find a person who had some chickens, offer them your cow, and negotiate to secure as many chickens as you could get.

But this system was problematic…

What if the person with the chickens did not want a cow? What if someone who wanted your cow did not have any chickens? What if you wanted different things, from different people, but only had one large item, your cow, to exchange?

Then some bright spark had a brainwave:

"Let's use some sort of token! You could sell your cow, receive some tokens, and use those tokens to buy whatever you want".

Abracadabra, alakazam, money was invented.

We all lived happily ever after.

***

There is just one itsy-bitsy problem with this tale. It never actually happened.

Throughout the Eighteenth and Nineteenth Centuries, explorers travelled the globe. They encountered innumerate peoples, with a plethora of different cultures. None of them, not a single one, relied on barter.

People have been known to barter *when currencies collapse*, due to hyperinflation. This was the case in Germany, in 1923, and in Twenty-First Century Zimbabwe. But this happens *after* they have become accustomed to using money, not before.

Barter also takes place between passing strangers…

The Nambikwara barter whenever they come into contact with a new clan. They send their women and children away, dance in a manner which mimics a military confrontation, and compliment any item they wish to possess. If they agree to exchange an item, they must tear it from the other person using force. If they do this too early, a mass brawl may ensue.

The whole charade is never far from violence. When it is over, the two clans go their separate ways. They may never meet again.

Such scenes are not uncommon...

When Gunwinggu Aborigines meet a new clan, the women hit the men with sticks, before dragging them into the forest for sex. Only then do they barter. Then they wander off in opposite directions.

It sounds like it might be fun, if not a little scary, but it is no basis for a system of ongoing trade between neighbours. It is far too hostile to offer the long-term stability an economy needs to survive. (Graeber, 2011)

THE SHARING ECONOMY

So, if our ancestors did not rely on barter, how did they trade?

They operated the sort of *sharing economies* we met at Burning Man...

You may recall the !Kung from the chapter on primitive democracy. The !Kung mocked each other whenever they were boastful - keeping the best hunters humble, in order to stop them from dominating the group.

The !Kung have an easy-come, easy-go sort of life. They hunt alone and in groups, going wherever they want, whenever they want. Invariably, Mother Nature provides.

Of course, one individual may be down on their luck, on any given day. Another individual may be a terrible hunter. But if they fail in the bush, their friends will come to the rescue - sharing whatever food they have. (Suzman, 2018) (Baker & Swope, 2004)

In a sixteen-day study, a single !Kung hunter killed four warthogs, supplying his clan with 65% of its meat. Four men did not even bother to hunt. Two captured enough meat to feed their families, three caught a little, and one failed to kill a single beast.

But this did not affect consumption. Everyone consumed an equal share of the spoils. Those who had spare meat gave it to those who did not, in much the same way that your neighbour might give you a cup of sugar. (Lee, 1979)

***

A more extensive study of their neighbours, the Kutse Basarwa, reached similar conclusions...

Over the course of one-hundred-and-seventy-five hunting trips, it became clear that "Hunter Five" consistently gave away more meat than he ate. But he received nothing in exchange. He was not given a lofty position in the group, special access to females, or any sort of trinkets. (Kent, 1996)

Hunter-gatherers like these do not have a concept of private property. Just because they capture an animal, does not lead them to believe that it is theirs alone.

Things belong to everyone and no-one, as one anthropologist discovered whilst studying the Pirahã:

"They are always incredulous when I'd come over to get (the item I had lent them)... I wasn't using it, and they needed it, so what's the big deal?... They frequently take each other's things, and there's no fuss about it". (Strauss, 2017)

Christopher Columbus told the Spanish courts something similar. Native Americans were, according to Columbus, "So naive and so free with their possessions that no one who has not witnessed them would believe it. When you ask for something they have, they never say no. To the contrary, they offer to share with anyone".

And Bartolomé de las Casas, who transcribed Columbus's voyages, said much the same thing of the Cubans:

"They lack all manner of commerce, neither buying nor selling, and rely exclusively on their natural environment for maintenance. They are extremely generous with their possessions. And, by the same token, they covet the possessions of their friends, and expect the same degree of liberality from them". (Zinn, 1980)

***

Then there are our old friends, the Iroquois...

As you might expect, things were more organised within the Five Nations. Whenever a person hunted or gathered some food, found or made an item, they would deposit it in the community's longhouse.

If they wanted something, they would make an appeal to a council of women. If the council deemed the request reasonable, it would give the person the items they desired. If not, they would have to go without. (Graeber, 2011)

***

These systems all have one thing in common. Money does not come into the equation.

The best !Kung hunter cannot sell his meat and use the money he receives to buy up his community's possessions. There is no plutocracy here.

Nor can anyone create new money, and use it to buy the best hunter's meat. People cannot come to dominate the supply of goods, by controlling the supply of money, because no such money exists.

THE ORIGIN OF MONEY

Before money, people did not rely on barter, *they relied upon themselves*.

They did not trade with their friends, because everything was owned collectively. They *shared* whatever they had. And they did not trade with strangers, because they were self-sufficient. They produced everything they needed, without having to rely on outsiders.

It was only when people began to farm, and form permanent villages, that things evolved. Individuals began to store grain at home - keeping it for themselves, not for the community.

Private property had been invented. (Strauss, 2017)

Now, rather than give something to a friend or a neighbour, because it was as much theirs as it was yours, people began to expect repayment. If I gave my brother some wood, I might not ask for anything in return. But if I gave that wood to one of two-hundred people in my village, I may very well expect them to give me something with a similar value sometime in the future. They would be in my *debt*.

As a one-off, I might make a mental note of this debt. But, in time, many such debts would be amassed. A whole load of people would owe a whole load of things to each other. Without some sort of accounting device, they would soon lose track.

And so people created "Commodity Money", to keep track of these debts. In Fiji they used whale teeth. In Tibet they used yak dung. The early Romans used salt. The Aztecs used cacao.

Such currencies were democratic. Anyone could go and find a cacao bean or a pile of yak dung. The people controlled the supply of money.

But there was a problem. Such currencies were quick to decay. And they were localised. A Tibetan might accept yak dung to account for a debt, but if she were to offer it to someone from outside of Tibet she would be greeted with some rather confused looks. (Hoffman, 2015)

The first record we have of formal money, which did not decay, dates back to 3500BC. In Mesopotamia, debt contracts were chiselled into clay tablets and deposited in palaces or temples. Similar artefacts existed in Egypt (from 2650BC) and China (from 2200BC). These tablets *could* be passed from one person to another, like money, but there is no evidence to suggest this happened on a regular basis. They served as a unit of account, perhaps to pay taxes, but were seldom used as a means of exchange.

The first coins we know of were made in Sardis, West Asia, in the Seventh Century BC. They reached Greece within a hundred years. But those coins were more like medals than money. They were stamped with the logos of aristocratic families, and given as gifts to secure alliances.

The Greek aristocracy aspired to self-sufficiency; commanding their slaves and servants to produce everything they desired. To resort to trade, because they were incapable of producing things for themselves, was seen as a sign of abject failure. Gifts were exchanged, items were plundered, but trade was a rarity. Merchants were looked down upon with contempt.

This situation changed when the wealthy Greek families united to form nations - employing magistrates, jurors and soldiers to protect their power. Those public servants needed to be paid wages. And so taxes were collected, paid for with gold and silver coins.

Greece's aristocratic families were forced to *sell* things, such as food and cloth, in order to receive the coins they needed to pay their taxes. The public servants, in turn, had to use the coins they had been paid to *buy* the things they needed - things like food and cloth.

Markets were created and money began to flow, at exactly the same time that the rich created *states* to consolidate their power.

The Greeks used their taxes to fund a huge army and navy. They invaded new lands; imposing states, money and markets onto the territories they conquered.

This story repeats itself through history...

In Europe, it was the Romans who took the baton from the Greeks. They formed a state, raised taxes to fund an army, expanded their empire, and imposed metal money upon vast swathes of Europe. The British, French and Spanish Empires forced metal money onto peoples across the globe.

Coins were an essential tool for imperialistic expansion. Whereas it would have been costly to transport heavy items back to the motherland, and inefficient to transport perishable items, it made sense to exchange those items for silver and gold, transport those precious metals across the seas, and use them to buy things at home.

Unlike commodity money, which was perishable, silver and gold stood the test of time. The Wushu coin in China retained its value for five-hundred years. The Solidus coin in Constantinople retained its value for seven-hundred years.

But there was a caveat. The power to create new money now lay with the aristocrats who owned the gold and silver mines, and the states who verified the purity of precious metals - stamping their official seal onto any new coin that was minted. The power to create new money no longer lay with the people. (Schoenberger, 2008) (Graeber, 2011) (Sheldon, 2017 (b)) (Hoffman, 2015)

FIAT FEUDALISM

Silver and gold were not without their problems. They could be melted down and mixed with cheaper metals. People could cut corners from their coins. If they were lost or stolen, they could not be re-issued.

A safer alternative was required ...

***

Pilgrims, headed for the holy land, required a large sum of money to pay for food and accommodation on the way. But travelling with silver and gold was a risky affair. You could be robbed at any time.

So, around the year 1150, those pilgrims began to deposit their money with the Knights Templar, at one of their many castle-like temples. In return for their gold, they were issued a receipt, a "Letter of Credit". Such receipts have been called the first "Cheques". They might just be the first sort of *paper money*.

The pilgrims headed on their merry way, arrived at another temple, showed their letter of credit, and withdrew the coins they needed for the next leg of their journey.

So the Knights Templar acted as a bank. They held people's wealth, issued them with paper money, and charged them fees for their services. They were also the first capitalists. They reinvested their profits in farms, wineries, vineyards, tanneries and tile factories.

But they were not democratic. They were an army, who got their initial power with the sword, fighting in the Crusades. And they were a religious order, who got their initial capital from the aristocracy, who made large donations in an attempt to buy a place in heaven.

Everyday folk could not raise such capital. They could not establish such a network of temples. And so they could not issue the sort of money that the Knights Templars were able to issue. (Bartlett, 2008)

***

In the East, a century later, it was the political class that led the way...

The Khans' administrators made money from the bark of the mulberry tree, turning it into black paper before stamping it with the official seal of the Mongol Empire. Anyone who forged that money, or who refused to accept, was executed for their crime.

***

And in England, it was the rich who took charge...

When a group of wealthy gentlemen lent King William the £1.2m he needed to fund his war with France, they incorporated themselves into a new company, The Bank of England, which was given a licence to take deposits of gold from the public and issue banknotes as receipts. (Hoffman, 2015) (Lanchester, 2019)

There was just one problem with the Bank of England's notes. They came in large denominations. They were no good for buying and selling small, everyday items, and they were beyond the reach of poor individuals.

In stepped the goldsmiths...

The goldsmiths had already grown rich, exchanging foreign coins for domestic ones, and profiting from the discrepancies in weight and size. But their real breakthrough came when they employed the same trick used by the Knights Templars. To protect themselves on their journeys from London to Amsterdam, traders stored their gold in the goldsmiths' sturdy vaults. The goldsmiths then issued them with receipts. (Kim, 2011)

At first, when the traders arrived at their destination, they would find a goldsmith, exchange their receipt for gold, and use that gold to buy the things they wished to export. In time, however, such a process became unnecessary. The traders simply spent the *receipts*, without ever withdrawing the gold.

The goldsmiths realised what was happening...

Noticing that most of the gold in their safes was left untouched, they began issuing *more* receipts than they had gold. They just needed to hold enough gold to repay the few people who actually cashed their notes.

They created that new money, out of thin air, whenever they issued loans. And then they charged interest on those loans. (Even, 1936)

The goldsmiths had evolved into banks.

In 1844, the "Bank Charter Act" made this practice illegal. But the act took several decades to enforce. Fox & Co. of Wellington was still creating its own banknotes seventy-seven years later. (Outing, 2017)

***

Then came "Electronic Money" - the money we spend on debit and credit cards, when transferring money online, and when taking out mortgages and loans.

Such money is also created by private banks.

They perform the same trick as the goldsmith-bankers - issuing way more electric money than they have notes and coins in their vaults. Again, they just need to hold enough money in their vaults to repay anyone who actually requests it. But most people will not request it. They will spend their bank-issued electronic money instead.

The process is so simple, it is hard to believe...

When a private bank issues a loan or mortgage, it simply increases the balance in the recipient's account. That's it! No gold is moved from one vault to another, no cash is transferred in wheelbarrows across town. The lending bank simply changes some numbers in their database - increasing the balance of the recipient's account, without doing anything else at all.

They create new, *electronic money*, out of thin air.

The recipient of the loan then transfers that money, perhaps when purchasing a home or furnishing a factory. The electronic money takes on a life of its own; moving around the economy, as if it were banknotes or coins.

It sounds absurd.

If you were to tell the average person on the street that bankers create new money out of thin air, whenever they issue a loan, they would probably think you were mad. But you do not have to take my word for it. Listen to the experts...

"The essence of the contemporary monetary system is (the) creation of money, out of nothing, by private banks", Martin Wolf, The Financial Times. (Wolf, 2010)

"Banks extend credit by simply increasing the (balance in the) borrowing customer's current account... That is, banks extend credit by creating money", Paul Tucker, Deputy Governor of the Bank of England. (Tucker, 2007)

"Rather than banks receiving deposits when households save and then lending them out, *bank lending actually creates deposits*... Viewing banks simply as intermediaries ignores the fact that, in the modern economy, *commercial banks are the creators of deposit money"*, Bank of England Quarterly Bulletin. (McLeay, Radia & Thomas, 2014)

SO WHAT?

Originally, there was no such thing as money. No-one could use it to control anyone else. The original money, commodity money, was democratic. Anyone could create it. But modern money is not democratic. The majority of people are not allowed to create banknotes or electronic money. That privilege remains with a small cabal of bankers, who create new money whenever they issue a loan. Those bankers are not beholden to the people, but their decisions do have far-reaching consequences.

These are the words of Cahal Moran, of the London School of Economics:

"The privately-made decisions of banks can determine whether or not particular businesses succeed, fail, or even exist in the first place. As banks create money when making loans, this expands activity in whichever area of the economy the money goes". (Moran, 2019)

The banks play God. They have the power to decide which sectors boom and which ones fail.

***

So how, exactly, does this work?

Imagine that everyone needs a mortgage to buy their homes. They do not have any savings. Now let's say the banks issue £50k mortgages to anyone who applies. Well, houses will all sell for £50k. Any house on the market for a greater price will be left unsold, because people will not have the money to buy them.

Now the banks have a change of tact. They start to issue everyone with £100k mortgages. House sellers will increase their asking price to £100k. Buyers have the funds to pay this price. They would be foolish to ask for less.

In this example, house prices double because the banks decide to create more money for mortgages.

But what about the people?

They have two choices. They could work double as hard, for double as long, to repay their super-sized mortgages. Or they could give up on the idea of house ownership altogether, and spend the rest of their days as tenants.

If they take the first option, they must subjugate themselves to their bosses. If they take the second, they must subjugate themselves to their landlords.

This is no democracy. The people are not in charge.

***

This example is, of course, purely hypothetical. The real world is more complex. But the numbers speak for themselves...

In the UK, a whopping 97% of money is electronic money. Around half this money, well over £1t, has been created when issuing mortgages. Pumping so much new money into the housing market *has* inflated prices...

In the 1950s, the average house in the UK cost £2,530. That is about £60,900 in 2016's prices. But in 2016, the average house cost £211,000 - three-and-a-half times that amount!

Private banks have also pumped almost £500b of new money into the financial sector - inflating the price of shares. Meanwhile, they have put less than £200b of their new electronic money into the real economy - helping businesses to form and expand. (PositiveMoney.Org)

***

Now ask yourself this: If you could allocate new money, would you do so in this manner?

Or, rather than issue so much money for mortgages, which inflate the price of existing houses, would you not prefer that it was used to build *new* houses - an act that could make housing more affordable? Would you have banks create new money to fund hostile takeovers of existing businesses? Or would you prefer them to use that money to fund the creation of *new* businesses?

In a direct democracy, you would have a say. You would be able to vote on how much money was created, and where that money went.

In a more extensive representative democracy, you would be able to vote for the top bankers, based on the policies in their manifestos.

But our money supply is not democratic. The bankers run amok, unchecked by the people, limited only by how much money they are able to lend.

***

We have already considered one solution to this problem - abolishing money altogether.

Whilst this may seem a little far-fetched, it does work for the !Kung and the Kutse Basarwa. It works when passing the salt or giving your neighbour a cup of sugar. And it works at places like Burning Man.

In the remainder of this chapter, we shall consider a few other solutions: Democratising our central banks. Creating public banks, beholden to the people. Turning to peer-to-peer lending, community currencies and cyber currencies...

100% RESERVE BANKING

The Federal Reserve, the national bank of the United States, remains a private institution. It is owned by America's private banks. But the Bank of England was nationalised in 1946. Since then, it has been overseen by the British government.

The Bank of England still has a monopoly on the production of banknotes and coins. But we tend not to buy things like houses, cars or businesses with cash. We buy these things with electronic money, created by private banks, who serve their shareholders, not the people.

But what if this was to change?

What if the government was to update the Bank Charter Act, to make it illegal for private banks to create electronic money?

***

The years following the Wall Street Crash were a time of soul-searching for economists. America's GNP had fallen by nearly 50%, car production was down 80%, and house-building had almost come to a halt. Over a hundred-thousand firms had closed their doors. Over two-thousand banks went out of business in 1931 alone.

A team of economists got to work. Building on the theories of Nobel Prize winning chemist, Frederick Soddy, they formulated the "Chicago Plan".

Under the Chicago Plan, laws would be introduced to stop banks from creating money out of thin air. They would only be allowed to lend government-issued money - crediting their customers' accounts with the notes and coins in their vaults, but not a cent more.

They called it "100% Reserve Banking" because banks would keep "100%" of the money they loaned in "Reserve". This differs from the current system, known as "Fractional Reserve Banking", in which banks only hold a "Fraction" of the money they lend - inventing the remainder.

The economists behind the Chicago Plan were no fans of big government. They were the darlings of Reagan and Thatcher, who would go on to form the "Chicago School", which sung the virtues of low taxes and market deregulation. Yet they made an exception for banking. They argued that governments should have a monopoly on money creation, and gathered statements from bankers who claimed it would be a "Simple" thing to do.

For them, the benefits were clear. 100% reserve banking would eliminate credit-driven booms and busts, allow governments to issue money at zero interest (rather than borrow it), and therefore reduce the national debt.

There was just one problem. Their plans never became a reality. They were put on a shelf to gather dust, until history repeated itself in 2008...

***

The Global Economic Crash inspired economists to cast their minds back to this long-forgotten plan. And, in 2012, a report by the International Monetary Fund concluded that the theory was sound. The benefits would be real. (Benes & Kumhof, 2012) (Wolf, 2014)

But the financial world had become convoluted, bloated by a plethora of complex financial products with confusing names - securities, derivatives, equities, commodities, and whatever else some dollar-eyed financier just happened to magic up on a whim.

Along came "Limited Purpose Banking", a system which has won the backing of five Nobel laureates...

Under limited purpose banking, banks would be stripped down to their basic form, with no financial reserves of their own. The actual business of banking would be done on a peer-to-peer basis, with lenders lending *their* money directly to borrowers. The banks would be intermediaries; asset managers, who would oversee the process, without adding or creating any money themselves.

"Mutual Funds" would be established to manage different financial products...

Say someone wishes to apply for a mortgage. Lenders would club together, form a "Mortgage Mutual Fund", and bid for that mortgage. The banks would act as intermediaries - operating such funds and advising their investors.

The lenders would probably be cautious. It is unlikely they would risk *their* money on subprime loans, in the same way the bankers risked *other people's* money in the lead up to the Global Economic Crash.

Mutual Funds could also be established for managing insurance policies, pension funds, business loans, stock portfolios and derivatives.

Every liability would be backed by capital - the government-issued money supplied by lenders. If the loans were repaid, those lenders would win. They would receive interest on their capital. If the loans were not repaid, those lenders would lose a part of their capital. But in either scenario, the banks, other lenders and other borrowers would be unaffected. There could not be a financial recession based on the over-lending of bad banks, because the banks would not be lending.

The system would provide *stability*. And it would also provide *simplicity*. Its proponents would establish a single regulatory body to replace the hundreds of regulators which exist in the United States today. (Kotlikoff, 2010) (Sandbu, 2010) (Kotlikoff & Leamer, 2009) (Smolo & Mirakhor, 2008)

***

In the wake of the Global Economic Crash, people were rather miffed:

"Why trust those dodgy banks to make investments? They've crashed our frigging economies! We should be able to invest *our* money *ourselves*".

And so were born the "Social Lending" sites, which are a little like the aforementioned mutual funds. Prosper and Lending Club appeared in the States. Zopa popped up in the UK. They were joined by the likes of SoFi, Greensky, Kabbage and Funding Circle.

These were not traditional banks. These were platforms, matchmaking websites that connected lenders and borrowers - everyday people who wished to do banking themselves. These platforms did not need high street branches or skyscrapers in financial districts. They were not tied down by clunky technology or rigid regulation. They were lean organisation who could offer better interest rates and lower fees.

They got off to a flying start, brokering $1.8b in loans by the end of 2012.

But they have hardly taken over the world...

Peer-to-peer lending sites have had to spend big to lure borrowers. Rather than empower individual lenders, they have turned to banks, asset managers and hedge funds, to service those debts. Most social lending platforms still make a loss. And only Kabbage and Funding Circle invest in small business. The other sites fund personal loans and mortgages, helping to create the inflationary bubbles we were seeking to avoid.

Such sites are nice in theory, but they still have a long way to go. (Armstrong, 2019) (Fishkin, 2014)

***

For limited purpose banking to become a reality, *every* bank would need to be turned into a clearing platform for peer-to-peer lending. This would stop them from creating new money out of thin air. But even then, control of the money supply would not necessarily pass to the people. To ensure it does, we would need "Sovereign Money"...

SOVEREIGN MONEY

Under the current system, central banks set interest rates. This is not the interest rate you or I might pay on a mortgage or student loan. It is the "Inter-Bank Lending Rate", at which private banks borrow money from the central bank, should they ever run out of reserves.

Based on this interest rate, private banks create as much electronic money as they can.

So we have two variables. The interest rate, which is set by the central bank. And the quantity of money, which is set by the market.

In a system based on sovereign money, these roles would be reversed. The central bank, not the market, would determine the quantity of money in circulation. Based on this quantity of money, the market would set the rate of interest. Lenders would lend whatever money they had to lend, for whatever rate of interest borrowers were willing to pay.

With sovereign money, the central bank would still have some sort of decision-making panel - "The Monetary Policy Committee" in the UK, the "Federal Open Markets Committee" in the USA, or the "Governing Council of the European Central Bank". These panels would still be tasked with achieving some sort of goal - keeping inflation at a certain level, maintaining growth or reducing unemployment. It is only their toolbox that would change. They would achieve their goals by controlling the money supply, not the interest rate.

To create new money, the central banks would simply credit the government's bank account with "Central Bank Digital Currency" (CBDC). The new credit in the government's account would be backed on the central bank's balance sheet by bonds which had an equal value. These bonds would not bear interest. They would have no maturity date. They would not need to be repaid, so should not be considered a part of the national debt.

At this point, the treasury would take over, distributing the "Digital Cash" in the government's account in one of four ways...

It could pay an equal amount to every citizen. A form of universal basic income, otherwise known as "Helicopter Money", this would also help to solve the plutocracy problem.

The government could spend the money itself - giving a pay rise to public servants, building homes for the poor, or opening post offices in remote locations.

The government could reduce taxes.

Alternatively, the government could partner with commercial banks to lend its digital cash to new and expanding businesses. (Dyson, Hodgson & Van Lerven, 2016)

***

Whilst such a system is not inherently *democratic*, it is easy to imagine how it might be *democratised*.

In a direct democracy, we could vote on the quantity of new money to be created, *and* the channels through which it should be distributed.

In a representative democracy, we could hold elections to choose our central bankers.

In a liquid democracy, we could find an expert with whom we agree, and delegate our vote to them.

Any one of these solutions would be more democratic than the system we have today.

The results are likely to benefit us all. It is unlikely that people would vote to pump so much new money into the housing market, forcing them to pay a higher price for the same houses. It seems far more likely that they would vote for that money to be used to build *new* homes or establish *new* businesses.

Furthermore, once this new money is in the financial ecosystem, banks would be forced to act responsibly, thanks to limited purpose banking. This would mean an end to the credit booms and busts that ruined so many lives in the aftermath of the 1929 and 2008 economic crashes.

***

Will any of this happen?

I do not know.

But back in the real world, the Bank of England *is* attempting to reform itself. It has recruited twelve sets of "Citizens' Panels" in each region, giving people from all corners of society the chance to grill the nation's central bankers - having their say about "Jobs, pay and the cost of living" - talking about their "Experiences of the housing market", borrowing and saving. (Allsey, 2019)

***

Whether you like it or not, central banks are political beasts. But they often operate independently of any sort of democratic framework.

Through quantitative easing, the Bank of England bailed out the private banks. The top 1% of Brits gained two-hundred-and-seventy-eight times more from this process than the poorest 14%. (Youel, 2018)

Sovereign money can give us a democratic framework through which we can hold our national banks to account; ensuring they serve the poor *as well as* the rich.

But why stop there?

These are supposed to be *our* banks, operating in *our* interest. There is an argument which says they should offer us banking services too...

***

Not so long ago, if you wanted to book a holiday you went to a travel agent - a retailer of holidays. These days, it is more common to book directly with the wholesalers - the airlines, hotels and restaurants.

Likewise, if you wanted to buy a newspaper, the chances are you went to a newsagent. These days, you are just as likely to go to the paper's website.

However, most people still use a high street bank - a retailer, who banks with the national bank on our behalf. It is as though we are stuck in the Twentieth Century.

There is nothing to stop central banks from offering online accounts to their citizens. By cutting out the middlemen, they would reduce risks and costs. They could also fund "Safe" lending, for mortgages and takeovers, offering lower rates of interest than the high street banks. This would push the private banks out of these markets, forcing them to invest in the real economy - in new and growing businesses. (Gruen, 2016)

PUBLIC BANKS

If the previous section filled you with hope, please do not get carried away. Unlike the rest of this book, most of it dealt with theoretical solutions, not real-world examples.

These solutions are by no means as radical as they may appear...

The paper I referenced when writing of the Chicago Plan was published by the International Monetary Fund. Limited purpose banking was proposed by Laurence Kotlikoff, a professor at Boston University. Sovereign Money is supported by Mervyn King, the former governor of the Bank of England.

These theoretical solutions may not yet be a reality, but progress *is* being made. In 2015, the Icelandic government considered a new financial system based on sovereign money. In 2018, the Swiss held a referendum on this very subject. Faced with vociferous opposition, from the financial sector and Switzerland's main political parties, only 24.3% of voters supported the initiative. Yet, for its proponents, this was a victory of sorts. It raised awareness of how money was created. They may push for another vote in the future. (Atkins, 2018)

***

So much for the future. What of the present?

Over in the States, a mass-movement is gaining momentum, calling for the introduction of "Public Banks". It is inspired by events which took place over a hundred years ago...

***

Back in the early 1900s, North Dakota was still a sparsely-populated frontier-state, sustained by the small-time farmers who pockmarked the otherwise unadulterated prairie.

Their isolation left them vulnerable...

With no other buyers in town, those farmers were forced to sell their crops to the grain monopolies, who kept prices artificially low. The farmers made a loss, they went into debt and, when the banks increased their interest rates, they found themselves in dire straits.

The state's government was no help. It was controlled by Alexander McKenzie, a corrupt former railroad agent who ran the local Republican Party with an iron fist, using it to serve the tax-dodging railroads, rather than the electorate.

When, in 1891, the state *did* try to introduce regulation, the grain monopolies threatened to close their mills. The state buckled.

The locals felt helpless; beholden to private banks in far-off Chicago and Minneapolis. They could not choose who got credit, or decide how to market their produce. Their government was too feeble to defend them.

It was little wonder, then, that the people elected the "Nonpartisan League" - an administration which is remembered for two acts. It took the mills into public ownership, ensuring that the locals, not the grain monopolies, would profit from their hard work. And, in July 1919, they established a public bank, owned by the state's residents. "The Bank of North Dakota" was backed with $2m in capital, and given responsibility for managing the state's account, thereby ensuring that state taxes would flow through this new institution.

***

Owned by the people, beholden to the electorate, the Bank of North Dakota takes local funds and spends them on local projects. They call it "Economic Sovereignty". Instead of sending their money to Wall Street, where it would be invested in risky financial products, the North Dakotans invest it in local projects which cannot get support from the private sector, but which do provide a public good. Their bank invests in infrastructure, deals with natural disasters, and provides students with low-interest loans - all without accruing unsustainable debt, destroying the environment or increasing taxation.

The Bank of North Dakota also partners with the private sector, providing liquidity for over a hundred small banks, and offering guarantees when those banks lend money to new firms. It even lends some of that money itself; helping to drive down the interest rate and therefore reduce the cost of borrowing.

The results are there for all to see…

Having survived an early counterattack by Wall Street, which boycotted the state's bonds, the Bank of North Dakota lent $41m to sixteen-thousand farmers, helping them to reclaim control of their farms.

The bank helped North Dakota to withstand the Wall Street Crash; paying its teachers in full, whilst other states could only pay them with vouchers. It survived the Dot Com Crash, handing $40m to the state government, to help it cover its deficit. And, having steered clear of subprime mortgages, to focus on the real economy, it was one of the few banks to come out of the Global Economic Crash unscathed.

In fact, it thrived. Whilst other banks lost billions, the Bank of North Dakota made a record profit. In 2008, it handed a dividend of $60m to the state government. In 2018, it paid out $159m. Its initial endowment of $2m had been transformed into $8b of assets. (Hanna & Simpson, 2019) (Harkinson, 2009) (Peischel, 2019)

***

The Bank of North Dakota is by no means perfect. It was criticised for funding the policing of protests against the Dakota Access Pipeline. It has been accused of serving the establishment, not the people. But the benefits seem to outweigh the costs. The bank puts monetary control back in the hands of the electorate; insulating the people from financial crises, and making real investments that benefit residents.

It has inspired a movement…

In California, over a hundred unions, community groups, environmental organisations, political parties and city governments have united to demand a public bank. Despite fervent opposition from vested interests, their calls were heeded, in October 2019, when Governor Gavin Newsom signed "The Public Banking Act". This allows the state's cities and counties to establish banks that will invest in affordable housing, new business, infrastructure and green energy. (Hanna & Simpson, 2019) (Johnson, 2019)

Elsewhere, however, attempts to establish public banks have not been so successful. Efforts have been thwarted in no less than twenty-four different American states. Half the British electorate would like to nationalise their country's banks, according to one poll, but their politicians have not yet responded to their calls. (Peischel, 2019) (BBC, 2019)

***

In the here and now, it may be best to turn to Germany, where public development banks are widespread.

They come in three forms...

The KFW, the third biggest bank in Germany, funds investments in the *national* infrastructure. *State*-owned "Landesbanken" take a lead on industrial strategy. And "Sparkassen" develop relationships with businesses and consumers on a *local* level. (Jones, 2017)

The first Sparkassen was established in Hamburg, back in 1778. Today, there are roughly four-hundred. They are mandated by law to focus on public service and regional development.

These banks are held accountable to the local government. County and municipal politicians, elected by the people, sit on their boards. In 83% of cases, elected officials actually head up these banks.

The results achieved by the Sparkassen are there for all to see...

Between them, these public banks hold 15% of Germany's domestic banking assets. They provide 70% of all the funding that is received by small and medium enterprises. (Irigoyen, 2017) (Markgraf & Véron, 2018)

***

So are public banks the solution?

They report to the democratic mass, not a shareholding minority. They make physical investments which benefit the people, in areas such as housing, infrastructure and enterprise. They tend not to create new money to fund speculation, creating inflationary bubbles and causing markets to crash.

"National Investment Banks" and "Sovereign Wealth Funds" can be found across the globe, in capitalist and communist nations, and in rich and poor countries alike - in Mexico, Ireland, South Korea, Canada, Australia, France, Singapore, India, Hong Kong, the UAE, Kazakhstan, Kuwait, Angola, Saudi Arabia, Venezuela, Ireland, Botswana, Senegal, Rwanda and Palestine.

The Chinese have several such banks.

Norway used the money it made from North Sea oil to establish the largest sovereign wealth fund on the planet, despite being a nation of just five-million people. (Clark, 2017)

So far, so good.

Still, public banks continue to share an ecosystem with private banks, who retain the power to create new money, out of thin air - using it however they choose, with scant regard for public opinion.

Furthermore, such institutions can go AWOL...

The KFB part-owned a lender, IKB, who dabbled in American mortgage-backed securities. The Sparkassen dumped excess savings into the Landesbanken, which invested in foreign property and Greek debt - projects which ended in disaster. (Coppola, 2017)

Ultimately, any system beholden to politicians is likely to be as frail as the politicians who lead them.

Perhaps we need a system in which public banks report directly to the people, via some form of direct democracy.

Perhaps we need more "Cooperative Banks", owned and run by their members. We have already spent a lot of time discussing cooperatives, so I do not wish to labour the point *too* much. But it should be noted that they are sizeable. Three-quarters of cooperatives in the United States are financial institutions. Most of them are credit unions; not-for-profit banks, run by a board of volunteers, who are elected by their members. In France, 60% of retail banking is done through cooperatives. In Asia, forty-five-million people are members of credit unions.

I bank with one of the UK's forty-five building societies. I have the right to vote for its top dogs. That is certainly more democratic than your average bank! Such institutions are less likely to dabble in dubious financial markets. They are *more likely* to fund worker and customer cooperatives. But again, they do still inhabit the same ecosystem as the private banks. (Kaiser, 2019) (Rifkin, 2014)

Perhaps what we need is some sort of mechanism through which we can cut out the banks completely; borrowing and lending money amongst ourselves....

CUTTING OUT THE MIDDLEMEN

We have already introduced the "Social Lending" movement, which offered so much, but failed to live up to the hype. A different type of peer-to-peer finance, however, has been far more successful...

"Crowdfunding" allows individuals to invest as little as a few dollars in a project or start-up. They can do so as a gift, as an interest-bearing loan, or in return for some shares in the new enterprise. More often than not, they make their investment in exchange for some sort of discounted or exclusive product.

The king of crowdfunding is *Kickstarter*...

Any budding artist or entrepreneur can propose a project on the Kickstarter site, although to really stand out, their pitches need polished videos, glitzy pictures and brand-name reviews.

Each project comes with a budget and a deadline. If sufficient funds are pledged by the time that deadline arrives, the money is collected and the project goes ahead. If it is not, investors do not part with a dime. Kickstarter, meanwhile, takes a small commission. It is not a bank. It does not fund or propose investments itself. It is more like a clearing-house.

The Kickstarter website sorts projects into one of eight categories: "Arts", "Comics and Illustration", "Design and Tech", "Film", "Food and Craft", "Games", "Music" and "Publishing". When I checked it out, "In Search of Tomorrow", a four hour science-fiction documentary, had pride of place at the top of the site's homepage. The film's producers, CreatorVC, called it a "Love-letter to the Sci-Fi films we grew up with". They called themselves, "An independent producer of community-powered entertainment - long-form factual content that is funded, inspired, and shaped by a dedicated community of fans".

Investors could pledge as little as £10, not to gain a return, but "Because you believe in it". For £30, they could grab the "Marty McFly Package". This did generate a dividend - a digital copy of the documentary, access to the "Community", an invitation to the virtual premiere, and a mention in the credits. Seven such packages were available in all. The "Luke Skywalker Package", which was selling for £4,800, offered an executive producer credit, two tickets to the Hollywood premiere, tickets to its after-party, and a meet-and-greet with the crew.

The packages were proving popular. With six days remaining, the project had already raised £273k - far more than its £35k target. It was going to go ahead.

A number of other projects were also enticing investors...

Creality were offering a 3D printer to anyone who was willing to stump up $319, to help them get their project off the ground. Investors in SunTable, a solar-powered table, could invest $299 upfront, and receive a SunTable worth $499 when the firm began production. Fairafric was looking for funds to start a solar-powered chocolate factory in Ghana. Detestable Games had already raised all the money it needed to produce its "Dodos Riding Dinos" board game. And Oliver Dahl's, "Between Places: A Photo Book", had received 92% of the funding it needed to go to print.

These are all real investments, in real projects. Crowdfunding does not create financial bubbles in financial markets. And it does pack a punch...

By the time I visited the site, in May 2020, about eighteen-million investors had pledged almost $5b. Of this, $4.45b had been invested in over one-hundred-and-eighty-thousand successful projects.

***

Peer-to-peer lending does not stop banks from creating money when they issue loans. But it does take a chunk of their business away. It stops them from issuing *so many loans*, and so it stops them from creating *so much money*.

It is progress, in an evolution-not-revolution sort of way.

But sites like Kickstarter still deal in dollars, pounds and euros; the sort of money that is created, from the top down, by big banks and big government.

Perhaps we need a system that does not rely on any such corporations and states - on private banks, central banks, public banks *or* cooperative banks - on bankers *or* politicians...

Perhaps we, the people, need to create *our own* currencies...

***

Such an idea is nothing new. We have already mentioned how commodity money could be created by absolutely anybody. In more recent times, "Tally Sticks" served a similar purpose. Two people took a piece of wood, cut notches to mark the size of a debt, and snapped it in two. Whoever held the "Counterfoil" owed a debt to the "Stockholder". Whilst waiting for the debt to be repaid, the stockholder's half, the "Stock", could be used to make purchases and pay taxes as if it were actual money.

Commodity money and tally sticks were democratic currencies. They could be created and used by anyone. (Baxter, 1989)

Today, over four-thousand such "Micro Currencies" still exist alongside traditional currencies. One of the most popular is *time...*

Time is democratic after all. We each have twenty-four hours a day to spend as we choose. The rich cannot hoard more time than the poor. Banks cannot create new time out of thin air.

Thanks to "Time Banks", we can now treat our time as if it was a currency...

We might spend three hours tutoring a schoolchild, save those three hours in a time bank, and then hire an electrician to spend three hours installing some extra plug sockets in our home. In this example, we earn three hours, save three hours, and then spend three hours. Our time, measured in hours, does the job of a traditional currency.

The idea is nothing new. It has its roots in the early Nineteenth Century labour movement. It was revisited in the 1980s, by Edgar Cahn, who was inspired by his local blood bank. But it came alive with the internet revolution.

Karla Ballard created the Ying time bank, having recalled a practice from her youth:

"One neighbour might pick up another's children from school. She might then call in the favour as a cup of borrowed milk the next week".

She asked herself a question:

"What if that system could be formalised and digitised, even if the neighbours don't know each other?"

Ballard was essentially proposing a barter-based system for the modern age...

A keen DIYer could perform plumbing and maintenance jobs. In return, an amateur cook could provide her with home-cooked meals. A green-fingered neighbour might weed her garden. Professionals could even get involved, offering help with her tax returns or performing keyhole surgery.

The Hour Exchange, in Maine, enables people to pay for their healthcare with "Time Dollars". It offers everything "From mental health and counselling services to herbal medicine... bodywork, midwifery and childbirth support". It also provides access to the arts and education, as well as a "Farm-to-Pantry" network.

Hong Kong is investigating a scheme that will allow people to save credits, when volunteering, which they can cash-in for care when they are old. Stanford University has trialled a program through which doctors spend their time mentoring students, and receive services such as home cleaning in return.

Such exchanges can have a sizeable footprint...

The Ying website claims to be active in thirty-eight nations, with over four-hundred locations in the USA alone, at the time of writing. Hourworld, which connects different time banks across the globe, had forty-five-thousand members.

Not all such exchanges succeed. A lot were formed in the wake of the Global Economic Crash, and many went kaput soon after. But a few are getting stronger by the day. (Matchar, 2018) (Fishkin, 2014)

***

Time-based currencies are clearly democratic. They are created by individuals, to help them provide and receive services from other individuals, without a corporation or government in sight.

"Community Currencies", by contrast, put businesses front and centre. They might not appear so democratic. But they do chip away at the power of the corporate banks. Businesses that use community currencies *rely on each other* for support, instead of the big financial institutions. They sell their wares to other businesses that use the community currency, earn credit, and then spend that credit to buy the things they need.

Let's explain this with an example...

When times are good, a Swiss furniture maker buys wood from a lumberyard using Swiss Francs. But when a recession hits, customers stop buying their furniture, and they begin to make a loss. Mainstream banks will not cover their losses. It looks like they are going to fold.

So the furniture maker offers to pay the lumberyard using the WIR currency. The lumberyard accepts the offer, takes the WIR, and uses it to pay for its electricity. The furniture manufacturer, meanwhile, has saved a fortune in Swiss Francs. It takes the few Swiss Francs it is still earning from the sale of furniture, and pays them to its workers, who all keep their jobs. To repay the WIR it has spent buying wood, it sells office furniture to other businesses, not for Swiss Francs, but for WIR.

The WIR, which was created in response to the Wall Street Crash, has been going strong since 1934. It is used by fifty-thousand Swiss businesses, mainly in the hospitality, construction, manufacturing, retail and professional services sectors. WIR exchanges account for between 1% and 2% of Swiss GDP. As our example shows, it is especially useful during recessions. It can help to keep businesses solvent and workers employed.

More significantly, from the viewpoint of democracy, *the WIR is a cooperative*. If businesses participate in the WIR ecosystem, they achieve full membership and have voting rights at its general assembly. They essentially own the WIR bank, and the currency it creates. (Institute of Social Currency, 2020)

***

Another community currency, the BerkShare, bridges the gap between businesses and individuals...

Residents of Berkshire County, in Massachusetts, can buy a BerkShare for $0.95, and then spend it as if it was a whole dollar. So, if someone wanted to take their family out for a $100 meal, they could go to a not-for-profit bank, exchange $95 for one-hundred BerkShares, and then use those BerkShares to pay for their meal - saving themselves $5 in the process. The restaurateur could either spend the BerkShares they received, perhaps to buy food from a local farm, or they could swap them for the $95 their customer had originally exchanged.

The BerkShare is a standard paper-based currency, which comes in five denominations. But unlike most such currencies, created by distant governments, the BerkShare is created by local people. It can be spent at around four-hundred local businesses, including hotels, salons, spas, medical centres, arts centres and sports venues. So it helps to keep money in the community; creating local jobs for local people.

Unlike bank-created money, BerkShares are not used to create inflationary bubbles in the housing market and stock market. It is a clean currency, used in the real economy, to buy goods and pay wages.

And, like the WIR, BerkShares are run by a cooperative. Locals can become members for twenty-five BerkShares a year. They can elect the board of directors and ratify major decisions. (Rifkin, 2014)

***

Micro currencies can come in many shapes and forms, but they all help to take power from the banks and give it to the people.

"Cyber Currencies" attempt to do something similar...

BANKING ON BITCOIN

The godfathers of cyber currency had a dream. They wished to invent a democratic currency for the digital age.

These were the "Cypher-Punks"...

They were inspired by David Chaum - a pioneer whose early attempts, in the late 1990s, had never gained momentum. And they learned from Bernard Van NotHaus - the man who created the "Liberty Dollar", in 1998, before spending two years in federal prison for "Counterfeiting, fraud and conspiracy".

Chaum inspired the Cypher-Punks to code; creating a raft of cyber-currencies such as "Hashcash", "RPOW", "B Money" and "Bit Gold".

But it was Van NotHaus who inspired Satoshi Nakamoto - the anonymous coder who created Bitcoin and then vanished, evading the authorities whilst his invention lived on... (Hoffman, 2015) (Cannucciari, 2016) (Gonon & Sayanoff, 2018)

***

To understand Bitcoin, we must first consider the "Blockchain"...

A blockchain consists of "Blocks" of data, bound to each other in a "Chain". It is a *ledger*, which records every time a Bitcoin is created, split and exchanged.

Since it is open-source and transparent, anyone can look up any record at any time. The entire history of a Bitcoin can be traced on the blockchain.

The blockchain exists across an unlimited network of computers, without a central hub. It is not owned by any people, governments or firms. It has no central authority.

It is wholly *democratic*. And it is *secure*. Unlike a single central server, owned by a bank or government, a network of thousands of computers cannot be hacked. (Rosic, 2019)

***

Bitcoin is a digital currency, just like the electronic money created by bankers whenever they issue loans. It is also a computer code; created, stored and exchanged on the blockchain - open-source and transparent - written and maintained by hundreds of cyber-geeks.

A Bitcoin is *not* a file. Files can be copied, shared and deleted.

A Bitcoin is an entry on the blockchain database, held in a digital wallet rather than a bank account. When you send a Bitcoin, you are simply handing over control of that part of the database.

Bitcoins cannot leave the blockchain. They cannot be debased with cheap metals, printed at will, or created out of nothing through quantitative easing. No lobbyist, politician or banker can create more Bitcoins on a whim.

New Bitcoins *are* created. They are given to the people who *mine* them, connecting their computers to the ecosystem and contributing code. But these new coins are created at a pre-determined rate, which halves every four years. The last ever Bitcoin will be created in 2040, at which point there will be twenty-one-million in circulation.

The supply of Bitcoin, therefore, is finite; much like the supply of gold and silver coins. Both should, in theory, maintain their value. Inflation should not devalue your share of the pie.

This is not to say there are no risks. Bitcoins are like digital cash. If you lose a dollar bill, it is unlikely you will ever see it again. In the same way, if your computer is hacked, or you give your password away, you may very well lose your Bitcoins. The blockchain is secure, but the means through which individuals access it is not. (Hoffman, 2015)

***

So is Bitcoin money?

It is certainly a store of *some* value. In September 2010, one Bitcoin was worth $0.07. At its peak, in late 2017, its price almost hit $20k. The bubble burst during the *Cryptocurrency Crash* of January 2018. But the Bitcoin has bounced back. It was worth almost $10k at the time of writing; way more than ten years before. The dollar, thanks to inflation, is worth less as each year passes.

The Bitcoin is also a unit of account...

But is it a medium of exchange?

If you walked into a shop and offered to pay with Bitcoin, the cashier may very well think you were mad.

That said, it has been used to buy and sell goods online, most notably on the *Silk Road* - an anonymous marketplace, frequented by drug users and dealers, which the FBI closed down in 2013.

Looking forward, Bitcoin is thought to have mass potential in the world of international remittances. Unlike bank transfers, and the services offered by the likes of Western Union, who might charge a fee of up to 10%, you can send Bitcoin to a loved one in a distant country for free. They can then exchange it into their local currency for next to nothing. Given that two-and-a-half-billion people do not have bank accounts, the potential here is huge. (Hoffman, 2015) (Cannucciari, 2016)

***

So what are the risks?

The blockchain may be safe, stable and democratic. But to gain access, you need to go through a clearing-house.

In the early days, there was only one such exchange - Mount Gox.

Owned and run by Mark Karpeles, a "Twenty-year-old French guy sitting in Tokyo with his cat", Mount Gox controlled 98% of Bitcoin transactions.

Problems arose when customers began *storing* their Bitcoins with Mount Gox. Whilst the blockchain is secure, because it is spread across an unlimited number of computers, Mount Gox was based at a single location. It was vulnerable.

When the American government closed the Silk Road, they seized $5m from Mount Gox's accounts. Kapeles cooperated with the authorities, but the Japanese banks were spooked. They placed limits on the number of transactions Mount Gox could perform. The company had $100m in their accounts, but they were only allowed to make ten international wires a day.

Kapeles had to withdraw millions of yen each morning, carry it across town, and then wire it to anyone who wanted to make a withdrawal.

When the price of Bitcoin hit $1000, Kapeles could not maintain the act. Mount Gox folded.

Worse was to follow...

It emerged that hackers had infiltrated Mount Gox's main server; creating a hole in the system, through which Bitcoins had trickled out. At least eight-hundred-and-sixty-five-thousand Bitcoins, worth up to a $1b, had been lost.

Mount Gox was by no means alone. A hacker collective, "The Mongos Group", had also stolen from other exchanges. Thousands had lost their coins.

***

So did the collapse of Mount Gox mark the end of Bitcoin?

Not at all. Bitcoin, and several other cyber-currencies, are still going strong.

When the railways were invented, there were all sorts of scams, bankruptcies, injuries and accidents. Still, we got the railways. Cyber-currencies are experiencing the same sort of growing-pains today. There are risks and there will be losers, but the gains might outweigh the losses. (Gonon & Sayanoff, 2018)

Crypto-currencies can solve all the issues outlined at the beginning of this chapter...

Because their supply is limited, they maintain their value. They are controlled by the people; not by banks or governments, bankers or politicians. They have not, as yet, been used to create inflationary bubbles in the housing market - making housing unaffordable, whilst depriving businesses of the funds they need to make investments in the real economy.

But there have been problems, as the Mount Gox debacle shows. The establishment is fighting back. The FinCEN ruling of 2015 has added extra regulation to the market. And a "Bitcoin Aristocracy" has started to form. A small number of players have accrued a massive proportion of the cyber-currencies, exacerbating the very inequalities these currencies were supposed to overcome. (Cannucciari, 2016) (Kostakis & Giotitsas, 2017)

It would be wise to proceed with caution.

CONCLUSIONS

So where, exactly, does this leave us?

Whilst writing "Democracy: A User's Guide", I was filled with both hope and despair, and not always in equal measures! I discovered some beautiful islands of democracy, encountering democratic schools for the first time, and coming across some pretty revolutionary ideas, such as liquid democracy and the Zero Marginal Cost Society. At the same time, I was left frustrated. The final eight chapters of this book focused on some very real challenges, but I could only find partial solutions. Democratic alternatives do exist, but the majority of our schools, media outlets, police forces, armies, workplaces, economies and currencies are still managed from the top down.

Let's not be under any illusions. Our so-called "Democracies" are far from democratic...

In the UK, we currently have an unelected royal family, an unelected House of Lords, an unelected judiciary, and a House of Commons ruled by a party that is under no obligation to fulfil its manifesto promises, and which may very well implement a raft of policies which were never mentioned during its election campaign. They have the right to impose policies which are not supported by the majority, and to ignore ideas which do have the people's support.

The Conservatives won the 2019 General Election with just under fourteen-million votes. Three-quarters of eligible voters did not vote for the party. Of the fifty-six-million people who had the right to vote, about nine-million were not even registered, and another fifteen-million did not cast a ballot. (Chocqueel-Mangan, 2020)

This is not a lone example. The last time the Labour Party won an election, in 2005, it only received nine-and-a-half-million votes. The turnout was even lower.

We could ask ourselves a pertinent question: Do people even want to live in a democracy?

A YouGov poll, conducted in May 2018, found that 69% of Brits wish to keep the monarchy. Perhaps these people genuinely prefer feudalism to democracy. Perhaps they like a feudalist-democratic mishmash. Or perhaps they just like to stick with the status quo. Whatever the case, to see so much support for a highly undemocratic institution might lead us to question the population's appetite for democracy itself. (Smith, 2018)

We should not scoff. There are some very legitimate arguments *against* democracy...

Plato argued that democracy is unjust, because it gives unequal people an equal say - allowing the unqualified to outvote the experts. It allows the ill-informed to say, "My ignorance is just as good as your knowledge".

In the Nineteenth Century, Utilitarian philosopher John Stuart Mill argued that people with university degrees should receive additional votes. He believed everyone should have a say, but he did not believe that everyone should have an *equal* say.

Others argue that democracy is "The dictatorship of the majority", "Mob rule" and "Unstable" - doomed to be replaced by another, less democratic system.

People might prefer "Theocracy", in which priests impose God's laws. They might like "Epistocracy", in which the wise are granted control, or some sort of "Benevolent dictatorship". And of course, plenty of Brits still have a taste for monarchism.

That said, there are plenty of arguments *for* democracy...

Amartya Sen has argued that democratic nations do not suffer from famines. Other scholars have pointed out that democracies almost never go to war with each other, they rarely murder their own populations, they nearly always have peaceful transitions of government, and they are more likely to respect human rights. (Crain, 2016)

It was never the intention of this book to make an argument for *or* against democracy. Perhaps it included some ideas that you liked, and others that left you scratching your head, thinking, "I'd rather have *less* democracy than see that crazy idea in my backyard". That is fine. This book was intended to be entertaining and informative. Despite the subtitle, "A User's Guide", it was never meant to be a manifesto.

Nor was it meant to be exhaustive. I mentioned in the introduction that several topics missed the cut, because "The subject of 'Democracy' is so gargantuan that even the greatest minds would struggle to do it justice".

We did not cover *democratic healthcare*, for example. But I would like to think you could extrapolate to see how it might work. Objectives could be set by the people, through referenda or participatory budgeting. Hospitals and hospices could be run by their workers, using the sort of methods we met at Semco.

Indeed, "Patient-driven healthcare" *is* a thing. Patients are already sharing their stories on the internet; telling other patients what to expect from their treatment, warning them of potential side-effects, offering them emotional support, and suggesting alternative therapies. Together, they are launching advocacy groups to win the public's attention. (Rifkin, 2014)

We could apply the tools we met in this book to *almost anything…*

We could create *democratic families*, by taking the Summerhill model, which gave adults and children an equal voice, and importing it into the home. We could introduce *democratic wages*, by holding referenda to set the salaries of nurses, refuse collectors and merchant bankers.

In the chapter on policing, we came across Jane Jacob's idea of "Democratic Town Planning". In the chapter on plutocracy, we saw how the internet is providing us with "Democratic Information". Graffiti could be seen as a form of "Democratic Art".

There are, however, some limits…

Many things *cannot* be democratic. Take the truth. A majority of people can believe our planet is flat, but such a belief will not affect its actual shape. Or take science. People can decide that gravity is a bad thing, and vote to have it abolished, but they will have a hard time changing the laws of nature.

There will have to be compromise. Consumer cooperatives put customers first, whilst producer cooperatives put workers first. As both customers *and* workers, we must choose who we wish to prioritise.

There will be mistakes.

But mistakes can lead to beautiful things…

Alexander Fleming discovered penicillin when he forgot to pack away his bacterial cultures. Wilson Greatbatch invented the pacemaker when he used the wrong resistor, whilst building a measuring device. Charles Goodyear created vulcanised rubber by spilling a mixture of rubber, sulphur and lead onto a hot stove. Coca Cola was the result of a failed attempt to make a headache medicine. Thomas Edison failed three-thousand times before he eventually created the light bulb. (Stewart, 2013)

Those people took risks. And the ideas covered in this book *are* risky. Would you want your government to spend billions, turning every school into a democratic school - something that has never tried on such a scale before? Would you be prepared to abolish parliament and instigate some sort of direct democracy? Would it not be safer to leave things the way they are?

Safer? Yeah, for sure.

Easier? You bet!

But better?

Ask yourself this: What is the worst thing that has ever happened when a nation, industry or organisation, tried to be *too* democratic?

And ask yourself this: Do the rewards not outweigh the risks?

This book asks many questions, such as these, but provides few concrete answers. As a writer, I would not wish to impose my views on my readers. That would be authoritarian. I wish only to ask that people consider these questions *for themselves*, so we can derive our solutions together.

Because that, at the end of the day, is what democracy is all about.

***

And now, before we go our separate ways, some shameless self-promotion...

In the introduction, I mentioned that I was motivated to write this book, "To add some substance to the topics covered somewhat more whimsically in my novels". Perhaps you are not a big fan of fiction. Or perhaps you have had enough of my writing already! But if not, please do allow me to make some recommendations...

If you enjoyed the chapters on democratic education and workplace democracy, you might just like "The Little Voice" - a satire that exposes the pitfalls of our current system, in which pupils and workers are so enfeebled.

If you enjoyed the introduction to the last chapter, you may very well like "Money Power Love" - a work of magical realism, which tells the story of the Victorian bankers; those crafty devils who created money out of thin air, and then used it to conquer the world.

And if you are aghast at the corporate control of society, a topic we covered in Chapter Fourteen, or if you fancy a return to the sort of primitive democracies we met in Chapter One, then "Individutopia" might just be your cup of tea.

Whether you give these a go or not, I would like to end by saying a big "Thank-you" for reading "Democracy: A User's Guide". I wish you and your loved ones a long, happy, peaceful life.

Goodbye.

REFERENCES

Aaltonen, Tiina. "Finnish Media Education". 2013. National Audiovisual Institute (KAVI)

Adair, James. "History of the American Indians". 1775. E and C Dilly Publishers.

Adelman, Asher. "Survey". June 23 2008. Workplace democracy Association.

Akala. "Full Address and Q&A". November 26 2015. Speech at the Oxford University Union.

Alejo, Diego; Pimentel, Vázquez; Aymar, Iñigo Macías; Lawson, Max. "Reward Work, Not Wealth". January 2018. Oxfam.

Allsey, David. "Bank Of England Hold Their First Citizens Panel Event Of The Year At Toynbee Hall". April 26 2019. Toynbee Hall.

Alston, Cyprian. "Benedictine Order" in "Catholic Encyclopedia". 1907. Robert Appleton Company.

Alvaredo, Facundo; Chancel, Lucas; Piketty, Thomas; Saez, Emmanuel; Zucman, Gabriel. "World Inequality Report". 2018. World Inequality Lab.

Anderson, Jenny. "American Democracy Is Fracturing. Libraries Say They Know How To Help". October 5 2018. Quartz.

Anonymous. "Indymedia Fighting Spirit Carries on 20 Years After Seattle Protests". November 30 2019. Indy Bay.

Argentieri, Benedetta. "Syria's War Liberates Kurdish Women As It Oppresses Others". February 29 2016. Reuters.

Ariely, Dan. "Predictably Irrational". February 19 2008. HarperCollins.

Armstrong, Robert. "Failed Promise Of Marketplace Lending Faces A New Test". September 22 2019. The Financial Times.

Artamonov, Nikita. "You're In The Army Now: An Expat Recruit's Experience In Switzerland's Militia". November 20 2019. Global Geneva.

Ashiagbor, Sefakor. "Political Parties And Democracy In Theoretical And Practical Perspectives". September 2013. National Democratic Institute.

Associated Press. "Albuquerque Residents Attempt Citizen's Arrest Of Police chief". May 8 2014. The Guardian.

Atkins, Ralph. "Swiss Voters Reject 'Sovereign Money' Initiative". June 10 2018. The Financial Times.

Attkisson, Sharyl. "Astroturf and Manipulation of Media". February 6 2015. TED Talk.

Augustyn, Adam et al. "Comitia". March 23 2018. Encyclopædia Britannica.

Austin. "The Communal Defense Committee: An Alternative to Police (Rojava Excerpt)". July 15 2008. Neighbor Democracy YouTube Channel.

Azzellini, Dario; Ressler, Oliver. "Occupy, Resist, Produce: RiMaflow". September 8 2014. Azzellini.

Azzellini, Dario; Ressler, Oliver. "Occupy, Resist, Produce: Scop Ti". October 27 2018. Azzellini.

Azzellini, Dario. "The Communal State: Communal Councils, Communes, and Workplace democracy". Summer 2013. North American Congress on Latin America, Volume 2, Number 46, Pages 25-30.

Baker, Andrew; Epstein, Gerald & Montecino, Juan. "The UK's Finance Curse? Costs and Processes". September 2018. Sheffield Political Economy Research Institute.

Baker, Matthew; Swope, Kurtis. "Sharing, Gift-Giving, and Optimal Resource Use Incentives in Hunter-Gatherer Society". 2004. Research Net.

Bandyopadhyay, Siddhartha. "Was The Election Of Police Commissioners A Mistake?". June 21 2013. The Conversation.

Barnes, Peter. "Capitalism 3.0". Peter Barnes. Oct 15 2006. Berrett-Koehler Publishers

Barrett, Amy. "Peaceful Protests: Are Non-Violent Demonstrations An Effective Way To Achieve Change?". 27th October 2019. Science Focus.

Barthel, Michael. "Newspapers Fact Sheet". July 9 2019. Pew Research Centre.

Bartlett, David. "Trial Of The Knights Templar". September 23 2008. Timeline.

Bastani, Aaron. "Billionaires Control The Media". November 19 2019. Novara Media.

Bates, Stephen. "The Bloody Clash That Changed Britain". January 4 2018. The Guardian.

Baxter, WT. "Early Accounting: The Tally And Checkerboard". December 1989. The Accounting Historians Journal, Volume 16, Number 2, Pages 43-83.

BBC. "Labour Plans National Bank Using Post Office Network". March 21 2009. British Broadcasting Corporation.

BBC. "Enforcing Law And Order". Accessed September 2019. British Broadcasting Corporation.

Beard, Mary. "Meet The Romans With Mary Beard". April 17 2012. British Broadcasting Corporation.

Ben, Cool. "Georgia's Rose Revolution". November 13 2015. Association for Diplomatic Studies and Training.

Benedict of Nursia. "The Rule of St. Benedict". 516 (1931 edition). A Pax Book.

Benes, Jaromir; Kumhof, Michael. "The Chicago Plan Revisited". August 2012. International Monetary Fund.

Bennett, Trevor; Holloway, Katy; Farrington, David. "Does Neighbourhood Watch Reduce Crime? A Systematic Review And Meta-Analysis". 2006. Journal of Experimental Criminology, Volume 2, Pages 437-458.

Bennett-Jones, Owen. "Excerpts: Annan Interview". September 16 2004. British Broadcasting Corporation.

Berlin, Peter. "The Barcelona Election". July 17 2015. Politico.

Bernburg, Jón. "Economic Crisis and Mass Protest: The Pots and Pans Revolution in Iceland". April 2016. Routledge.

Berti, Francesco. "E-Politics for 'The People'?". September 27 2017. The Good Lobby.

Bibby, Andrew. "Is There A Co-Op Solution To Britain's Railway System?". September 30 2013. The Guardian.

Biswas, Asit; Tortajada, Cecilia. "From Our Ancestors To Modern Leaders, All Do It: The Story Of Corruption". September 7 2018. The Conversation.

Bjartveit, Kjell. "Norway: Ban on Advertising and Promotion". July 7 2003. World Health Organisation.

Blackwell, Christopher (1). "The Development of Athenian democracy". January 24 2003. Harvard University's Center for Hellenic Studies.

Blackwell, Christopher (2). "Athenian democracy: A brief overview". February 28 2003. Harvard University's Center for Hellenic Studies.

Blakeman, Chuck. "DaVita: A 65,000 Person Corporate Village, Or Just A CEO's Nutty Dream?". November 11 2015.

Bloom, Joshua; Martin, Waldo. "Black Against Empire: The History and Politics of the Black Panther Party". 2013. University of California Press.

Bloy, Marjie. "Chartism". March 4 2016. History Home.

Bloy, Marjie. "The Spa Fields Riots". August 30 2003. The Victorian Web.

Boddewyn, Jean. "Control of Advertising". 2015. International Encyclopedia of the Social & Behavioral Sciences, Pages 201-207.

Boehm, Christopher. "Egalitarian Behavior and Reverse Dominance Hierarchy". June 1993. Current Anthropology, Volume 34, Number 3, Pages 227-254.

Boehm, Christopher. "Hierarchy in the Forest". 1999. Harvard University Press.

Borges, Ian. "Why Semco Doesn't Want Your Company To Be Like Semco". 2019. Corporate Rebels.

Boyle, Dave. "Good News: A Co-Operative Solution to the Media Crisis". 2012. Co-Operatives UK, Fresh Ideas 2.

Bridges, Lucas. "Uttermost Part of the Earth". 1948. Hodder and Stoughton.

Briggs, Jean. "Never in Anger: Portrait of an Eskimo Family". 1970. Harvard University Press.

British Library Learning. "Women's Suffrage Timeline". February 6 2018. British Library.

British Library. "Chartism: A Historical Background". Accessed November 2019. The British Library Board.

Brownlee, Frank. "The Social Organization of the Kung Bushmen of the North-Western Kalahari". July 1943. Africa: Journal of the International African Institute. Volume 14, Number 3, Pages 124-129.

Butler, Patrick. "At Least 320,000 Homeless People In Britain, Says Shelter". November 22 2018. The Guardian.

Butler, Patrick. "More Than 8 Million In UK Struggle To Put Food On Table, Survey Says". May 6 2016. The Guardian.

Calvetti, Oswald. "Face Au Succès Des Thé "1336" Et "Scop-Ti", Les Ex-Fralib Ont Besoin De Trésorerie". July 6 2019. Parti Communiste Français.

Cammaerts, Bart; DeCillia, Brooks; Magalhães, João; Jimenez-Martínez, César.

"Journalistic Representations of Jeremy Corbyn in the British Press: From Watchdog to Attackdog". July 1 2016. London School of Economics and Political Science.

Cannucciari, Christopher. "Banking On Bitcoin". 2016. Periscope Entertainment, Downtown Community Television Center & Dynamic Range.

Carlile, Clare. "History of Successful Boycotts". May 5 2019. Ethical Consumer.

Casalicchio, Emilio. "Explained: How To Deselect A Tory MP". February 11 2019. Politics Home.

Cassidy, John. September 10 2018. "The Real Cost of the 2008 Financial Crisis". New Yorker.

Cathcart, Abby. "The John Lewis Model Reveals The Tensions And Paradoxes At The Heart Of Workplace democracy". July 30 2013. Democratic Audit UK.

Caulkin, Simon. "Gore-Tex Gets Made Without Managers". November 2 2008. The Guardian.Cave, Tamasin; Rowell, Andy. "A Quiet Word: Lobbying, Crony Capitalism and Broken Politics in Britain". March 1 2014. Random House UK.

Cecchetti, Stephen G & Kharroubi, Enisse. "Why Does Financial Sector Growth Crowd Out Real Economic Growth?". February 2015. BIS Working Papers Number 490.

Cesale, Alessandro. "Cooperative Housing: A Key Model For Sustainable Housing In Europe". April 26 2012. Cooperatives Europe.

Chandler, Simon. "Thousands of Misleading Facebook Ads Help Conservatives To 'Crushing' U.K. Election Victory". December 14 2019. Forbes.

Charlton, Emma. "How Finland Is Fighting Fake News: In The Classroom". May 21 2019. World Economic Forum.

Chenoweth, Erica. "The Success Of Nonviolent Civil Resistance". November 4 2013. TEDxBoulder.

Chenoweth, Erica; Dahlum, Sirianne; Kang, Sooyeon; Marks, Zoe; Shay, Christopher; Wig, Tore. "This May Be The Largest Wave Of Nonviolent Mass Movements In World History". November 16 2019. The Washington Post.

Chertoff, Emily. "No Teachers, No Class, No Homework; Would You Send Your Kids Here?". December 12 2012. The Atlantic.

Chisolm, Alastair. "The Tolpuddle Martyrs". July 15 2009. BBC Dorset.

Chitanondh, Hathai. "Thailand Country Report on Tobacco Advertising and Promotion Bans". 2003. World Health Organisation.

Chivers, Tom. "From Magna Carta To Universal Suffrage, The 1000-Year History Of British Democracy". 7 June 2017. The Daily Telegraph.

Chocqueel-Mangan, Matt. "2019 Wrap-Up: Good Result For VfP, Bad Result For Democracy". January 9 2020. Vote For Policies.

Chrisafisi, Angelique. "Advertising Breaks Your Spirit: The French Cities Trying to Ban Public Adverts". December 23 2019. The Guardian.

Clark, Thomas. "I'd Like To Hear An Example Of A Country Where Corbyn And McDonnell's Ideas Have Worked". November 17 2017. Another Angry Voice Blog.

Clement, Jessica. "Global Social Networks Ranked By Number Of Users 2019". November 21 2019. Statistica.

Cohen, Deborah. "Inside The UK's Drug Buyers' Clubs". June 5 2019. BBC Newsnight.

Cohen, Nick. "In Britain Now, The Richer You Are, The Better Your Chance Of Justice". April 21 2018. The Guardian.

Cohen, Nick. "What Did The Squatters Do For Us?". January 23 2006. The New Statesman.

Coleman, Alison. "Banishing The Bosses Brings Out Zappos' Hidden Entrepreneurs". April 7 2016. Forbes.

Coppola, Frances. "The Wondrous German Public Sector Banks Aren't All They Are Cracked Up To Be". Oct 24 2017. Forbes.

Crae, Ross. "In Your Garden: Sharing Allotment Plots Allows Everyone To Have A Go At Growing". February 26 2016. The Sunday Post.

Crain, Caleb. "The Case Against Democracy". October 31 2016. The New Yorker.

Daboín, Eduardo. "Simón Bolívar Communal City: An Experience Of Self-Government In The Venezuelan Plain". August 13 2018. Revista Pueblos.

Dahl, Robert. "Democracy". August 26 2019. Encyclopædia Britannica.

Dahlum, Sirianne; Knutsen, Carl; Wig, Tore. "Who Revolts? Empirically Revisiting the Social Origins of Democracy". October 2019. The Journal of Politics, Volume 81, Number 4.

Daniels, Chris. "Rise Of An Auckland Electricity Behemoth". July 1 2005. New Zealand Herald.

De Waal, Frans. "Chimpanzee Politics: Power and Sex Among Apes". 1982. John Hopkins University Press.

Deer, John Fire Lame Deer. "Lame Deer, Seeker of Visions". 1976 (October 1 1994 Edition). Simon & Schuster.

DEFRA (a). "Agriculture In The United Kingdom 2018". 2018. UK Government.

DEFRA (b). "Food Statistics In Your Pocket 2017 - Global And UK Supply". October 9 2018. UK Government.

Deloire, Christophe. "World Press Freedom Index 2020". April 21 2020. Reporters Without Borders.

Dias, Nelson. "Hope For Democracy: 25 Years Of Participatory Budgeting Worldwide". April 2004. In Loco Association.

Dilouambaka, Ethel. "Things You May Not Know About Democracy in Ancient Greece". September 19 2017. The Culture Trip.

Dodd, Vikram; Grierson, Jamie. "Greenpeace Included With Neo-Nazis On UK Counter-Terror List". January 17 2020. The Guardian.

Doherty, Iwan. "Why We Need More Housing Co-ops". April 24 2020. Tribune.

Donadio, Rachel. "France's Fuel-Tax Protests Expose The Limits Of Macron's Mandate". December 4 2018. The Atlantic.

Doucleff, Michaeleen; Greenhalgh, Jane. "How Inuit Parents Teach Kids To Control Their Anger". March 13 2013. NPR.

Downie, Andrew. "Learn What You Want". February 9 2004. The Telegraph.

Dracott, Edd. "General Election 2019: The Unofficial Facebook Pages Reaching

Millions Of Voters". December 11 2019. The Belfast Telegraph.

Drutman, Lee. "The Business Of America Is Lobbying: How Corporations Became Politicized And Politics Became More Corporate". April 16 2015. Oxford University Press.

DuVernay, Ava. "13th". 7 October 2016. Forward Movement.

Dyck, Joshua; Lascher, Edward. "Initiatives without Engagement: A Realistic Appraisal Of direct democracy's Secondary Effects". February 28 2019. University of Michigan Press.

Dyson, Ben; Hodgson, Graham; Van Lerven, Frank. "Sovereign Money: An Introduction". December 2016. Positive Money.

Ellis, Lee; Beaver, Kevin; Wright, John. "Handbook of Crime Correlates". April 1 2009. Academic Press.

Ellis, Sian. "King John And The Sealing Of Magna Carta". November-December 2014. Britain Magazine.

Emmerson, Owen. "No To The Cane". January 13 2020. Tribune Magazine.

Endicott, Kirk. "Property, Power and Conflict Among The Batek Of Malaysia" in "Hunters and Gatherers 2: Property, Power and Ideology". January 1988. Berg Publishers.

Engels, Frederick. "The Iroquois Gens" in "Origins of the Family, Private Property and the State". 1902. Charles H. Kerr Publishing Company.

Epstein, Edward. "Have You Ever Tried to Sell a Diamond?". February 1982. The Atlantic.

Evans, Rob; Dodd, Vikram. "Police Anti-Extremism Unit Monitoring Senior Green Party Figures". April 26 2016. The Guardian.

Even, Louis. "The Goldsmith Who Became a Banker: A True Story" in "This Age of Plenty". 1936. The Pilgrims of St Michael.

Falk, Tyler. "In Billboard-Less City, Can Businesses Survive?". January 2 2012. ZD Net.

FC Barcelona. "How The Voting Went At The 2019 Assembly". October 6 2019. FCBarcelona.Com.

Feinberg, Robert; Kuehn, Daniel. "Does a Guaranteed Basic Income Encourage Entrepreneurship? Evidence From Alaska". 2019. Working Papers 2019-02, American University, Department of Economics.

Feloni, Richard. "Here's What Happened To Zappos' HR Boss When The Company Got Rid Of Managers And Her Job Became Obsolete". February 12 2016. Business Insider.

Feloni, Richard. "Inside Zappos CEO Tony Hsieh's Radical Management Experiment That Prompted 14% Of Employees To Quit". May 16 2015. Business Insider.

Ferguson, Euan. "One Million. And still they came". February 16 2003. The Observer.

Finley, Klint. "A Year Without Net Neutrality: No Big Changes (Yet)". December 14 2018. Wired.

Firth, Raymond. "Extraterritoriality And The Tikopia chiefs". 1969. Man Journal, New Series, Volume 4, Number 3, Pages 354-78.

Fishkin, James. "Democracy When The People Are Thinking: Reflections on Deliberative Designs, Micro and Macro". 2018. European Consortium for Political Research.

Ford, Hugh. "St. Benedict of Nursia" in "Catholic Encyclopedia". 1907. Robert Appleton Company.

Foster, Colin. "When School Students Fought The System". October 6 2006. Workers' Liberty.

Frances, Ryan. "£13bn In Unclaimed Welfare? It's Just Fuel For The Tories' Big Benefits Myth". May 11 2016. The Guardian.

Frank, Thomas. "The Wrecking Crew: How Conservatives Rule". August 5 2008. Henry Holt and Company.

Freeman, Edward. "Strategic Management: A Stakeholder". 1984. Cambridge University Press.

Friend, Nick. "Wimbledon's 'Most Sought-After Tickets' Go On Sale For $105,000". March 29 2019. CNN.

Frost, Ashleigh. "The Bentley Blockade". April 16 2014. One Million Women.

Fuentes, Federico. "Venezuela's Crisis: A View from the Communes". May 10 2019. Green Left Weekly.

Fuller, Steve. "Newspaper Market In Europe: Statistics & Facts". Sep 16 2019. Statista Research Department.

Fulton, Lionel. "Worker Representation In Europe". 2015 Labour Research Department and European Trade Union Institute for Research.

Garzia, Diego; Cedroni, Lorella. "Voting Advice Applications In Europe: The State Of The Art". 2010. ScriptaWeb.

Geberer, Raanan. "Neighbourhood Watch Groups: Looking Out for Each Other". December 2014. The Cooperator.

Geiser, Urs. "Swiss Give Green Light For Renewables And Nuclear Phase Out". May 21 2017. Swiss Info.

Gelman, Valeria; Votto, Daniely. "What If Citizens Set City Budgets?". June 13 2018. World Resources Institute.

Gillin, John. "The Origin of Democracy". May 1919. American Journal of Sociology, Volume 24, Number 6, Pages 704-714.

Giraud, Eva. "Has Radical Participatory Online Media Really 'Failed'? Indymedia And Its Legacies". 2014. Convergence: The International Journal of Research into New Media Technologies, Volume 20, Issue 4, Pages 419-437.

Goldmacher, Shane; Martin, Jonathan. "Alexandria Ocasio-Cortez Defeats Joseph Crowley In Major Democratic House Upset". June 26 2018. The New York Times.

Gonon, Vincent; Sayanoff, Xavier. "Bitcoin Big Bang: The Unbelievable Story Of Mark Karpeles". October 7 2018. Brainworks.

Goodley, Simon; Ashby, Jonathan. "A Day At 'The Gulag': What It's Like To Work At Sports Direct's Warehouse". December 9 2015. The Guardian.

Goodman, Amy; González, Juan. "Don't Hate The Media, Be The Media: Reflections On 20 Years Of Indymedia". November 27 2019. Democracy Now.

Gorenflo, Neal. "What If Uber Was Owned And Governed By Its Drivers?". 2016. Evonomics.

Graeber, David. "Bullshit Jobs: A Theory". May 15 2018. Simon & Schuster.

Graeber, David. "Debt: The First 500 Years". 2011. Melville House Publishing.

Graeber, David. "Foreword" in "Revolution in Rojava". 2016. Pluto Press.

Graeber, David; Wengrow, David. "Are We City Dwellers Or Hunter-Gatherers? New Research Suggests That The Familiar Story Of Early Human Society Is Wrong, And The Consequences Are Profound". Winter 2018. The New Humanist Quarterly.

Gray, Peter & Chanoff, David. "Democratic Schooling: What Happens To Young People Who Have Charge Of Their Own Education?". February 1986. American Journal of Education, Volume 94, Number 2, Pages 182-213.

Gray, Peter. "A Brief History Of Education". August 20 2008 (b). Psychology Today.

Gray, Peter. "Children Educate Themselves III: The Wisdom of Hunter-Gatherers". August 2 2008 (a). Psychology Today.

Gray, Peter. "Children Teach Themselves To Read: The Unschoolers' Account Of How Children Learn To Read". February 24 2010. Psychology Today.

Gray-Donald, David. "Will Campaigns To Revive Community TV In The New Digital World Work?". March 16 2017. J Source.

Greenberg, Daniel. "Free At Last: The Sudbury Valley School". June 1 1995. Sudbury Valley School Press.

Greene, Nelson. "Dekanawida and Hiawatha" in "History of the Mohawk Valley: Gateway to the West 1614-1925". 1925. The S. J. Clarke Publishing Company.

Gregory, Alice. "Running Free in Germany's Outdoor Preschools". May 18 2017. The New York Times Style Magazine.

Grice, Andrew. "General Election 2015: Sixty Per Cent Of People Want Voting Reform, Says Survey". May 5 2015. The Independent.

Griffin, Ben. "Ex-SAS Soldier / Veterans For Peace Activist Speaks Out". September 9 2016. It's Just Myself, So It Is Youtube Channel.

Griffin, Ben. "The Making Of A Modern British Soldier". October 23 2015. Independent POV YouTube Channel.

Grinde, Donald; Johansen, Bruce. "Exemplar Of Liberty: Native America And The Evolution Of Democracy". 1990. American Indian Studies Center, UCLA.

Gruen, Nicholas. "Why Central Banks Should Offer Bank Accounts to Everyone". December 16 2016. Evonomics.

Hadfield, Miles. "Making A Difference: Community Ownership Is Saving Pubs". July 2 2018. Coop News.

Haft, Lara. "Don't Repeat The Maccabees' Mistake: Safety Through Solidarity, Not Surveillance". December 26 2019. Mondoweiss.

Hall, Jez. "PB In Schools: Has Its Time Come In The UK?" March 27 2019. PB Network.

Hamel, Gary. "The Hidden Costs Of Overbearing Bosses". December 1 2009. Labnotes, Issue 14.

Hamil, Sean; Walters, Geoff; Watson, Lee. "The Model Of Governance At FC

Barcelona: Balancing Member Democracy, Commercial Strategy, Corporate Social Responsibility And Sporting Performance". 2010. Soccer & Society, Volume 11, Pages 475-504.

Hampson, Martha; Patton, Alec; Shanks, Leonie. "10 Schools For The 21st Century". 2013. Innovation Unit For Public Services.

Handley, Lucy. "São Paulo Ad Ban Makes Marketers More Creative". August 28 2012. Marketing Week.

Hanna, Mega. "BDS Movement: Lessons From The South Africa Boycott". February 26 2016. Al Jazeera.

Hanna, Thomas; Simpson, Adam. "100 Years Ago, Farmers and Socialists Established the Country's First Modern Public Bank". July 28, 2019. In These Times.

Hardman, Isabel. "Why We Get The Wrong Politicians". September 6 2018. ". Atlantic Books UK.

Hardt, Steve; Lopes, Lia. "Google Votes: A liquid democracy Experiment On A Corporate Social Network". June 5 2015. Technical Disclosure Commons.

Harkinson, Josh. "How the Nation's Only State-Owned Bank Became the Envy of Wall Street". March 28 2009. Mother Jones.

Harte, Julia; R. Smith, Jeffrey. "Constitutional Sheriffs: The Cops Who Think the Government Is Our 'Greatest Threat'." April 18 2016. NBC News.

Hay, George. "Law Enforcement In Britain Before And After Peterloo". November 2 2018. The National Archives.

Hellpern, Will. "Inside The Anti-Advertising Movement That's Recruiting Ad Agency Workers To Destroy Billboards And Replace Them With Art". April 6 2016. Business Insider Singapore.

Hempel, Jessi. "Social Media Made The Arab Spring, But Couldn't Save It". January 26 2016. Wired.

Henley, Jon; Kassam, Ashifa; Letsch, Constanze; Goñi, Uki. "May Day: Workers Of The World Unite And Take Over Their Factories". May 1 2015. The Guardian.

Heutlin, Josephine. "The Rise And Fall Of The Pirate Party". September 19 2016. The New Republic.

Higdon, Nolan; Huff, Mickey. "United States Of Distraction: Media Manipulation In Post-Truth America". 2019. City Lights Books.

Hill, Christopher. "The English Revolution 1640". 1940. Lawrence and Wishart.

Hill, Christopher. "Puritanism And Revolution: Studies In Interpretation Of The English Revolution Of The 17th Century". 1958. Palgrave Macmillan.

Hjalmarsson, Randi; Lindquist, Matthew. "The Causal Effect Of Military Conscription On Crime". August 2019. The Economic Journal, Volume 129, Issue 622, Pages 2522–2562.

Hoeschele, Wolfgang. "Sharing Cities: Activating the Urban Commons". March 13 2018. Shareable.

Hoffman, Torsten. "Bitcoin: The End Of Money As We Know It". July 2015. 3D Content Hub.

Hornblower, Simon. "Ancient Greek Civilization". August 29 2019. Encyclopædia

Britannica.

Howe, James. "How The Cuna Keep Their chiefs In Line". December 1978. Man Journal, Volume 13, Number 4, Pages 537-553.

Howgego, Joshua. "Universal Income Study Finds Money For Nothing Won't Make Us Work Less". February 8 2019. New Scientist.

Hublin, Jean-Jacques; Abdelouahed, Ben-Ncer; Bailey, Shara. "New Fossils From Jebel Irhoud, Morocco And The Pan-African Origin Of Homo Sapiens". June 2017. Nature Journal, Edition 546, Pages 289-292.

Institute of Social Currency. "The WIR. The Supplementary Swiss Currency Since 1934". Accessed May 2020 The Economy Journal.

Ipsos MORI. "Perceptions Are Not Reality: What The World Gets Wrong". December 14 2016. Ipsos MORI.

Irfan, Umair. "America's Record High Energy Consumption, Explained In 3 Charts". Apr 18 2019. Vox.

Irigoyen, Claudia. "Sparkassen Savings Banks in Germany". March 27 2017. Centre For Public Impact.

Jacobs, Ben; Gambino, Lauren. "Democrats See Major Upset As Socialist Beats Top-Ranking US Congressman". June 27 2018. The Guardian.

Jacobs, Jane. "The Death and Life of Great American Cities". 1961. Vintage Books.

Jakes, Susan. "Dabbling In Democracy: No One Knew What To Expect When A Chinese Town Tried Listening To Its People". April 16 2005. Time Asia Magazine.

Jeffries, Stuart. "How The Web Lost Its Way: And Its Founding Principles". August 24 2014. The Guardian.

Jefferies, Tanya. "What Happened To Thatcher's Share Ownership Dream?". October 9 2015. This Is Money.

Jenness, Diamond. "The Life of the Copper Eskimos: Report of the Canadian Arctic Expedition, 1913-1918". 1922. Ottawa.

Jindar, Beritan. "Rojava Asayish: Security Institution Not Above But Within The Society". June 6 2016. ANF News.

Johansen, Bruce. "Dating The Iroquois Confederacy". Autumn 1995. Akwesasne Notes New Series, Volume 1, Number 3 & 4, Pages 62-63.

Johansen, Bruce. "Forgotten Founders: Benjamin Franklin, The Iroquois And The Rationale For The American Revolution". 1982. Harvard Common Press.

Johnson, Eric. "Survival Of The Nicest? Check Out The Other Theory Of Evolution". Spring 2013. Yes! Magazine.

Johnson, Jake. "Stunning Rebuke To Predatory Wall Street Megabanks". October 03 2019. Common Dreams.

Jones, John. "Why Is Hugo Chavez Called A Dictator?". Jan 31 2011. Venezuela Analysis.

Jones, Owen. "British Banks Can't Be Trusted – Let's Nationalise Them". October 19 2017. The Guardian.

Jones, Owen. "Kurdish Afrîn Is Democratic And LGBT-Friendly. Turkey Is Crushing It

With Britain's Help". March 16 2018. The Guardian.

Jones, Owen. "Sorry, David Cameron, But Your British History Is Not Mine". June 15 2014 (a). The Guardian.

Jones, Owen. "The Establishment: And How They Get Away With It". September 4 2014. Penguin Books.

Jones, Terry. "Monty Python's Life of Brian". August 17 1979. HandMade Films.

Jordan, Mary; Clement, Scott. "Rallying Nation". April 6 2018. The Washington Post.

Kaiser, Jo. "Media Cooperatives: Challenges And Opportunities". February 3 2019. Medium.

Kangas, Steve. "A Timeline Of CIA Atrocities". November 22 1997. Global Research News.

Kasmir, Sharryn. "The Mondragon Cooperatives: Successes And Challenges". February 13 2016. Global Dialogue, Volume 6, Issue 1.

Kasmir, Sharryn. "The Myth Of Mondragon". 1996. State University of New York Press.

Kaufmann, Bruno. "The Way To Modern direct democracy In Switzerland". April 16 2019. The Federal Department of Foreign Affairs.

Kendall, Graham. "The Science That Makes Us Spend More In Supermarkets, And Feel Good While We Do It". March 4 2014. The Conversation.

Kent, Susan. "Cultural Diversity Among Twentieth Century Foragers". 1996. Cambridge University Press.

Kentish, Benjamin. "British People Hugely Overestimate The Number Of Muslims In The UK, Says New Survey". December 15 2016. The Independent.

Kettle, Martin. "Don't Romanticise Putney". October 31 2007. The Guardian.

Kia, Annie; Ricketts, Aidan. "Enabling Emergence: The Bentley Blockade And The Struggle For A Gasfield Free Northern Rivers". 2018. Southern Cross University Law Review, Volume 19, Pages 49-74.

Kim, Jongchul. "How Modern Banking Originated: The London Goldsmith-Bankers' Institutionalisation Of Trust". October 2011. Business History, Volume 53, Number 6, Pages 939-959.

Kinna, Ruth. "An Anarchist Guide To...ACAB". June 2012. Strike, Issue 12.

Klein, Joe. "How Can a Democracy Solve Tough Problems". September 2 2010. Time Magazine.

Klein, Naomi. "The Shock Doctrine: The Rise Of Disaster Capitalism". 2007. Random House of Canada.

Knapp, Michael; Flach, Anja; Ayboğa, Ercan. "Revolution In Rojava: Democratic Autonomy And Women's Liberation In Syrian Kurdistan". 2016. Pluto Press.

Kobach, Kris. "The Referendum: direct democracy in Switzerland". 1993. Dartmouth Publishing.

Kohari, Alizeh. "Hunger Strikes: What Can They Achieve?". August 16 2011. British Broadcasting Corporation.

Kollewe, Julia. "Number Of Empty Homes In England Rises To More Than 216,000".

March 11 2019. The Guardian.

Kostakis, Vasilis; Giotitsas, Chris. "Beyond Bitcoin". Evonomics. January 8 2017.

Kotlikoff, Laurence. "Jimmy Stewart Is Dead: Ending The World's Ongoing Financial Plague With Limited Purpose Banking". March 8, 2010. Wiley.

Kotlikoff, Laurence; Leamer, Edward. "A Banking System We Can Trust". April 23 2009. Forbes.

Krouwel, André. "The Selection Of Parliamentary Candidates In Western Europe: The Paradox Of Democracy". 1999. Paper for the ECPR Mannheim workshop "The Consequences Of Candidate Selection".

Kurtz, Lester. "The Anti-Apartheid Struggle In South Africa (1912-1992)". June 2010. International Centre on Nonviolent Action.

Lamehdasht, Bahrum. "Money In The Star Trek Universe". September 25 2017. 1st Class Economics.

Lanchester, John. "The Invention Of Money". August 5 & 12 2019. The New Yorker.

Langle, Alison. "Amid Rising Skepticism, Why Swiss Trust Their Government More Than Ever". February 20 2019. OZY.

LaSalle, Martin. "FC Barcelona: More Than A Club!". June 19 2012. Coop News.

Laughland, Olive; Saner, Emine. "Tony Blair And The Protesters Who Keep Trying To Arrest Him For War Crimes". 16 Nov 2012. The Guardian.

Lee, Alexander; Paine, Jack. "Did British Colonialism Promote Democracy? Divergent Inheritances And Diminishing Legacies". August 28 2016. University of Rochester.

Lee, Christina. "Employee Job Satisfaction And Engagement: The Doors Of Opportunity Are Open". 2017. Society For Human Resource Management.

Lee, Richard, "Politics, Sexual And Nonsexual, In An Egalitarian Society" in "Politics And History In Band Societies". 1979. Cambridge University Press.

Lee, Richard. "The !Kung San: Men, Women, And Work In A Foraging Society". 1979. Cambridge University Press.

Lee-Miller, Heaven. "What Happened To France's Monarchy?" November 29 2018. Royal Central.

Leeson, Peter. "The Invisible Hook: The Hidden Economies Of Pirates". March 31 2009. Princeton University Press.

Leeson, Peter. "The Law and Economics of Pirate Organisation". 2007. Journal of Political Economy, Volume 115, Number 6, Pages 1049-109.

Leonard, Mark. "China's New Intelligentsia". March 2008. Prospect Magazine, Issue 144.

Levering, Robert. "How Anti-Vietnam War Activists Stopped Violent Protest From Hijacking Their Movement". April 4 2017. Open Democracy.

Levi-Strauss, Claude. "The Social And Psychological Aspects Of Chieftainship In A Primitive Tribe: The Nambikuara Of Northwestern Mato Grosso". 1967. Natural History Press.

Litman, Todd. "Evaluating Carsharing Benefits". January 2000. Transportation Research Record Journal, Volume 1702, Pages 31-35.

Livingston, Michael. "Here's When Boycotts Have Worked: And When They Haven't". March 1 2018. Los Angeles Times.

Lo, Joe. "Secretively-Funded Think Tank Celebrate 'Most Free-Market Cabinet Since Thatcher'." July 19 2019. Left Foot Forward.

London, Tom. "Everyone Should Know Who Owns The Press – For The Sake Of Our Democracy". Left Foot Forward. June 8 2013. Left Foot Forward.

Lothian-McLean, Moya. "These Students Staged A Mass Walkout After Their Teachers Were Fired 'For Being Gay'." February 20 2020. The Independent.

Lowe, Sid. "The Battle For Barcelona: A Day In The Life Of Presidential Candidate Joan Laporta". July 17 2015. The Guardian.

Lumiar. "Agreements At School: Why They Are Important Since Early Childhood Education". September 10 2019. Lumiar Santo Antônio do Pinhal.

Lüscher, Sandro. "The Four Ingredients Of A Successful People's Initiative". October 12 2018. Swiss Info.

Lyons, Izzy. "Eight Facts You Didn't Know About The Suffragette Movement". April 24 2018. The Daily Telegraph.

Macleod, Calum. "A Private Force Isn't The Answer To The UK Policing Crisis". February 17 2018.

Mahdawi, Arwa. "Can Cities Kick Ads? Inside The Global Movement To Ban Urban Billboards". August 12 2015. The Guardian.

Major, Guy; Preminger, Jonathan. "Overcoming The Capital Investment Hurdle In Worker-Controlled Firms". 2019. Journal of Participation and Employee Ownership, Volume 2, Issue 2.

Mallet, Victor. "France Seeks To Defuse Protests With Pension Climbdown". January 11 2020. The Financial Times.

Markgraf, Jonas; Véron, Nicolas. "Germany's Savings Banks: Uniquely Intertwined With Local Politics". July 18 2018. Bruegel.

Márquez, Braulio. "The Simón Bolívar Socialist Peasant Community City Is Strengthened And Advanced". July 16 2018. Bolívar y Zamora Revolutionary Current Press.

Marr, Andrew; Chomsky, Noam. "Noam Chomsky on Propaganda: The Big Idea". February 14 1996. British Broadcasting Corporation.

Martin, Ben. "Communal Ownership Drives Denmark's Wind Revolution". September 20 2017. Green Economy Coalition.

Martin, Brian. "Protest In A Liberal Democracy". January-June 1994. Philosophy and Social Action, Volume 20, Numbers 1-2, Pages 13-24.

Mason, Paul. "How Did The First World War Actually End?". August 1 2014. Channel Four.

Mason, Paul. "PostCapitalism: A Guide to Our Future". 30 July 2015. Allen Lane.

Matchar, Emily. "Time Banking Is Catching On In the Digital World". June 25 2018. Smithsonian Magazine.

Mathews, Race. "The Mondragon Model: How A Basque Cooperative Defied Spain's Economic Crisis". October 19 2012. The Conversation.

Maverick, JB. "The Top 6 Shareholders of Facebook". November 25 2019. Investopedia.

May, Alex. "Beyond Politics? The Limits of Extinction Rebellion's Strategy Are Beginning to Show". December 7 2019.

Maynard, Roger. "Pirate Radio Tries To Beat Repression In Paradise". August 22 2010. The Independent.

McCarthy, Donnachadh. "The Prostitute State: How Britain's Democracy Has Been Bought" September 30 2014. Lulu Press.

McCarthy, Justin. "Most Americans Support Reducing Fossil Fuel Use". March 22 2019. Gallup.

McCarthy, Tom. "Spotlight". September 3 2015. Participant.

McDermott, Quentin; O'Brien, Kerry. "WikiLeaks: The Forgotten Man". June 19 2012. Four Corners for ABC.

McGeown, Kate. "People Power at 25: Long Road To Philippine Democracy". February 25 2011. British Broadcasting Corporation.

McGuire, Alan. "Labour International Is Backing Open Selections For MPs: Here's Why". June 28 2018. Labour List.

McLeay, Michael; Radia, Amar; Thomas, Ryland. "Money Creation In The Modern Economy". March 14 2014. Bank of England Quarterly Bulletin, Volume 54, Number 1, Pages 14-27.

Merry, Stephanie. "Kitty Genovese Murder: The Real Story Of The Woman Killed 'In Front Of 38 Witnesses' In Queens In 1964" July 4 2016. The Independent.

Milne, Richard. "Olafur Hauksson, The Man Who Jailed Iceland's Bankers". December 9 2016. The Financial Times.

Minutaglio, Bill. "The Real Legacy Of The Real Dallas Buyers Club Is That It Didn't Really Have One". March 2 2014. The Guardian.

Mitra, Sugata. "Kids Can Teach Themselves". February 2007. LIFT 2007 Ted Talk.

Møller, Jørgen. "Democracy First Or State First? A Historical Perspective On The Sequencing Debate". 2014. APSA 2014 Annual Meeting Paper.

Møller, Jørgen. "The Birth Of Representative Institutions: The Case Of The Crown Of Aragon". Summer 2017. Social Science History, Volume 41, Pages 175-200.

Monbiot, George. "Why Common Ownership Is A Route To Social Transformation". March 11 2017. Evonomics.

Moore, Heidi. "Merchants Of Truth By Jill Abramson Review – Journalism's Troubles". January 30 2019. The Guardian.

Moore, Michael. "Where To Invade Next". September 10 2015. Dog Eat Dog Films & IMG Films.

Moores, Chris. "Thatcher's Troops? Neighbourhood Watch Schemes And The Search For 'Ordinary' Thatcherism In 1980s Britain". 2017. Contemporary British History, Volume 31, Pages 230-255.

Moran, Cahal. "Yes, Money Is Endogenous. Who Cares?". December 9 2019. Rethinking Economics.

Morgan, Lewis. "Ancient Society". 1877. University of Arizona Press.

Morkis, Stefan. "Monday Matters: Dundee Decides Is A Vote Winner". April 2 2018. The Courier.

Morris, Ian. "The Illusion Of Democracy". May 6 2015. Stratfor Worldview.

My Voucher Codes. "The European Football Index". 2018. My Voucher Codes.

Myers, Rupert. "A Legal Guide To Citizen's Arrest". August 9 2011. The Guardian.

Myre, Greg. "Why Can't The Former Soviet Republics Figure Out Democracy?". February 19 2014. NPR.

Nadler, Ronald. "Rann Versus Calabar: A Study In Gorilla Behaviour". 1976. Yerkes Newsletter.

Nash, Gary. "Class And Society In Early America". 1970. Prentice- Hall.

Neill, Alexander. "Summerhill: A Radical Approach to Child Rearing"

Nelson, Jon. "Advertising Bans In The United States". May 21 2004. Department of Economics, University of Pennsylvania.

Newnham, David. "Risinghill Revolution". February 3 2006. Times Education Suppliment.

Newton , William. "The Monastic Roots Of Western Democracy". July 11 2013. Blog of the Courtier.

Nguyen, Duc-Quang. "How direct democracy Has Grown Over The Decades". June 12 2018. Swiss Info.

Noble, Oliver. "13 Peaceful Protests And Whether They Worked". October 20 2011. Mental Floss.

Noguchi, Yuki. "Zappos: A Workplace Where No One And Everyone Is The Boss". July 21 2015. NPR.

Noonan, Laura; Tilford, Cale; Milne, Richard; Mount, Ian; Wise, Peter. "Who Went To Jail For Their Role In The Financial Crisis?". September 20 2018. Financial Times.

Norris, Sian. "Don't Forget The Working-Class Women Who Made Suffragette History". January 9 2019. Open Democracy.

OECD. "Self-Employment Rate" in "OECD Labour Force Statistics 2019: Summary Tables". 2019. OECD Publishing Paris

Olson, Mancur. "Dictatorship, Democracy, and Development". September 1993. The American Political Science Review, Volume 87, Number 3, Pages 567-576.

Orwell, George. "Homage To Catalonia". April 25 1938. Secker & Warburg.

Ostrom, Elinor. "Governing The Commons: The Evolution Of Institutions For Collective Action". 1990. Cambridge University Press.

Outing, Roger, "An Introduction To English Banking History". Retrieved 2017. The British Museum.

Panetta, Grace; Reaney, Olivia. "Today Is National Voter Registration Day". Sep 24 2019. Business Insider.

Parker, Marina. "Anna: The Woman Who Went to Fight ISIS". July 3 2019. BBC This World.

Parliament UK (a). "Anglo-Saxon Origins" in "Birth Of The English Parliament".

Accessed November 2019. Parliament UK.

Parliament UK. "Forceswatch Briefing: Conscientious Objection In The UK Armed Forces". February 2011.

Partington, Richard. "Britain Risks Heading To US Levels Of Inequality, Warns Top Economist". May 14 2019. The Guardian.

Partington, Richard. "How Unequal Is Britain And Are The Poor Getting Poorer?". September 5 2018(a). The Guardian.

Paulin, Alois. "Through liquid democracy To Sustainable Non-Bureaucratic Government". 2014. Journal of eDemocracy and Open Government, Volume 6, Pages 216-230.

PB Partners. "Dundee Pilot Participatory Budgeting Programme". 2017-2018. PB Partners.

Pearson, Tamara. "Wage Limits Set For State Officials In Venezuela".February 15 2011. Venezuela Analysis.

Peischel, Will. "How A Brief Socialist Takeover In North Dakota Gave Residents A Public Bank". October 1 2019. Vox.

Perraudin, Frances. "Extinction Rebellion Arrests Pass 1,000 On Eighth Day Of Protests". 22 Apr 22 2019. The Guardian.

Perry, Kellen. "10 Things You Should Know About Citizen's Arrest Before You Try It". 2019. Ranker.

Petersen, Miriam. "Energy Remunicipalisation: How Hamburg Is Buying Back Energy Grids". October 19 2016. World Future Council.

Pew Research Centre. "Public Wary Of Military Intervention In Libya". March 14 2011. People Press.

Platt, Edward. "Inside the Morning Star, Britain's last communist newspaper". August 4 2015. The New Statesman.

Pletcher, Kenneth. "Opium Trade". Apr 17 2015. Encyclopædia Britannica.

Plutarch (Author) & Perrin, Bernadotte (Translator). "Plutarch Lives, VII, Demosthenes and Cicero. Alexander and Caesar". 1914. Harvard University Press.

Pomeroy, Sarah; Burstein, Stanley; Donlan, Walter; Roberts, Jennifer; Tandy, David. "Ancient Greece: A Political, Social, and Cultural History". 2011. Oxford University Press.

Powers, Ashley. "The Renegade Sheriffs: A Law-Enforcement Movement That Claims To Answer Only To The Constitution". April 23 2018. The New Yorker.

Press, Susan. "How Members Kept The Presses Running At Morning Star Newspaper". December 7 2011. The Coop News.

Price, David. "Nambiquara Leadership". November 1981. American Ethnologist, Volume 8, Number 4, Pages 686-708.

Pridmore, Jason; Mols, Anouk; Wang, Yijang; Holleman, Frank. "Keeping An Eye On The Neighbours". 2019. The Police Journal, Volume 92, Number 2, Pages 97-120.

Putz, Catherine. "Turkmenistan Set To Rollback Subsidies For Good". September 27 2018. The Diplomat.

Ramos, Jose. "Re-Inventing Democracy: "Wenn Liquid Wird Kommen", An Interview With Axel Kistner And Andreas Nitsche". September 27 2016. P2P Foundation.

Reiner, Robert. "Conservatives And The Constabulary In Great Britain: Cross-Dressing Conundrums" in "The Politics of Policing". 2016. Emerald Publishing. Pages 79-96.

Reland, Joël. "Tax Dodging: How Big Is The Problem?". November 9 2017. Full Fact.

Renard, Georges. "Guilds In The Middle Ages". 1918 (2000 Edition). Batoche Books Kitchener.

Rhodes, Chris. "Financial Services: Contribution To The UK Economy". April 25 2018. House of Commons Library.

Riddell, Fern. "The 1910s: 'We Have Sanitised Our History Of The Suffragettes'." February 6 2018. The Guardian.

Rifkin, Jeremy. "The Zero Marginal Cost Society". April 1 2014. Palgrave Macmillan.

Robertson, Brian. "Holacracy: A Radical New Approach To Management". July 2 2015. TEDxGrandRapids.

Robinson, Edward; Valdimarsson, Omar. "This Is Where Bad Bankers Go to Prison". March 31 2016. Bloomberg Markets.

Robson, David. "The '3.5% Rule': How A Small Minority Can Change The World". May 14 2019. BBC Future.

Rosenberg, Tracy. "Why Public Access Television Is Important And You Should Fight For The CAP ACT". December 4 2010. Huff Post.

Roy, Nilanjana. "Want To Build Democracy? Then Build Libraries". November 29 2019. Financial Times.

Rushkoff, Douglas. "Team Human". February 19 2019. W. W. Norton & Company.

Sabbagh, Dan. "Priti Patel Accused Of Conflict Of Interest In Mod Contract". August 26 2019. The Guardian.

Sabin, Lamiat. "Left Wing? You May Be On Police Extremism List". January 17 2020. The Morning Star.

Sadofsky, Mimsy. "What It Takes to Create a Democratic School". February 1 2014. SudburyValley.org

Safi, Hiba. "Radical Maximum Wage In Egypt: Who Pays the Bill?". April 21 2015. The Tahir Institute For Middle East Policy.

Sahlins, Marshall. "Notes On The Original Affluent Society" in "Man the Hunter". 1968. Aldine Publishing Company.

Salem, Fadi; Mourtada, Racha. "Civil Movements: The Impact Of Facebook And Twitter". May 2011. Arab Social Media Report, Volume 1, Number 2.

Sandbu, Martin. "A Less Wonderful Life For Bankers". March 21 2010. The Financial Times.

Satell, Greg. "Why Some Movements Succeed And Others Fail". May 31 2015. Digital Tonto.

Scarpetta, Stefano. "Risks That Matter". 2019. OECD.

Scherer, Sophia. "Breaking Through The Information Blockade: Participatory

Journalism and Indymedia". October 12 2014. New Media For Social Change.

Schneider, Megan. "The Guardians Of Truth: The Role Of Journalism In Today's World". March 27 2019. The Gateway.

Schneider, Nathan. "Owning Is the New Sharing". December 21 2014. Shareable.

Schoenberger, Erica. "The Origins Of The Market Economy: State Power, Territorial Control, And Modes Of War Fighting". July 1 2008. Comparative Studies in Society and History, Volume 50, Pages 663-691.

Schuler, Martin; Dessemontet, Pierre. "The Swiss Vote On Limiting Second Homes". March 11 2012. Journal of Alpine Research.

Scott of the Insurgency Culture Collective. "The Anarchist Response To Crime". Retrieved October 2019. The Anarchist Library.

Scott, James. "Against The Grain: A Deep History Of The Earliest States". August 22 2017. Yale University Press.

Scott, James. "Seeing Like A State: How Certain Schemes To Improve The Human Condition Have Failed". March 1998. Yale University Press.

Scott, Roger. "Roots: A Historical Perspective Of The Office Of Sheriff". Retrieved September 2019. National Sheriffs' Association.

Semler, Ricardo. "How To Run A Company With (Almost) No Rules". 2014. Ted Global.

Semler, Ricardo. "Managing Without Managers". September-October 1989. Harvard Business Review.

Semler, Ricardo. "Maverick". 1993. Penguin Random House LLC.

Serhan, Yasmeen. "The Common Element Uniting Worldwide Protests". November 19 2019. The Atlantic.

Service, Elman. "Origin Of The State And Civilization: The Process Of Cultural Evolution". 1975. New York.

Shafer, Byron. "Bifurcated Politics: Evolution And Reform At The National Party Convention". July 11 1988. Harvard University Press.

Shakespeare, Stephan. "Voters Support Ban On Second Jobs For MPs". February 25 2015. YouGov.

Shancjan, Scott. "Spotlight Again Falls On Web Tools And Change". January 29 2011. New York Times.

Sharp, Lauriston. "People Without Politics: The Australian Yir Yoront" in "Systems Of Political Control And Bureaucracy In Human Societies". 1958. American Ethnological Society.

Shaw, Maureen. "History shows that sex strikes are a surprisingly effective strategy for political change". April 14 2017. Quartz.

Shaw, Randy. "Beyond The Fields: Cesar Chavez, The UFW, And The Struggle For Justice In The 21st Century". October 8 2010. University of California Press.

Sheldon, Joss. "Money Power Love". 2017. Rebel Books.

Sheldon, Joss. "States Created Markets. Markets Require States. Neither Could Continue Without The Other". Oct 8 2017 (b). Medium.

Sheldon, Joss. "The Magic Money Tree". Oct 10 2017 (a). Medium.

Shiva, Vandana; Wallach, Lori. "20 Years After The Battle of Seattle". November 27 2019. Democracy Now.

Shoebridge, Brendan. "The Bentley Effect". October 22 2016. Smiling Dragonfly Productions.

Shultz, Doug. "The French Revolution". January 17 2005. The History Channel.

Silberbauer, George. "Political Process in G/Wi Bands" in "Politics and History in Band Societies". 1982. Cambridge University Press.

Simkin, John. September 1997. "Operation Mockingbird". Spartacus Educational.

Smith, Andrew. "76% Of UK Adults Oppose The Promotion Of Military Exports To Human Rights Abusers". September 27 2017. Campaign Against The Arms Trade.

Smith, Hilary. "Leveller Democracy : Political Theory And Political Reality". Spring 1990. University of Richmond Scholarship Repository.

Smith, Matthew. "Who Are The Monarchists?". May 18 2018. YouGov.

Smolo, Edib; Mirakhor, Abbas. "Limited Purpose Banking And Islamic Finance ". 2012. Business Islamica, Volume 6, Issue 5, pages 34-36.

Soniak, Matt. "Can Anyone Just Make a Citizen's Arrest?" December 13 2013. Mental Floss.

Souza, Celina. "Participatory Budgeting In Brazilian Cities". April 2001. Environment & Urbanization, Volume 13, Number 1.

Spinney, Laura. "Searching For Doggerland". December 2012. National Geographic.

Spirova, Maria. "Corruption And Democracy: The 'Colour Revolutions' In Georgia And Ukraine". December 2008. Taiwan Journal of Democracy, Volume 4, Number 2, Pages 75-90.

Stasavage, David. "When Distance Mattered: Geographic Scale And The Development Of European Representative Assemblies". 2010. American Political Science Review, Volume 104, Number 4, Pages 625-643.

Stefon, Matt. "Fairness Doctrine: United States Policy, 1949–1987". December 30 2018. Encyclopædia Britannica Inc.

Stelter, Brian; Stone, Brad. "Web Pries Lid Of Iranian Censorship". June 22 2009. The New York Times.

Stephan, Maria; Chenoweth, Erica. "Why Civil Resistance Works: The Strategic Logic of Nonviolent Conflict". Summer 2008. International Security, Volume 33, Issue 1, Pages 7-44.

Stephan, Maria; Gallagher, Adam. "Five Myths About Protest Movements". December 13 2019. The Washington Post.

Stewart, Henry. "Can A Workplace Be Democratic?". April 12 2013 (b). The Huffington Post.

Stewart, Henry. "Seven Reasons Why Collaborative Hiring Works Better". February 23 2016. The Huffington Post.

Stewart, Henry. "The Happiness Manifesto". January 3 2013 (a). Kogan Page.

Stone, Jon. "What have strikes ever achieved?". June 15 2015. The Independent.

Strauss, Ilana. "The Original Sharing Economy". January 3 2017. The Atlantic.

Suzman, James. "How Hunter-Gatherers May Hold the Key to our Economic Future". February 10 2018. Evonomics.

Swierczek, Björn. "5 Years Of liquid democracy in Germany". August 17 2011. The liquid democracy Journal, Issue 1.

Tackley, Graham; McAlister, Matt. "2017 In Review". 2018. Kaleida.

Taibbi, Matt. "The Divide: American Injustice in the Age of the Wealth Gap". October 21 2014. Spiegel & Grau.

Tamblyn, Nathan. "The Common Ground Of Law And Anarchism". April 30 2019. Liverpool Law Review, Volume 40, Issue 1, pages 65–78.

Tarry, Nick, "Religious Courts Already In Use". February 7 2008. British Broadcasting Corporation.

Tatchell, Peter. "WW1: The Hidden Story Of Soldier's Mutinies, Strikes And Riots". August 1 2014. Left Foot Forward.

Tharoor, Shashi. "'But What About The Railways?': The Myth Of Britain's Gifts To India". March 8 2017. The Guardian.

The Economist Intelligence Unit. "Democracy Index 2018: Me Too, Political Participation, Protest And Democracy". 2018. The Economist.

Tomasian, Bethany. "Q&A With John Bunch: Holacracy Helps Zappos Swing From Job Ladder To Job Jungle Gym". March 29 2019.

Travis, Alan. "Support For War Falls To New Low". January 21 2003. The Guardian.

Trejos, Amanda. "Why Getting Rid Of Costa Rica's Army 70 Years Ago Has Been Such A Success". December 15 2019. USA Today.

Tremlett, Giles. "Mondragon: Spain's Giant Co-Operative Where Times Are Hard But Few Go Bust". March 7 2013. The Guardian.

Tremlett, Giles. "The Podemos Revolution: How A Small Group Of Radical Academics Changed European Politics". March 31 2015. The Guardian.

Tsai, Marisa. "Eight Countries Taking Action Against Harmful Food Marketing". June 2016. Food Tank.

Tsolakidou, Stella. "The Police in Ancient Greece". May 30 2013. Greek Reporter.

Tucker, Paul. "Money And Credit: Banking And The Macroeconomy". 13 December 2007. Monetary Policy and The Markets Conference, London.

Tully, James. "Modern Constitutional Democracy And Imperialism". Autumn 2008. Osgoode Hall Law Journal, Volume 46, Number 3, Pages 461-493.

Ungku, Fathin. "Factbox: 'Fake News' Laws Around The World". April 2 2019. Reuters.

Vergano, Dan. "Half-Million Iraqis Died in the War, New Study Says". October 16 2013. National Geohraphic.

Wahlquist, Calla. "Incredibly Worrying': Legal Fight Looms Around Australia Over Clampdown On Protest". October 5 2019. The Guardian.

Wallop, Harry. "Allotment Waiting Lists Reach Up To 40 Years". June 2 2009. The Daily Telegraph.

Watkins, J; Wulaningsih, W; Da Zhou, C et al. "Effects Of Health And Social Care Spending Constraints On Mortality In England: A Time Trend Analysis". 2017. BMJ Open.

Weatherford, Jack. "Indian Givers: How The Indians Of The Americas Transformed The World". November 29 1989. Ballantine Book.

Whitehouse, David. "Origins Of The Police". December 7 2014. Works In Theory.

Whitfield, Bronte. "My Boyfriend Just Tried to Citizen's Arrest Tony Blair". 20 January 2014. Vice.

Wilde, Matt. "Contested Spaces: The Communal Councils And Participatory Democracy In Chavez's Venezuela". 2017. Latin American Perspectives, Volume 44, Number 1, pages 140-158.

Wilkinson, Richard. "How Economic Equality Harms Society". 2011. TedGlobal.

Williams, Granville. "A Ruthless Masterclass In Media Control". December 12 2019. The Morning Star.

Wolf, Martin. "Strip Private Banks Of Their Power To Create Money". April 26 2014. The Financial Times.

Wolf, Martin. "The Fed Is Right To Turn On The Tap". November 9 2010. The Financial Times.

Wood, Zoe. "The John Lewis Model And What Others Could Learn From It". January 16 2012. The Guardian.

Wooloch, Isser. "The French Revolution Introduced Democratic Ideals To France 1789 To 1799". 1998-2000. Frank Laughter.

World Health Organisation. "A Report On Smoking Advertising And Promotion Bans In The Islamic Republic Of Iran". 2003. World Health Organisation.

Wright, Iain. "Sports Direct Workers Aren't The Only Ones Unprotected In Our 'Gig Economy'." July 22 2016. The Guardian.

Wynter, Coral; McIlroy, Jim. "Marta Harnecker: Venezuela's Experiment in Popular Power". Dec 9 2006. Green Left Weekly.

Youel, Simon. "Latest Wealth Data Shows Disproportionate Gains Between The Richest And Poorest Since QE". February 1 2018. Positive Money.

Zingales, Luigi. "A Capitalism For The People: Recapturing The Lost Genius Of American Prosperity". February 11 2014. Basic Books.

Stephan, Maria; Gallagher, Adam. "Five Myths About Protest Movements". December 13 2019. The Washington Post.

Zerbisias, Antonia. "Canada Jumps On The Anti-BDS Bandwagon". February 26 2016. Al Jazeera.

Zimmerman, Bill. "The Four Stages Of The Antiwar Movement". October 24 2017. The New York Times.

Zinn, Howard. "A People's History Of The United States". 1980. Longman Group UK Limited.

www.joss-sheldon.com

BE ONE OF THE FIRST PEOPLE TO FIND OUT ABOUT JOSS SHELDON'S NEXT BOOK. SIGN UP FOR HIS NEWSLETTER TODAY...

www.joss-sheldon.com/newsletter/4592876008

If you enjoyed this book, please leave a review online. Joss Sheldon does not have a professional marketing team behind him – he needs your help to spread the word about his books!

Printed in Great Britain
by Amazon

57690769R00236